CW00553637

THE NORDIC PARLIAMENTS

THE NORDIC PARLIAMENTS

A Comparative Analysis

BY

DAVID ARTER

C. HURST & COMPANY, LONDON

First published in the United Kingdom by
C. Hurst & Co. (Publishers) Ltd.,
38 King Street, London WC2E 8JT

ISBN 0-905838-88-2
Printed in Great Britain

PREFACE

Exactly a third of a century of formal co-operation between the Danish, Finnish, Icelandic, Norwegian, and Swedish legislatures via the annual sessions of the Nordic Council, extensive informal contacts among delegates and even a regional journal of parliamentary affairs, *Nordisk Kontakt*, have curiously failed to inspire a comparative investigation of the Nordic parliaments. That an Englishman should venture a preliminary attempt to fill this important gap in the literature without the resources that a Nordic-based project would command, and condemned in an austere Britain to relatively short visits to the field, is plainly to risk the slings and arrows of outraged criticism. The aim of this present volume, however, is modest: namely, to essay a systematic exposition of the participation of the Nordic parliaments in the policy process. The primary objective is to present basic information about the five sovereign and three devolved assemblies in the region in a consistently comparative manner in order to highlight the different patterns of assembly involvement in decision-making. There is also a consideration of the evolving role of the Nordic Council. Ultimately, a tilt is taken at the corporatist orthodoxy which, somewhat unfairly, it is argued, has consigned the Nordic parliaments to the obituary columns of political science.

I gained immense encouragement in my research from the friendship and co-operation of countless persons, and still blush at the bemused expressions of interviewees on being told I was putting together a book on the Nordic parliaments — all of them? Special mention, however, must go to Dr Magnus Isberg and Thorsteinn Magnusson who were unstinting in their help during the early stages of the research for this book. I should like to thank the Social Science Research Council, the Swedish Institute and the Foreign Ministries of Denmark, Finland, and Norway, for financial assistance in undertaking study visits; Dr Richard Tötterman, the former Finnish ambassador in London, Bent Skou, Torbjørn Støverud, Jan Lundblad and Tom Söderman for arranging the details; Erik Mo, Elise Stenbæk, Kurt and Bente Andersen, Peter Bohlbro, Jouni Vainio, Dr Claes Linde and Professor Tatu Vanhanen for responding to my requests for information at long range; and, finally, Eila Hedqvist for *auld lang syne*. My wife, Eeva-Kaisa, roundly (and rightly) cursed the enterprise at times, but then invested in an essential *aide-de-combat* of the home-based author — a good set of earplugs. Her support made the whole thing possible.

September 1983 DAVID ARTER

CONTENTS

Part II. THE INVOLVEMENT OF THE NORDIC PARLIAMENTS IN POLICY ADOPTION: LEGISLATING OR DELIBERATING ASSEMBLIES?

TABLES

1

THE NORDIC PARLIAMENTS: A ROUTINE CASE OF DECLINE?

'There is emerging in all liberal democracies a more intense concern with the representative dimension of government than at any time since the 1930s. Then the challenge came from ideologies that consciously rejected parliamentary democracy. Now there are doubts and anxieties among supporters of parliamentary democracy themselves.' — D. Coombes and S.A. Walkland, *Parliaments and Economic Affairs* (1980), pp. 4–5

This volume sets out to analyse and compare a distinctive group of '*tings*', namely the Danish *Folketing*, Icelandic *Althing* and Norwegian *Storting* together with the corresponding national parliaments in Sweden and Finland, the *Riksdag* and *Eduskunta* respectively. '*Tings*' do not end there: included in the study are the legislatures on the three Home Rule territories in the Nordic region, the *Landsting* in Greenland and *Lagting* on the Faeroe Islands, both autonomous communities within the Kingdom of Denmark, along with the *Landsting* on the Åland islands, a self-governing province within the Finnish republic. Together with the Nordic Council, *Nordisk Råd*, a consultative assembly founded as a result of a Danish initiative in 1952, these bodies make up the Nordic parliaments.

The 87-member Nordic Council is not a parliament in the orthodox sense of a deliberative organ with powers — or, at the very least, the formal power to enact laws that are binding unless and until repealed by the same legislative body. It might reasonably be expected that as a supranational assembly, the Nordic Council's law-making competence would be restricted to a circumscribed category of Nordic legislation; but in fact it is not authorised to pass laws at all, nor can it require the implementation of any of its recommendations. Unlike the European Parliament in Strasbourg, moreover, the Nordic Council is not directly elected by the people — its delegates are nominated separately by the five national and three devolved assemblies — and in consequence it has suffered from a very low profile, a problem compounded by the fact that it meets for only one week annually and lacks a chamber of its own. The venue for Nordic Council proceedings rotates between the five national parliament buildings in the region, and each of these assemblies has a short spring recess so as to release its delegation to attend the Nordic Council's session. Importantly too, there exist in reality a number of proscribed areas of debate: it has thus become conventional to preclude matters of security, defence and, invariably, foreign policy from the agenda of the Nordic Council. In large part, this has been to preserve the notion of a *Nordic Balance* viz. a delicate equilibrium deriving from the security arrangements formed in the aftermath of the Second World War and involving a strongly-armed and neutral Sweden, flanked on the one side by Finland which since 1948 has been militarily linked to the Soviet Union by a Treaty of Friendship, Co-operation and Mutual Assistance and, on the other, the two NATO members, Norway and Denmark. A recent instance of the Nordic Council's customary silence on defence-related matters will serve to illustrate the general point. When at its 1983 session in Oslo, the Folketing delegate, Erlendur Patursson, a Faeroes' representative, tabled a private proposal recommending that a committee of researchers be set up to prepare a Nordic Council initiative on international peace and disarmament, the Nordic Council's standing committee on Economic Affairs (significantly there is no standing committee on defence and security matters) declined to proceed with the measure. It noted that the standing committee had in its day handled questions of a military and security character — the issue of the atomic weapon-free Nordic zone in 1961, 1964 and 1966, for example, and in 1974 the question of a North Atlantic peace proclamation — and had consistently held that it was not beyond the formal competence of the Nordic Council to deal with such matters. Nonetheless, the Economic Affairs committee decided both to respect and support the convention of not handling foreign policy matters with military and security implications and the matter ended there.[1]

Plainly then, as a non-elected assembly lacking legislative powers, the Nordic Council is a parliament only in the minimal etymological sense of a body where a degree of 'parleying' takes place. To be fair, participation in plenary debates has increased markedly following the acquisition in the early 1980s of facilities for the simultaneous translation of speeches. The Finns, in particular, have benefited from this provision. With its infrastructure of specialist standing committees, plenary sessions, party group meetings and so on, the Nordic Council has also borne a strong procedural resemblance to the national parliaments in the region. Yet the Nordic Council was not designed to be a legislative assembly. Rather it was created to act as a vehicle for pressurising the individual governments of the region on matters involving joint action and for developing further already existing projects of a specialised, sectoral and cross-national character. The Nordic Council's remit has remained solely to make recommendations to the various national goverments and in turn it is informed by them of action taken on its proposals. In a real sense, however, the Nordic Council has been immeasurably more important an assembly than a review of its formal powers might indicate. Indeed, it has symbolised and expressed the strong sense of regional affinity felt among its member-states and their continuing desire to develop practical forms of co-operation. The Nordic Council, of course, has itself developed as an institution in more than three decades of existence, a matter which will be taken up in chapter 6. For the moment, it will suffice to note that its membership rose from 78 to 87 in 1983 following plenary acceptance of the Legal Affairs committee's proposal that Greenland should have separate representation in the Nordic Council for the first time as part of the Danish delegation (see Table 1.1).[2]

All three Home Rule territories therefore now have a separate, albeit as yet not fully independent, voice in the Nordic Council. They are also represented at the national parliamentary level: the Faeroes and Greenland each elect 2 delegates to the Danish Folketing and Åland returns a single member to the Finnish Eduskunta. At the heart of the local political system of the self-governing provinces are devolved assemblies elected every four years by universal suffrage. If the Nordic Council is not a parliament in so far as it does not possess legislative powers, the devolved assemblies enjoy extensive legislative authority — in the case of the Greenlandic Landsting, for example, in the areas of local government, taxation, trade, industry, agriculture, social policy, public health and labour law, planning and the environment, internal transport, education and culture and church affairs. True, in both Greenland and the Faeroes, matters such as defence, foreign policy and criminal law remain the exclusive preserve of the Danish central government, whilst in the Åland Landsting, so-called 'Presidential proposals'

Table 1.1. REPRESENTATION IN THE NORDIC COUNCIL, 1983

National assembly	*No. of delegates nominated*
Folketing	16
Eduskunta	18
Althing	7
Storting	20
Riksdag	20
Lagting (Faeroes)	2*
Landsting (Greenland)	2*
Landsting (Åland)	2*
Total	87

* Part of Danish delegation.

emanating from Helsinki and usually concerning agreements between Finland and another state — for example to avoid double taxation, as in the case of the agreement with the Republic of Korea in 1982[3] — are normally approved without so much as a discussion in the chamber. A rare exception in December 1974 related to a proposed agreement between Finland and Sweden to avoid double taxation which the Landsting refused to approve on the grounds that no provision had been made for those coastal communes which would suffer from a tax shortfall as a result of the fact that many local Åland seamen worked on Swedish vessels. Nonetheless, it needs emphasis that all three Home Rule assemblies possess wide legislative powers over issues of local concern, and this has created a high level of regional autonomy within the framework of the unitary Danish and Finnish states.

The way the devolved assemblies exercise their legislative powers may be seen from the activities of the Åland Landsting. During its two-month spring session in 1983, no less than fifteen laws were approved, ranging from a successful private member's bill pressing for better air connections between Åland and Sweden (at present there is only one flight a day in each direction) to a law requiring the use of car headlights throughout the year, thus bringing practice in Åland into line with that in Finland and Sweden.[4] Relations between the Home Rule territories and the 'mother-state' have not always been without their strains, of course, and may in any event be depicted as evolving in an organic manner. Hence a dispute over ownership of Greenland's mineral resources in 1979 resulted in a compromise which granted the Greenlanders fundamental rights and a qualified veto-right with regard to exploitation.[5] For its part, the Danish government permitted a special referendum in 1982 at which 52% of the Greenland population opted in favour of abandoning membership of the European Community (EC) a vote which the Danish Government respected when Greenland decided to withdraw the following year. The referendum result reflected two primary anxieties in Greenland: one, a concern on the part of the 50,000 Inuit-speaking Eskimo population that unduly generous fishing rights were being granted to West Germany around the coast of Greenland, and secondly, that the indigenous, nomadic *Inuit* lifestyle was being threatened by the (voluntary) EC seal import ban, which was ruining the market for pelts. Elsewhere, the report of a committee set up by the Åland Landsting — and at present in the hands of the Finnish Ministry of Justice — could, if approved, substantially enhance the visible autonomy of the Åland islands through granting them *inter alia* the right to issue their own postage stamps. We will examine the work of the Home Rule legislatures in more detail, although it bears emphasis at this stage that the structure and operation of the devolved assemblies corresponds closely to that of the mother-parliaments. As Jógvan Sundstein, its Speaker, has observed, 'all bills in the Faeroese Lagting are handled three times on the floor of the House, but as in other parliaments, the lion's share of the work is undertaken in the specialist standing committees to which all proposals must be dispatched.'[6]

As to the mother-parliaments, the sovereign assemblies of Denmark and Finland, together with their counterparts in Iceland, Norway and Sweden, their size is laid down in the national constitutions or, in the Finnish case, the constitution-level Parliament Act, *Valtiopäiväjärjestys* (VJ) which dates back to 1928. In Denmark the new constitution of 1953, *Danmarks Riges Grundlov* (DRG) which replaced the 1915 instrument of government, states that the Folketing shall comprise at most 179 members, two of whom shall be elected for the Faeroes and two for Greenland. The Eduskunta in its turn is to consist of 200 delegates, one of them to represent the single-member constituency of Åland. According to the 1944 Icelandic constitution *Stjórnarskipun* (IC), drafted when the country declared its full independence from Denmark, the Althing shall comprise 60 members, no less than 12 of them elected from the capital, Reykjavík. In Norway the 1814 constitution, *Norges grundlov* (NG), stipulates that the Storting is to number 155 delegates, all of whom must have been resident in the kingdom for ten years and be eligible to vote. Incidentally, the 1814 constitution was formulated by the Eidsvoll National Assembly, *Riksforsamlingen*, a constituent assembly convened by Prince Christian Frederik to elect a new monarch in the aftermath of the Napoleonic wars and Norway's separation from Denmark. The 1814 constitution has remained in force ever since amended, as Elder *et al.* have observed, 'more in spirit than in letter'.[7] Finally in Sweden, the amended 1974 *Regeringsformen* (RF) specifies that the Riksdag shall comprise 349 delegates and their deputies. The total number of Riksdag delegates was in fact reduced from 350 (in the 1974 Constitution) to 349 in 1976 to avoid deadheats and the recurrent need — as occurred during the so-called 'lottery Riksdag' of 1973–6 — for the Speaker to cast lots to decide the result. Elsewhere the size of the legislatures in the region has remained constant in recent years — the number of Storting delegates has not varied since 1814! — and with the growth in the size of the national populations, this has meant a marked deterioration in the ratio of voters to elected delegates. In Finland one delegate represented 14,300 citizens in 1908 whereas by the 1980s the number of his constituents had risen to 23,700.[8] To recreate the 1908 voter-delegate balance, 330 Eduskunta members

Table 1.2. THE SIZE OF THE NORDIC PARLIAMENTS

	No. of delegates
Althing	60
Storting	155
Folketing	179
Eduskunta	200
Riksdag	349
Lagting (Faeroes)	32
Landsting (Greenland)	26
Landsting (Åland)	30

Source: DRG 4:28, VJ 1:2, RF 3:1, IC 3:31, NG:57, 61, RF 3:1.

would be necessary. The devolved assemblies are much smaller than the five sovereign legislatures in the Nordic region: there are 32 delegates in the Faeroese Lagting, 26 in the Greenlandic Landsting and 30 members in the Landsting of the Åland islands (see Table 1.2).

Delegate recruitment to the Nordic legislatures

The general elections that determine the composition of the Nordic assemblies are held every four years in all the states of the region except Sweden, where the Riksdag sits for a three-year term. In Sweden, in fact, there has been a recent discussion of increasing the length of parliaments to four years, while in Finland, before the 1983 general election, the Prime Minister Kalevi Sorsa proposed that the Eduskunta term be extended to six years (precisely as for the Head of State) so as to facilitate the government's task of economic management. In both countries, however, opponents of change have pointed to the rapid developments that can occur in political and economic conditions and the fundamental need to allow citizens the opportunity to react to them promptly through the ballot-box.[9] There *are* provisions for dissolving parliament and calling premature elections in much of the region: in Denmark for example, it is the Prime Minister's prerogative to decide to go to the country early, whereas in Finland it is the President who exercises this right. However, in the event of an early election in Sweden, the extraordinary Riksdag sits only until the next constitutionally-prescribed general election. In theory, this may only be a matter of months — undoubtedly an important consideration in preventing a premature dissolution of the Riksdag when Thorbjörn Fälldin's first and second non-socialist coalitions got into difficulties in 1978 and 1981. There have been no unscheduled dissolutions of parliament under the new Swedish constitution; in contrast, the dynamics of the parliamentary situation have made them commonplace in both Denmark and Finland. Only in Norway is there no provision whatsoever for a government to go to the country early, because a fixed Storting term of four years is laid down in the 1814 Constitution.

In the four mainland Nordic states, voting rights are held by all citizens of eighteen years and over; in Iceland, however, the franchise threshold is higher at twenty years of age. Ironically, it was in Finland, at the time the most economically and politically backward nation in the region, that mass democracy was first achieved when in 1907 it became the first European country to incorporate women into the electorate. Then the age qualification was fixed at twenty-fours years, it was subsequently lowered in stages until by 1970 it reached its present level of eighteen. In Denmark, legislation reducing the voting age must be submitted to the people at a popular referendum; indeed, in 1969 a referendum on a proposal to reduce the voting age from twenty-one to eighteen received the support of only 21.2% of the active electorate and only in September 1978 before a referendum majority for the change could be found. In Sweden, moreover, where economic expansion in the 1960s attracted a significant foreign labour force — of Finns, Turks and Yugoslavs in particular — immigrants must have been resident in the country for five years to be eligible for citizenship status and thereby for the franchise at national elections. In any event, elections in the Nordic nations have not only been regular but in Denmark frequent occurrences: in the period 1971–84, there were no less than seven Folketing elections.

The voting system employed at elections throughout the region has been a fairly standard Proportional Representation (PR) list system, albeit with more variations in the arrangements for calculating seat allocations — the d'Hondt method with its consecutive whole number divisor (1, 2, 3, 4 etc.) is used in Finland, while a modified version of the Saint-Laguë method with its successive odd number principle (1.4, 3, 5, 7, 9 etc.) operates in Denmark, Norway and Sweden. Indeed, the radical innovation of single transferable voting (STV) for elections to the Danish Upper Chamber in the 1860s and a period of French-style single member double ballot voting in Norway and Sweden at the turn of this century gave way to a common type of PR list voting in the Nordic region by the 1920s — spawned, as elsewhere in Europe, by the thoroughly conservative ambition of preventing the tyranny of workers and farmers that constituted the majority of the nation. In the process, the principle of territorial representation replaced the notion of functional representation by 'estates'. Since the 1920s, the electoral systems in the region have been adjusted and re-adjusted: the introduction of a 4% threshold in Sweden and a 2% one in Denmark, for example, have made it more difficult for small parties to gain a parliamentary toehold. On the other hand, these thresholds may well have encouraged a certain amount of tactical voting from which small parties have benefitted. At the 1982 Swedish general election it is thus conceivable that a number of Social Democrats defected and voted Left-Communist in weaker SDP areas so as to give the projected Social Democratic government radical leftist support in the Riksdag in the event of it falling short of majority status.[10] In Finland, moreover, small parties have been able to protect themselves by forging electoral alliances with a large party, i.e. producing a joint slate of candidates: in the Uusimaa constituency flanking Helsinki in March 1983, this enabled a candidate from the miniscule Finnish Christian League (it gained only 3 parliamentary seats) to topple the veteran Centre Party Speaker of the Eduskunta, Johannes Virolainen. Small parties must generally concentrate their votes on one leading candidate per list. By successfully doing this, 2 Green delegates were returned to the Eduskunta, admittedly far less than succeeded in making the West German Bundestag in the same month, but nonetheless the first Green member in the Nordic parliaments. Denmark, Iceland, Sweden and the Faeroes, moreover, operate a system of floating seats distributed not on a constituency basis, but in accordance with a party's overall national poll. In Sweden, there are presently 39 of these 'compensation seats', *utjämningsmandater*, from which small parties stand to profit; in the Faeroes up to 5 of the 32 seats are allocated in this manner. Overall, however, the Nordic voting systems have had an inherent bias towards the larger established parties while not preventing the election of broadly representative multi-party legislatures.

When viewing the occupational background of members of these multi-party Nordic legislatures over the six decades from the breakthrough of mass democracy to the early 1980s, the evidence tends to confirm the existence of three trends which have also affected the majority of West European assemblies during the same time span. First, there has been a consistent under-representation of manual workers in the Nordic parliaments relative to their numerical strength in the economically active labour force. Certainly the election of the first working-class delegate, a railwayman, to the bicameral Swedish Riksdag in 1878[11] and of the first blue-collar representative to the Storting in 1891 — 4% of the Storting in 1903 were listed as workers — seemed portentous enough. However, as early as the turn of this century, there are indications that leaders of the various Norwegian labour-market organisations were ditching the Storting with the explanation that their political objectives could be attained more effectively by establishing direct contacts with the government and central administration.[12] In truth, the adoption in Norway at this time of a French-style single member double ballot electoral system also contributed significantly to reducing the number of working-class representatives in parliament.[13] Even the rise of mass-based parties of the newly-enfranchised working class had only a limited impact on patterns of delegate recruitment in the region. In Finland, for example, high-status social groups have always been well-represented in the Social Democrats and Communists, so much so that during the early years of the unicameral Eduskunta the ratio of working-classs to middle-class delegates was approximately one to one;[14] this constituted a curious shortfall of blue-collar members, particularly since both left-wing parties organised pre-selection primaries. To adapt Edouard Herriot, it seemed very much a case of '*restaurant ouvrier, chefs bourgeois*'. A slow decline in the numbers employed in primary industry after the Second World War, reinforced the 'embourgeoisement' of the Nordic parliaments: in 1977 only 4.5% of Folketing delegates listed themselves as workers, skilled or unskilled.

Secondly, there has been a paucity of industrialists and businessmen in the Nordic parliaments. In Sweden, for example, the number of directors and/or owners of enterprises, both large and small, fell from 46% of the total Riksdag seats in 1920 to 27% in 1953. This contributed to a clear lack of industrial experience and expertise on the parliamentary standing committees and in turn prompted the increased participation of industrialist groups on pre-legislative commissions of inquiry, *utredningar* — a development which had the inevitable effect of weakening the Riksdag's role in the adoption of public policy.[15] By the 1980s, the situation had deteriorated to the point where, according to the chairman of the Skåne Chamber of Commerce, himself a bank director, Swedish industry had only a handful of representatives in the Riksdag.[16] Indeed, it is symptomatic of a growing concern over the dearth of parliamentary delegates with a background in trade and industry that in Norway there has been recent discussion of the parties organising a scheme of in-service industrial experience for Storting members.[17]

Thirdly, there has been a progressive 'professionalisation' of the office of parliamentarian in the Nordic states, something reflected in the growing number of career politicians found in the national assemblies. Career politicians or 'professionals' — many with a pre-parliamentary background of service in the party machine —

may be regarded as those delegates who have served at least three consecutive legislative terms, and who accordingly lack a recent knowledge and/or experience of the world of work and the crucial policy field of labour-market affairs. In Finland, Pekka Väänänen has estimated that in recent times 'professionals' have amounted to about one-third of all Eduskunta members and that they are most frequently from parties of the left.[18] More generally, conversations with many of the older generation of parliamentarians has confirmed that there is a growing body of career politicians in the five national legislatures. As one elderly Swedish Liberal delegate put it ruefully, 'In twenty years time, they will all be professionals!'

Careerists aside, there has been a decline throughout the Nordic legislatures in two formerly well-represented groups. The proportion of high-ranking civil servants has fallen, as has the number of farmer delegates — although the latter remain over-represented in relation to their numerical strength in the country in several of the states. In contrast, there has been an increase in the *corps* of teachers sitting in the parliaments of the region.

Thus far, patterns of delegate recruitment in the region have largely mirrored those occurring in the bulk of west European assemblies. True, nationally-known personalities may occasionally be successful: the tax lawyer Mogens Glistrup, founder of the Danish Progress Party, made his name on television before entering the Folketing in 1973 and Antti Kalliomäki, a Finnish Social Democrat and newcomer to the Eduskunta in March 1983, was a household name as the national pole-vault champion. Incidentally, at the same time, Lasse Viren narrowly failed to enter parliament for the Conservatives. Television presenters have generally met with less success in their parliamentary aspirations, and the exceptions have usually survived only a single term in the assembly (part of the popular Nordic sentiment that politics is best left to the 'professionals'?). In the devolved assemblies of the Faeroes, Greenland and Åland, moreover, local roots and/or a known position on local issues may still be as important as the party label in ensuring results at the polls. In one important respect, however, the composition of the legislatures in the region has been distinctive: thus the representation of female delegates in the Nordic assemblies has been consistently the highest in Western Europe since the war. Finland has led the way here. As early as 1908 no less than 12.5% of Finnish parliamentarians were women, and this at a time when only one other country, Australia, had even gone so far as to extend eligibility to women. To this day, there have been proportionately more female legislators in Finland than in any other non-socialist country.[19] At the general elections of 1983, over 30% of the newly-elected parliamentarians were women, no less than ten times more than in the British House of Commons elected the same year.

Ironically, the political status of Finnish women at the turn of this century was anything but good. They were denied the right to vote (as well of course as the opportunity of standing for parliament), despite the fact that in 1865 all women paying local rates had been enfranchised on communal matters. In 1897 the Diet of Peasants, part of the quadricameral Diet of Estates abolished in 1906, had proposed extending the suffrage to women — pointing to their growing involvement in social affairs — but this proposal proved too radical and was unable to get majority parliamentary backing.[20] Even the radically-minded parliamentary reform committee which reported in 1906 failed to achieve unanimity on the question of women. Regarding female suffrage, the committee recognised that doubling the size of the electorate would have an undoubted impact on the final outcome of elections. However, it did not view it as self-evident that men and women would line up against each other in different parties; rather it believed, that on many issues, women would probably underscore the same principles as men. The committee added that when the central role of women in the temperance and education movements was taken into account, their impact on the final composition of parliament was likely to prove healthy. Even so, there was disagreement on the subject of women's eligibility as parliamentary candidates. In a dissenting statement to the committee's report, one Hermanson stated bluntly that in his opinion women had no place in national political life and, pointing to the likelihood of extremist voting by women, recommended that eligibility as parliamentary candidates should be confined to men who had obtained the age of twenty-four in the year before election.[21]

Women were granted full suffrage rights in Norway in 1915 — eight years after their Finnish counterparts — but it was 1921 before Karen Platou was elected on a Conservative, *Højre*, list for Kristiania, so becoming the first female delegate to enter the Storting. As with prospective working-class entrants to parliament, the single-member double ballot system militated against female nominations, and although the introduction of a PR list system in 1921 facilitated their task, the numbers of women in the legislature remained very low in Norway until after the Second World War. By 1961, however, 9% of Storting delegates were women, with the largest share belonging to the Labour Party — not until 1961 in fact was the first female delegate elected for the farmer-based Centre Party — and the majority hailing from the greater Oslo area. Indeed, northern

Norway had traditionally been arid ground for female candidates and in this respect Margith Munkebye's parliamentary success in Nordland in 1957 marked a turning-point.[22] It might be mentioned in passing that the majority of female Storting delegates have boasted a comparatively modest social background as farmers' wives, teachers and workers. Up to the late 1960s all the women delegates from working-class homes had represented the Labour Party, but then as Ingunn Nordeval Means has observed so, too, did a professor's daughter and a number of teachers.[23] The proportion of women in the Norwegian Storting has grown consistently in recent years: in the 1973–7 session the percentage of female delegates was 15.5%; in 1977–81 it had risen to a fraction over 23% and in the 1981–5 Storting, the figure stands at slightly over 25%.

A longitudinal view of female representation in the Swedish parliament since the achievement of universal suffrage (1919–21) reveals a very similar pattern to that in Norway: at no point before the Second World War did the proportion of women delegates in the bicameral Riksdag exceed 5%; by the transition to unicameralism in 1971, however, this figure had risen to 14% and by 1976 it had climbed still further to 22.9% The first woman returned to parliament was Kerstin Hesselgren, who in 1922 was elected to the First Chamber and remained the only woman there till 1934. In the same year, four women were successful at elections to the Second Chamber — a Liberal, Conservative and two Social Democrats. Precisely as in Norway, there has also been a marked imbalance in the partisan distribution of women in the assembly. The Centre Party was a veritable male bastion until the late 1960s and the same was true of the Left-Communists' parliamentary group.[24] This position changed dramatically in the 1970s, however, and following the 1982 general election, the Centre Party's parliamentary group comprised 32.1% women delegates and the Left-Communists' 20% in a Riksdag in which the overall share of female representatives stood at 27.5%.

The vote was extended to women in Denmark and Iceland in 1915. In the former, developments in the Folketing have conformed to the typical post-war surge in the level of female representation found in the other mainland Nordic legislatures: by 1971, 17% of Danish legislators were women and in 1984 this rose to no less than 26%. Iceland has been a notable exception to the significant post-war increase in female members of parliament found elsewhere in the region; in 1974 their proportion in the Althing was only 5%. Indeed, it may have been a desire to remedy this deficiency which prompted the organisation of feminist lists in three constituencies at the general elections of April 1983. The list for Reykjavik won a seat outright and this was occupied by Sigríður Dúna Kristmundsdóttir, an anthropologist and part-time university lecturer with a B.A. degree from the London School of Economics. In addition, the total feminist vote was sufficient to produce two 'compensation seats', making a grand total of three feminists in the new Althing. Iceland may in fact be moving slowly into line with the other Nordic states as regards female representation: 15% of the present parliament consists of women and of the five parties currently represented in the Althing, only the Progressive Party has not a single female delegate.

To sum up on the occupational composition of the parliaments in the region, it should be plain that the Nordic parliaments are a long way from being social microcosms of the societies they serve. Indeed, it might be contended that while the electoral systems permit the Nordic assemblies broadly to reflect the will of the people as expressed through the ballot boxes (significantly, turn-out has been relatively high in comparative perspective), the parties via their control of the selection procedures have contributed to producing assemblies that are in essence social élites. Strictly, of course, it matters less that parliaments are not representative in a social sense — they never could be fully so — than that they are (not prevented from being) representative in the classical sense of acting as a forum for the articulation of the public interest. In line with Edmund Burke's celebrated address to the electors of Bristol, members should mediate on behalf of the national interest above the clash of competing factions and be subject only to their conscience: a member owes his constituents 'not his industry only, but his judgement'[25] and betrays instead of serving the voters if he sacrifices his viewpoint to their opinion. Article 48 of the Icelandic constitution echoes these sentiments by stating that members of the Althing are bound solely by their convictions and not by any orders from their constituents. It follows from this classical formulation of representative democracy that there is no inherent reason why nobles should not be capable of representing knaves and vice versa — the ability to represent is not dependent upon social or economic station, but solely on the exercise of judgement. There is some survey evidence that Nordic parliamentarians do perceive their role in something approximating these terms, i.e. primarily as free agents adjudicating on behalf of national rather than sectional or partisan interests. When Finnish delegates were asked to rank-order a number of factors bearing on the process of personal decision-making, the majority set of priorities put individual judgement ahead of the party line, the wishes of the electorate or the interests of a pressure group.[26] It is doubtful, however, how far this is seen to be the case. Certainly when the dramatic Finnish election of 1970 and the meteoric rise of the radical rightist Rural Party drew attention to the plight of the so-called 'forgotten nation', it became apparent that the legitimacy of the Eduskunta and its capacity to represent the interests of the whole country was being questioned. According to a local councillor and handicraft teacher from the southern city of Lahti, 'the worst thing is that the whole parliament including the Communists is full of wealthy people who have detached themselves from the nation at large'.[27] Small wonder perhaps that in Pesonen and Sänkiaho's study of 'People and Democracy' in Finland, it emerged that among the most politically alienated citizens there was a desire to strengthen the position of the Presidency at the expense of parliament.[28]

Full parliamentary delegates apart, a system of deputy members operates in each of the Nordic parliaments except Finland. Indeed, by legislation in 1828 Norway became the first nation in the world to introduce a system of parliamentary deputies; Iceland followed suit in 1845; Denmark adopted the system in 1953 and finally Sweden did so in 1974. The expansion of the system of parliamentary deputies represents an historic case of institutional diffusion within the region. Iceland, for example, almost certainly emulated Norwegian practice because when the Althing was re-established on a consultative basis by the Danish King in 1844, each delegate was permitted a replacement member.[29] True, the 1874 constitution contained no such provision, and if a member died a by-election was held. However, as PR was gradually introduced in the twentieth century the deputy system developed, and since 1959 each delegate has had his own replacement.

The classical Norwegian system of deputies, *varamann*, has a number of obvious advantages as delineated by Svenn Groennings. First, it ensures that both district and party have the parliamentary voting strength to which they are entitled. Next, it stimulates political interest and gives a greater number of persons legislative experience. Last, it provides a stepping-stone for subsequent election to the Storting as well as offering a vehicle for rewarding the party faithful.[30] Equally, two evident drawbacks suggest themselves. At a practical level, the long journey from Finnmark has traditionally been extremely difficult in winter (the development of domestic air links has now largely overcome this problem), while more seriously it might be argued that a deputy, either through lack of parliamentary experience and/or the time to acquire the relevant substantive knowledge, can rarely be as effective as a full member. In Norway particularly, arrangements for calling in parliamentary deputies have given this last point particular force. Thus a deputy is not infrequently enlisted for a single day only[31] though according to a former Storting Speaker, a regular member should be absent for over two days before a replacement is called in.[32] Not surprisingly, therefore, something in the order of 250 leaves of absence are granted annually to Storting members. In Iceland, replacement members have a greater chance of making a meaningful legislative contribution for in general they are brought in only if the regular delegate is going to be absent for at least two weeks. Indeed, the custom is that deputies retain their place for a minimum period of two weeks even if, as sometimes happens, the regular member is absent for only a day or two and may actually be present in the Althing building. In Sweden, the primary reservation of Riksdag Speaker Ingemund Bengtsson regarding the system of parliamentary deputies concerned its abuse by members in the habit of taking off periods of two months to engage in what was essentially party work. Bengtsson favoured replacements for ministers and members of the Speaker's Council, though less so for ordinary delegates, and determined to take a stricter line in granting future leaves of absence.[33] Incidentally Bengtsson, who started a second term as Riksdag Speaker following the Social Democrats' electoral victory in September 1982, has had recently to act strictly on other matters — notably before the 1983 summer recess when he was forced to reprimand a Left-Communist delegate for admitting members of the 'Women for Peace' movement into parliament enabling them to demonstrate at the entrances to the plenary chamber.[34]

Occasionally, deviant voting from deputy members has contrived to upset the party apple-cart. Most celebrated, perhaps, was the Norwegian member who, on assuming the seat vacated by the newly-appointed Prime Minister, voted against the Premier's intentions and in opposition to membership of the EC at the crucial division in 1972. Less dramatically, a Swedish Centre Party deputy, Ulla-Britta Larsson, supported a Social Democratic counter-proposal on a traffic law in March 1981 and with the resulting tied vote of 148-148 forced the matter back to standing committee. Larsson, who was acting for two months as deputy for Gunnar Björk, voted in favour of the extra 50 million kronor proposed by the Social Democrats and designed to replace ferry services by permitting the building of bridges over certain waterways.[35] Deputy members can also err inadvertently. In December 1981, another Swedish Centre Party deputy (this time the Prime Minister's sister-in-law) accidentally pressed the wrong voting button and so backed an opposition motion adding an extra 2 million kronor to the proposed expenditure on election literature to immigrants![36]

Distinctive institutional features of the Nordic parliaments

While all five sovereign Nordic states at present have single-chamber assemblies — the Danish upper house was abolished as part of the constitutional reforms of 1953 and its Swedish equivalent seventeen years later — it is a peculiarity of the region that unicameralism has been modified in Norway and Iceland by an historic system of legislative 'divisions'. In short, our earlier list of '*tings*' must be extended. The Storting thus divides into a *Lagting* and *Odelsting* for the purposes of considering the special category of 'law' proposals, i.e. bills affecting the criminal code, the rights of individual citizens and so on, and similarly the Icelandic Althing constitutes itself after a general election into two divisions, *Efri Deild* and *Nethri Deild*. Unlike Norway, however, the latter have equal powers: all bills must negotiate three readings and at least one committee stage in both chambers, making the Icelandic legislative process by far the most complicated in the region. Significantly, the inception in 1907 of a democratically-elected Eduskunta in Finland was accompanied by the creation of an 'upper tier' Grand Committee, *suuri valiokunta*, modelled on Norwegian practice and intended to inject checks and balances into the enactment process. In contrast to the Lagting in Norway, however, the overwhelming majority of bills (though not the budget) are considered in the Grand Committee after first going to one of the specialist standing committees — a procedure investing the Finnish legislature too with features of *modified unicameralism*. Finally, if qualified unicameralism is a distinctive trait of the legislative systems of Finland, Norway and Iceland, a unique form of *mitigated bicameralism* characterised the Swedish assembly before the transition to a single-chamber Riksdag in 1971. In contrast to the United States Congress and the British Houses of Parliament, the Riksdag had joint standing committees (as late as the 1940s many of their chairmen came from the Upper House), and their reports, which were sent to both Houses simultaneously, were considered as far as possible on the same day.[37] In this way, possible differences between the two chambers had to be faced and solutions sought at an earlier stage in the adoption process than in traditional bicameral systems.

To assert that in all the Nordic states the parliamentary principle is a matter of constitutional prescription as well as being indigenous to political practice risks the charge of ingenuousness. In fact, however, the realisation of the parliamentary principle was a very gradual process which developed contiguous with, though not as a direct result of, incipient industrialisation in the late nineteenth century and in particular the emergence of political groupings based on the new working class.[38] Ultimately, indeed, this process — especially in the 'colonies' of Norway and Finland — involved nothing less than the struggle of *nation against state* and conjoined farmers, workers and urban middle-class radicals in opposition to the central officials of the King in the various national capitals: the Swedish King in Oslo and Stockholm and the Danish monarch in Copenhagen and Reykjavík. It first led to the acceptance of parliamentarism in Norway — Norway and Sweden were conjoined in a loose union until 1905 — when in 1884 the Left, *Venstre*, acquired power from the officials and upper class on the Right, *Højre*. Elsewhere, the adoption of the parliamentary principle pre-dated the achievement of universal suffrage in Denmark and Sweden (see Table 1.3) but succeeded the completion of mass democracy in Finland, where it was integrally connected with the fall of Czarism — Finland had been a Grand Duchy of the Russian empire between 1809–1917 — and impending Bolshevik revolutions in Moscow and Helsinki. In Iceland, parliamentary government was an effective reality before the break with the Danish crown and the acquisition of full independence in 1944.

If parliamentarism was established in the region soon after the First World War, it might be added that in the two former 'imperial' states of Denmark and Sweden, the formal constitutional commitment to the parliamentary principle was extremely belated and then closely bound up with the shift from bicameral to unicameral assemblies in the 1950s and 1960s. Friction between the farmer-dominated Folketing and the plutocratic upper chamber, Landsting, both created by the 1849 constitution, had characterised Jacob Estrup's Premiership between 1875 and 1894 when the government, lacking majority support, could not gain approval for its finance bills in the more representative lower chamber. However, it was not until the emergence of a Social Democratic-Radical Party majority in both chambers that the salience of the Landsting as a political factor was reduced and (in 1939) an attempt made to abolish it'[39]

Table 1.3. THE COMPLETION OF MASS DEMOCRACY AND THE INTRODUCTION OF PROPORTIONAL REPRESENTATION IN THE NORDIC STATES

	Introduction of mass democracy	*Advent of PR voting*
Denmark	1918	1915
Finland	1906	1906
Iceland	1915	1915
Norway	1915	1921
Sweden	1921	1909

Even so, a move to introduce a Norwegian-style system of modified unicameralism failed at a popular referendum, and it was 1953 when the Landsting was finally abolished and the parliamentary principle incorporated into a new constitution. That the breakthrough of parliamentarism in the region was long and hard is well exemplified in the Swedish case: the first tentative steps towards the notion of responsible government were taken, according to Olle Nyman,[40] as early as the 1840s, and thus substantially precede the abolition of the 'estates' and introduction of bicameralism in 1866. Yet it was 1969 and the so-called 'partial constitutional reform' of that year before the parliamentary principle in Sweden gained formal constitutional status. Indeed, it was not until 1917 and the formation of Nils Edén's Social Democratic-Liberal coalition that the question of whether the government's power derived from 'the King or the People', *kungamakt eller folkmakt*, was resolved in favour of the latter and over fifty years thereafter before this principle was finally laid down in the form of government.

Throughout the Nordic region today, governments are recruited from, and in turn responsible to, parliament and in line with the vast majority of West European polities, the primary pathway to cabinet office is via a period of service in the national assembly. Rare exceptions to this rule have been the appointment — in the wake of a government crisis or indecisive election — of Finnish cabinets comprising civil servants or experts and the (often tactical) nomination of so-called 'non-party' specialists to one or two portfolios elsewhere, a strategy invariably deployed to resolve disputes about the tenure of particular ministerial posts at the time of the formation of a new cabinet. An important development has been the strengthening of the role of parliament in government-building in Sweden since the constitutional reforms of the 1970s by the obligation placed upon the Speaker (rather than the King as earlier) to nominate a candidate for the post of Prime Minister, that candidate — precisely as in the case of the West German Federal Chancellor — being subsequently affirmed or rejected by a ballot of delegates at a plenary session of the House. Indeed, in all three constitutional monarchies in the region, Denmark, Norway and Sweden, the Head of State has been reduced to a ceremonial role outside the legislative process. It is true that in Denmark and Norway the monarch still attends the formal meetings of the cabinet or Council of State — a Left-Socialist attempt in May 1983 to abolish the Norwegian monarchy was overwhelmingly defeated in the Storting[41] — but this is purely to ratify decisions taken earlier at the ordinary cabinet sessions when the Prime Minister is in the chair. In Sweden since 1973, however, the King has been excluded from meetings of the government, albeit — curiously — not the consultative Foreign Affairs Council, *utrikesnämnden*, an organ which the government is obliged to inform of important foreign policy developments.

In the two Nordic republics of Finland and Iceland, the formal constitutional status of the legislature is inferior to that elsewhere in the region. In accordance with article 1, paragraph 2, in both the Finnish constitution of 1919 and the Icelandic constitution of 1944, the legislative power is vested jointly in parliament and the President. Only in Finland, however, is a bifurcation of legislative authority a reality, with power divided between a Head of State elected for a six-year term of office — popular polling is followed by balloting in an American-style electoral college of 301 members — and a cabinet nominated by the President, but answerable to parliament in the orthodox way. A complex multiparty system, seemingly endemic government instability (at least until the mid-1960s) and the absolutely crucial importance of the President's constitutional duty of directing the nation's foreign policy and, in particular, maintaining amicable relations with the Kremlin have combined to explain much of the increased power of the Finnish Presidency since the war. Indeed, during the long tenure of President Kekkonen (1956–81) the authority of the Finnish President was directly comparable to that of the French office under General de Gaulle. In contrast, the functions of the Icelandic Head of State have been essentially ceremonial: the President (currently Vigdís Finnbogadóttir, a former theatrical director and Western Europe's first directly-elected female Head of State) has indeed the right to appoint cabinets and dissolve the Althing. However, Duverger's inclusion of Iceland in his category of 'semi-Presidential regimes' is based on the formal powers of a President whose role, like that of her Irish, West German and Austrian counterparts, is in practice purely symbolic.[42]

Earlier mention of the tangled complexities of the Finnish party system prompts the observation that in keeping with the majority of countries in Western Europe, the parliaments of the sovereign Nordic states became party politicised well before the completion of mass democracy and the introduction of PR systems of voting in the first two decades of this century. The selection of candidates at general elections, the choice of parliamentary officers and the nomination of the personnel of standing committees have thus been dominated by the parties for nearly 100 years, while much of the significant work of the assemblies has been conducted in the parliamentary party groups, even if they are barely recognised in the various parliamentary standing orders. Moreover, the composition of the national delegations to the Nordic Council is also determined along party lines and not surprisingly therefore the ten years form the early 1970s have witnessed the development of cross-national party groups centred on the work of the Nordic Council. The picture in the three devolved assemblies in the region, however, has been markedly different.

Political parties in Greenland only just pre-date the Home Rule Act of November 1978.[43] Of the three parties currently represented in the 26-seat *Landsting*, the miniscule Marxist *Inuit Ataquatiquit*, which demands complete independence for Greenland, was formed in precisely the same month as the Home Rule statute was issued,[44] while the two major parties — the ruling left-centre *Siumut* which opposed Greenland's membership of the EEC at the special referendum on the island in 1982, and the right-centre, pro-Market *Atassut* which advocates the continuation of political, economic and cultural co-operation with Denmark — were both founded in 1977. Following the second elections since Home Rule, held in April 1983, both *Siumut* and *Atassut* had twelve seats (see Table 1.4), but the former remained in office committed *inter alia* to a defence of the native population of Greenland, the *Inuit*, along with its language and culture. In the Faeroes, a self-governing community under the Danish crown since 1948, political parties in the 32-member *Lagting* are more institutionalised than in Greenland, albeit still relatively

Table 1.4. THE DISTRIBUTION OF SEATS IN THE THREE DEVOLVED ASSEMBLIES IN THE NORDIC REGION, 1983

Assembly	*Party*	*Seats*
Greenlandic Landsting	Siumut	12
	Atassut	12
	Inuit Ataquatiquit	2
	Total	26
Faeroese Lagting	People's Party	6
	Unity Party	8
	Social Democrats	7
	Independence Party	3
	Republicans	6
	Progress Party	2
	Total	32
Åland Landsting	Social Democrats	3
	Liberals	9
	Centre	14
	Right	4
	Total	30

new manifestations. Their profile, however, has been sharpened lately by the question of independent representation for the Faeroes on the Nordic Council, a matter which the Republicans, in particular, have pushed hard.[45]

On the Swedish-speaking Åland islands, which became a self-governing province of Finland on December 28, 1951, the party politicisation of the 30-seat *Landsting* has been an extremely recent phenomenon. The landmarks were the Landsting elections of 1967 and 1971; thereafter the partisan allegiance of delegates became the decisive factor in the selection of legislative standing committees, and though no reference was made either to 'party' or 'parliamentary group' in the revised Landsting standing orders in 1972, the Landsting's parliamentary office did record party affiliation in the official list of delegates it compiled in 1974. Even so, not until 1979 was the Speaker elected from the largest parliamentary group — in the 1978–9 session, the Speaker actually hailed from the smallest Landsting party! At approximately the same time, the practice of party spokesmen making statements on the budget developed although it was the autumn session of 1980 before the assembly amended its work procedures so that seating arrangements in plenary session were organised on a party basis rather than alphabetical order as earlier. Finally in December 1981, another amendment to the Landsting's work procedures set aside regular weekly times for parliamentary group meetings.[46] The distribution of seats among the four parties presently represented in the Åland Landsting is outlined in Table 1.4.

The primary cause of the belated party politicisation of the Åland Landsting may be located in the distinctive nature of the social structure on the islands. As Wrede and Wrede have observed, the grounds for political discontent were naturally weaker on the small fishing boats than in the large factories on the Finnish and Swedish mainland; the proportion of blue-collar workers was much smaller than elsewhere in the Nordic states and hence class differences remained insignificant; also important, in contrast to Finland, the language factor tended towards unity, not conflict.[47] Moreover, because the Home Rule campaign dominated political life on the Åland islands between the wars, other issues (and potential divisions) tended to be subordinated to it. We should recall here the influence of Julius Sundblom, the Home Rule leader and so-called 'King of Åland', who was strongly opposed to political parties. Finally, of course, the very nature of the small island communities, with their close *gemeinschaftlich* relations between governors and governed, tight kindred and neighbourhood networks, small populations and small distances, meant that essentially local questions could be resolved without resort to ideological (partisan) solutions.

The death of Sundblom in 1945 did not immediately change this picture. As early as 1957 an umbrella organisation, the Åland Union, *Åländsk Samling* was founded, and controlled local and national elections, but it was the 1960s before the Social Democrats stepped up their activities and 1971 before they put up candidates under their own name. The Presidential elections of January 1982 marked a turning point in the party political history of the Åland islands. It was then that a candidate backing the successful Social Democratic candidate Mauno Koivisto carried the single-member Åland constituency and the Social Democrats succeeded in holding on to it at the general election the following year. Earlier the Åland delegate had traditionally aligned himself with the Swedish-speaking group in the Eduskunta. Indeed, possibly to accommodate him, the designation Swedish People's Party's parliamentary group — the Swedish People's Party is the official name of the mainland party — has been trimmed to read simply 'the Swedish parliamentary group', *Svenska riksdagensgruppen*. As to factors in the growing party politicisation of the Åland Landsting in the late 1960s, they need not detain us; suffice it to note that urbanisation has played its part. In 1921 only 6% of the islands' population lived in the capital Mariehamn, compared with 42% forty years later when an agricultural society had been transformed into a predominantly service society. Geographic and social mobility have increased, mass tourism has produced closer contacts with neighbouring countries — particularly Sweden — and through television Swedish political life has found its way into most Åland homes. Even so, levels of electoral mobilisation have remained distinctively low on the Åland islands: until the 1980s the highest turn-out at any election was only 63%, and the absence of well-organised political parties and therefore established voter allegiances doubtless had much to do with this.[48]

The party landscape of the sovereign Nordic assemblies

Away from the devolved assemblies, political parties have long played a central role in the work of the Nordic legislatures. Historically the largest parliamentary group in the region has been the Social Democrats. In 1983 the party could claim well over a quarter of the active electorate in Finland, just below and rather more than one-third of the vote in Denmark and Norway respectively and as much as 45.6% in Sweden. Only in Iceland has support for social democracy been relatively weak at under one-fifth of the total poll. The regional strength of the movement has been founded upon notably high levels of political cohesion among the industrial working class. At the Swedish general election in September 1982, for example, 72% of the industrial working class voted for the Social Democratic Party compared with only 8% of the blue-collar population supporting the Conservatives.[49] Outside Iceland, in fact, where distinctively liberalism and conservatism fused in 1929 to form a broadly-based Independence Party drawing significant support from the blue-collar electorate, working-class conservatism in the Nordic region has been conspicuous by its absence. In contrast, by stripping away the Marxist rhetoric from their programmes in the 1960s, the Social Democratic parties were able to make substantial inroads into the middle-class vote and so become catch-all parties in the mould of the West German SPD.

Over the five decades up to 1970, the bourgeois seats in the Nordic legislatures were dominated by three political groupings — the centre-based Agrarians and Liberals and the moderate right-wing Conservatives. Historically this non-socialist tripartism was a corollary of the superimposition of mass democracy and proportional representation on largely rural societies, for this created the conditions for the emergence of a numerically significant and highly durable genus of agrarian parties, and in turn institutionalised bourgeois politics along a rural-urban axis. In the very early phases of the mobilisation of a mass electorate in the late nineteenth century, a non-socialist Left, an alliance of peasant farmers and a few urban intellectuals had opposed the Right, a loose union of officials, senior clergy and industrialists based in the towns and capital cities (there are interesting comparisons here with the contemporary leadership role of the academics in the populist *raznochintsy* movement in Czarist Russia). The Right, which by degrees modernised its programme and became Conservatives, has remained predominantly town-based; the 'old Left', however, split with the advent of universal suffrage and PR, the urban intellectuals forming the core of the Liberals, leaving the farmers to found their own party. This they did successfully: on two occasions in Finland, in 1929 and 1962, the Agrarian Party, *maalaisliitto*, was the largest single party.[50] However, a steady decline in the size of the farming population, accelerating after the Second World War, led the agrarian parties in the 1950s and 1960s to re-name themselves Centre parties with a view to adding an urban string to their bow. Incidentally, although interest-specific farmers' parties never emerged on any scale in Denmark and Iceland, the Agrarian Liberals, *Venstre*, in Denmark and the Progressive Party, *Framsóknarflokkurinn*, in Iceland have relied above all on agricultural support.

The balance of electoral and parliamentary power between the three 'historic' non-socialist parties has varied from country to country and over time. However, overall support for the Centre parties seems at present to be on the decline, ranging from a mere 6.7% for the Norwegian party and 15.5% for the Swedish party — a drop of almost 10% from the heady days of the early 1970s when the party capitalised on the ideas of the 'new left', particularly a growing public concern with environmental issues — to 17.6% for the Finnish party. Significantly, the bulk of the support for the Centre parties continues to derive from the farmers. Nearly three-quarters of the farming population voted for the Swedish Centre Party in September 1982 compared with only a little over one-fifth of small businessmen. For its part, the future of liberalism in the Nordic states is beginning to look rather bleak. The Liberal parties have struggled to project a distinct identity in the crowded multi-party market places of the region and, unlike their British counterparts, have failed to articulate the obvious protest mood of a section of voters over the years since the late 1960s. The Norwegian party disappeared from the Storting for long periods in the 1970s; the Finnish Liberals failed to get a single Eduskunta seat in 1983, while the Swedish Liberals were reduced to the status of a minor party at the general election the previous year. Indeed, in Finland the Liberals have merged with the Centre Party — although contesting elections under their own name — and there has been ephemeral discussion of a similar move in Sweden. Finally, the Conservatives have gained ground over the last decade to become the largest bourgeois party across the region and achieve as much as 31.7% of the poll in Norway in 1981. There has even been talk of a 'Norwegian model', i.e., two leading parties in the form of the Social Democrats and Conservatives, developing in Sweden and elsewhere in the region. However, backing for conservatism is still dominated by its original core elements — the civil servants, professional groups and large entrepreneurs. In 1982 the Swedish Conservatives, *moderata samlingspartiet*, gained the support of almost half of all senior public officials and employees. In short, the Independence Party in Iceland remains the only real catch-all party of the Nordic right comparable to the Conservative Party in Britain or the West German Christian Democrats.

Looking at the region as a whole before 1970, significant anti-system parties of radical left or radical right were confined to Finland and Iceland. In the latter, the People's Alliance, a loose grouping of communists, pacifists and left-wing socialists, polled almost one-fifth of the vote on several occasions in the 1940s and 1950s. In Finland a substantial radical left — in the form of the Socialist Workers' Party, a puppet of the Moscow-based Finnish Communist Party — emerged in the wake of the Civil War of 1918, while fear of the growing strength of communism touched off the only Nordic neo-fascist movement of any size — the black-shirted and fervently anti-communist Patriotic People's Movement (IKL), which at its peak in 1936 gained 14 Eduskunta seats and 8.3% of the poll. The Finnish Communist Party, banned in 1930, but relegalised in 1944 and subsequently operating within the umbrella organisation the Finnish People's Democratic League (SKDL), polled 23.2% of the active electorate in 1958, equalling the Social Democratic vote and bettering that of any of the bourgeois parties. Since the late 1960s and the appearance of a deep-seated reformist-hardline split in its ranks, the Communist Party has declined, and in 1983 it reached its post-war nadir of 14.0% of the vote.[51] Contemporaneous with the decline of Finnish communism, a decade of recession and high electoral volatility in the 1970s (no less than 40% of voters shifted parties in Denmark in 1973) saw the emergence of radical rightist parties in Denmark, Finland and Norway and a marked polarisation within the bourgeois bloc throughout the region. Most notably, Mogens Glistrup's anti-tax Progress Party in Denmark, formed only six weeks before the 1973 general election, claimed almost 20% of the poll in its first campaign. Moreover, recent signs of a decline in this new radical right in the Nordic region were confounded by the performance of the Finnish Rural Party in March 1983. Acting as a mouthpiece for a strong undercurrent of electoral protest directed against a number of malpractices involving established politicians that surfaced in the weeks before polling, the Rural Party contrived to gain almost 10% of the vote, almost equalling the level of its breakthrough year of 1970. Furthermore, in a manner quite unprecedented in Western Europe since the war — with the possible exception of the governmental accommodation of the once populist Democrats '66 in the Netherlands in the 1970s — the Rural Party achieved what no other protest movement has achieved, namely government office and two ministerial posts in Kalevi Sorsa's fourth Social Democratic-led coalition formed in May 1983. Indeed, the radical rightist party gained the very two portfolios of taxation and labour formerly held by the radical leftist People's Democratic League.[52]

Summing up on the Nordic party systems from a parliamentary viewpoint, a number of observations are in order. First, that in the absence of deep-seated religious and linguistic divisions on the scale of the Netherlands and Belgium, social class has been the dominant electoral cleavage in the region and as a result conflict in the Nordic legislatures, as expressed at Final Reading ballots, can largely be depicted on a left-right continuum. True, centre-based parties representing both religious and language groups have enjoyed a parliamentary toehold. Thus the Christian People's Party in Norway and latterly parliamentary-based Christian parties in Denmark and Finland have drawn heavily on low-church revivalist elements within the State Lutheran churches, while the Swedish People's Party in Finland, the only ethnic minority party in the Nordic assemblies, represents the 6% or so of the population speaking the second official language Swedish as a mother-tongue. Incidentally, the Swedish People's Party parliamentary delegation, like that of the Free Democrats in West Germany, is located rather anachronistically on the extreme right of the debating chamber, a reminder of its separatist ambitions in the early Independence era. However, parliamentary divisions tend mainly to reflect a basic left-right, socialist non-socialist duality, and class voting has remained very high by Western European standards. The class index of voting in Sweden between 1956–82 is set out in Table 1.5.

Secondly, and despite the socialist non-socialist dichotomy in parliament, no clearly-defined socialist non-socialist alternation in power has occurred in the region with any degree of regularity. On the contrary, the historic fragmentation in the bourgeois camp has meant that tripartite non-socialist majority government has been a relative rarity (at least until recently) and then, as the three Swedish bourgeois coalitions between 1976–82 demonstrate, it has rarely proved particularly stable. The centre of gravity in Nordic politics, in short, has been to the left of centre even though there has been a narrow bourgeois electoral plurality across the region *as a whole* over the sixty years of mass democracy. The state of the parties at the polls in the 1980s is presented in Table 1.6.

Parliamentary assemblies in the Nordic region are notably old, and one of them can trace a lineage back earlier than the Magna

Table 1.5. THE INDEX OF CLASS VOTING IN SWEDEN, 1956–82*

1956	+53
1960	+55
1964	+47
1968	+42
1970	+40
1973	+44
1976	+36
1979	+37
1982	+38

Source: Sören Holmberg of the University of Gothenburg at a meeting of the Scandinavian Politics Group of the Political Studies Association of the United Kingdom. University of Newcastle, 12.4.1983.

*The index of class voting devised by Robert Alford is obtained by subtracting the percentage of the middle-class voting for parties of the left from the proportion of working-class electors supporting parties of the left.

Carta. Although a number of vestiges of this long tradition remain, the Nordic legislatures are today essentially modern, functional bodies eschewing ceremonial in favour of a purpose-specific approach to the business of law-making. Highly-sophisticated electronic voting equipment has thus been widely installed and well-accoutred offices for members constructed — in the case of delegates representing outlying constituencies, complete with overnight facilities. In Norway, the result of an assembly division is photographed, written out and distributed automatically to delegates within one minute of the vote taking place. So efficient has this advanced Norwegian technology proved that the Swedes adopted it in October 1983 when the Riksdag moved from *Sergels torg* in the main city square back to Helgeandsholmen in the Old Town. In recent decades, moreover, a number of innovations in the internal structures and proceedings of parliament have contributed to strengthening the formal position of the Nordic assemblies in respect of the executive authority, while at the same time expressing a growing concern with what Coombes and Walkland (the citation at the beginning of this chapter) have referred to as 'the representative dimension of government'. It is worth taking up these points briefly in turn before launching into the debate about the supposed decline in the position of parliament throughout the western world.

The antiquity of the parliamentary institutions in the region is well illustrated in the Icelandic case. The establishment of the Althing as early as AD 930 marked the unification of the various Norse settlements within a single nation-state and the creation of one of the oldest legislative assemblies in the world. This ancient republic of Iceland survived for nearly three hundred years. Moreover, over the course of the four centuries which followed Iceland's incorporation into the Norwegian crown in 1262, the Althing shared legislative responsibility with the King, although the subsequent supremacy of royal absolutism led to a decline in its status, and it was abolished altogether in 1800. The resurrection of the Althing on a consultative basis in 1843 owed much to the general surge of liberalism across Western Europe in the mid-nineteenth century — significantly, the Danish King, who had replaced the King of Norway as Iceland's Head of State in 1814, ran into domestic difficulties and granted a constitution in 1849 which reformed the Danish legislature. This in turn forced the constitutional issue to the forefront of Icelandic politics, cast the Althing in its historic role as symbol and champion of Icelandic nationhood, and spawned parliamentary leaders like Jón Sigurðsson to lead the fight for independence. In many respects, the period until January 1874 when the Danish King

Table 1.6. PARTY REPRESENTATION IN THE NORDIC PARLIAMENTS IN THE 1980s

	Radical Left	*%*	*Left*	*%*	*Centre*	*%*	*Right*	*%*	*Radical Right*	*%*
Denmark (1984)	Socialist People's Party	11.5	Social Democrats	31.6	Radicals	5.5	Conservative People's Party	23.4	Progress Party	4.0
	Left Socialists	2.7			Centre Democrats	5.0				
					Christian People's Party	2.7				
					Liberals	12.1				
		14.2		31.6		25.3		23.4		4.0
Finland (1983)	Finnish People's Democratic League	14.0	Social Democrats	26.7	Centre Party	17.8	National Coalition	22.2	Rural Party	9.7
					Swedish People's Party and Åland Union	4.6			Greens	1.5
					Christian League	3.0			Constitutional Right Party	0.4
		14.0		26.7		25.4		22.2		11.6

Country	Party	%	Party	%	Party	%	Party	%	Party	%
Iceland (1983)	People's Alliance	17.3	Social Democrats	11.7	Progressives	18.5	Independence Party	38.7	League of Women's Lists*	5.5
			Social Democratic League	7.3						
		17.3		19.0		18.5		38.7		5.5
Norway (1981)	Left Socialists	4.9	Labour Party	37.2	Centre Party	6.7	Right (Conservatives)	31.7	Progress Party	4.5
					Christian People's Party	9.3				
					Liberals	4.0				
		4.9		37.2		20.0		31.7		4.5
Sweden (1982)	Left Communists	5.6	Social Democrats	45.6	Centre Party	15.5	Moderates (Conservative)	23.6		
					Liberals	5.9				
		5.6		45.6		21.4		23.6		

*In some cases, the spatial positioning of the parties is rather arbitrary — the League of Women's Lists in Iceland is difficult to place on a left-right continuum as, indeed, are the Greens in Finland.

conceded a constitution providing Iceland with self-government in domestic affairs could be considered the golden era of Icelandic parliamentary politics.

When compared with the ritual and ceremony of proceedings in the British House of Commons, tradition in the Nordic assemblies is less immediately conspicuous. The Speakers are not bedecked in silk robes and knee breeches; the job of the Sergeant-at-Arms is undertaken by a head janitor; members do not indulge in the archaic rhetoric of 'calling for candles' and there are no 'maiden speeches'. True, the opening of the Riksdag session was formerly preceded by a fanfare of mounted heralds, and this pageantry was revived in 1935 to commemorate the five hundredth anniversary of the original Riksdag assembly at Arboga. In all three monarchies in the region, moreover, the traditional Speech from the Throne at the State opening of parliament has been preserved, like the Queen's Speech in the United Kingdom, even if it is not always delivered by the monarch in person. Otherwise, the parliamentary tradition in the Nordic assemblies is not so visible as at Westminster. That it does exist can be seen *inter alia* in the seating arrangement of members by region rather than by party in Norway and Sweden; the convention which allows the Storting Speaker to contribute a plenary speech having first handed his responsibilities to a deputy-Speaker; and the universality of members' request proposals, a time-honoured form of private initiative in which the monarch (nowadays, of course, the government) is petitioned for some form of action. Interestingly, there are Riksdag members who want a return to the sumptuous festive opening of the Riksdag and for whom the recent spectacle of the Speaker slowly ascending from below the plenary chamber on an elevating podium has had more in common with the theatre (or farce?) housed in *Sergels torg* before the Riksdag moved there in 1976 than a 'proper' opening ceremony.

The post-war period has witnessed a degree of modernisation in Nordic legislative practice which has contributed to strengthening the formal position of the assemblies in the region. Relevant reforms have included the widespread introduction and/or consolidation of a Westminster-style Question Time; the advent of formal provisions for a no confidence vote in Sweden; investing the Riksdag Speaker with powers to nominate the Prime Minister-designate; the appointment for the first time of parliamentary Ombudsmen in Denmark and Norway, complementing those already existing in Sweden and Finland; the reform of the parliamentary standing committee systems in Denmark, Sweden and latterly Finland (where in February 1983 the number of permanent Eduskunta committees was increased from 5 to 13); the widespread introduction of reply speeches in plenary debates; and the televising of important parliamentary proceedings with the approval of the Speaker's Council. Indeed, symptomatic of the intent of these reforms has been the way the Danish monarch is now confined to a box in the public gallery at the opening of the Folketing. The Swedish King fares only marginally better: when he attends the Riksdag opening he is seated alongside the Speaker, but no longer reads the Prime Minister's speech. There have been recent proposals, moreover, from the Praesidium to enliven the proceedings of the Nordic Council and these have included limiting the time of plenary speeches to create more opportunities for reply speeches, extending the institution of questions so that written questions may be tabled throughout the year and increasing plenary control over the budget.[53]

The 'decline of parliaments' thesis

Why have such *ad hoc* parliamentary reform measures been (seen to be) necessary? Has the policy function of the Nordic parliaments been enhanced as a result or has there been a continuing decline in the institutional role of the assemblies in the region? Why, furthermore, have there been growing 'doubts and anxieties among supporters of parliamentary democracy' (in Coombes and Walkland's phrase) in western Europe today? Finally, how realistic is it to apply the label 'post-parliamentary democracy' when attempting to describe the decision-making process in the Nordic states? In sum, when analysing and comparing the Nordic parliaments, are we faced with no more than a routine case of decline? The second part of this introductory chapter is concerned to identify an approach to answering this last question rather than embarking on a detailed examination of the subject itself. To do this, however, we must present briefly the three convergent strands in the 'decline of parliaments' thesis. What then are the main arguments in support of the widespread presumption of a decline of parliament in western Europe?

First, attention is drawn in the general body of the literature to the way the basic infrastructure of parliaments — the plenary sessions, standing committees, question periods etc. — has been appropriated, so to speak, by highly cohesive political parties, the corollary of this process being a weakening in both the legislative and deliberative functions of modern assemblies.

In the British case, the 'colonisation' of the Commons by mass-based, centrally-organised and highly cohesive political parties has ensconced in power a distinctive genus of parliamentary potentate or 'vote baron', the party whips. This at least is how many new delegates perceive things. In fact, the authority of the whips can be exaggerated: their real sanction lies in the ability informally to jeopardise a political career rather than in issuing formal reprimands or official letters of expulsion. They are best regarded as 'business managers' confronted with the often daunting task of getting 200 or 300 MPs through the Division Lobby in the eight minutes allocated to voting. Small wonder that, as one experienced parliamentarian put it, a good whip must be a combination of 'psychologist, actor and night-club bouncer'![54] In France the equivalent of the Government Chief Whip is the Parliamentary Liaison Minister, and he heads a disciplinary machine which, though organised through the twin and sometimes conflicting channels of the Elysée President's Palace and the Prime Minister's Office, is every bit as strict as that operating in Westminster. Delegates are expected to toe the party line and outside the small, centre-based groups, levels of partisan cohesion are high right across the party spectrum. In the French Communist Party, for example — and notwithstanding the fact that the office of parliamentarian tends to be de-emphasised by the movement — newly-elected members sign an undated letter of resignation which they are duly sent in the subsequent event of errancy at ballots. Elsewhere in Western Europe the notion of whipping is weaker, although levels of partisan unity remain generally high. For example, convention contradicts the provisions of article 21 of the 1949 *Grundgesetz* (Basic Law) of the Federal German Republic requiring parties to be 'inwardly democratic', i.e. conform to democratic principles, because it is wholly customary for the leadership to require the complete loyalty of rank-and-file delegates at crucial votes. Party discipline, in short, is as strict in Bonn as in Westminster and, in line with the majority of legislatures in Western Europe, MPs may be regarded as members of their parties before members of parliament.

It goes almost without saying that the penetration of the internal machinery of assemblies by solidaristic political parties has significantly limited the efficacy of parliamentary activity. Briefly stated, party control has tended to mean that the *legislative function of assemblies* i.e. the successful initiation of proposals, has been subordinated to their role of deliberators or scrutineers: law-making, in other words, has become a prerogative of governments and private members' bills have assumed an essentially demonstrative character. Certainly a private initiative is not infrequently tabled with the primary aim of putting pressure on a government or simply airing a controversial issue rather than in any serious expectation of the measure being adopted. This was probably the case early in 1983 when, against the backdrop of the fisheries dispute with the

British government and other EC nations, Glistrup and six other Progress Party delegates tabled a private measure concerning the question of compensation for losses incurred by the owners of Danish-registered fishing vessels.[55] In the absence of Westminster-style Supply Days and with the Danish government and Folketing's standing committee on Market Relations (a unique body where EC legislatures are concerned — see chapter 9) deadlocked on the issue[56] it seemed that Glistrup's initiative was mainly designed to ensure a plenary debate at which party standpoints on this contentious issue could be publicised. Parliamentary government, according to the nineteenth-century British constitutional authority Walter Bagehot, is "government by discussion" and yet the entrenchment of mass parties in the century since Bagehot has also served to reduce the *deliberative function of legislative assemblies.* Through control of the parliamentary agenda and use of technical devices like the *clôture* and guillotine, governments can truncate discussion on their bills. Moreover plenary debates, albeit not of the topical kind Glistrup sought, are invariably sparsely attended. The degree of 'parleying' on the floor of modern parliaments is therefore limited, not least because the need to conform to the party line has made the outcome a foregone conclusion. So much then for the purported impact of mass parties on the policy role of the legislature.

A second thread of explanation in the 'decline of parliaments' orthodoxy has focussed on the vast growth in the scale and scope of government after the Second World War — the elaborate superstructure of new departments, public corporations and central boards this has entailed — and its corollary, namely a growing ministerial reliance on the specialists, trained advisers and permanent officials that comprise the central technocracy.

The transformation of the West European state needs little documentation. Viewed as an (admittedly oversimplified) three-stage progression, the state has developed from the minimal role of nightwatchman, *État-Gendarme*, fundamentally concerned to provide citizens with external protection and internal law and order, to a *welfare state* guaranteeing 'womb-to-tomb' protection for its citizens in the event of need, to a *managerial state*, basically an economic conception in which governments attempt by manipulating the strings to achieve such widely-desired goals as growth and prosperity. Symptomatic of the expansion of the activities of central government has been the increase in government revenues as a proportion of gross national product — over one-third in many West European systems — and the sharp rise in the level of personal taxation needed to fund elaborate welfare structures. In Sweden in 1983, for example, over 50% of GDP derived from government tax receipts. The West European states, moreover, are large employers of labour, they own and direct key sectors of industry, and assume in varying degree responsibilities for planning, forecasting and programming the economy. The multi-sided character of the modern state is well depicted by Mattei Dogan who asserts that 'having assumed functions as organiser, producer and protector, the state invests, subsidises, nationalises and redistributes.'[57]

This vast post-war growth in the scale and scope of government has also involved the significant bureaucratisation of central policy-making, something which has prompted a swelling chorus of criticism directed at the unacceptable power of officials. The traditional conception of bureaucrats as mere 'executors' or 'implementers' of policies, it is argued, has become plainly untenable. Lord Hailsham in his book *The Dilemma of Democracy* thus claims that 'Britain is governed by a bureaucracy of mandarins and their subordinates,[58] while, still more menacingly, the American political scientist Robert Dahl has sighted a 'Democratic Leviathan' — a giant bureaucratic whale threatening to overwhelm those plying the democratic waters surrounding cabinet and parliament. In their survey of senior civil servants and parliamentarians in the United States, Britain, France, Germany, Italy, the Netherlands and Sweden, Aberbach, Putnam and Rockham concur with Hailsham to the extent of stating that classical theories excluding bureaucrats from any role in creating policy no longer fit reality, if ever they did.[59] In an analysis of social policy development in Sweden and Britain, Hugh Heclo also emphasises the vital role officials play at the prelegislative stage of policy-making and observes that in so far as policy has evolved as a corrective to social conditions, 'civil servants have played a leading role in identifying these conditions, and framing concrete alternatives to deal with them.'[60] Other studies of the political role of senior civil servants have reached similar sorts of conclusions. Thus emphasising the modern role of departmental officials in bridging the gap between experts and cabinet ministers in the Danish policy process, Erik Damgaard has pointed to the way in which administrators are required to sift the evidence presented and make recommendations from a range of options when ministerial guidelines may be broad, unhelpful or even contradictory.[61] In such circumstances, civil servants must proceed on the basis of personal evaluation and anticipated reaction in drafting proposals. Their role is a far cry from the neutrality and impartiality associated with Max Weber's classical delineation of the administrator's role.

Viewed from a parliamentary standpoint, an important consequence of the post-war growth in the scale and scope of government and the concomitant tendency for decision-making to devolve from elected ministers to non-elected officials has been the growing enormity of the task of monitoring the activities of the executive — *the control or policing function of assemblies.* The significance of these developments may be gauged more clearly when account is taken of the widespread view that historically, parliaments existed 'to curb and limit the activities of governments, and found their main function in the imposition of restraints and checks on the discretionary power of the executive.'[62] How effective, however, can these checks really be, given that as a result of their high individual workload and the increasingly technical nature of the subject-matter with which they have to deal, ministers have come to rely extensively on civil servants to co-ordinate the legislative work of their departments, and they in turn are not directly responsible to parliament? For an elected delegate pressed by a constituent, it may be desirable to know who in practice was responsible for a particular decision, the basis upon which it was made and whether the correct procedures were observed. Attempts to strengthen the parliamentary surveillance of the central administration in recent decades have taken a number of institutional forms: the creation of Ombudsmen, Parliamentary Commissioners and *Médiateurs*, for example, and the formation by the first Thatcher government in 1979 of a select 'watchdog' committee system. There has also been extensive discussion in several West European states of adopting the type of open hearings staged by the standing committees of the United States Congress. The question of the efficacy of such measures in the Nordic context will be taken up in Part III of this volume.

A third and final area in the literature on the 'decline of parliaments' has concentrated on pressure group/executive relations and the way in which, as a consequence of the evolution of the West European state towards economic management, there has been a growing involvement of organised, 'corporate' interests in the policy-making processs.

Governments, in short, tend to govern in co-operation with the major labour-market organisations, and the probabilities are that the salient discussions on leading economic questions will be held in conjunction with the affected interests either on an *ad hoc* informal basis or, more routinely, at annual rounds of negotiations on incomes and prices. Indeed, it has become commonplace for reference to be made to a 'corporate channel', denoting the (analytically distinct) sector of policy-making in which the government and major economic groups or "corporations" convene to formulate the guidelines of future economic programmes. True, a corporate channel may be said to have developed further in some systems than in others: in a number of West European democracies the overarching goal of post-war reconstruction prompted a significant degree of *concertation* between government and the major sectional interests, whether in the form of Monnet-style economic planning in France or the type of 'consociational' relationships between the major political and economic élites described by Arend Lijphart in the Netherlands. Perhaps the last-mentioned cases should be regarded as 'ideal-types': French economic planning may well have passed its heyday, while the recessionary 1970s caused chinks in the consociational armoury, not least because there were then less economic pickings to go round. The fundamental *modus operandi*, however, has remained the same, and it is still broadly valid to assert that with the expansion of government into the economic sphere, the activity of modern cabinets has come, as Coombes and Walkland indicate, 'to resemble foreign policy in that it is conducted under what John Locke called "federative powers" — powers based on prerogative and involving negotiations and even decision-making with elements essentially outside parliament.'[63] The 'parliamentary channel' in sum appears to have taken second place *vis-à-vis* the 'corporate channel'. Indeed even in Britain, where the notion of the corporate state has been anathema to wide sections of opinion on the centre-right of the political spectrum, A.H. Halsey was able to argue in 1978 — significantly just before the accession of Margaret Thatcher as Prime Minister — that 'the state in Britain has become less parliamentary and more the centre of attempts to incorporate and pacify competing economic interests.'[64]

The literature on interest group/executive relations has also followed a line at something of a tangent to 'corporate analysis' though in its way wholly complementary to it, taking as its starting point the increasingly technocratic nature of public administration and accordingly the need for governments to enlist the aid of experts in the pursuit of rational outcomes. As in the writing on corporatism, emphasis is placed on the evolution of a new policy style in which the government, and more particularly the senior bureaucrats serving it, are engaged in consulting with the spokesmen of affected interests on the plethora of committees, commissions and departmental working groups that constitute an essential part of the modern state. Briefly stated, it is argued that there has been a growing tendency for governments to 'co-opt' pressure groups on to committees and commissions at the vital pre-legislative stage. In his study of Norwegian interest groups, Robert Kvavik alludes to a 'secularisation of the administration' resulting from the increased participation of pressure group representatives,[65] while Kenneth E. Miller contends that in Denmark interest groups constitute in practice a branch of the state administration.[66] Heisler and Kvavik's all-embracing 'European Polity model' describes a decision-making system characterised by continuous, regularised access for a wide range of interest organisations up to the highest level of the political system.[67] Methodologically innovative was their assertion that pressure groups be viewed as 'insiders' rather than 'outsiders', knocking on the door of government, so to speak, in the hope of being admitted; they are perceived as 'withinputs' rather than simply 'inputs', to deploy the terminology of David Easton's classical behavioural analysis.

The twin impact of the processes of corporatism and co-optation has been, it is argued, to threaten and reduce the deliberative function of modern assemblies. Parliaments, the argument goes, have too often been confronted with situations that are cut and dried — *faits accomplis*—permitting the assembly to do little more than rubber-stamp executive recommendations. As Bob Jessop, considering the transformation of the British state, has thus observed, 'The deliberative stage of legislation has been largely incorporated into the executive branch. . . .'[68] All in all, it appears that the legislative function of parliaments is minimal; their deliberative function is threatened; and their control-policing function is compounded by the sheer complexity of the apparatus of the modern state. Small wonder that the 'decline of parliaments' thesis has become part of the accepted wisdom of political science. Indeed, in their persuasive study of decision-making in Britain, Richardson and Jordan have even ventured to dub Britain a '*post-parliamentary democracy*' and the House of Commons merely 'a constitutional procedural device for legitimising decisions'.[69] Whether the 'decline' thesis constitutes an exhaustive truth or not represents the paramount question of this study. Before discussing an analytical approach to answering it, however, it is worth reviewing the debate about the role of parliament from an exclusively Nordic perspective.

The 'decline of parliaments' thesis from a Nordic perspective

In a speech in May 1982 to mark the seventy-fifth anniversary of the inception of the reformed unicameral legislature, Antero Juntumaa, a delegate from Finland representing the small Christian League in that country, doubtless echoed the sentiments of many Finnish parliamentarians when stating that the Eduskunta's powers had devolved both to the large party machines (at the expense of the parliamentary party groups) and the labour-market organisations.[70] Only a little earlier, the leading weekly current affairs' magazine, *Suomen Kuvalehti*, had run a piece entitled simply 'Powerless Parliament'.[71] The forthright views of the leader of the Danish Progress Party, Mogens Glistrup, differ from those of Juntumaa more in perspective than in substance: 'Parliament is controlled by organised interests because pressure groups finance the leading parties and in consequence expect Folketing delegates to push excessive group demands for increased expenditure.'[72] The increased subordination of the legislature to corporate interests, according to Glistrup, had contributed substantially to Denmark's poor post-war record of economic management.

The appearance of a significant shift of power away from the democratically-elected institutions of government has concerned Swedish parliamentarians too. As Ola Ullsten, the leader of the Swedish Liberals, put it in January 1983 at an extraordinary party conference called to discuss the party's calamitous showing at the general election the previous September, 'there is a threat to freedom in a society in which power has passed insidiously to the central bureaucracy, unions and other large corporate interests.'[73] Some, of course, have refused to accept such developments lying down. A Finnish Liberal candidate claimed at an election meeting in March 1983 that if the burden of taxation were lifted from incomes — a matter decided in the corporate channel — on to consumers, this would strengthen the influence of parliament[74]; others including the controversial right-wing veteran Tuure Junnila, who in the 1960s wrote a highly critical account of the management of Fenno-Soviet relations, contented themselves with maintaining that if successful at the polls, they could at least improve the standard of parliamentary debate.[75]

Signs of a growing awareness on the part of Nordic delegates of a drift of power away from parliament should not be regarded as evidence that legislators necessarily perceive their role as largely futile. Many indeed feel they can exert a measure of policy influence either in their parliamentary party group or on the relevant legislative standing committee provided, of course, that the case they are putting is sufficiently well researched and effectively elaborated. True, there will always be a few parliamentarians wanting to see the creation of new standing committees as vehicles for heightening their influence in desired policy areas. The Danish Christian People's Party delegate, Inge Krogh, for example, suggested the creation of an extra Folketing standing committee to deal with Family Affairs.[76] However, talk of a decline in the standing of parliament has coincided with data indicating a possible drop in the popular legitimacy afforded the parliaments in the region. Most strikingly, 70% of those persons of voting age interviewed in Finland early in

1983 held that the status of parliament had deteriorated in recent years, and the rather disreputable image of the Eduskunta became a background issue in the general election campaign some weeks later. 41% of respondents alluded to the so-called 'day allowance question', *päivärahakysymys*, as the primary cause of this sorry state of affairs — the Chancellor of Justice had in fact exposed the cases of four senior delegates illegally claiming the allowance — but, significantly, 39% of those interviewed simply pointed to a problem of 'general confidence'.[77] In Sweden, moreover, the Liberal delegate, Olle Wästberg, contributing an article in the nonpartisan daily, *Dagens Nyheter*, during the 'silly season' in September 1981 noted how no less than two-thirds of the public felt that Riksdag members quickly lost touch with ordinary citizens.[78] Survey information has tended to confirm such findings elsewhere in the region.

Even so, it is important not to exaggerate the extent to which the popular legitimacy of parliament has declined of late. Importantly, the Finnish study did not contain a question on what position the Eduskunta actually enjoyed among the public — only one as to whether it had declined or not. The legislature, moreover, remains a favourite target of activist pressure and for mass lobbies seeking to influence the course of proposals before the assembly. The Nordic parliaments, therefore, are frequently the focus of popular and media attention. Just a few recent instances will suffice to illustrate the point. Thus in 1979 demonstrators against a parliamentary decision to construct a hydroelectric power project across the river Alta in northern Norway went on a dramatic hunger strike outside the Storting — the Lapps in the Alta area feared the loss of their salmon catch as well as the use of the river valley for grazing their reindeer. There were protests too in *Sergels torg* in Spring 1982 when the Fälldin III non-socialist coalition in Sweden moved a bill introducing a number of benefit-free sickness days, *karensdagarna*, into the health insurance system as a means of effecting marginal cuts in public spending. In September 1980, moreover, a long 'beer march' proceeded from Senate Square to the steps of the Eduskunta in an attempt to mobilise support for the withdrawal of so-called 'middle beer', *keskiolut*, from the grocers and supermarkets and its return to the state-owned alcohol shops. The model urged on legislators was the Swedish and, it was argued, there had been numerous positive effects of Sweden ceasing production of a similar type of lager, *mellanöl*. In addition, as we see in Chapter 4, there have been a number of controversial, cliff-hanging debates media and public alike have followed with interest. So it seems fair to conclude that the public status of both parliaments and parliamentarians in the Nordic region remains reasonably secure, notwithstanding survey evidence of declining legitimacy and the intermittent feeling among many delegates that things could be better.

It is in the realm of academic research that the decline in the institutional position of the Nordic parliaments appears most starkly etched. A mass of neo-corporatist analyses has thus condemned the legislatures in the region to the status of appendages in the policy process — bit-part actors, with the personnel of the pre-legislative commissions cast in the starring roles. In particular, attention has been focused on the deleterious consequences for the elected assembly of the increasingly ensconced position of interest groups within the executive arm of government. Seemingly against the main thrust of Glistrup's argument that pressure groups pull the parliamentary strings through their financial stake in the main parties, Nordic political scientists have emphasised the operational distance separating corporate and parliamentary channels: groups, it is held, display a diminishing interest in both parliament and parliamentarians. So much does not in itself, of course, invalidate Glistrup's view, although it appears that only rarely do groups display a manifest interest in the legislature as an arena in which to exert pressure. Group contacts with legislators appear a last resort rather than first option.

Kvavik notes therefore that Norwegian groups initiate direct contacts with parliamentarians only when all other means of influencing proposals before their consideration in the Storting have been exhausted.[79] Nils Elvander reaches a similar conclusion in Sweden, claiming that the least important focus of pressure is the Riksdag, although he allows that interest organisations do maintain contact with the parliamentary party groups.[80] Indeed, it seems that the traditional concept of parliamentary democracy has been not only threatened, but largely superseded in Nordic political research by a notion of *functional representation* — that is, policy-making conducted in close collaboration with the nexus of sectional interests that comprise the corporate channel of influence. The corporate channel is, in fact, a Nordic invention. It was in a seminal discussion of policy-making in Norway in the mid-1960s that the late Stein Rokkan drew the celebrated distinction between the electoral and corporate channels and proceeded to postulate what has become the predominant view in the Nordic states, namely that 'votes count in the choice of governing personnel, but other resources decide the actual policies pursued by the authorities'.[81] Even in Finland, where traditionally the structure of the party system has maintained a delicate numerical balance between legislature and executive, the emergence of a stable centre-left *majorité* in the late 1960s and the corresponding development of an incomes policy system inspired recourse to corporatist formulations. As Voitto Helander has observed, 'There are signs that the Finnish political system is changing into a two-tier system with a parliamentary and corporate subsystem in the manner that Stein Rokkan has described in regard to the Norwegian system'.[82]

The most recent and certainly most ambitious investigation into the whole question of the inter-relations between the main policy actors — parliament, government, civil servants, pressure groups etc. — has been the government-sponsored Power Commission, *maktutredning*, which was set up in 1972 to analyse the distribution of power in Norwegian society and completed its final report a decade later. From a parliamentary viewpoint, a depressing scenario emerges in which power rests in the hands of non-elected élites at the expense of the elected representatives of the people in parliament. The report argues that those elements most concerned with a particular policy area are overrepresented on the state machinery dealing with it and, as a result, can fix both the desired goals in that sector as well as the means of achieving them. This segmentation of the policy process in Norway, the report continues, has tended to militate against the basic principle of parliamentary democracy. Put another way, the enormous influence of civil servants, pressure group spokesmen, experts and the personnel of the media has contributed to the professionalisation of politics and made the democratic process all the more inaccessible to citizens. Thus power in public policy matters is not exercised by the elected representatives of the people in parliament so much as by small, specialised, elite groups in a highly segmented central administration.[83]

An analytical approach to a comparative analysis of the Nordic parliaments

Whether the policy role of the Nordic parliaments really is as minimal as the work of the neo-corporatist school would indicate represents the central question of the present analysis. Although undeniably an ambitious remit, a systematic and comparative account of the legislatures in the region would seem timely on at least two counts. First, there is reason to surmise that significant changes occurring in the economic and political climate of the Nordic states in the 1970s and early 1980s have challenged the extent of corporate cohesion in the policy process and possibly in turn contributed to something of a revival in the position of parliament. Interestingly, a recent study of the reformed unicameral

Riksdag over the first decade of its operation revealed an *increased* parliamentary involvement at the crucial pre-legislative stage of policy-making.[84] Secondly, the general revival of academic research in the area of legislative behaviour has tended to by-pass the Nordic region. National legislative studies, in other words, have been relatively few in number and, ironically, although more than three decades have elapsed since the formation of the Nordic Council as a vehicle for regional co-operation, a comparative investigation of the Nordic parliaments has simply not been undertaken. The present work thus attempts to fill a notable gap in the literature, and it should finally be added that in embarking on it, any expectation that its content might read like an obituary or an extended memorial oration on the demise of parliament as a significant institution of government had to be consciously rejected. Instead, the volume proceeds from the premise that in the absence of a thorough medical examination, so to speak, little can really be known about the patient's general condition. There are even grounds for cautious optimism because, as Loewenberg and Patterson refreshingly assert, 'unexamined assumptions about the dominance of the executive in modern government and the decline of legislatures have led to unwarranted conclusions about the minimal role of legislatures in policy-making.'[85]

The economic and political changes forming the backdrop to a possible revival of parliament warrant a brief note and this will be followed by a word about the relative paucity of academic research on the Nordic legislatures. As in much of Western Europe, Scandinavia was affected by the symptoms of world depression during the mid-1970s. The politico-economic impact of recession varied from one individual Nordic state to the next: Norway, for example, was largely cushioned against the worst effects by the discovery of North Sea oil and gas — a source of income as well as collateral for foreign borrowing — and this enabled governments to maintain a low level of unemployment, around 2%. Finland, too, was buttressed by her trade with the Soviet Union under the terms of the Treaty of Friendship, Co-operation and Mutual Assistance: this currently amounts to about a quarter of the national total and has principally involved exchanging high-quality consumer durables for Soviet supplies of natural gas. Throughout the region, however, the economic malaise dictated a number of common denominators. In particular, it created widespread pressure for fiscal restraint and demands for cuts in public spending which contributed to or at least threatened 'a waning in the welfare state'. The ensuing tensions between governments and labour-market organisations over measures such as wage and price freezes and the need to slice a smaller economic cake into smaller pieces than previously, tended to be compounded by the advent of right-wing or non-socialist governments inherently less well disposed to a collectivist style of policy-making — although, in truth, nowhere in the region was there an assertion of the stark Thatcherite philosophy that it is the government's task to govern unfettered by interference from back-seat drivers in the corporate sector.

At the non-élite level, the main corollary of recession was a deterioration in industrial relations and recourse by the workforce to strike threats and, indeed, 'wildcat' action. In Norway in the summer of 1980, workers on the offshore platforms obtained a staggering 30% wage increase by threatening a strike which would have halted oil production, and this triggered off a spiral of wage demands which included an 18% increase secured by the merchant seamen. It was all part of a familiar syndrome: a fall-off in world markets accentuated the uncompetitiveness of traditional industry (the problem affected even Norway); unemployment rose and in Denmark touched 10%; and there were widespread demands for wages to keep pace with inflation. In Sweden the resultant outbreak of unofficial strikes during the winter of 1980 was deeply shocking to observers of a country whose industrial relations record had long been admired throughout the Western world. It was all a far cry from the 1950s and 1960s and the episode related by Andrew Schonfield of how during a visit of British trade unionists to Sweden to try and find out the secret of the outstanding industrial tranquility there, an incredulous group was told by a shop-steward that when conflict threatened to break out, 'we simply has a meeting.' 'We has a meeting! I'd like to see how they'd make out with our blokes over here,' commented one of the British delegation.[86]

In Denmark, whose foreign debt has been the largest of any country in the region, the government went on to the offensive in 1981 with the slogan, 'We must produce ourselves out of our troubles.' More recently, however, signs of a possible upturn in the world economy have raised great hopes, and led the Nordic states to look to West Germany to take the lead in furthering the economic recovery reputedly taking place in the United States. All in all, however, the protracted recession has strained relations in the corporate channel on two interacting levels: first, the austerity programmes imposed by governments have tested inter-élite cooperation in the management of the economy, and secondly, the fact that key labour federations have on occasions found themselves faced with wildcat grassroots action has tended to reduce their authority and bargaining power *vis-à-vis* the executive.

A wind of change started to blow through the politics of the Nordic region in the 1970s and there were those who felt the draught. The electorate became more mercurial, new and often radical parties enlivened the proceedings of parliament and, above all, there were historic alternations of power in Norway and Sweden. In Norway, the Labour Party, which can claim none other than the ex-Chancellor of West Germany, Willy Brandt, among its members, had monopolised government since the war save for two short periods, 1963–5 and 1972–3. Yet in October 1981 the pendulum finally swung and an era of Labour government gave way to the first Conservative (minority) administration since the 1920s, and this in turn was transformed into a three-party non-socialist coalition in the summer of 1983 with the incorporation into the cabinet of the Conservatives' legislative allies, the Christian People's and Centre parties. In Sweden, a virtually unbroken 44-year spell of Social Democratic rule, beginning ironically at the time of the first world recession in the early 1930s, ended in electoral defeat for the party in 1976 and then an interlude in which no less than four non-socialist cabinets held office in the space of six years was itself concluded by the return of a Social Democratic minority government under Olof Palme in October 1982. Table 1.7 shows the changes taking place in government across the region between 1976–84. On the presumption that a measure of continuity in government is a desirable, if not sufficient, condition for the maintenance of a cohesive corporate sector, it is clear that Norway and Sweden have failed in recent years to meet these conditions of stability. Whether the policy role of parliament has been strengthened by the combination we have mentioned of economic and political forces working to reduce the cohesion of the corporate channel must remain for the time being an open question. On the same theme, however, it might seem a fair speculation that the legislative function of the Folketing will have been enhanced by the almost perennial problem of building stable, majoritarian government in Denmark; that the deliberative role of parliament is likely to have been consolidated by the fact that outside Iceland the Social Democrats are the largest single party in the Nordic assemblies, but presently participate in government only in Sweden and Finland; and that the control-policing function of the legislature could well have been reinforced as a result of the industrious scrutineering of the various protest parties sustained by the continuing electoral volatility in the region. Whatever the case, the policy contribution of the Nordic parliaments has undoubtedly acquired a heightened interest and significance in the changed political and economic climate of the last decade and a half. The 'decline of parliaments'

Table 1.7. CHANGES IN THE PARTISAN COMPOSITION OF NORDIC GOVERNMENTS, 1976–84

	Term	*Type of government*	*Alternation in power*
Denmark	1976–82	4 Social Democratic minority administrations	
	1982–4	Centre-Right coalition	1982 Schlüter's Conservative-led coalition
Finland	1976–84	Centre-Left coalitions with or without the Communists and from May 1983 including the Rural Party	No alternation
Iceland	1976–8	Non-socialist coalition	
	1978–9	Centre-Left coalition	
	1979–81	Social Democratic minority	
	1981–3	Broadly-based coalition spanning the political spectrum with the Prime Minister from an opposition group within the Independence Party	Indeterminacy
	1983–4	Centre-Right coalition	
Sweden	1976	Social Democratic minority administration	
	1976–82	3 Non-socialist coalitions and a Liberal minority government (1978–9)	
	1982–4	Social Democratic minority	1976 advent of Fälldin (I) 1982 return of Palme (III)
Norway	1976–81	Social Democratic minority governments	
	1981–3	Conservative minority administration	
	1983–4	Centre-Right coalition	1981 advent of Willoch's Conservative minority

thesis may not after all be an exhaustive truth, but rather one open to serious question. What is not in question is that if the Nordic parliaments are discovered to be no more than 'legitimising assemblies',[87] the value of the entire democratic machinery in the region would be seriously reduced.

The absence of a substantial literature on the individual Nordic parliaments is surprising because, with the notable exception of Iceland, the discipline of political science is well developed in the region. The Swedish situation is typical enough: there is the classic study in 1957 entitled *The Parliament of Sweden* by Elis Håstad, sponsored by the Hansard Society for Parliamentary Government (in Great Britian) and growing out of an all-party Riksdag initiative in January 1955; Sören Holmberg's investigation based on a questionnaire survey of Swedish parliamentarians in 1969, the final year of the operation of the bicameral legislature; and the short work published in 1982 by Magnus Isberg, a member of the staff of the Riksdag's Constitutional Committee, which draws mainly on quantitative data on commissions, parliamentary questions and interpellations, private initiatives and so on, along with interviews with staff of the Riksdag parliamentary parties. Elsewhere in the region, research on the national legislature has become synonymous with particular individuals — Gudmund Hernes in Norway, who conducted an exhaustive set of verbal interviews with Storting delegates in the late 1960s, and Erik Damgaard whose doctoral dissertation completed in 1977 took as its theme 'The Folketing at a Time of Change'. In Finland, there is an interview survey of Eduskunta delegates by Matti Oksanen undertaken, like the Holmberg and Hernes studies, in the late 1960s and contributions on various institutional facets of the Finnish assembly including Voitto Helander's short paper on the Grand Committee. In Finland, as in Norway and Sweden, there are also official histories of parliament commissioned by the parliaments themselves and with something of an historical orientation. For this reason the historical material in the present study is kept to a minimum. As to Iceland, the only completed work on the Althing is a brief general pamphlet by Benedikt Gröndal, a former Social Democratic Party chairman and longstanding parliamentarian. (Thorsteinn Magnusson at the University of Exeter was engaged at the time of writing on research into its standing committee system). The devolved legislatures in the region are no better covered in scholarly literature. There is a recent work on the Åland Landsting commemorating the sixtieth anniversary of the 1922 statute on self-government, but nothing exists on the Faeroese and Greenlandic assemblies. All the major legislative studies will be drawn upon and cited in detail in the following chapters. However, they are *par excellence* national studies which eschew a comparative perspective, and *inter alia* the task of charting the strong diffusional currents affecting the parliamentary institutions in the region, in favour of an in-depth analysis of individual assemblies. Comparison based on this material — and hence the legislative topography of the Nordic region — is complicated by the different methodological approaches employed by the different authors, variations in the type of questions put to parliamentary respondents (in those which use survey evidence) and discrepancies in the periods covered by the investigations. Moreover, although stimulating in their contrasting ways, a number of these works have inevitably become rather dated.

The sources used in the present volume are multiple. In addition to the available academic literature, they include the parliamentary standing orders, official minutes of legislative proceedings, official statistics, newspaper articles, political biographies, and interviews with parliamentarians, parliamentary staff members, ministers, civil servants, experts and labour-market leaders. It has not been possible to emulate the national surveys and interview all the members of each parliament in the Nordic region, and in consequence the sum product of the book necessarily stands squarely in the British tradition of judgements based on 'informed opinion'. Although the conclusions should be seen in such a light, they are nonetheless predicated on a systematic, comparative approach which, in line with other legislative studies — e.g. Loewenberg and Patterson's *Comparing Legislatures*, and indeed Isberg's recent report on the Riksdag — examines the participation of the Nordic assemblies in the three central stages of the policy process: formulation, adoption and implementation. To establish the extent of parliamentary involvement in these main decision stages is not in itself to comment on the degree of policy *influence* exerted by the legislature, which is considerably more difficult. To assess such influence, it would be necessary to show, for instance, that not only was a parliamentary commission (see chapter 2) set up at the request of say the Riksdag, but also that it would not have been created without specific pressure from that source.[88] The detailed case-study material necessary to this end can be used only sparingly given the broad scope of this book; yet it would seem pedantic not to infer a measure of real influence from the differential patterns of parliamentary involvement that emerge from the examination in the ensuing chapters. We will seek briefly to illustrate the three stages of the policy process that constitute the analytical framework of this study.

The formulation stage of public policy entails, self-evidently, the detailed investigation, preparation and final drafting of legislative proposals — a task undertaken either by a commission of inquiry operating outside the formal confines of a government ministry (even though the commission's directive will formally emanate from a cabinet minister) or in the nexus of intra-departmental advisory committees and working groups. As a general rule, the engagement of West European parliamentarians at the policy formulation stage appears to be low: in Britain MPs never participate at the pre-legislative stage and this is also basically true of West Germany. However, since the 1969 parliamentary reforms, which permit the *Bundestag* to set up special commissions of inquiry, the so-called *Enquête-kommission*, the level of delegate involvement in the generation of longer-term proposals has risen slightly.[89]

The adoption of policy follows its deliberation on the floor of the House and in standing committee and requires the acquiescence of at least a simple parliamentary majority. While the efficacy with which bills are scrutinised is likely to be affected by the type of standing committee system, i.e. whether it is subject-specific as in the Bundestag or bill-specific as in the House of Commons, the impact of the West European assemblies at the policy adoption stage is invariably limited by the high levels of partisan cohesion. Free votes are rare and are reserved for questions of a controversial character on which the government wishes to avoid taking an official stance — e.g. the Commons' vote on the restoration of capital punishment in July 1983. Incidentally, among the citizenry at large there is no shortage of misconceptions about the routine work of the assembly. In West Germany, only important 'non-legislative' debates (see chapter 8) like that on the Government's Policy Declaration, *Die Regierungserklärung* are televised.[90] The routine proceedings, when attendance at plenary sittings is sparse, are not broadcast, which inevitably leads to a certain public naivety about delegate participation in the collective deliberation and adoption of bills.

The implementation of policy occurs when measures adopted by parliament and ratified by the Head of State are put into effect. At this stage, in other words, officials in the government departments, central agencies and boards administer the decisions of the House and ensure that laws are faithfully executed. Clearly, however, no legislation is so exhaustive in its detail as to provide guidance on how each and every case under the law should be dealt with and in an advanced technocratic state there is therefore considerable scope for administrative discretion. Equally, West European parliaments have developed techniques for monitoring the implementation of public policy — the creation of the office of Ombudsman is perhaps the best known. Even so, it appears that the growth in the scale and scope of government has made the parliamentary task of policing the executive through its regular standing committees extremely difficult.

In this last-mentioned context of parliamentary control over the executive, the individual delegates in the region have a considerably increased workload. Precisely because the scale and scope of government have grown, so too has the burden placed on legislators since the Second World War. Members of the Nordic parliaments, in short, have countless time-consuming demands on their time: reading through mountains of frequently technical documentation, preparing speeches, attending a host of meetings both inside and outside the assembly building, and getting through their extensive correspondence. To that extent they are, of course, no different from parliamentarians elsewhere in Western Europe. Equally, it is doubtless as true in the Nordic region as it is reputed to be in Britain that the people get the members of parliament they deserve. For the vast majority of industrious and dedicated delegates — the legislative culture of delegates is discussed in chapter 5 when their commitment to standing committee work is stressed — the secret of lasting sanity may well be the ability to put their activities into perspective and to recognise that patience and perseverance are probably the greatest assets parliamentarians can have. There is not likely to be an immediate or obvious legislative dividend on effort, and a persuasive speech or a telling intervention is unlikely in itself to set the world to rights. Delegates should not assume a monopoly of virtue either — the best conceived intentions do not necessarily make the best laws, or indeed laws at all. The caption on two sections of the Folketing lobby frieze painted by Rasmus Larsen as long ago as 1919 sums up wryly the need for legislators to be persevering and pragmatic and to take the rough with the smooth. "Not every cock that crows heralds a new day" reads the one, and, to anticipate charges of male chauvinism, the text on the adjoining picture reads 'Not every hen that clucks lays an egg'.

REFERENCES

1. 'Fred och nedrustning'. *Nordisk Kontakt* 3/83, pp. 180–1.
2. 'Nordisk håndslag til Grønland'. *Nordisk Kontakt* 5/83, pp. 333–6.
3. *Ålands författningssamling* 1982, 3.
4. 'Arbetsdryg vår för Ålands landsting.' *Nordisk Kontakt* 10/83, pp. 692–3.
5. Gudmundur S. Alfredsson, 'Greenland and the Right to Self-Determination.' *Nordisk Tidsskrift for International Ret* 51, 1982, pp. 39–44.
6. Jógvan Sundstein, 'Lagtingets historie og funktion'. *Nordisk Kontakt* 7/83, pp. 483–4.
7. Neil Elder, Alastair H. Thomas & David Arter, *The Consensual Democracies? The Government and Politics of the Scandinavian States*. Oxford: Martin Robertson, 1982, p. 3.

8. Pekka Väänänen, 'Kansanedustajien vaihtuvuus', *Kanava* 3, 1979, pp. 162–5.
9. 'Neljä vuotta sopiva istuntokausi'. *Kristityn Vastuu* 3.2.1983.
10. Information provided by Dr Sören Holmberg of the University of Gothenberg at a meeting of the Scandinavian Politics Group of the Political Studies Association of the United Kingdom, University of Newcastle, 12.4.1983.
11. Lennart Bodström, 'Industrins, handelns och hantverkets folk i riksdagen 1920–1953', in *Näringslivets folk i riksdagen*. Stockholm: Gernandts Boktryckeri, 1956, p. 25.
12. Bernt Krohn Solvang & Jorolv Moren, 'Partsrepresentasjon i Komitéer: Litt om utviklingen over tid', in Jorolv Moren (ed.) *Den Kollegiale Forvaltning. Råd og utvalg i sentraladministrasjonen*. Oslo-Bergen-Tromsø: Universitetsforlaget, 1974, pp. 33–6.
13. Ottar Hellevik, *Stortinget — en sosial elite? En undersøkelse av sammanhengen mellom sosial bakgrunn og politisk karriere*. Oslo: Pax Forlag, 1969, p. 36.
14. Pekka Väänänen, *Kansanedustajat kautta aikojen. Tutkielma edustajain yhteiskunnallisen ryhmityksen muutoksista*. Helsinki: Otava, 1975, p. 15.
15. Folke Petrén, 'Politiskt intresse-ett foretaga intresse', in *Näringslivet folk i riksdagen*, p. 11.
16. 'Näringslivet dåligt representerat i riksdagen'. *Nordisk Kontakt* 16/80, p. 1137.
17. *Norinform* 1.6.1982.
18. Väänänen (1975), pp. 18–19.
19. Pirkko Haapanen, Tapio Koskiaho & Aino Saarinen, *Women and Politics*. Tampereen yliopiston politiiken tutkimuksen laitoksen tutkimus 33a, 1974, p. 13.
20. Martti Noponen, *Kansanedustajien sosiaalinen tausta Suomessa*. Helsinki: WSOY, 1964, p. 26.
21. *Keisarilliselle Majesteetille eduskunnanuudistus-komiteelta alamaisimmasti*, 28.2.06
22. Tertit Aasland, 'Kvinner i Stortinget', in *Det Norske Storting gjenom 150 år*. Bind IV, Oslo: Gyldendal, 1964.
23. Ingunn Norderval Means, *Kvinner i Norsk Politikk*. Oslo: Cappelens, 1973, p. 75.
24. Maud Eduards, *Kvinnor och politik. Fakta och förklaringar*. Stockholm: Liber, 1977, pp. 28–31.
25. Cited in *Parliamentary Reform*. London: Cassell (for Hansard Society). 2nd edn, 1967, p. 119.
26. Voitto Helander, *Kansanedustaja ja painostusryhmät: vuorovaikutus, legitiimiys ja vaikutus*. Turun yliopiston valtio-opin laitos. Tutkimussarja C, 26, 1975, p. 23.
27. Mikko Vainio, Käsityönopettaja, kaupunginvaltuutettu, Lahti. *Unohdetun kansan siivellä* 1. Helsinki: Otava, 1971, p. 112.
28. Interview with Professor Pertti Pesonen, editor of the Tampere-based daily newspaper, *Aamulehti* 15.7.1980.
29. Benedikt Gröndal, *Althingi a Tjaldabaki*. Reyjavik: Al Pingi, 1981, p. 48.
30. Svenn Groennings, *The Varaman*. Oslo: Stortingsbiblioteket, 1960.
31. Interview with the Secretary-General of the Storting, Erik Mo, 1.10.1981.
32. Interview with Storting Speaker, Svenn Stray 30.9.1981.
33. Interview with Riksdag Speaker, Ingemund Bengtsson 10.9.1981.
34. 'Talmannen läxade upp riksdagskvinna', *Aftonbladet* 17.5.1983.
35. 'C-kvinna fronderade om väganslag', *Dagens Nyheter* 27.3.1981.
36. 'Släkten är värst'. *Dagens Nyheter* 17.12.1981.
37. Elis Håstad, *The Parliament of Sweden*. London: Hansard Society for Parliamentary Government, 1957, pp. 86–94.
38. Rune Nordin, *Den Svenska Arbetarrörelsen*. Stockholm: Tidens, 1978, pp. 82–90.

39. Olle Nyman, *Utländska statskick. En jämförande översikt över regeringsmakt, parlament, förvaltning och press i de flesta länder i världen.* Stockholm: Bonniers, 1978, p. 88.
40. Olle Nyman, *Svensk Parlamentarism 1932–36. Från minoritetsparlamentarism till majoritetskoalition.* Stockholm: Almqvist & Wiksell, 1947, pp. 2–3.
41. 'Republikken Norge lar vente på seg'. *Nordisk Kontakt* 10/83, p. 730.
42. Maurice Duverger, 'A New Political System Model: Semi-Presidential Government'. *European Journal of Political Research* 8, 1980, pp. 165–87.
43. *Lov om Grønlands hjemmestyre.* Lov nr. 577 af 29 Nov. 1978.
44. Philip Lauritzen, 'Grönland — från Koloni till Hjemmestyre'. *Världs politikens dagsfrågor* 1979, 9, pp. 20–1.
45. Eiden Muller, 'Færøernes repræsentation i Nordisk Råd'. *Nordisk Kontakt* 3/83, pp. 149–50.
46. Henrik Gustafsson & Lars Ingmar Johansson, '1972 års landstingsordning som grund för landstingets arbete', in *Åland i Utveckling. Festskrift utgiven av Ålands landsting med anledning av självstyrelsens 60-årsjubileum de 9 juni 1982.* Helsingfors: Frenckellska Tryckeri, 1982, pp. 88–9.
47. Magnus Wrede & Casper Wrede, 'Landstinget som arena för den Åländska politiken — partibildningen och valdeltanget', in *Åland i Utveckling*, pp. 128–50.
48. Casper Wrede, *Åländska väljartyper. Meddelanden från ekonomisk-statsvetenskapliga fakulteten vid Åbo akademi.* Åbo 1981.
49. Information provided by Sören Holmberg 12.4.1983.
50. For a detailed examination of the emergence and development of the Nordic party systems, see Elder, Thomas & Arter (1982), chapters 2–3.
51. 'Skdl lupaa hallitukselle asiallisen opposition'. *Helsingin Sanomat* 8.5.1983.
52. David Arter, 'The Finnish Elections — 1983'. *West European Politics* 6,4,1983, pp. 252–5.
53. 'Nordisk Räd skal være engagerende'. *Nordisk Kontakt* 9/83, p. 623.
54. Interview with Conservative Party MP, Julian Critchley. 'People and Power', BBC 1 Television 8.2.1983.
55. Glistrup et al(FP), *Forslag til Lov om fiskeriomkostninger.* L 102, Folketinget 1982–3.
56. 'EC sopuun kalastussodassa'. *Helsingin Sanomat* 26.1.1983.
57. Mattei Dogan, 'The Political Power of the Western Mandarins: Introduction', in M. Dogan (ed.) *The Mandarins of Western Europe. The Political Role of Top Civil Servants.* New York: Sage, 1975, p. 5.
58. Lord Hailsham, *The Dilemma of Democracy.* London: Collins, 1978.
59. Joel D. Aberbach, Robert D. Putnam & Bert A. Rockman, *Bureaucrats and Politicians in Western Democracies.* Cambridge, Mass.: Harvard University Press, 1981, p. 239.
60. Hugh Heclo, *Modern Social Policies in Britain and Sweden: From Relief to Income Maintenance.* New Haven: Yale University, 1974, pp. 301–3.
61. Erik Damgaard, 'The Political Role of Nonpolitical Bureaucrats in Denmark', in Dogan (1975), pp. 286–7.
62. D. Coombes & S.A. Walkland (ed.), *Parliaments and Economic Affairs.* London: Heinemann, 1980, p. 18.
63. Coombes & Walkland (1980), p. 12.
64. A.H. Halsey, 'The Rise of Party'. Reith Lecture BBC Radio 4, 1978.
65. Robert B. Kvavik, *Interest Groups in Norwegian Politics.* Oslo-Bergen-Tromsø: Universitetsforlaget, 1976, pp. 119–20.
66. Cited in M. Heisler (ed.) *Politics in Europe.* New York: MacKay, 1974, p. 50.

67. M.O. Heisler & R.B. Kvavik, 'Patterns of European Politics: The "European Polity" Model', in Heisler (1974), pp. 27–89.
68. Bob Jessop, 'The Transformation of the State in Post-War Britain', in Richard Scase (ed.) *The State in Western Europe*. London: Croom Helm, 1980, p. 58.
69. J.J. Richardson & A.G. Jordan, *Governing under Pressure. The Policy Process in a Post-Parliamentary Democracy*. Oxford: Martin Robertson, 1979, pp. 121–36.
70. 'Eduskunta kansalaisten vallan väline'. *Kristityn Vastuu*, 27.5.1982.
71. 'Vallaton Parlamentti'. *Suomen Kuvalehti*, 6.2.1981.
72. Interview with Danish Progress Party leader, Mogens Glistrup, 22.4.1982.
73. 'Folkpartiet förnyar i partitoppen'. *Nordisk Kontakt* 2/83, pp. 122–3.
74. Tuula Trygg, *Keskustan Uudenmaan vaalipiirin tilaisudessa Nurmijärvellä*, 18.3.1983.
75. 'Mies, jota eduskunnassa nyt tarvitaan. Tuure Junnila'. *Uusi Suomi*, 19.3.1983.
76. Interview with the Danish Christian People's Party delegate, Inge Krogh, 22.4.1982.
77. "'Yleinen luottamuspula' vie eduskunnan arvovaltaa'. *Helsingin Sanomat*, 17.3.1983.
78. Olle Wästberg, 'Politiker, sluta upp med hemligsmakeriet'. *Dagens Nyheter*, 11.9.1981.
79. Kvavik (1976), pp. 119–20.
80. Nils Elvander, *Intresseorganisationerna i dagens Sverige*. Lund: Gleerup, 1966, pp. 203–4.
81. Stein Rokkan, 'Numerical Democracy and Corporate Pluralism', in R.A. Dahl (ed.) *Political Oppositions in Western Democracies*. New Haven: Yale University Press, 1966, p. 106.
82. Voitto Helander, *A Liberal Corporatist Sub-System in Action: The Incomes Policy System in Finland*. Turun yliopiston yleisen valtio-opin tutkimuksia, 1, 1979, p. 29.
83. Bo Lindensjö, 'Makten — Politiken och Demokratin'. *Svenska Dagbladet*, 17.5.1983.
84. Magnus Isberg, *The First Decade of the Unicameral Riksdag*. The Role of the Swedish Parliament in the 1970s. Stockholms Universitet, Statsvetenskapliga Institutionen. Forskningsrapporter 1982: 1.
85. Gerhard Loewenberg & Samuel C. Patterson, *Comparing Legislatures*. Boston and Toronto: Little, Brown & Co., 1979, p. 226.
86. Andrew Schonfield, *Modern Capitalism: The Changing Balance of Public and Private Power*. London: Oxford University Press, 1965, p. 199.
87. Loewenberg & Patterson (1979), p. 198.
88. Isberg (1982), p. 84.
89. Peter Schulz, *Die deutsche Demokratie*. München-Wien: Gunter Olzog, 1974, p. 93; Klaus von Beyme, *Das politische System der Bundesrepublik Deutschland*. München-Zürich: R. Piper, 1980, pp. 165.
90. Kurt Sontheimer, *Grundzüge des politischen Systems der Bundesrepublik Deutschland*. München-Zürich: R. Piper, 1980, pp. 170–1.

Part I

POLICY FORMULATION IN THE NORDIC STATES: THE EXTENT OF PARLIAMENTARY INVOLVEMENT

2

POLICY-MAKING: THE PRE-LEGISLATIVE STAGE

> 'The development of the co-optive structure has been accompanied by a shift in the locus of decision-making . . . from the parliament and parties to the administrative agencies. Authority to formulate and implement public policy has been delegated in substantial degree to the administrative sub-system . . . Concomitantly, the parliament has come to resemble a rubber stamp in many of the most important policy areas.' — Martin O. Heisler and Robert B. Kvavik, 'Patterns of European Politics: The "European Polity" Model'[1]

With a justifiable element of simplification, the initial stage in the legislative process in the Nordic region can be depicted as comprising three analytically distinct steps. First, the 'registration' of policy problems and issues — as a result of either parliamentary questions, pressure group campaigns or media perseverence — and their thorough elucidation and deliberation on commissions of inquiry set up by the government. In this way, the matter is formally placed on the political agenda. Secondly, the completion of a commission report containing recommendations (and sometimes reservations), which in turn is followed by written responses to them from relevant interest organisations and ultimately the translation of the sum input into draft proposals — a task undertaken by civil servants in the various government ministries. Finally, the consideration of these draft proposals by individual ministers, their undersecretaries, often too in cabinet committees and subsequently their ratification by the cabinet as a whole. Thereafter, the bill is submitted to the Office of Parliament and shortly after that announced by the Speaker. Together, these three stages constitute the policy formulation stage in the Nordic states. Accordingly, the two chapters that make up the first part of this volume have twin objectives:

first, to trace the policy sequence from the creation of a commission inquiry to the approval of proposals by the cabinet and their placement before parliament; and secondly and concurrently, to examine the role and influence of the various policy actors — particularly parliamentarians — at this pre-legislative stage. Significant intra-regional differences emerge.

The commission procedure

Throughout the region, the pre-legislative stage of policy-making has been characterised by the extensive use of commissions of inquiry designed to effect a systematic investigation and deliberation of issues before the preparation of draft proposals by civil servants in the government ministries. At this stage in the policy cycle the Nordic style is markedly open and consultative: commissions thus facilitate a structured dialogue between relevant actors in a policy area, while the *remiss* or report stage promotes specialist feedback to the commission report. The culture of the *remiss* stage varies across the region: in Norway and Sweden it is highly formal, in so far as all the affected bodies are requested to respond in writing to commission proposals; in Denmark and Finland, by contrast, it tends to be informal and discretionary, the onus falling on the minister and his departmental staff to proceed as is seen fit. The receipt and synthesis of corporate reactions at *remiss* can be time-consuming; yet within the norms of this consultative framework, there is a tendency for the affected organisations to talk themselves into agreement and, in the small and personalized élite systems of the Nordic states, for anticipated reaction to be a major form of legislative co-ordination.

Although the real expansion of the commission system coincided with the growth of welfarism and the increased role of the state in social and latterly economic management, the regularised and systematic involvement of interest groups and policy experts — the so-called corporate sector — via commissions of inquiry is notably old in some parts of the region. In Norway commissions, *midlertidige komitéer for utredningsarbeid,* had an ensconced position in the formulation of policy throughout the nineteenth century. Between 1814 and 1900 there were 894 at work — which meant that an average of about ten new commissions were set up each year, compared with a mean of twenty new ones yearly in 1900–36. Storting delegates were well represented on these early commissions; between 1814 and 1934 no less than 17.6% of their total personnel were parliamentarians. Paradoxically, parliamentary representation on commissions was highest during the mid-nineteenth century when the Storting was convened only every second or third year and the notion of the 'civil service state', *embetsstaten*, aptly captured the paramount position of the officials who acted as advisers to the King.[2] The strengthening of the Storting's position with the introduction of annual sessions and the breakthrough of parliamentarism in 1884 signified a decline in parliamentary involvement on commissions of inquiry. Indeed, with the real expansion of the commission system after the Second World War, pressure groups and civil servants have come to dominate their composition throughout the region. Robert Kvavik's examination of the membership of Norwegian commissions in the late 1960s revealed that 42% of commission members were recruited from interest organisations.[3] Before proceeding further along this road, however, a brief description of the basic operational mechanics of the commission system is in order. Although in what follows the focus is on Swedish practice, the procedure for preparing legislative proposals through commission and *remiss* is fundamentally the same throughout the region.

Before a new piece of legislation is produced or an existing policy significantly amended, the government invariably appoints a commission of inquiry to undertake a thorough investigation of the measure. The appropriate ministry lays down the broad guidelines within which the commission must operate, this directive having been vetted by the Minister of Finance and approved by the cabinet as a whole. Commissions are extremely assiduous in their work and usually take a considerable time to complete their report: the average life of the 300–400 Swedish commissions continuously in existence has been estimated at about two and a half years[4] and in Norway it is closer to three.[5] Commission directives do indeed often contain a deadline or target date for the completion and submission of a report, but these are invariably exceeded. Some of the seemingly protracted nature of commission deliberations is explained by the fact that the chairman and members of the commission conduct their assignment over and above their normal duties and are thus unable to devote more than about two days per month to commission work. At the same time, the chief secretary and his staff are full-time employees and undertake much of the initial research which largely forms the basis of the commission's discussion. In Sweden particularly, the commission secretariat is a highly developed institution, secretaries often having served on previous inquiries, though not necessarily in the same policy area: Bernt Öhman, for example, who in July 1982 was appointed chief secretary to the commission examining the activities of the Swedish Labour-Market Board, *AMS-utredning*, had previously been secretary to the controversial Wage-Earner Funds Commission which reported in September 1981. In Denmark, in contrast, staffing arrangements are less developed, with commission secretaries frequently working on two or even three inquiries at the same time. The proceedings of commissions in the region are secret and confidential. Commission reports, however, are public documents which are kept in libraries; not surprisingly, many are long and extremely detailed. That of the Danish Commission on Low Incomes, which was set up in 1976 and reported six years later, filled no less than 428 pages.[6] True, these reports frequently prompt a debate in the media when the public is reminded of the original directive, the background to the creation of the commission and its main recommendations, as well as hearing reaction from the political parties and other affected interests. However, much of this has relatively little impact on Sven Svensson, the typical Swede, or Matti Suomalainen, the 'Finn in the street'. With the commission report in mind, officials in the relevant government department prepare a draft bill which is then submitted for comment to the organisations concerned — the *remiss* stage. Often in a substantially modified form, the bill is finally submitted to the Riksdag.

There are two main types of commission of inquiry. The majority in Sweden today consist solely of civil servants, *ämbetsmannautredning*, and indeed not infrequently just a single official. Before 1950 one-man commissions were relatively rare, but they have become increasingly common as experience has confirmed that the higher the size of a commission's membership, the lower its overall level of efficiency has tended to be. A one-man investigator has, of course, a small secretariat and can call on the advice of experts when necessary. The so-called parliamentary commissions, *parlamentariska utredningar*, by contrast, involve representatives of the parliamentary parties as well as groups and departmental officials, and are usually set up on controversial issues that divide the parties — energy and environmental questions, for example, or the costs of the country's defence programme. Occasionally, there is dissent on the floor of the Riksdag over the rightful composition of a commission. In November 1980 the Social Democrat Lisa Mattson demanded in a question to the Minister for Social Affairs that the one-woman civil service commission preparing recommendations on a reform of Swedish prostitution law be transformed into a broadly-based parliamentary commission. Mattson held that because the matter was so controversial, it could only be dealt with properly by a parliamentary investigation.[7] Generally, however, the commissions meeting in the Riksdag building on week-day mornings proceed largely unnoticed, except for a few questions from delegates about the likely timing of their reports.

Historically, the development and growth of the commission system in Sweden has been integrally connected with the relatively small size of government departments: all the ministries except the Foreign Office have staffs of less than two hundred — including typists and caretakers — and distinctively the responsibility for the implementation of policies has devolved upon a variety of quasi-autonomous central administrative agencies and boards.[8] This has meant that in practice the essential function of ministries (the constitutional theory is rather different, see p. 100) has been to plan new policies — a task which, given the limited manpower resources at their disposal, departments have undertaken with the aid of commissions. In the course of their work, Swedish commissions have drawn extensively on the experience of the other Nordic countries. In 1981, for instance, Gunnar Hecksher led a Swedish commission to Oslo to examine the Norwegian system of holding local and national elections in separate years rather than, as in Sweden, at the same time every third year.[9] The Hecksher commission subsequently recommended a return to the earlier Swedish practice, i.e. bringing Sweden into line with Norway, but with opposition from the Social Democrats this proposal has yet to be carried out. Interestingly, there has been a recent attempt to encourage the intra-regional circulation of commission reports. According to a directive of the Nordic Council of Ministers in November 1981, reports completed under the auspices of one government department are to be distributed among their regional counterparts so as to build up documentation banks in the range of public policy fields.[10] Clearly such a scheme offers a potentially important vehicle for the diffusion and cross-fertilisation of ideas and initiatives in the Nordic area.

As may be inferred from the several years it takes Swedish commissions to complete their work, the policy formulation process is long and slow-moving. It is invariably a protracted sequence of events from the initial perception of a policy need — usually by government experts or specialists in pressure groups — to the creation of a commission of inquiry, the submission of its report, the collation of *remiss* 'feedback', the drafting of legislative proposals by ministry officials and ultimately the presentation of a bill to parliament. As Thomas J. Anton has observed in the Swedish context, policy-making is 'extraordinarily deliberative'.[11] Certainly, some variation in the degree to which the commission system is institutionalised is evident within the region. The Finnish commission system is nothing like as open and consultative as the Swedish. Since the early 1970s, an increasing body of legislative planning has been undertaken by departmental working groups, *virkatyöryhamät*, on which even interest groups are only occasionally represented. The number of commissions, therefore, has been significantly lower than in Sweden: in 1977 there were only 98 in existence compared with 123 in 1976 and 146 in 1975.[12] Even so, the point about the elongated nature of the policy formulation process in the region stands. As one Norwegian Under-Secretary of State put it frankly, 'If there were more consultation than there is today, nothing would ever be done!'[13]

From a governmental viewpoint, of course, a great merit of this time-consuming process of preparing legislation has been that the routine involvement of affected interests on commissions, advisory committees and other executive working groups has contributed in a significant way towards promoting inter-élite compromise, so expediting matters at the policy adoption stage in parliament. Regularised access to commissions of inquiry, in other words, has tended to promote a readiness ultimately to reach pragmatic solutions, and this in turn has effectively defused the more highly-charged issues before they come before the legislature for scrutiny. As Erik Damgaard and Kjell Eliassen conclude in their study of the impact of corporate participation on Danish law-making, 'if bills are drafted by the active participation of external actors, they are likely to be passed at a relatively low level of conflict in parliament.'[14] In the same vein, Johan P. Olsen notes that if a consensus is achieved at the pre-legislative stage in Norway, the Storting or Cabinet is highly unlikely to intervene.[15] From a parliamentary viewpoint, in contrast, the entrenched position of the commission system and the systematic deliberation of issues it facilitates has threatened the assemblies of the region with effective redundancy in the policy process, apparently reducing them to ratifying proposals emanating from the executive machine. Heisler and Kvavik put the dilemma forcibly: 'The development of the co-optive structure has been accompanied by a shift in the locus of decision-making in the European polity from the parliament and parties to the administrative agencies. Authority to formulate and implement public policy has been delegated in substantial degree to the administrative subsystem which, in turn, has passed some of its responsibility to the "private sector". Concomitantly, the parliament has come to resemble a rubber stamp in many of the most important policy areas.'[16] In this volume, of course, we are centrally concerned to examine the validity of this claim in the Nordic states; but for the moment it is timely to look at the reverse side of the coin — the means available to the parliaments in the region to exert influence at the crucial policy formulation stage.

In general, the Nordic parliaments can influence policy at the formulation stage in three ways. First, through tabling questions and interpellations in the House and/or as a result of the united proposal of a legislative standing committee, parliament is not infrequently the force behind a government decision to create a commission of inquiry. Thus on 21 October 1980 the Riksdag Finance Committee reported on three members' request proposals urging the government to create a commission to examine differential living standards following the impact of inflation in the 1970s.[17] The Finance Committee obtained statements from the Institute of Social Research and Central Statistical Office before backing the case for an inquiry with the argument that continuous research into living standards was essential to the generation of sound social and economic policy. When the Riksdag subsequently supported its Finance Committee's report, the case for a commission was irresistible. Indeed, the government of the day invariably complies with a Riksdag request to set up a commission of inquiry, although it should be noted that pressure from the assembly is by no means always the only reason underlying a cabinet decision to set up a new commission. Obviously the fact that the government appoints the chairmen and determines their partisan balance normally permits it to control the commission system. Moreover, commission recommendations are not necessarily accepted in total and may in fact be substantially modified in the ensuing legislative proposal. In any event, it bears restatement that pressure from parliament is commonly cited in the ministerial guidelines as a reason for the creation of a commission of inquiry. A recent study showed that during the early 1970s just under 15% of all Swedish commission directives made reference to Riksdag demands for an inquiry, and this figure had risen to about a quarter of all directives by the end of the same decade. Significantly, there was a clear increase in the number of directives giving Riksdag petitioning as the *only* reason for the creation of a commission.[18]

Secondly, pariiamentarians can be appointed members of commissions of inquiry, often following pressure in the House. The creation of two of the four parliamentary commissions in existence in Denmark in January 1981 was the direct result of pressure exerted in the Folketing. The Matrimonial Law Reform Commission, *udvalget angående ægteskabslovgivningen*, set up by the Minister of Justice in 1969 stemmed from the parliamentary rejection of proposals based on an earlier commision which did not include parliamentary delegates. The commission appointed by the Minister of the Interior to investigate *inter alia* the preparation of homeopathic and natural medicines similarly followed a Folketing initiative in June 1973: it was given almost ten years to complete its work and included the Radical delegate Erik Nordqvist.[19]

Thirdly, a delegate can attempt to influence the corporate interests represented on a commission — a Social Democratic member, for example, can clearly channel his views through the spokesmen of the labour organisations on the commission. In Mikko Eklin's study of the controversial Finnish commission on counter–cyclical economic policies, *suhdannevarauskomitea*, set up by the so-called broad centre-left Popular Front government in November 1970, it is significant that the main opposition Conservative Party possessed at least 'absentee representation' in the form of persons representing the employers' organisations.[20] When the selection of interest groups precludes such linkages, a parliamentarian can then attempt to influence the public debate which invariably accompanies both the creation of a commission and the publication of its report. Moreover, most commission proposals involve at least an informal *remiss* stage during which a minister gets feedback from the organisations most affected. As parliamentarians may well have contacts with these organisations there is further opportunity for delegates to exercise influence at this distinctive phase in the policy process. In short, in so far as they can deploy informal means to persuade the corporate interests represented on a commission, it is obvious that parliamentarians do not necessarily require a seat on a commission of inquiry to affect policy-making at its pre-legislative stage.

It needs emphasis, however, that outside Sweden the direct involvement of Nordic parliamentarians in the initial development of public policy has been minimal. A brief review of delegate participation on commissions of inquiry will illustrate the point: in most of the region it is exceptional for elected politicians to be engaged in the formulation of legislative recommendations and proposals. The Danish situation is typical, for commissions — which are extremely numerous despite the larger size of Danish ministries compared with their Swedish counterparts — only rarely include members of the Folketing. There have been a number of notable exceptions. In the 1960s, a Social Law Reform Commission containing parliamentarians enjoyed important policy functions, while in November 1950, a 21-member Defence Commission, also comprising Folketing (and former Folketing) delegates, was set up to make recommendations for a new defence system. It delivered its report in May 1951 and this became the basis of the first so-called 'defence package', *forsvarsforlig*, between the three pro-Nato parties — the Social Democrats, Liberals and Conservatives.[21] In the 1970s too, a commission appointed to examine the question of Home Rule for Greenland contained seven parliamentarians and deliberated for three years in all.[22] These have been the exceptions, however. On 1 January 1970, there was a total personnel of nearly 3,000 involved on non-permanent pre-legislative committees, but only 3% were members of the Folketing.[23] Eleven years later, on 1 January 1981, there were 279 operational commissions of inquiry in Denmark — the highest proportions linked to the Departments of Education and the Environment respectively — out of which only four, or less than $1\frac{1}{2}$% included members listed as Folketing delegates.[24] Even allowing for the fact that not all the committees listed in the 1981 statistics were preparatory organs (many were concerned with the administration, co-ordination and implementation of existing legislation), this is an extremely low percentage.

The situation is fundamentally similar in Norway, although, unlike Denmark, the present minimal level of delegate involvement on commissions of inquiry — only 1.4% of the total membership of commissions in 1981 comprised parliamentarians — represents a significant decline over the course of this present century as table 2.1 demonstrates. In their study of trends in the composition of Norwegian commissions, Solvang and Moren point to four historic explanations for the decline in delegate participation. First, the consolidation of parliamentarism by the beginning of this century prompted a growing involvement of delegates in Storting work, and this, coupled with the heightened significance of standing committees, reduced both their available time and their interest in participating in policy work outside the legislature. Secondly, about 1900, leaders of the labour-market organisations began to eschew election to the Storting, arguing that their objectives could be more effectively attained through direct consultation with the government and central administration. At the same time, the increasingly specialised

Table 2.1. PARLIAMENTARY INVOLVEMENT ON NORWEGIAN COMMISSIONS OF INQUIRY SINCE WORLD WAR I

	No. of commissions	*Total personnel*	*Storting former Storting delegates*	%
1921–35	365	2,033	366	18.1
1951	125	—	—	10.0
1966	147	1,103	26	2.4
1981	167	1,353	19	1.4

Sources: Solvang and Moren (1974), pp. 33–4; *Storting melding nr 7A* (1981–2) Forbruker- og administrasjonsdepartementet.

nature of policy formulation and the complementary emergence of a network of subject-specific interest groups created plentiful resources of expertise with which to fill commission places. Finally, Solvang and Moren note that in recent years commissions of inquiry have tended to remain in existence longer — a mere 6–8 months was typical before the Second World War — and, in addition, the fact that the size of their membership has also grown has obviously been a factor accounting for the declining proportion of parliamentary members on commissions.[25] It could, of course, be argued that the greater the extent of delegate involvement in policy formulation, the more binding commission recommendations — particularly unanimous proposals — are likely to be both on government and parliament. This may or may not be a desirable state of affairs. Certainly it is interesting that in the 1959–60 Storting session, Halvor Bunkholt introduced a private member's bill attempting to amend article 62 of the constitution so as to preclude parliamentary involvement on commissions of inquiry. Bunkholt argued that it heightened a delegate's workload, caused misunderstanding in the country, but above all tied the hands of the Storting in the scrutiny of legislative measures. Although the Storting ultimately followed its standing committee on Foreign Affairs and the Constitution and rejected Bunkholt's bill as unnecessarily restrictive,[26] there has been little or no pressure from delegates to increase the very low level of parliamentary participation on commissions of inquiry in either Norway or Denmark.

In contrast to Norway, the trend has been towards a greater degree of parliamentary participation on commissions of inquiry in Finland, although — precisely as in Denmark and Norway — overall levels of delegate involvement have been low. Members of the Eduskunta were indeed quite extensively involved on commissions of inquiry directly after the Second World War. In 1945, in fact, one-third of all commissions contained at least one parliamentarian. Thereafter, a decline in the 1950s and 1960s was followed by a revival of delegate participation on commissions in the 1970s. In 1975, 11% contained at least one member of parliament, as Table 2.2 shows, and while commissions consisting predominantly of parliamentarians (reflecting the partisan balance in the legislature) were rare in the 1950s and 1960s, they became increasingly common — at least in absolute terms — in the 1970s. Recent parliamentary commissions have investigated, *inter alia*, Constitutional Reform, Traffic and Media Communications.

Three points need to be made by way of a postscript on the marginal involvement of elected politicians on policy-making commissions in Denmark, Norway and Finland. First, to note the low level

Table 2.2. THE COMPOSITION OF FINNISH COMMISSIONS OF INQUIRY, 1945–75

	1945 %	1955 %	1965 %	1975 %
Commissions with mainly parliamentarians	5	0	1	2
Commissions with at least one parliamentarian	28	9	3	9
Commisions without parliamentarians	67	91	96	89
	100	100	100	100
n =	(39)	(53)	(118)	(117)

Source: Voitto Helander, *Etujärjestöt ja komitealaitos*. Turun yliopisto: Politiikan tutkimuksen ja sosiologian laitos. Respo 33/1979, p. 20.

of delegate participation on commissions in these countries is not necessarily to imply a paucity of 'partisan' representation at the pre-legislative stage. True, the onus is on the government to determine the nature and composition of a commission — whether it shall consist of parliamentarians, civil servants or a mixture of politicians, experts and pressure group spokesmen — and this normally gives it an important tactical initiative.

But the political parties enjoy considerable discretion in selecting individual members of commissions on which they are invited to participate. In contrast to Sweden, moreover, where the parties have tended to regard parliamentarians as more reliable commission members — not least because they are less likely to view the commission system as a career channel to be used for personal ends[27] — the convention in Denmark, Norway and Finland has been to nominate members from outside the parliamentary groups.

Secondly and paradoxically, the incorporation of partisans on commissions of inquiry (parliamentary or otherwise) does not in itself guarantee the expression of a partisan viewpoint: the Commission on Central Public Administration in Finland which reported in 1978 noted that in reality political parties frequently do not possess well-defined views on matters under deliberation, nor are they able to generate them in the lifetime of a particular commission.[28] A significant inference can be made, namely that on a number of the parliamentary or party-based commissions in Finland, politicians, lacking clearly-defined directives from their organisations, have operated more as individuals than partisans.[29] A similar conclusion may be reached from research into the commissions set up by the Department of Communications in Norway in 1945–70, for Olav Grimsbo has shown that of the 4% of the total commission personnel in the period who were Storting members, no less than one quarter tabled individual reservations to commission reports and often did so not as partisans, but as representatives of particular regional interests.[30]

Finally, it is widely felt in governing circles in the three countries, especially in Denmark, that the systematic deployment of parliamentary commissions weakens the government's freedom to govern in the way it thinks fit. It was precisely a concern to defend traditional notions of responsible party government, albeit in this case strong minority government, that emerged from the remarks of Ole Espersen, the Minister of Justice in Jørgensen's fifth Social Democratic minority government in Denmark in 1982. Espersen was adamant in his opposition to including Folketing members on pre-legislative commissions. He felt that this was almost certain to increase a minister's workload, since his party's parliamentary spokesman on a commission would seek out his advice and guidance, and a minister might also find himself in the position of having to go against his own party's stance on the commission. In addition, a minister could find his hands effectively tied by the achievement of inter-party consensus on a commission. In sum, Espersen argued that the government should endeavour to present its programme to parliament — the rightful arena, he believed, for the collective deliberation of proposals. If compromises were then necessary, they would at least be enforced and in turn ratified at a meeting of all the elected representatives of the people in plenum. Only a revision of the constitution would change his practice of nominating expert non-parliamentary commissions.[31]

Distinctively in Western Europe, the proportion of the total number of Swedish commissions of inquiry that include parliamentarians in their membership (i.e. at least one) has not fallen below one-fifth at any time this century: it stood at an average of 47% between 1905 and 1954, fell to 23% in 1967, but rose sharply again during the 1970s. As table 2.3 demonstrates, the general elections of 1973 and the parliamentary deadheat between socialists and non-socialists that followed marked a turning-point. The proportion of the total number of new commissions of inquiry containing at least one parliamentarian thus rose from under one-third for the period 1968–73 to over half during the 'lottery Riksdag' of 1973–6. Furthermore, the proportion of multi-member commissions with Riksdag representation increased from 48% for the period 1970–3 to no less than 67% in 1973–6 and remained only a fraction lower than this to the end of the decade. It is interesting that there was a strengthened presence of opposition parties on commisssions of inquiry in the 1970s.[32] During the Fälldin non-socialist cabinet of 1976–8, almost half of the new commissions with a parliamentary

Table 2.3. COMPOSITION OF SWEDISH COMMISSIONS OF INQUIRY, 1968–79

	Period	*Commissions with at least one Riksdag member* %
1968–70	1) Social Democratic majority in both Chambers	31
1970–3	2) Social Democratic minority government in unicameral assembly. Majority with support of Left-Communists	32
1973–6	3) Social Democratic cabinet in the 'lottery Riksdag'	51
1976–8	4) Three-Party Bourgeois majority government	39
1978–9	5) Liberal single-party minority government	33
	Mean	38
	n = 994	

Source: Magnus Isberg. *The First Decade of the Unicameral Riksdag* (1982), p. 48.

membership contained delegates from all three governing parties *plus* the main opposition group, the Social Democrats, and commissions with this same four-party composition rose to 61% during Ullsten's Liberal minority in 1978–9. It is important also to note that the overall decline after 1976 in the number of commissions with at least one Riksdag member was related to the growth in the number of single-member commissions — they almost tripled between 1973 and 1979 — and this in turn was probably connected to the concern of incoming governments (particularly after 44 years of social democracy) to press on quickly with the preparation and introduction of legislative proposals, aware doubtless that their tenure of office might be limited. This was almost certainly true of the Ullsten minority. The majority of single-member commissions, of course, function more expeditiously than their multi-member counterparts and generally cost less — a not inconsiderable factor during recessionary times. In any event there seems a strong *prima facie* case for arguing that the heightened Riksdag representation on commissions of inquiry generally in the 1970s was integrally tied to the delicate legislative-executive balance which was maintained throughout the decade. As Isberg has remarked, 'the cabinet needed more consultations with the Riksdag under the more insecure parliamentary conditions of the lottery Riksdag, coalition government and weak minority government.'[33]

However, even during the long period of majoritarian Social Democratic government beginning in 1932, the dividing line between executive and legislature was blurred by the significant involvement of opposition politicians in the development of public policy. Indeed, unlike Denmark, it is part of the Swedish policy-making style — not only when cabinets lack majority backing in the Riksdag — to incorporate representatives of the parliamentary opposition on to commissions in an attempt to generate broad-gauge consensus on a reform measure before its introduction into the legislature. Not surprisingly, therefore, work on parliamentary commissions has constituted a not inconsiderable proportion of the average delegate's weekly programme. In a study which focused on a routine Riksdag week in late November 1974, it was calculated that a typical parliamentarian spent 6% of his time during the week on commissions of inquiry, compared with 10% on one of the Riksdag standing committees and another 8% on parliamentary party group work. There were no marked inter-party differences to be observed in the time allocated to these various activities.[34] At the same time, the conflict between keeping the size of commissions manageably small and endeavouring to satisfy wide-ranging demands for membership has been resolved, in the case of Riksdag delegates, by selecting parliamentarians who can simultaneously articulate a variety of interests — for example, those of a professional body or trade union along with a particular regional industry. Although the point should not be exaggerated, the tendency to combine various group interests in a single Riksdag delegate has produced a situation in which, as Hans Meijer has observed, 'a relatively limited number of individuals within the political parties, who are able to represent several interests, are tapped for many commission appointments.'[35]

While the level of Riksdag participation in the formulation of legislative measures has been remarkably high, one of the objectives of involving delegates in Sweden has been fundamental to parliamentary commissions throughout the Nordic region: namely, the resolution of inter-party disagreement so as to facilitate the gestation of proposals in sensitive areas. This much was recognised in the report of the Commission on Central Public Administration in Finland in 1978, which stated that parliamentary commissions should be employed in connection with the preparation of recommendations in all controversial questions. What needs emphasis, however, is that in Sweden the *conflict resolution function* of parliamentary commissions is considerably more institutionalised than elsewhere in the region: if a matter is essentially political rather than technical in character, and divides the main parties, parliamentarians will invariably be included as commission members.

On the face of it, the nature of the party system might indeed seem the vital clue to explaining differential levels of parliamentary involvement at the pre-legislative stage. The more extreme the party system — Finland traditionally and more recently Denmark — the fewer parliamentary commissions there are likely to be, it might be hypothesised, and the more the government will adopt an *ad hoc*, piecemeal approach to policy consultation. In reality, of course, the picture is more complicated, although the recent decline in the already small number of parliamentary commissions in Denmark could certainly be seen as being bound up with the proliferation of new parties in the early 1970s. With the leaders of the neo-Stalinist wing of the Communist Party and radical rightist Rural Party both represented, it was also not to be wondered at that the Finnish Constitutional Reform Commission of the early 1970s — in sharp contrast to its Swedish contemporary — failed to make any significant progress and was ultimately dissolved. Clearly, if a particular matter is contentious and the likelihood of inter-élite agreement is remote, it would be the height of folly to create a parliamentary commission and give the oppposition a foothold at a critical stage in the policy process.

In Sweden, however, the appointment of parliamentary commissions has not been seen to challenge governments in this way; on the contrary, the practice of nominating parliamentary commissions, which was consolidated during the uniquely long period of majoritarian Social Democratic administration in 1932–76, contributed to the growth of norms and conventions favouring compromise — a willingness on the part of participants to abide by the informal rules of the commission system on a 'win some, lose some' basis. As Folke Johansson's study indicates, the fact that a significant proportion of Swedish parliamentary commissions contrive to produce unanimous proposals suggests that they do play an important role in creating cross-party consensus.[36] This point should not be overstated. One obvious cost of an open and consultative policy style is that it affords opposition elements a high degree of visibility at the formulation stage. Reservations to commission reports can be tabled and dissent formally registered even before the formal deliberation of a measure in the Riksdag. However, the reality that three-quarters of all Swedish commissions during this century have managed to present unanimous recommendations tells its own story.

It is probably fair to assert that at any given time only a minority of Swedish parliamentary commissions are engaged in the deliberation of questions of 'high politics', i.e. controversial matters of a radical, innovative character to which the government gives high priority. Clearly, the delegates represented on such commissions function first and foremost as 'partisans' or, in the terms of David Donnison's role analysis of the membership of British commissions of inquiry, as 'advocates of a particular philosophy'.[37] The number of parliamentary commissions primarily directed at the resolution of inter-party conflict has, it is true, been consistently greater in absolute terms than elsewhere in the region. Yet a distinctive characteristic of the policy formulation process in Sweden has been the routine involvement of parliamentarians on commissions of a plainly less controversial and partisan kind — typically when the matter at hand has involved the amendment and modification of existing legislative provisions and where delegates are cast in the role of experts or 'representatives of an interest' more than advocates of a particular philosophy.[38] When the Immigration Minister in Fälldin's 3-party bourgeois coalition, Karin Andersson, set up a commission in June 1980 to investigate a wide range of issues relating to the sizeable immigrant population in Sweden, it was natural to include among several parliamentarians with non-Swedish origins the only Finnish-born Riksdag delegate, Lahja Exner, a former textile worker representing the Social Democrats.[39] Obviously, the extensive involvement of Riksdag members as articulators of particular interests has contributed to enhancing the legitimacy of the policy formulation process. The *policy legitimation function* of Swedish parliamentary commissions deserves emphasis, since the achievement of broad cross-party consensus at the pre-legislative stage had only a weak functional logic during the long era of Social Democratic majority government.

The long-term exclusion of the parliamentary opposition from pre-legislative policy organs might conceivably have prompted the bourgeois parties to join electoral forces to displace the ruling Social Democrats before 1976; and taking this line of argument, parliamentary commissions would be viewed, in part at least, as tactical sops designed to draw the teeth of an almost permanent opposition. In reality, however, commission recommendations could be revised by the responsible minister — albeit at the cost of raising the temperature in the Riksdag — using the cushion of a Social Democratic majority in the House. It therefore seems that the Swedish tradition of engaging parliamentarians on policy commissions developed alongside an acceptance of the desirability, in the interests of rational policy-making, of harnessing the knowledge and experience of Riksdag delegates above partisan considerations even if not wholly divorced from them. The extent and regularity of the practice would tend to confirm this view: parliamentary commissions are not confined to issues where inter-party conflict is paramount, but examine questions of a technical, pragmatic kind.

As such, those in Sweden form part of a policy style which is distinctive not only in the Nordic region, but throughout Western Europe.

A few examples from the period August–October 1982 illustrate the point. In August, a parliamentary Rescue Service Commission, *räddningstjänstkommittén*, impressed with the record of the helicopter ambulance service in saving life in the mountain areas and archipelagos, supported an expansion of the service, while there were other parliamentary commissions dealing respectively with local adult education and leisure accommodation, the latter recommending *inter alia* that increased state support should be given to youth hostels and holiday villages with tax concessions for individuals leasing summer cottages. In September 1982, a parliamentary commission was set up to examine the implications for the structure of the mass media in Sweden of the technological developments occurring in the communications industry — especially in the electronics field — with the advent of cable and satellite television, videograms etc. There were also a couple of one-man parliamentary commissions, one to evaluate the need for more official information and/or publications directed towards improving the quality of the Swedish environment, and the other to produce a more cost-effective manpower structure in the various boards and agencies in the defence policy sector. At the beginning of October 1982, a parliamentary commission on national recreation and tourist policy, *Turek*, received a supplementary directive calling on it to investigate ways of improving the facilities for local outdoor leisure pursuits, while another, the result of a Riksdag decision in the spring of 1981, set out to produce a reform in the organisation of the police force so as to devolve more authority to the local level.[40] Finally, it was decided at the end of October 1982 to set up a parliamentary commission to examine the situation of the Lapps with a view to three things: 1) strengthening their legal position on questions relating to reindeer farming; 2) considering the need for an organ to represent Lappish opinion, and 3) proposing measures to protect and develop the Lappish language, *samiska språket*. A parliamentary commission also recommended a new system for providing economic support to handicapped persons in need of cars, even when not in gainful employment, while another suggested that immigrant children and children from other linguistic minorities should have the right to at least four hours' weekly instruction in their own language in nursery schools. It was essential, according to the commission report, that parents and children should have a language in common. It should be noted here that decisions to create commissions taken by the outgoing Fälldin government were mainly respected by the new Social Democratic administration, and that as a result an important element of continuity in the formulation of policy was maintained.

It does not follow, of course, that the omission of parliamentarians from most pre-legislative commissions elsewhere in Scandinavia necessarily leads to the significantly reduced legitimacy of the policy formulation process: in many cases, delegates would not welcome the increased workload, and anyway they accept the need for the technical clarification of issues before their consideration in the legislature. However, it can be surmised that in so far as commissions serve as useful vehicles for the consolidation of technical knowledge, the ability of individual Nordic parliamentarians outside Sweden to assess proposals at the adoption stage in the assembly is prejudiced by their exclusion from pre-legislative involvement. It might be added in parenthesis that Mogens Glistrup, the leader of the Danish Progress Party, although insisting that the composition of each commission should be adjudged on its merits — i.e. issue by issue, rather than as a matter of general principle — nonetheless felt that members of the legislature could usefully be included when the matter at hand meant the acquisition of information that would enhance the efficiency of delegates as parliamentary scrutineers. Glistrup saw participation on commissions investigating questions related to micro-technology and, more generally, the problems of the post-industrial revolution as especially pertinent to the older generation of Folketing members.[41]

While the involvement of parliamentarians on commissions of inquiry in most of the Nordic region is minimal, it is essential to avoid presenting an idealised picture of the role of the numerous parliamentary commissions in Sweden. Some 'routine' commissions fail to produce unanimous proposals: in the summer of 1982, a parliamentary commission's majority recommendation that the County Council, *landstinget*, elect all the members of the state-backed County Boards on Employment, Schools, Forestry and Fisheries produced a joint reservation from the two leading opposition parties, the Social Democrats and Conservatives, who argued that this would involve undue party politicisation of these bodies.[42] Parliamentary members of commissions, moreover, are not always nominated on the basis of proven expertise, and as a result their contribution may be largely nominal, with decisions effectively taken by the commission secretariat or non-parliamentary members. This is invariably the case with the few Danish parliamentary commissions. Thus according to one of the Justice Department experts on the long-standing Matrimonial Law Reform Commission (wound up in 1982) the Folketing delegates constituted a kind of 'upper chamber', with the other members forming a sub-committee that in practice did most of the spadework.[43] Incidentally, the Matrimonial Law Reform Commission was the only commission to meet in the Christiansborg Palace — unlike Sweden where many are convened in the Riksdag building — although even then meetings proved to be highly fragmented with the Folketing members departing to the plenary assembly to vote at the sound of the division bell — sometimes as many as four or five times in the course of a single commission meeting. In Sweden parliamentary commission meetings are normally held on Wednesdays and Thursdays[44] and avoid a clash with Riksdag votes, but the relatively high number of commissions in existence at any one time has stretched the personnel resources of the parliamentary groups and led to some delegates sitting on more than one commission while others belong to commissions outside their immediate area of interest or experience. As in Denmark, therefore, parliamentary members are frequently reliant on the initiatives of civil servants and experts on commissions.

Finally, it is important to note that the creation of a Swedish parliamentary commission can perform a strictly tactical function, namely the postponement of legislative issues of a highly divisive, partisan character. An excellent example of this *policy deferral function* was the commission set up by Fälldin to examine the planned rundown of the nation's nuclear energy programme, a commission created against a background of marked divisions over the issue between the three non-socialist governing parties and a tactical desire on the Prime Minister's part to shelve it so as to give the new government vital breathing space. Equally, a government may decide to set up a parliamentary commission to investigate a controversial issue in order to appear to be doing something, safe in the knowledge that as the inter-party conflict generated by the question is unlikely to be resolved, it will be possible to defer the matter until it is judicious to institute a new commission.

The much-discussed Swedish Commission on Wage-Earners' Funds, *utredningen om löntagarna och kapitaltillväxten*, which was reconstituted in 1977, suffered precisely this fate. The original commission was a by-product of the first so-called Haga agreement in May 1974 between the governing Social Democrats and one of the parties in opposition, the Liberals (see p. 207) and was given its directive by the Finance Minister, Gunnar Sträng, in January 1975. However, its secretariat was not at work much before 1977 when, following the accession of the non-socialists to power, membership of the commission was increased from 9 to 13 with the inclusion for the first time of a member of the Conservative Party's parliamentary group. Even then, the intensive period of commission deliberations did not occur until 1979–80. Indeed, although the commission produced an interim statement on the background to the problem under investigation as well as several interim 'expert papers', its final and very brief report was not published until September 1981. The Wage-Earners' Funds Commission, in short, was in existence for seven years and in that time witnessed government changes on no less than five separate occasions. A number of points need to be made here. First, the Conservatives who were initially excluded from the commission served after their incorporation in 1977 in a wholly adversarial capacity, opposed to any funds scheme which smacked of socialism by the backdoor. The main labour-market organisation, LO, in turn, adopted a similarly dogmatic stance in favour of its own radical blueprint, and the result was in Donnison's words a discussion of 'general principles deriving from a frame of reference extending well beyond the task in hand'.[45] Secondly, and a direct corollary of the above, nearly seven years of intermittent activity produced a final report which contained only five background chapters: the sixth on operational method prompted serious disagreements and was not published, while the seventh which was to have contained the commission's proposals was stillborn.[46] As a result, despite the publicity which surrounded the commission's final report, the matter could safely be shelved. As the chairman of the commission, Bernt Öhman, was later to observe, 'the issue was too big for a commission with the result that the parties were continually seeking how best to exploit the whole exercise.'[47]

To be fair, the Wage-Earner Funds Commission was exceptional: there have been very few parliamentary commissions which have failed to produce some moderation of conflict in the form of at least a majority set of recommendations. In any event, for the Social Democrats, under pressure from LO to introduce profit-sharing proposals, but divided on the matter and faced by a general election in the autumn of 1976 at which the whole issue could prove to be a vote-loser, the original Wage-Earner Funds Commission represented a way of buying time, while at the same time demonstrating a concern ultimately to legislate on the matter, i.e. to move forward on the traditional Swedish basis of pre-legislative consensus. Significantly, however, when the Social Democrats returned to power in 1982 following an election dominated by the "funds issue", they did not set up a new commission, but instead proceeded directly to introduce proposals on the matter: in highly controversial questions touching on the very essence of party creeds, this may well be the only way of proceeding.

A brief postscript on parliamentary commissions in Sweden is in order, because although the extensive involvement of individual parliamentarians on commissions of inquiry has served to legitimise the policy formulation process and allow Riksdag delegates to participate significantly in the development of public policy, it has imposed restraints on the efficacy of parliament *as a whole* to scrutinise and criticise the executive. This stems from the fact that it is extremely difficult for a party to dissociate itself from the line taken by one of its senior delegates who has a seat on both a parliamentary commission and on the corresponding parliamentary standing committee. That such a person, acting as party spokesman and rapporteur, tends to monopolise subsequent plenary discussion of the issue has rendered largely ineffectual the majority of delegates without a stake in the preparation of the matter at hand. As a result, the status of the legislature at the policy adoption stage is considerably reduced. Delegates are not unaware of the dilemma though, as mentioned earlier, the feeling seems to be that it is preferable to have Riksdag delegates who can be relied on, rather than experimenting on commissions with ordinary party members, thereby creating a career channel capable of being exploited by ambitious individuals possibly to the prejudice of desired results in terms of policy.[48]

Thus there is a sharp contrast in policy-making styles between Sweden and the rest of the Nordic region when it comes to the inclusion of parliamentarians at the formulation stage. In Sweden delegates participate extensively and accept the extra workload involved in commission membership; elsewhere, the functional separation between an executive arm of government which is directed to the preparation of proposals and a legislature which subsequently debates them is defended. True, a Finnish Communist Party delegate, Inger Hirvelä, contended that in the conditions of highly stable centre-left majoritarian government continuing now for nearly two decades, the greater involvement of parliamentarians with policy formulation commissions would be desirable as part of an attempt to redress the balance away from the executive.[49] But Folketing opinion on the matter is generally typical. In Glistrup's view, commissions exist to provide an informed basis for discussion, not to legislate themselves. Only on the commissions examining questions arousing much general discussion should parliamentarians be recruited as a general rule: Glistrup thus regretted the termination in the spring of 1982 of the parliament-based Matrimonial Law Reform Commission.[50] Other Folketing delegates implied that acceptance of membership of commissions might entail tacit acquiescence in the directive's terms of reference, with the result that parliamentarians could in practice become the hostages of ministers.[51] Even when this danger was not expressed, the question of incorporating Folketing delegates on to commissions of inquiry was given low priority. The Left-Socialist, Steen Folke, for example, stressed that bridging the growing gulf between citizens and their elected representatives was more important than the integration of parliamentarians into the policy formulation process.[52] It should be noted here that delegates are, anyway, often members of preparatory bodies created by the various labour-market organisations. The Radical delegate, Aase Olesen, noted that in her (admittedly small) parliamentary group, delegates were involved on three or four such bodies.[53] Though not a sentiment expressed by delegates to the author, it might of course be added that the distinctively high level of parliamentarians' involvement on Swedish commissions of inquiry does not in itself reflect the actual influence exerted by parliamentarians in the development of public policy. The plain fact is that whatever the composition of commissions, proposals are drafted in the ministries by a wide range of departmental officials and we will now briefly consider the policy role of civil servants.

But before doing so, it should be added, as a postscript to our consideration of parliamentary involvement at the formulation stage in Sweden, that throughout the 1970s governments expressed growing concern at the time-consuming and increasingly costly nature of commissions of inquiry. Shortly before the Social Democrats left office in 1976 the government noted in a letter to the Riksdag that 'restrictions on the use of commissions would probably have important direct and indirect effects on public expenditure.'[54] On assuming power again six years later, the Social Democrats returned to the same theme. Indeed, the deputy Prime Minister, Ingvar Carlsson, set out to rationalise the structure of the commission system, discontinuing fifteen commissions while expressing the hope that by the beginning of July 1983, the work of another seventy-five would have been completed. In the future, he made it clear, all commissions should in principle have completed their task within two years, new ones would not be created in areas previously investigated, and the ministries would assume responsibility for organisational matters hitherto delegated to the commission network.[55] Commissions would also take rather differing forms — ongoing investigations concerning Children and Young Persons, Narcotics, and Economic Crimes such as fraud were cited as ones deemed suitable for commissions of inquiry — and it was stated that both their members and the commission secretariat would be asked to work intensively for a delimited period to produce recommendations on larger and more controversial questions.[56] If these measures were dictated by the recessionary climate of the 1980s, they may also reflect a real concern to make governments — and the policy formulation process — more flexible and sensitive to changing circumstances than previously in Sweden.

Civil servants and policy formulation

'I believe that somebody who has a strong interest in politics and the way society should develop will get a good return on his work in the *kanslihuset*. Formally, to be sure, civil servants are not thought to take political decisions; in reality, they take them every day.' So observed a senior civil servant in one of the Swedish government ministries when interviewed by Anders Mellbourn in the early 1970s.

The influence of civil servants in the policy formulation process is a subject we can only consider briefly; and it is anyway extremely difficult to gauge and by no means uncontroversial. At the lowest level, few would doubtless dissent from the view that contiguous with the expansion of the post-war state, significant legislative responsibilities have devolved to the career officials in the government departments. They occupy a pivotal position in the sequence beginning with the formulation of recommendations in a commission or working group and culminating in the finalisation of proposals for cabinet approval. Civil servants, in short, are centrally engaged in *policy-making*.

There are nonethelsss enormous intra-regional differences in their formal powers. Distinctively in Finland there are about 800 senior officials, *valtioneuvoston esittelijät*, about half nominated by the President and half by the government as 'extraordinary appointments', who introduce measures on behalf of their ministers at ordinary cabinet meetings. The system of 'sponsoring officials' is an old one and has changed little since its origins in the nineteenth century. The 'sponsors' introduce proposals at ordinary cabinets, albeit with the authorisation of the minister concerned, and put their own views forward on the matter. The minister, who customarily has the next speech, is naturally free to disagree with them and it is he alone who has voting rights. But if it is easy to exaggerate the importance of the 'sponsor system' — the senior officials involved are generally extremely loyal to their minister — it is equally clear that their potential influence is considerable, especially when the minister is less experienced. In Sweden, in contrast, civil servants are not formally vested with any legislative role nor has there developed a convention of 'implicit authorisation' as in Britain, where the civil servants are enabled to 'interpret the minister's mind' in the production of draft proposals. Throughout the Nordic region, however, civil servants play a vital role in the formulation of public policy in so far as they determine how a matter is to be handled, the methods and approaches to be adopted in resolving it, and the shape of the draft proposal.

This, of course, is not to suggest that civil servants set out to exert political influence, or indeed perceive themselves as affecting policy outcomes. Anders Mellbourn's study of the role conceptions of top Swedish civil servants (interviewed in 1971) showed that politically-minded officials, i.e. those deriving satisfaction from the political dimension of their work and entering public service out of political interest, accounted for no more than 10% of his sample and were not partisan in their orientation; rather, they were able to present themselves as the obedient servants of their governmental masters, whoever those masters might be.[58] Even allowing for the emergence of a generation of senior bureaucrats socialised in the radical political climate of the late 1960s, the picture is unlikely to have changed significantly. Obviously, too, in small government departments, as in Sweden, an energetic and determined minister can make an enormous difference: in departments such as Education and Employment, moreover, matters are directed by twin managers, viz. two ministers of effectively equal status. Yet the point here is that civil servants can have a cumulatively significant impact on both the nuance and detail of policy without the exercise of political influence being necessarily one of their manifest objectives. This they can do on the plethora of policy commissions as well as in the various ministries. Almost the majority of commission personnel are civil servants, albeit recruited mainly from central boards, agencies and public services rather than the ministries themselves. Commissions do contain departmental officials, particularly from the legal secretariat, but their formal participation on commissions should not be exaggerated. However, it is the secretariat of commissions which, in producing extensive guideline documents for members about a week before commission meetings, effectively direct proceedings. Moreover, when the commission's work is complete, departmental officials, often of quite low rank, produce policy statements which — inasmuch as they may be the product of some two years of concentrated work, extensive consultation with organisations outside the ministry and subsequent discussion with superiors in the department, especially the Heads of Section, *departementsråd* — are extremely difficult for the minister, confronted by the official in person, to resist. Formally, the matter will have been at first referred to the minister's right-hand man, the Under-Secretary of State, though only very rarely will guidance in the form of policy directives have been given. As a result, when the matter is handled in the weekly meeting between civil servants and the minister, *departementsberedning*, it will invariably be rubber-stamped.

The minister's task is further compounded by the sheer volume of business handled in his department. In the Ministry of Education in Sweden, to take a concrete illustration, there are five sections — Schools, Higher Education, Adult Education, Culture and Media — which together generate between 50 and 100 matters weekly that are presented for resolution in the formal sitting of the cabinet and on which the ministers are required to make recommendations. In effect the only technical assistance in perusing and considering these matters comes from the Permanent Secretary, *expeditionschef*, a lawyer, who examines the possible repercussions of ministerial recommendations (notably their consonance with the law) and advises on precedents. The Permanent Secretary might investigate, for example, whether the impending appointment of a district Director of Education should follow the recommendations of the local School Board or the wishes of the community itself.[59] Not infrequently, problems are anyway interdepartmental: officials in the Ministry of Education thus have extensive contacts with the Ministry of Employment over such questions as job training schemes for young persons and the level of Swedish-language instruction to be given to immigrants. In all this, the minister is necessarily reliant on the guidance of civil servants.

It should also be emphasised that there is a considerable personnel overlap and indeed extensive informal contact between the civil servants making up the secretariat of commissions and officials in the ministries: the secretary of the commission is frequently a departmental official on temporary leave of absence. So although Swedish civil servants do not enjoy conventional powers of legislative initiative and are not permitted to "interpret the minister's mind', they do exercise legislative initiative in so far as they are required independently to decide how the problem is to be formulated.

In the longer term, the effective autonomy enjoyed by individual civil servants in the drafting of policy proposals raises the central question of the development of a possible conflict between the legislative increment of permanent administrators and the programmatic intentions of elected governments. Does a class of civil servants represent a major structural constraint on governments by constituting a normative sub-system in its own right?

Although much West European literature emphasises the elements of conflict in the relationship between administrators and elected politicians, these should not be exaggerated in the Nordic context. An interview survey of senior Norwegian civil servants conducted in the late 1960s showed relatively little evidence of perceived conflict between the two groups, while another study of the national budget process in Norway pointed to the widespread élite consensus that civil servants should assume responsibility for the detailed formulation of the budget.[60] Moreover, although Claes Linde's recent analysis of Departments and Central Boards, *verk*, in Sweden demonstrated that there were more Riksdag members than civil servants — 59 against 36% — who held the simplistic belief that it was primarily the political element which differentiated Departments from Boards,[61] little or no evidence emerged of hostility towards the work of the public administration on the part of parliamentarians. Even so, there is no shortage of unfavorable accounts of the growing power of civil servants.

In a highly critical study of the Swedish civil service written in 1981, Mats Svegfors, a former Conservative Party Under-Secretary at the Ministry of Housing, argued that Sweden is witnessing a 'revolution in small steps' prompted by civil servants and leading inexorably to an expansion of state control. The revolution is not socialist but incrementalist — a gradual process of 'piecemeal social engineering' involving civil servants, who in their policy reports and draft legislative proposals generate the tens of thousands of details that go to make up government policy decisions.[62] These decisions, Svegfors contends, exhibit a nuance which reflects the values and culture of the civil service and which effectively frustrates the leadership function of elected politicians. The fundamental cause of this situation, it is argued, is the narrow recruitment base of administrators. (While the number of lawyers in the ministries has declined,[63] the number of entrants with a social science degree has risen. Here would seem to be implicit recognition of the need for a training relevant to the policy role civil servants currently perform.) Svegfors' point, however, is that the previous experience of appointees to the civil service has been predominantly in positions in public administration — on central boards or commissions of inquiry — and that they therefore lack both the theoretical and practical knowledge of the society they are supposed to be serving in their task of drafting legislative proposals. Their perspective is markedly bureaucratic, tending towards a defence and indeed promotion of regulations and controls. The revolution in sum has created 'a democratic Leviathan'.

Svegfors' study is predicated on two central claims: first, that the various policy sections, *sakenheter*, within the ministries enjoy much functional autonomy (see diagram 2.4) and are the productive

Table 2.4. STRUCTURE OF A SWEDISH GOVERNMENT MINISTRY

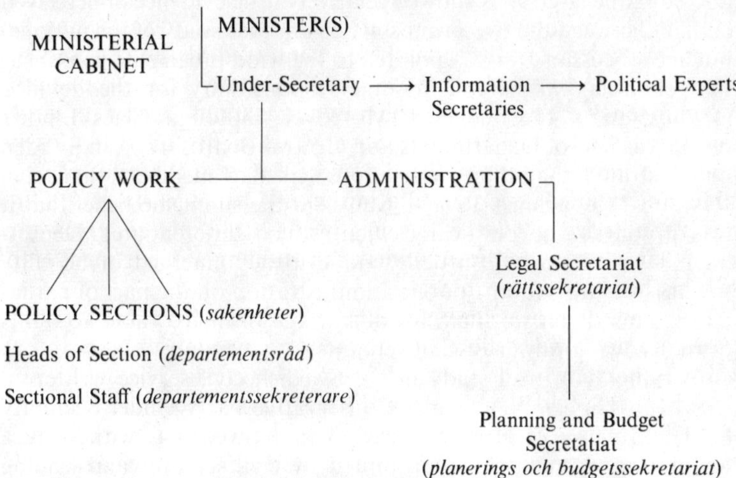

organs of central government;[64] and secondly that the directives to civil servants preparing drafts are generally brief and do not serve as an adequate instrument of political control. Accordingly, Svegfors holds that the decisive contribution to the formulation of public policy is made by departmental civil servants. Certainly the picture presented is less monolithic than might appear the case: for example, officials are depicted as engaged in resolving inter-departmental differences in the drafting of a directive for a commission of inquiry, though even then the compromise is reached at the level of civil servants. Doubtless Svegfors would willingly have posed in Sweden the question posed by Ole Berrefjord, a member of the so-called Power Commission, set up in 1972 to analyse the bases of power in Norwegian society: 'Has Norway evolved from a civil service state to a civil service state?'[65]

A number of objections can be raised to Svegfors' thesis. First, and in the broadest terms, the political equation is dynamic and changing: there are strong governments and weak governments, while in any event the degree of internal pluralism within the *kanslihuset* is rather greater than Svegfors allows.

Next, when personal and/or political tensions occur between cabinet ministers in jointly-led departments, this is invariably reflected in a parallel division of loyalties between civil servants. The policy process within the ministry may accordingly be blocked. In the Ministry of Housing in 1976–9 problems of dual management meant that only three commissions of inquiry were appointed, well below the level of the other ministries.

Thirdly, although compromises over commission directives worked out in inter-departmental committees of officials may be taken as evidence of decisions being contained at the civil service level, recourse to such committees could equally be interpreted as a contingency measure undertaken by bureaucrats faced with weak ministerial leadership. If a minister appears ineffectual, it is clearly politic to mobilise support for a policy — even at the price of possible concessions — by consultation with other departments. Certainly, interview evidence among Swedish officials supports the view that what is vital for a minister in running a department is to win his/her battles in cabinet.

Fourthly, directives and guidelines to officials from under-secretaries are not always short, and the autonomy enjoyed by civil servants is not always as great as Svegfors suggests. His experience doubtless reflected the situation during the non-socialist coalition in 1979–81 and the probable concern in the wording of a directive not to be so specific as to risk causing unnecessary inter-party disagreement.[66]

Finally, there have always been problems that cannot be satisfactorily resolved by civil servants, especially policy questions which in their nature cut across departmental boundaries. Thus environmental questions, although handled primarily by the Ministry of Agriculture, have frequently involved the Ministries of Industry and Housing; and energy questions, as Torbjörn Larsson has shown, cut across ministries and constitute areas of potential inter-departmental conflict that can only be resolved at the political level.[67]

If it would be an exaggeration to portray the Nordic polities as 'civil service states', there is still implicit support for the main thrust of Svegfors' argument in the ephemeral talk in Sweden of effecting an American-style politicisation of the civil service,[68] an issue raised by the governing Social Democrats in the late 1960s.[69] However, although this might strengthen the leadership function during periods of single-party government, it could prove far more problematical at times of coalition. In the exceptional case of Finland, the partisan basis of permanent civil service appointments has progressed so far that even the traditional obligation of civil servants to remain politically neutral has been questioned.[70] In the second half of the Kekkonen era, middle-ranking officials were nominated on a party basis, officially by the President (as required by the constitution) but invariably following the recommendations of the pro-Kekkonen group of parties, i.e. the Centre and Social Democrats.

This inevitably had a damaging effect on the leadership function in the departments.

In the Ministry of Education in the late 1970s, the department appeared divided between the 'Red' and 'Green' appointments, each serving their own party's interest rather than the approach of the responsible minister.[71] Small wonder perhaps that in 1975 26 public figures, academics and journalists addressed an open letter to the President condemning the appointments system as unfair and ultimately inefficient.[72] The Eduskunta Speaker, Johannes Virolainen, remarked in 1980 that over the previous twenty years it had been necessary for an interviewee for a civil service position to have all the different party membership cards in his pocket, to be on the safe side![73]

In Finland the penetration of the state machine by partisan appointments has been endemic. Even the apex of the administrative system, the Cabinet Office, has not been immune to the prevailing trends: the General Section still comprises only 'classical' nonpartisan civil servants in the best Whitehall tradition, but the Planning Section of the Cabinet has been totally party-politicised. Moreover, the distinctive and long-standing system of 'sponsoring officials' has been similarly affected and there have even been proposals to appoint Permanent Secretaries, *kansliapäällikkö*, on a partisan basis, although the idea seems unlikely to be realised in the near future. The partisan character of civil service appointments obviously does not mean that the officials so nominated are necessarily incompetent, blinkered or even hard to integrate into the department. However, a few have given the Finnish civil service a decidedly bad name, and confidence in the national bureaucracy is lower in Finland than at any previous time.

The Finnish situation is unique among the Nordic states. Yet throughout much of the remainder of the region and in response to the heightened administrative workload of ministers, there have been attempts to strengthen the leadership function in government departments by the creation of 'ministerial cabinets', i.e. essentially partisan teams of advisers and experts assisting the minister in the co-ordination of his department. In Norway, Sweden and Iceland this team is led by an under-secretary of state and includes a number of political experts and information officers. In Finland, senior ministers are assisted by political secretaries who, like under-secretaries, serve only during the tenure of a particular minister. True, there is nothing in the Nordic states approaching the size of the French 'ministerial cabinets' which average between fifteen and twenty persons, 90% of them seconded civil servants frequently with a training at the École Nationale d'Administration.[74] Equally, ministerial advisers in the Nordic countries are predominantly partisan in their recruitment and constitute far more of a *political* directorate than appears to be the case in France.

In this latter context, the distinctive role played by the under-secretaries of state in the region deserves to be briefly noted. In Sweden, the office of the Under-Secretary, *statssekreterare*, is technically an administrative one and one of the three highest-ranking posts in a government department, along with Permanent Secretary, *expeditionschef*, and the Chief Legal Officer, *rättschef*. By the later stages of the Social Democrats' forty-four year tenure of power, however, the role of the under-secretary had evolved to the point at which it was plainly more political than narrowly administrative.[75] By the 1970s, as Mellbourn's study of top civil servants shows, almost half of the thirteen under-secretaries interviewed were classed as political figures on the basis of their organisational affiliations and the views they expressed.[76] The fresh appointments of under-secretaries by the non-socialist coalition in 1976 markedly accentuated the political character of the office so that by the early 1980s the under-secretaries were in many ways analogous to junior ministers[77] — relatively young persons (aged 35–45) engaged in assisting the minister with the running of his department. Interestingly, and paralleling developments in Sweden, when the long period of Christian Democratic domination in the German Federal Republic was broken by the entry of the Social Democrats into government in 1966, there was a marked strengthening of the party political élite in the government ministries. This involved the creation of a number of 'parliamentary state secretaries' who were in effect junior ministers and served the minister and party in the department concerned.[78]

The under-secretary in Sweden is involved in the writing of directives for commissions of inquiry as well as the appointment of commission personnel and, while not himself a parliamentarian, is conventionally called upon to represent a minister required to appear before a Riksdag standing committee. It is worth noting too that the report which provided the basis of the Constitutional Committee's investigation into the government's handling of the Russian submarine incident in the autumn of 1981 owed much to informal contacts between the committee secretariat and the Under-Secretary in the Defence Ministry.[70] In fact, on the basis of the Defence Department's diary tracing the whole episode in detail, the Prime Minister and Defence Secretary were called before the committee for a formal hearing. It needs emphasis that the co-ordination function of under-secretaries has extended beyond individual departments: there are regular under-secretary lunches on Mondays, convened and directed by the Under-Secretary in the Prime Minister's Department (a post created in 1964 not least to offset the influence of the civil servants in the Finance Department)[80] along with a number of one- or two-day planning meetings annually.[81] Indeed, the synchronisation of government work achieved through the under-secretary network has gone some way to compensating for the absence of cabinet committees in Sweden. Incidentally, although all twenty under-secretaries resigned after the defeat of Fälldin's third coalition in September 1982, a prior agreement obliged the incoming Social Democratic government to provide them with suitable employment.[82]

Before considering the development of the institution of under-secretary in Norway, it is timely to note recent evidence that in Sweden in the early 1970s the Social Democrats captured a number of leading permanent positions in the *kanslihuset* in addition to the under-secretary's post. According to Bert Levin who was appointed an under-secretary when Fälldin's first bourgeois coalition was elected in October 1976, a process of politicisation — comparable to, though not as deep-seated as that in Finland — had advanced to the point at which on arrival at his new job, Levin was confronted with 'a forest of red needles'.[83] Six of the eight leading civil servants in the Ministry of Education, he claims, were active Social Democrats, while in several sections of the Department the Social Democrats' dominance was overwhelming. True, Levin recalled only a few instances of this leading to disloyalty, i.e. of civil servants pursuing an Opposition rather than a Government line on a question. However, he speculated that because of the ingrained attitudes and outlook of the Social Democratic appointees, it was difficult for them to accept the political ambitions of the incoming non-socialist ministers. Most significantly, perhaps, Levin contends that when Pierre Vinde, a former Finance Ministry Under-Secretary, observed in his standard work on Swedish administration 'How Sweden is Governed", *Hur Sverige styres*, that recruitment to government departments, as elsewhere in the central administration, is not based on partisan considerations, he was stating at best a partial truth. Though plainly valid for the Finance Ministry under the long-serving Gunnar Sträng who possessed sufficient personal authority to pursue a Social Democratic policy without the aid of partisan officials, Vinde's thesis does not hold, Levin argues, for the *kanslihuset* as a whole and certainly not for the Ministry of Education which was markedly politicized under the direction of young and ideologically conscious ministers like Olof Palme and Ingvar Carlsson in the early 1970s. Levin, certainly, has no objections to a minister building up a political team of under-secretaries *et al.*, but insists that partisan nominees should be for no longer than the minister's tenure of office and should not occupy permanent positions, which he sees as constituting potential pockets of political resistance to the plans of an incoming minister.

The system of under-secretaries is more recent in Norway than in Sweden; it dates from 1947 when the post was introduced explicitly to strengthen the political leadership function in government ministries. Accordingly, the under-secretary was empowered to assist the minister with the co-ordination of his department although not permitted to deputise for him in the cabinet or Storting.[84] In the 1960s, attempts to strengthen the partisan element in government ministries still further followed the end of a long period of Labour Party government and significant changes that had taken place in the educational background of civil servants.

By the late 1960s, 29% of senior Norwegian civil servants were graduates (or the equivalent) in economics, rather than the traditional lawyers — parallel changes were occurring elsewhere in the region — and as such tended to have a disposition towards macro-economic planning and an expansion of the public sector. This created a natural empathy between the bureaucracy and the long-serving Labour governments. As Higley, Brofoss and Groholt have observed, 'the suspicion of excessive ideological compatibility between some top civil servants and the Labour Party underlay the efforts of the bourgeois coalition government which took over in 1965 to broaden and strengthen political control of the civil service.'[85]

Bolstering the under-secretary's position seemed an obvious means to this end. However, there was no shortage of critics of the office. It was argued, for example, that persons vested with political responsibilities should be answerable to parliament for their actions and that in any event the introduction of under-secretaries blurred the command structure in the ministries, particularly the division of authority between the under-secretary and the leading civil servant, the Permanent Secretary, *departementsråd*. When a commission of inquiry reported on the matter in 1974, its majority recommended that the under-secretary be permitted to participate in Storting proceedings in order to answer questions from delegates.[86] However, in a statement to the Storting in March 1976, the government declined to go as far as the commission: the *status quo ante* was maintained and under-secretaries continued to be precluded from parliamentary meetings.[87] In both Norway and Sweden, 'ministerial cabinets' include a variety of officers in addition to the under-secretary — e.g. personal secretaries to ministers in Norway; and information secretaries and so-called political experts, *sakkunniga,* in Sweden. The information secretaries are partisans often recruited from the ranks of the party organisation, while the political experts have very occasionally also been parliamentarians. Daniel Tarschys, a Liberal delegate, was a political expert in the Budget Department in 1981–2, although his duties involved little more than two or three hours work per week. Altogether, Fälldin's third coalition employed a total of 20 under-secretaries, 16 information secretaries and 36 political experts.

The institution of under-secretaries has not been paralleled in Denmark and Finland. In Finland, senior ministers have indeed nominated one or more political secretaries from the ranks of their party, much as in Britain where the convention since the third Wilson government came to power in 1974 has been that each cabinet minister shall have at most two party political advisers.[88] Not infrequently, these political secretaries — they are not parliamentarians — are subsequently appointed to senior positions on public boards and administrative agencies, making the post an attractive career stepping-stone for favoured partisans. Although the institution of the Prime Minister's Political Secretary has existed throughout the entire Independence era — he is allowed at most four such advisers — the network of political secretaries in Finland only developed to the full in the 1970s. Political secretaries were thus nominated during the Paasio Social Democratic minority government in 1972 and provisions for their formal remuneration were included in the 1974 budget. Yet the position of the political secretary remains fluid, and the status of the post is lower than that of under-secretary in Sweden. As to the duties of the office, the political secretary is in daily contact with his minister's department, acts as the minister's personal adviser, but never himself attends cabinet meetings. Initially, the political secretaries were viewed with a good deal of suspicion by the permanent ministry officials, and there were tensions between them. However, in the view of the Head of Cabinet Office, *valtioneuvoston kansliapäällikkö*, the system of political secretaries has come to work smoothly enough.[89] Equally, as the Prime Minister's Political Secretary for Foreign Affairs insisted, the importance of the political secretaries should not be exaggerated.[90] In the main they are relatively young men with careers to build. Many of them are recruited from the minister's party; others are seconded civil servants. Several political secretaries have gone on to achieve ministerial office themselves: Paavo Väyrynen, for example, at present Chairman of the Centre Party and Minister of Foreign Affairs in the Sorsa IV government formed in May 1983, was the Prime Minister's secretary in 1971–2.

In Denmark, the distinctive absence of under-secretaries (and indeed of political secretaries) has been linked to the rule that civil servants should remain strictly neutral and to a belief that ministers should have sole responsibility for the direction of their departments. These were in essence the sentiments expressed as early as 1921 by K.K. Steincke, then a permanent secretary and subsequently a long-serving minister in Stauning's Social Democratic government, when responding to a questionnaire by *Nordisk Administrativt Tidsskrift* probing the attitude of senior Danish civil servants to the Swedish system of under-secretaries.[91] They were echoed, too, by a working group under the direction of the Danish High School for Administration, which in the 1970s examined the possibility of strengthening the leadership function of ministers by setting up either under-secretaries, Finnish-style political secretaries or the type of Minister without Portfolio (albeit with special policy responsibilities) found in Britain and occasionally too in the other Nordic countries. In its report in 1979, the working group concluded that the creation of an under-secretary network could well threaten the prevailing notions of the rightful role of the cabinet minister as well as undermining the existing hierarchical structure of central administration.[92]

On rare occasions, individual ministers have not been averse to experimenting with political assistants: Per Hækkerup, as Foreign Minister, nominated a 'party secretary', *partifællesekretær*, who was authorised to make statements on the minister's behalf. The 'guinea pig' in question was a Foreign Ministry official, who as the son-in-law of H.C. Hansen had the appropriate political pedigree, although later returning to the ranks of the civil service. Clearly, too, a number of informal means exist for relieving the minister's administrative burden. With Social Democratic governments, it has not been rare for a foreign policy spokesman in parliament to alleviate some of the load by attending meetings of the Socialist International and by developing and using good contacts with the press and television — though the minister himself has continued to accept full responsibility. In contrast to the rest of the region, however, a network of under-secretaries has not developed and indeed it has been little discussed. Of course, to note the distinctive absence in Denmark of political support to cabinet members is not necessarily to suggest that the ministerial leadership function has significantly suffered relative to the other Nordic states for as Christian S. Nissen — citing Richard Crossman — has observed, 'the danger is, if you bring in two or three people . . . the Department makes sure nothing happens. A total frigidity sets in because Departments are very hostile to foreign elements.'[93]

The search for general conclusions about the role of civil servants — *vis-à-vis* the part played by ministers and their political assistants — in the formulation of public policy is not made easier by the constantly changing dynamics of the political situation. Some ministers obviously remain in a particular department longer than others (the matter is pursued in the next chapter), while the career patterns of civil servants in the region dictate varying lengths of service in any one ministry.

Following the 1965 reforms in Sweden, for example, departmental terms of about five years were advocated, although in recent years, not least because of the impact of recession, the mobility of civil servants into and out of government ministries has been much reduced. In other words, the traditional professional route of Swedish civil servants, who begin in a central board, gravitate to membership of a commission of inquiry, complete a relatively short period in a government ministry and finally obtain a position of seniority in a central board has been threatened by economic austerity.

In Norway, by contrast, officials tend to serve longer in the same ministry, so contributing to the development of what Gudmund Hernes has referred to as a 'departmental culture' — a set of institutionalised norms and attitudes — which new entrants to the civil service are in practice compelled to internalise and which can act as an obstacle in the path of a reforming minister. In Denmark, too, according to Erik Damgaard, promotion generally occurs within the ministry of the civil servant's initial appointment and despite a recent trend towards increased inter-departmental mobility, the Danish 'civil servant's whole career typically takes place within the fairly limited context of one ministry.'[94] The same is true in Finland. Moreover, although Finland has developed a network of central boards and agencies, *keskusvirastot*, comparable to Sweden, there is virtually no movement of officials between the central agencies that are mainly concerned with the implementation of laws and the government departments which serve as the policy formulation bodies. The personnel in both remain separate and distinct.

To a degree, of course, the policy influence of civil servants is tied to the extent to which they possess the right of independent legislative initiative (well-established in Finland, formally non-existent in Sweden), the degree of functional autonomy enjoyed by sections within ministries (generally high throughout the region), the centrality of the department in substantive terms (it is widely recognized that in recent years Finance Ministry officials in Denmark have been the most powerful group of civil servants) and not least the general attitude of the minister, i.e. whether his relations with civil servants are fundamentally adversary or collaborationist. Despite the complexities of the picture — and it is important to avoid seeing the relationship between minister and civil servant in zero-sum conflict terms — a number of tentative points may be made.

First, there is clearly much truth in Svegfors' assertion that ministers are primarily engaged in representing and promoting the interests of their department in the cabinet and the country, and consequently delegate much of the responsibility for co-ordinating the routine legislative work of the ministry to their under-secretaries. There is doubtless much validity too in Svegfors' claim that largely as a result of his predominantly 'ambassadorial' duties, 'a minister invariably believes he has more power than he really has.'[95] Secondly, although charged with the daunting task of overseeing the day-to-day policy activities of departments, under-secretaries are by no means always as ineffectual as Svegfors insists. They are in a position to resolve problems arising out of disagreements between officials, at a relatively late stage in the policy formulation process; and particularly during periods of single-party and/or cohesive coalition government, they can exercise considerable authority regarding the drafts of directives to civil servants. Even so, it is extremely doubtful if an under-secretary can adequately compensate for a weak minister, i.e. one losing his battles in cabinet and lacking the administrative competence necessary to manage a government department.

Yet evidence suggests that despite being vastly outnumbered by officials, a strong minister can make a substantial difference. A Minister of Labour like Svend Auken in Jørgensen's fifth Social Democratic government in Denmark in 1982 was able, as a university-trained specialist in labour economics, to engage in a far more active policy of economic management than his long-serving predecessor Erling Dinesen who, though Minister of Labour for twelve years (with breaks) between 1964 and 1976, respected throughout that time the tradition that the LO and Employers' Organisation should be left to attend to their own affairs. Ministers can also use a variety of methods to avoid being dominated by their departmental officials. The strategy of Ritt Bjerregaard, the successful Social Democratic Minister of Education in Denmark between 1975 and 1978, involved building what in effect amounted to an embryonic 'counter-bureaucracy' which afforded her primary loyalties. As her Liberal Party successor Bertel Haarder noted, 'Bjerregaard will be particularly remembered for her enormous display of force in authorizing the appointment of personally trusted people to the growing pyramid of committees and commissions which she protected herself with.'[96] Incidentally, while on the subject of commissions of inquiry, a minister reluctant to proceed to legislate on the basis of a commission's report can always claim that one or two questions have been left outstanding and then set up a committee of experts to look into them. As a former Danish Finance Minister, Poul Møller has noted, it is obviously not possible to set up a new commission altogether, for this would constitute an open disavowal of the first one: a body of specialist officials, however, will normally do the trick. Meanwhile, the minister can search for a higher authority to which to address his proposals before their final preparation in bill form. The Nordic Council, Møller notes, represents just such an organ, for 'he can consult and co-operate with it in the best Nordic spirit without the risk of being reproached and criticised!'[97]

Further examples of effective ministerial styles could be cited. Suffice it here to note that while a strong minister can clearly make a difference, his impact is likely to be first and foremost on the morale and overall cohesion of his department. Indeed, even when buoyed by what the former British Health Minister, Barbara Castle, called 'the vitamin of power', ministers have only a finite amount of time and energy to devote to policy activities as such. They can certainly give a lead, but ultimately the task of translating directives and commission reports into draft proposals falls to civil servants who thereby play a pivotal part in how a particular policy measure is to be formulated.[98] All this is not, of course, unique to the Nordic nations, nor does it justify their description as 'civil service states' in any significant sense. Officials do not set out to govern the country nor, indeed, generally to thwart the avowed intentions of elected politicians. But at the same time, it is essential to perceive the departmental role of ministers and their personal 'cabinets' in a realistic light, i.e. to see the partisans engaged less in attempting to concentrate the exclusive direction of policy in their own hands than in forming the summit of a mountain of legislative activity undertaken by permanent departmental officials. It is clearly impossible for even the most industrious minister and his advisers to do more than orchestrate and give authority to the vast bulk of this activity. Indeed, there seems a case for arguing, in line with Paul G. Roness' analysis of the changing structure of Norwegian government departments, that while ministers probably participate actively in the major decisions affecting their ministries, 'the process of change seems to a great extent to be impelled by the administrators themselves.'[99] In so far as this is true, the vital task facing ministers is then successfully to defend their departmental proposals at the cabinet stage of the policy process.

Parliamentary perceptions of the policy formulation process

Before turning to an examination of the cabinet stage in the policy process, however, it is worth pausing to inquire what the response of leading bureaucrats and — more interestingly from our viewpoint — parliamentarians has been to the changed policy role of senior administrators. In other words, given that the period after the Second World War has witnessed the emergence of an increasingly interventionist and technocratic state, which in turn has dictated that civil servants no longer simply apply laws neutrally and objectively in the classical Weberian mould, how do administrators perceive their changed role, and how do parliamentarians react to the situation? Most important, can it be said that a tension exists between the respective roles of civil servant and member of parliament? The question is particularly pertinent in Sweden, because that country has the distinctive concept of the 'neutral executor' legally entrenched — bureaucrats in short can be dismissed only by an order of the courts — and also because there has lately been growing concern about the influence exercised by the upper echelons of the civil service in the *kanslihuset*. Svegfors, it will be recalled, was highly critical of the role played by departmental civil servants in the formulation of policy, while in similar vein, Levin's criticism was directed at the partisan nature of a number of strategically-placed officials in the Swedish ministries. In the absence of recent data, only a few tentative observations can be made at this point.

First, congruous with the position in the other Nordic countries, the relationship between civil servants and politicians in Sweden is a complex one which should not be viewed in simple, antagonistic terms. On the contrary, leading civil servants and parliamentarians appear to share a common *Weltanschauung:* a commitment to uphold a pluralist model of society in which power is diffused and a multiplicity of organizations compete for influence within the framework of a broad consensus over basic systemic values. Despite the more heterogeneous origins of Riksdag delegates — there are significantly less lawyers than in the *kanslihuset* — and the relatively recent emergence of a democratically-elected parliamentary élite compared with the historic primacy of the central administration in the decision-making process, civil servants and politicians nonetheless tend to possess common beliefs and attitudes and in this sense constitute a cohesive power élite. Yet an unduly monolithic picture should not be painted. For example, there appears a clear discrepancy between parliamentarians' perceptions of the desirable characteristics of the civil servant and the role senior bureaucrats themselves want to perform. Thomas J. Anton's 1971 interview survey of a small group of forty-four Riksdag members — along with a much larger sample of 315 senior civil servants — reveals that most parliamentarians, irrespective of party allegiance, believe that the single most important quality of civl servants (at least those employed in the central boards and public authorities) should be their ability to act as 'neutral executors' or policy implementers — persons, in other words, loyally representing and serving the government of the day. Expertise, technical know-how and professional competence were rated of secondary importance, and no less than 98% of Riksdag respondents rejected the significance of 'policy-making qualities for civil servants'.[100] The overwhelming majority of civil servants for their part asserted their right independently to influence the administration of policy, i.e. not simply to carry it out mechanically but to bring to it their particular attributes.

If most of the Riksdag delegates accepted that civil servants should be neither more nor less than 'neutral executors', they also did not feel that civil servants were attempting in any way to pre-empt their own policy role as parliamentarians. Indeed, Anton's study reveals interestingly how Riksdag members believe in the orthodox view that the government should govern, i.e. take responsibility for the direction of policy. As a corollary of this, they place the representative qualities of the elected delegate — the importance of articulating constituency grievances etc. — ahead of any policy-making qualifications the delegate may possess. The main dividing line, it seems, is between the majority of interviewees adhering to the classical view of civil servants and parliamentarians as administrators and representatives respectively and a small minority of bureaucrats together with a rather larger body of parliamentarians — primarily on the Social Democratic side — advocating something of a conflation in the roles of the two sets of actors so that civil servants in the government ministries (though not the central boards and public authorities) along with parliamentarians (as well, of course, as government ministers) would participate conjointly in the formulation of public policy. This has in fact happened for decades because, as we have seen, considerable personal interaction between politicians and bureaucrats takes place on the plethora of government-appointed commissions of inquiry. Even so, while there is evidently a wide-ranging consensus among Swedish parliamentarians over substantive and procedural values, there is clearly less than wholehearted endorsement of the reality that these days ministry officials perform a legislative role. On the basis of Anton's work, it is apparent that bourgeois politicians in particular — both Svegfors and Levin belong to this lineage — are less likely to accept policy formulation as a legitimate role of the civil servant.

Elsewhere, the post-war transformation of the civil servant's role from that of neutral executor to co-ordinator and formulator of legislative proposals has prompted mixed reaction from parliamentarians. In Finland, a number of smaller opposition groups outside the Red-Green, Social Democratic-Centre Party Establishment, in focusing on the predominantly partisan basis of appointments to the civil service, have strongly deprecated the development in the last twenty years of an American-style 'spoils system'. Wholesale patronage and the *sotto governo* approach more associated with post-war Italian politics, it is insinuated, have no place in the government and administration of Finland.

In Denmark where traditional departmental relationships have been formally maintained by a continuing refusal to appoint political under-secretaries to assist ministers in the direction of policy, the growing influence of the civil service has been at least implicitly recognised in the recent attempts to safeguard against the phenomenon of 'departmentalism', i.e. resistance to ministerial directives on the part of long-serving administrators. There has thus been a concern to diversify recruitment and introduce new skills into the central bureaucracy. In 1976, for example, representatives from a number of government departments including the Ministry of Finance, along with the civil service unions, proposed that civil servants should be transferred at least three times between ministries during the first ten years of their employment.[101] Certainly the fact that personal contacts between ministry officials and parliamentarians are relatively extensive — on commissions of inquiry, legislative standing committees etc. — may well have tended to minimize the general level of mutual suspicion between the two groups, although a straight transference of roles as in West Germany from *Beamte* to *Bundestag*, civil service to parliament, and *vice versa* is rare in the Nordic region. Yet if criticism of 'politicised' administrators has been more trenchant in Sweden than elsewhere in the region (albeit primarily from under-secretaries rather than parliamentarians), the Nordic civil servant plainly is and will remain a political actor with a lynchpin position in the generation, preparation and formulation of policy proposals.[102] Voitto Helander and Dag Anckar's summation of the Finnish situation may be regarded as representative of that in the region as a whole: 'In planning and implementing the principal decisions made at the political level, officials have got more political responsibility and more political power too.'[103]

REFERENCES

1. Heisler (1974), pp. 62–3.
2. Moren (1974), p. 33.
3. Robert Kvavik, 'Interest Groups in a Co-optive Political System — The Case of Norway', in Heisler (1974), p. 105.
4. Arne Halvarson, *Sveriges statsskick*. Lund: Esselte Studium, 1980, p. 61.
5. Gunnar Svardal, 'Stortinget, regjeringen og statsadministrasjonen' in Leif H. Skare (ed) *Forvaltningen i samfunnet. En bok om byråkrati, og demokrati, planlegging og effektivitet*. Oslo: Tanum-Nordli, 1979, p. 91.
6. Indkomstfordelingen før og nu'. *Weekendavisen* 11–17.6.1982.
7. 'Svar på fråga 1980/81:98 om en parlamentarisk utredning för utforming av prostitutionsutrednings betänkande'. *Riksdagens protokoll* 1980/81:32/33, pp. 57–60.
8. Isberg (1982), p. 27.
9. Interview with Professor Henry Valen, University of Oslo 1.10.1981.
10. 'Utredningsarbetet', *Nordisk Kontakt* 1/82, p. 77.
11. Thomas J. Anton, 'Policy-Making and Political Culture in Sweden'. *Scandinavian Political Studies* 4, 1969, p. 94.
12. Voitto Helander, *Etujärjestöt ja komitealaitos*. Turun yliopisto: Politiikan tutkimuksen ja sosiologian laitos. Respo 33/1979, p. 20.
13. Johan P. Olsen, 'Governing Norway: Segmentation, Anticipation and Consensus Formation' in Richard Rose and Ezra N. Suleiman (eds), *Presidents and Prime Ministers*. Washington, DC: American Enterprise Institute for Public Policy Research, 1980, p. 249.
14. Erik Damgaard and Kjell A. Eliassen, 'Reduction of Party Conflict through Corporate Participation in Danish Law-Making'. *Scandinavian Political Studies* 3 (New Series), 2, 1980, p. 119.
15. Olsen (1980), p. 245.
16. Heisler and Kvavik (1974), pp. 62–3.
17. *Finansutskottet* 1980/81: 6.
18. Isberg (1982), p. 84.
19. 'Udvalget til undersøgelse af naturpræparater og ikke-autoriserede helbredelsesmetoder,' *Kommissioner, råd og nævn pr 1 Januar 1981*. Folketings Biblioteket.
20. Mikko Eklin, *The Role of a Planning Organisation in Collective Decision-Making: The Anatomy of a Finnish Government Commission*. Helsingin yliopiston yleisen valtio-opin laitoksen tutkimuksia. Sarja C, Deta 11, 1975, p. 13.
21. Dan Larsen, *Folketingets udvalg 1950–1975*. Århus: Danmarks Journalisthøjskole, 1977, pp. 149–50.
22. Lov om Grønlands hjemmestyre 1978.
23. Hans-Peter Hilden and Ole Zacchi, 'En analyse af kommissioner, nævn og udvalg 1.1.1970', in *Offentlige Udvalg. Rapport fra en arbejdsgruppe omkring Politikere, Administratorer og Eksperter under selskabet for samfundsdebat*. København, 1970, pp. 32–5.
24. Kommissioner, råd og nævn pr 1 Januar 1981.
25. Solvang and Moren (1974), pp. 33–6.
26. Innst. S. nr 82 (1963–4). *Innstilling fra utenriks- og konstitusjonskomiteen om forslag fra Halvor Bunkholt til endring i Grunnlovens §82.*
27. Discussion with John H. Hagard of the Riksdag's International Secretariat 10.10.1981.
28. *Valtion keskushallintokomitean 11 osamietintö*. Nide 1, Helsinki 1978, pp. 420–21. See also Liiteosa (1979), pp. 205–9.

29. For the typology of modes of interaction between parliament and administration drawn on in the present context, see Anthony King, 'Modes of Executive-Legislative Relations: Great Britain, France and West Germany'. *Legislative Studies Quarterly* 1, 1, 1976, p. 13.
30. Olav Grimsbo, 'Om utredningsutvalg og konflikter' in Moren (1974), p. 110–21.
31. Interview with Ole Espersen, Danish Minister of Justice, 26.4.1982.
32. Isberg (1982), pp. 48–9.
33. Ibid., p. 46.
34. Bengt Owe Birgersson, *Riksdagsarbetet i enkammarriksdagen*. Riksdagens protokoll bihang 1975/76. Saml.2. Förslag och redogörelser — 15. Bilaga 1. Stockholm, 1976, pp. 78–80.
35. Hans Meijer, 'Bureaucracy and Policy Formulation in Sweden'. *Scandinavian Political Studies* 4, 1969, pp. 108–9.
36. Folke Johansson, *Utredningars genomslag i politiska beslut*. Göteborgs universitet: Statsvetenskapliga Institutionen, 1979, Rapportserien 2.
37. David Donnison, 'Committees and Committeemen' in Martin Bulmer (ed.) *Social Research and Royal Commissions*. London: George Allen and Unwin, 1980, pp. 15–17.
38. Ibid., pp. 15–17.
39. *Invandrarpolitiska kommittén (A 1980: 04)*. Kommitté berättelse 1981. Del 1, pp. 322–3.
40. *Från Riksdag & Departement* 7, 25–30.
41. Interview with the Danish Progres Party leader, Mogens Glistrup 22.4.1982.
42. Ökat länsdemokratiskt inflytande föreslås via de politiska partierna. *Från Riksdag & Departement* 20.8.1982.
43. Discussion with Inger Margrethe Pedersen, a judge in the Justice Department and a member of the Matrimonial Law Reform Commission 22.4.1982.
44. Birgersson (1976), p. 81.
45. Donnison (1980), pp. 15–17.
46. *Löntagarna och kapitaltillväxten*. Slutrapport. Statens offentliga utredningar 44, 1981. Stockholm: Ekonomidepartement, 1981.
47. Interview with Bernt Öhman, Chief Secretary of the Commission on Wage-Earner Funds 16.9.1982.
48. Conversation with John H. Hagard of the Riksdag International Secretariat 10.11.1981.
49. Interview with Inger Hirvelä, a Communist Party member of the Eduskunta 23.3.1983.
50. Interview with Mogens Glistrup 22.4.1982.
51. Interview with the Chief Librarian in the Folketing, Kristian Hvidt 23.4.1982.
52. Interview with Danish Left-Socialist Party delegate, Steen Folke 25.4.1982.
53. Conversation with Danish Radical Party delegate, Aase Olesen 22.4.1982.
54. Cited in Isberg (1982), p. 37.
55. 'Carlsson låter kvasten gå'. *Nordisk Kontakt* 1/83, p. 58.
56. En rad utredningar läggs ned. Resten skall arbeta snabbare. *Från Riksdag & Departement* 11.2.1983.
57. Anders Mellbourn, *Byråkratins ansikten. Rolluppfattningar hos svenska högre statstjänstemän*. Stockholm: Liber, 1979, p. 73.
58. Ibid., pp. 74–5.
59. Interview with Birger Halle, Permanent Secretary in the Swedish Ministry of Education 21.9.1982.
60. John Higley, Karl Erik Brofuss and Knut Groholt, 'Top Civil Servants and the National Budget in Norway' in Dogan (1975), pp. 262–3.
61. Claes Linde, *Departement och Verk. Om synen på den centrala statsförvaltningen*

och dess uppdelning — i en förändrad offentlig sektor. Stockholms universitet: Statsvetenskapliga institutionen, 1982, p. 160.
62. Interview with former Conservative Party Under-Secretary at the Ministry of Housing, Mats Svegfors 21.9.1982.
63. Olle Nyman, 'Rekryteringen till de svenska centrala ämbetsverkens chefsposter 1915–1975'. *Statsvetenskaplig Tidskrift* 2, 1976, pp. 77–89.
64. Mats Svegfors, *Revolution i små steg*. Stockholm: Timbro, 1981, p. 47.
65. Ole Berrefjord, 'Fra embetsmannstat til embetsmannstat?' in Gudmund Hernes (ed.), *Forhandlingsokonomi og blandingsadministrasjon*. Bergen-Oslo-Tromsø: Universitetsforlaget, 1978, pp. 134–59.
66. Discussion with Torbjörn Larsson, a member of the Political Science Department of Stockholm University 24.9.1982.
67. Torbjörn Larsson, 'Från Energiforskningsprogram till Energiverk'. Unpublished paper kindly made available to the author.
68. Arne Hellden, *Regeringsmakt och demokrati*. Stockholm: Liber, 1966, pp. 149–52.
69. Interview with Claes Linde, a member of the Political Science Department of Stockholm University 24.9.1982.
70. Arno Hannus, "Virkamiesmoraalista'. *Kanava* 9, 1978, pp. 524–8. Tore Modeen, 'Virkamiehen itsenäisyys'. *Kanava* 9, 1978, pp. 558–9. Antti Kivivuori, 'Virkamiesten sidonnaissuhteet ja virkamiesmoraali'. *Politiikka* 4, 1979, pp. 271–85.
71. Interview with Professor Ilkka Heiskanen, Department of Political Science, University of Helsinki 22.7.1980.
72. 'Poliittisista virkanimityksistä paheksumiskirje'. *Helsingin Sanomat* 9.5.1975.
73. 'Talonpoika'. *Kanava* 2, 1980, p. 69.
74. Ella Searls, 'The Fragmented French Executive: Ministerial Cabinets in the Fifth Republic'. *West European Politics* 1, 2, 1978.
75. Gustaf Petrén, 'Forholdet mellem embedsmænd og politikere i et lille samfund'. *Nordisk Administrativt Tidskrift* 54, 1973, pp. 182–4.
76. Mellbourn (1979), p. 123.
77. Interview with the Chief Legal Officer in the Prime Minister's Office, Claes Eklundh 15.9.1982.
78. Gordon Smith, *Democracy in Western Germany: Parties and Politics in the Federal Republic*. London: Heinemann, 1982, p. 70.
79. Interview with Magnus Isberg, the secretary in the Constitutional Committee responsible for handling the matter, 19.9.1982.
80. Simon Andersson, Anders Mellbourn and Ingemar Skogö, *Myndigheten i samhället. Problem och utvecklingslinjer i statsförvaltningen*. Stockholm: Liber, 1978, p. 50.
81. Rättschefen (Statsrådsberedningen), *Regeringen och Regeringsarbetet*. 1.9.1982, pp. 7–8.
82. 'De faller med Fälldin'. *Dagens Nyheter* 18.9.1982.
83. Bert Levin, 'En skog av röda nålar. Om politiseringen av department och förvaltning' in Bengt Rydén (ed.) *Makt och Vanmakt. Lärdomar av sex borgerliga regeringsår*. Studieförbundet Näringsliv och Samhälle, 1983, pp. 91–100.
84. Svardal (1979), pp. 84–6.
85. Higley, Brofuss and Groholt (1975), p. 256.
86. 'Viktig ny ordning for statssekretærer'. *Nordisk Kontakt* 9/74, pp. 571–2.
87. 'Statssekretærer kan ikke opptre i Stortinget'. *Nordisk Kontakt* 6/76, p. 361.
88. Harold Wilson, *The Governance of Britain*. London: Sphere Books, 1977, pp. 239–47.
89. Interview with Uolevi Hakavuori, Head of the Cabinet Office in Finland, 23.3.1983.

90. Interview with Pentti Väänänen, the Finnish Prime Minister's Political Secretary for Foreign Affairs, 23.3.1983.
91. Christian S. Nissen, 'Den politiske ledelse i centraladministrationen'. *Nordisk Administrativt Tidsskrift* 60, 2, 1979, pp. 226–7.
92. Ibid., p. 221.
93. Nissen (1979), pp. 227–8.
94. Damgaard (1975), p. 278.
95. Interview with Mats Svegfors 21.9.1982.
96. Victor Andersen, 'Javel, hr. minister! Magtens virkelige tredeling'. *Weekendavi sen* 13.8.1982–19.8.1982.
97. Poul Møller, *Politik påvrangen*. Aalborg: Stig Vendelkærs Forlag, 1974, pp. 27–36.
98. Nils Ørvik, *Departmental Decision-Making: a Research Report*. Oslo: Universitetsforlaget, 1972.
99. Paul G. Roness, 'Organizing Processes of Administrative Change: An outline of a theoretical perspective with empirical illustrations from Norwegian government departments'. Paper at conference of the European Consortium for Political Research, Århus 29.3–3.4.1982.
100. Thomas. J. Anton, *Administered Politics: Elite Political Culture in Sweden*. Boston-The Hague-London: Martinus Nijhoff, 1980, p. 87.
101. Finn Bruun, *Changes and Conflicts. A Sketch of Danish Executive Reform Proposals since 1945*. University of Århus: Institute of Political Science, 1982, pp. 9–11.
102. Lennart Lundqvist and Krister Ståhlberg (eds), *Tjänstemän i Norden*. Åbo: Åbo Akademi, 1982.
103. Voitto Helander and Dag Anckar, *Consultation and Political Culture. Essays on the Case of Finland*. Helsinki: Societas Scientiarum Fennica, 1983, p. 161.

3
THE CABINET STAGE OF POLICY-MAKING

> 'Cabinet meetings are a valuable part of the work of the government because they bring ministers together and give them a sense of unity. A good deal is resolved when brought before the cabinet. But what takes place is in reality the final trial of policy recommendations agreed elsewhere.' — *Søren-Ole Olsen, Secretary to the Danish Prime Minister*

In common with most West European assemblies in the post-war era, the overwhelming majority of legislative initiatives introduced into the Nordic parliaments have been in the form of government bills. In some cases, the government may have found itself adopting or responding to a private initiative; in others, its proposal will have been amended in a standing committee of parliament and ultimately passed in a form which differs somewhat from the original bill. But the greater share of laws reaching the statute book has nonetheless emanated from measures approved in cabinet and introduced as government bills. Denmark may be taken as a representative case. From the transition to unicameralism in 1953 through to 1970, almost 99% of all successful measures were government bills[1] and, as Table 3.1 shows, this situation did not change significantly during the era of party volatility in the 1970s. Indeed, with the important exception of Iceland, successful private member's bills are a rarity in the region (see chapter 7) and governments are the primary initiators of legislation. Sometimes government bills are in the form of detailed proposals; alternatively, they may set out only the main guidelines of legislation, leaving its detailed finalisation and implementation to parliament and/or affected authorities. In Sweden, in particular, these government directives or 'framework proposals', *riktlinjepropositioner*, are becoming increasingly common, and in Finland too a former Deputy-Speaker has advocated greater use of them.[2]

The fact that the Nordic legislatures spend the bulk of their time considering government proposals rather than private bills does not necessarily imply that governments in the region legislate in a significant sense. As mentioned, government proposals can and indeed sometimes are modified in parliamentary standing committee, particularly when the government does not possess a majority in the assembly, while, more pertinently, the cabinet itself might well be regarded as functioning like a parliamentary standing committee

Table 3.1. SUCCESSFUL GOVERNMENT AND PRIVATE BILLS IN THE DANISH FOLKETING, 1973–1981

Parliamentary session	*Government bills*	*Private bills*	*Total*
1973–4	119	5	124
1974–5	174	17	191
1975–6	161	11	172
1976–7	186	4	190
1977–8	146	5	151
1978–9	146	1	147
1979–80	160	1	161
1980–1	152	7	159
	1,244	51	1,295

Source: Antal fremsatte og vedtagne lovforslag fordelt efter oprindelse 1953/4–1980/81. *Folketingsåret 1980–81*, p. 3.

in so far as it gives departmental proposals a general airing and discusses their major principles and consequences. This chapter examines the legislative role of the Nordic cabinets and in particular whether the governments in the region may be said to govern in more than a nominal sense. To take the analysis further, a distinction is drawn (sometimes one of nuance only) between the *policy direction* role of a cabinet, which presumes at best the collective deliberation and determination of major policy lines, and its *policy adoption* function, which can minimally involve little more than holding weekly consultations at which ministers are informed of routine measures and formally acquiesce in them. Some of the important constraints on the government's direction of policy are identified. It is then contended that in many ways the Nordic cabinets have not significantly deviated from their classical historic role of ratifying detailed proposals formulated by the permanent executive: this they do not as officials of the King as in the nineteenth century before the breakthrough of parliamentarism, but rather as a team of ministers acting as ambassadors for the various departments of state and the corporate interests associated with them.

Obviously, this picture is somewhat overdrawn: individually, ministers see themselves very much as legislators with responsibility for co-ordinating the detailed initiation of proposals falling within their policy sphere, while collectively the cabinet can take important decisions of principle, especially in the foreign policy and economic fields. However, there is evidence to suggest that the Nordic cabinets devote relatively little time to policy direction and that, faced with long agendas, they tend merely to adopt measures agreed elsewhere. At the very least, something of a deterioration in the status of plenary sessions of the cabinet may be observed. In addition to these broad themes, this chapter sets out to trace in detail what happens to a bill from the time it completes its drafting in a government ministry, usually following a commission inquiry and modification after *remiss*, to the point at which, through the Speaker's Council, it is lodged with parliament — in short, the cabinet stage of policy adoption.

The constitutional status of Nordic governments

Although government bills are overwhelmingly the primary source of laws enacted in the region's parliaments, the legislative status of the Nordic cabinets is barely recognised constitutionally. Outside Sweden, the actualities of modern practice are obscured by the considerable legal power which continues to be held by the Head of State. Article 3 of the Norwegian Constitution states unequivocally that the executive power is formally vested in the King, although in accordance with articles 12 and 13 he may, during his travels within the kingdom, leave the running of the country to the Council of State. This latter body is in any event chosen by the King, who also apportions business among its members. The Eidsvoll Constitution in Norway, which contains relatively few amendments, dates back to 17 May 1814: however, even in the new Danish Constitution of 27 May 1953, legislative power is divided equally between the King and the Folketing[3] and the monarch's duties include *inter alia* the appointment of the Prime Minister and other ministers.[4] In both countries, too, brief and generally formal meetings of a *Council of State* are still attended personally by the monarch, who is required to approve proposals both before they are submitted to parliament and again before they assume the force of law. With the Danish and Norwegian monarchs, this nowadays is purely procedural and has meant that the weekly sessions of the *ordinary cabinet* constitute the real workshops for government proposals. In Denmark, for example, the monarch attends purely formal meetings of the Council of State, *statsrådet*, organised on an *ad hoc* basis as little as fourteen or fifteen times a year.[5] In Iceland, too, decisions are in practice taken by the ordinary cabinet and merely ratified as Presidential rulings in the Council of State, despite the statement in article 15 of the 1944 Constitution that the President appoints the Council of State, determines the number of ministers, and assigns their duties.

The same cannot be said of Finland where, as in Iceland, legislative power is shared by the President and parliament,[6] but where in contrast to the latter, government bills have on occasions been subject to modification by the Head of State at the so-called 'Presidential session of the cabinet', *presidentin esittelyistunto*. In 1969, for example, President Kekkonen insisted that a bill relating to changes in the electoral system be presented to the Eduskunta in a form which differed significantly from that decided on after a vote in the ordinary cabinet, *ministeristön yleisistunto*.[7] It is true that in an overwhelming majority of cases, ministerial proposals have been duly countersigned by the Finnish President and this is unlikely to alter during the term of Mauno Koivisto. But what needs emphasis here is that only in Sweden, of all the Nordic states, is there an explicit constitutional statement of the modern governmental function of the cabinet along with its work and procedure. Indeed, since 1973 the King has not been permitted to attend cabinet meetings nor is his signature any longer necessary on government bills.

The preclusion of the King has made no difference to the fact that, as elsewhere in the region, the cabinet has continued to operate at two distinct levels: a formal meeting of the government, *regeringssammanträden*, which is prescribed by the constitution and takes place weekly (at 9 o'clock on Thursday mornings), lasts about 45 minutes, and involves nothing more than the routine ratification of decisions. Ministers put matters on the agenda of government meetings by registering them with the Prime Minister's Office which in turn produces a list of matters to be resolved — set out departmentally and with accompanying recommendations — and this is distributed to ministers immediately before the start of the formal session. Ministers then go summarily through their list of recommendations, which are almost always approved without discussion. However, an informal cabinet session or ordinary cabinet, *allmän beredning*, takes place directly after the formal meeting, although rarely considering the same questions, and this constitutes the real ministerial workshop — even though, rather paradoxically, decisions are sometimes taken first in the formal meeting of the government, viz. when it is politically expedient to show that the government is doing something — even if only taking a decision in principle — and only later worked out in the ordinary cabinet, sometimes months later![8] The point here, however, is that notwithstanding the two-tier operation of the Swedish cabinet, the constitution posits its function in unequivocally modern terms: 'The government governs the country and is responsible to the Riksdag'.[9]

The role of the cabinet in the *collective* direction of policy is given distinctive emphasis in the Swedish constitution. Technically a minister cannot make decisions independently of the cabinet, nor has he power over the various central boards and agencies falling within his policy area, which again are the exclusive responsibility of the cabinet as a whole. Formally, too, there is a marked separation of power between the government as the political arm of the executive and the civil servants in the central administration. The independent free-standing position of the civil servants is reflected in the rule that actions they take in central boards and government ministries may not be made the main substance of questions and interpellations in the Riksdag. Constitutionally, in short, the Swedish government governs exclusively as a team of ministers and it is the task of the fourteen government departments and Prime Minister's Office which collectively make up the government chancellery, *regeringskansli*, simply to prepare and implement matters decided in the meetings of the government.[10] In sharp contrast to the constitutional provisions in Sweden, governments elsewhere in the region are depicted as playing the type of supportive role to the Head of State which is a long way from the modern reality.

To note after this that cabinet government, at least in the British conception of the term, scarcely exists in the Nordic states may seem rather surprising. Yet in the strictest sense, the composition of cabinets in Scandinavia has differed from that in Britain: indeed, cabinets do not exist at all in the region if by the term is meant a core of ministers involved in directing a larger team of ministers and beyond them the entire government administration. Nordic cabinets, in other words, do not comprise a ministerial élite, but are rather meetings of the whole government. True, the size of the cabinets in the region has, if anything, grown somewhat in the post-war period. Gunnar Thoroddsen's Icelandic cabinet of 10 was in 1983 the largest in the history of the republic, while the lower constitutional limit on the size of the cabinet in Norway — a Prime Minister and at least seven other ministers[11] — was exceeded by nine when Kåre Willoch's Conservative minority administration was formed in October 1981. Notwithstanding some variation in their size, however, the point stands that members of Nordic governments have generally enjoyed cabinet status.

All four Ministers of State in Fälldin's third coalition (1981–2) were regular cabinet ministers despite being junior ministers without overall charge of a government department. The former Swedish constitution stipulated that Ministers of State, *konsultativt statsråd*, should function as legal advisers within the cabinet in a roughly similar manner to the Finnish Chancellor of Justice — although the latter is not a cabinet minister — and this role they performed well into the post-war premiership of Tage Erlander. The new constitution, however, makes no reference to the office of Minister of State, although the recent practice has been to appoint four or five cabinet members with that designation to hold the less prestigious portfolios — e.g. Wages, Health Care, Schools and Immigration in Fälldin's third administration. In the 19-strong cabinet of Olof Palme in October 1982 there were Ministers of State or 'assistant ministers', *biträdande minister*, as they are at present called, at Social Affairs, Labour-Market Affairs, Education and Industry. At the Department of Industry there were two assistant ministers; one, Birgitta Dahl, with special responsibility for Energy questions. From the beginning of 1983 the size of the cabinet increased to twenty with the appointment of Mats Hellström to the newly-created portfolio of Foreign Trade Minister, a junior ministerial post at the Foreign Office. All twenty are fully-fledged members of the cabinet. In Finland the so-called 'second' or assistant ministers allocated to the larger government departments also possess a full cabinet seat: indeed, their particular responsibilities are not clarified until the first plenary session of the new cabinet. Technicalities apart, the main lines of policy adoption at the cabinet stage have in practice been fundamentally the same in the British and Nordic cases: in both, the course a government proposal takes has involved a series of low hurdles, the first of which is invariably a cabinet committee. In short, bills drafted in a government department, usually after extensive consultation with the relevant policy actors, are referred to an appropriate cabinet committee.

The procedures for cabinet deliberation of bills

These small 'satellite' committees of 5–6 ministers, created by a decision of full cabinet, have a variety of functions. First, they modify or endorse departmental proposals and prepare recommendations for final resolution in plenary cabinet. Next, they provide the individual ministers with a valuable means of gaining political support for a measure 'across the table', so expediting its progress through cabinet and its ultimate submission to parliament. Thirdly, cabinet committees ensure that essential co-ordination work between ministers is undertaken — this is particularly important when (as increasingly happens) proposals cut across departmental boundaries. Finally, during periods of coalition, cabinet committees provide useful arenas for airing a range of partisan opinion and settling disagreements at an early stage in the process of cabinet policy adoption. The policy role of cabinet committees will be taken up again later in this chapter. However, it has invariably been the case during the repeated single party administrations (in Denmark since the war) that when a cabinet committee is involved in the elaboration of an important government proposal it will initiate discussions with the relevant policy committee of its parliamentary group. This has subsequently involved presenting full cabinet with little short of a *fait accompli* on the matter in question.

The degree to which the cabinet committee system is institutionalised varies considerably between the Nordic nations. Distinctively in Sweden, it is completely unknown. There are no cabinet committees: informal inter-departmental contacts take place, of course, particularly via the network of the under-secretaries of state. In Denmark, on the other hand, there are no less than 24 regular cabinet committees varying in size from 14 down to only 2 members. In Finland, there are only three cabinet committees with legal status — Foreign Affairs, Finance and the Political Economy committees — all chaired by the Prime Minister, although there have been fifteen *ad hoc* temporary cabinet committees in recent years — which has increased the workload of ministers who are now involved in membership of between ten and twelve of these committees.[12] Throughout the Nordic states, cabinet committees have mirrored contemporary concerns: in Denmark at the beginning of 1982, a ministerial committee was instituted to focus on the growing (regional) problem of youth unemployment, while another was given a remit to examine civil defence.[13] Across the region, cabinet committees are not the secretive organs of the British political system. Their position is formal, open, entrenched and widely held to be desirable. But in some parliamentary circles there is a feeling that cabinet committees could also provide valuable information, and even documentation, to members of the legislature and in so doing be subject to a measure of parliamentary scrutiny and control.

Cabinet committees apart, much important ministerial deliberation and policy discussion occurs off the record: e.g. in the so-called 'evening class', *iltakoulu*, in Finland — an informal ministerial get-together on Wednesday evenings to prepare matters for the full cabinet the following day — or the cabinet lunches, *lunchberedning*, in Denmark, Norway and Sweden where, crucially, ministers can exchange views free from the close attentions of civil servants. In Denmark an informal ministerial lunch follows directly after the cabinet meetings on Tuesday mornings — in the absence of the Prime Minister's Secretary;[14] in Norway, an informal ministerial lunch is held on Fridays;[15] while in Sweden the traditional cabinet lunch is eaten every day at noon! The level and importance of the questions raised by individual ministers at cabinet lunches inevitably varies within the region, dependent not least on how well developed the cabinet committee system is. In Sweden, for example, where cabinet committees do not exist but cabinet lunches are the most institutionalised, it is probable that the matters taken up at cabinet lunches are normally of sufficient importance for the responsible minister not to want to make a decision on them alone, but not important enough for the ordinary cabinet to be notified.

The importance of these relaxed cabinet gatherings at which easy-going discussions can take place in congenial surroundings should not be minimised. Ordinary plenary cabinets are, after all, largely routine affairs involving relatively little across-the-board discussion. In Denmark, the weekly cabinet lasts on average only $1\frac{1}{2}$–2 hours, yet it deals with an agenda containing as many as thirty items.[16] Over lunch immediately afterwards, there is thus the opportunity to take up any outstanding matters for further (or in some cases preliminary) deliberation and to attempt to achieve collective co-ordination and a common sense of direction on a wide range of issues. Cabinet lunches can serve therefore as an important unifying and integrating agency, bringing together ministers who, either singly or in tandem with a joint/assistant minister, are otherwise highly preoccupied with the business of their own department. Ministers have a chance to compare notes, so to speak, raise problems and relate their activities to the overall government programme, something which, it should be noted, politicians in the Nordic countries regard as of the utmost importance.

Some of the crucial challenges to collective policy management by a cabinet team — to the government governing in more than a nominal sense — have already been taken up in this book, and here we will only recall that in the executive arm of Nordic government, as elsewhere in Western Europe, 'partisans' or representatives (elected or appointed) of the governing party or parties are vastly outnumbered by non-elected officials. It was calculated that in Norway in 1977, 50 'partisans', i.e. cabinet ministers, undersecretaries of state and personal assistants of ministers, were expected to direct and control the operation of 2,730 central civil servants.[17] The odds were only slightly better in Sweden in the early 1980s, for there were more than 1,000 civil servants connected with policy-making compared with about 100 partisans — ministers, under-secretaries, information secretaries and political experts.[18]

Clearly co-ordinating the activities of these officials is a daunting task even for an experienced minister who is called upon to demonstrate a capacity for administration and decision-taking and yet must recognise that his tenure of office may be summarily terminated by the vagaries of an unforseen government crisis or the intervention of a scheduled election. For a newly-appointed minister, whose policy grounding is likely to be less secure and whose apprenticeship on the parliamentary backbenches is none too relevant to the acquisition of the organisational skills required of a cabinet minister, the job is still more demanding. Indeed, his reliance on the advice, guidance and experience of his civil servant can place the latter in a dominant role. This is not to suggest that the minister-civil servant relationship is necessarily an adversary one: in the small government departments in Sweden in particular, there are doubtless ministers who would echo the sentiments of Barbara Castle, who as a Labour Party cabinet minister in the third Wilson government was moved to write after a year in office that, 'I got very fond of my civil servants (or at any rate some of them). The outside world has no idea how human they are.'[19] However, it is obvious, that the civil servants play an important co-ordinating role in the policy process, and that therefore ministers can profit from occasions like cabinet lunches where they can consider government plans and tactics in a free atmosphere away from the tight marking of senior officials.

After cabinet committee and informal ministerial discussions, a measure is taken up (possibly again) in full cabinet. Plenary sessions of the cabinet are convened regularly, usually once a week, but they can be more frequent, and are then usually convened by the Prime Minister, although article 17 of the Icelandic Constitution provides for cabinet meetings to be held when one minister so desires. Several of the Nordic constitutions stipulate a minimum quorum for reaching valid decisions: in Sweden, at least five ministers must participate in cabinet meetings, the same number as in the Presidential session of the cabinet in Finland.[20] Several also set out rules on eligibility. In Sweden, only persons who have been Swedish citizens for at least ten years may hold cabinet office, and a minister is not allowed to hold any other public or private position.[21] In Norway, members of the cabinet must have obtained the voting age of eighteen and more than half of them should also belong to the State Lutheran Church.[22] In Finland, the Minister of Justice and at least one other minister must have been trained in jurisprudence.[23]

The procedures for full meetings of the Nordic cabinets vary both from country to country and over time, but in the absence of constitutional prescription are largely a matter of convention. In Denmark, proceedings of the ordinary cabinet are very informal: there are no constitutional rules relating to cabinet business and no regulations either on voting, which in practice has been extremely rare. However, in the event of the monarch being unavoidably prevented from attending a meeting of the formal Council of State, the constitution does require decisions to be taken on a majoritarian basis and votes entered in a minute book for subsequent inspection and approval by the monarch.[24] Far from being verbatim accounts of what has taken place, minutes of ordinary cabinets are no more than the personal impressions of the Prime Minister's Secretary.[25] They are neither accepted nor undersigned, simply identifying views to ministers, setting out some of the discussion, the reasons behind the decision and the decision itself. Indeed, the more controversial and confidential the matter discussed, the less elaboration it will tend to receive in the appropriate minute.[26] As far as preparations for ordinary cabinet meetings in Denmark are concerned, documentation is normally distributed to all ministers and permanent secretaries, *departementschefer*, by Friday if the matter is to be raised at the full cabinet session the following Tuesday. Matters to be introduced orally are to be registered with the Prime Minister's Office on Friday, while on Monday a provisional agenda is circulated to all ministers.[27]

Much as in Denmark, there are few formal provisions relating to the conduct of cabinet business in Norway. The Eidsvoll Constitution sets out only three relevant stipulations: first, that when the King is travelling and leaves the handling of government to the Council of State, matters shall be decided by a vote, and in the case of a tie the Prime Minister, or in his absence the next highest-ranking member present, shall have two votes;[28] secondly, that a record be kept of ordinary cabinet proceedings along with a special record of secret diplomatic matters;[29] and thirdly, that a cabinet minister not professing the official Lutheran faith shall not participate in the consideration of matters concerning the state church.[30] In general, Norwegian cabinets have been informal and pragmatic. True, there has been some formalisation of procedures since the early post-war premierships of Einar Gerhardsen when the longest-serving minister would simply present his case first and junior ministers would not infrequently find themselves without the opportunity to introduce a particular measure, however urgent and important. Nowadays, a minister wishing to place an item on the cabinet agenda registers it with the Prime Minister's Office and a two-page memorandum is then circulated to the other ministers. Discussions are thus better informed although, as Johan P. Olsen's interviews with the Bratteli cabinet of 1975 demonstrate well, the convention has been to keep controversial decisions and their corollary, formal splits, away from plenary cabinets.[31]

A similar intention has been extremely difficult to achieve in Finland since the advent of broad centre-left government in 1966 with several formal cabinet votes revealing the extent of the division between the coalition parties. One such in the spring of 1981 concerned the vexed 'red-green' question of increased milk marketing charges, although in this case the Social Democratic and Swedish People's parties managed to avenge their defeat by Centre and

Communist party ministers in a cabinet vote and to reverse the 'government' proposal on the floor of the Eduskunta.[32] The constitution itself makes no reference to voting in cabinet and only incidentally alludes to plenary procedures in stating that the cabinet is collectively responsible to parliament for decisions except when an individual minister has placed his dissension on record in the minutes.[33] In the only other reference to cabinet practice, the constitution posits in the most general of terms that all questions taken up in cabinet shall be prepared by the competent Ministry.[34] In this context, the limiting case in the Nordic region is Iceland where, despite the stipulation that cabinet meetings be held to discuss new legislative proposals and important political measures, the constitution makes no reference whatever to cabinet procedure.

In contrast, the constitutional reforms of 1974 led to some formalisation of cabinet practice in Sweden. Previously, no minutes of cabinet proceedings had been kept and no votes taken. The new form of government, however, specifically requires minutes of cabinet meetings and dissenting opinions to be recorded.[35] In practice the effect of these new stipulations has been minimal for, although open to inspection by parliamentarians and public alike, minutes of government meetings in Sweden have recorded only the decisions. The record of cabinet meetings is divided into a main minute, *huvudprotokoll*, containing information on the ministers present and the departmental items to be discussed, and a supporting minute, *underprotokoll*, set out on a departmental basis, and in reality presenting only a statement of government decisions.[36] In short, there is less elaboration of government business than in the impressionistic account produced by the Prime Minister's Secretary in Denmark. Formal votes prompted by deep-seated divisions have occurred only once since the implementation of the new constitution — in January 1981 when the five Liberal ministers disagreed with their coalition partners over the question of the government making exceptions to the ban on Swedish investment in South Africa and Namibia.[37]

We have seen that except in Sweden, the Head of State functions as chairman at the formal sittings of the Council of State. Yet in order to exonerate the monarch from legal and, indeed, political responsibility for a measure, the signature of the Prime Minister or a member of the government is required in Denmark and Norway, while in Iceland and Finland the Presidential signature, countersigned by a minister, validates a legislative proposal. Uniquely, Swedish constitutional proposals and government bills are signed by the Prime Minister and/or relevant cabinet minister on behalf of the government. In special cases and then by order of the cabinet, a civil servant can sign cabinet despatches.[38]

The procedures for the presentation and submission of government bills to the Swedish parliament are comprehensively set out in the third section of the Riksdag Standing Orders and correspond closely to the established practice elsewhere in the region. In the first instance, a government bill is to be accompanied by the appropriate cabinet documentation, i.e. a review of its earlier consideration, an explanatory preamble to the proposal and a ruling from the Law Council, *lagrådet*, where the matter warrants it or the bill's constitutionality is in any doubt.[39] It is then transmitted to the Office of Parliament, *kammarkansliet*, and notification of its impending introduction into the chamber is given by the Speaker at the plenary session following the bill's distribution to members of the Riksdag. The Standing Orders also set out a general timetable for the submission of government measures. Thus with the Swedish financial year beginning on July 1, the government is required to produce an outline finance plan and national budget by January 10 at the latest (or as soon as possible thereafter in the event of a new administration delaying proceedings) and follow this with a detailed budget proposal, *kompletteringsproposition*, by the end of April. Any other government bills relating to the forthcoming financial year shall be submitted to the Riksdag by March 10.[40] Government bills of a more general nature should be presented by March 31 if the government wishes them to gain parliamentary consideration in the same session of the Riksdag.[41] Finally, the Standing Orders urge the government to submit bills in such a way that work bottlenecks in parliament are avoided: the Speaker should be consulted to achieve this end. Incidentally, a government bill can be submitted even when the Riksdag is not in session.[42] The Standing Orders of the other Nordic parliaments do not specify procedures for the presentation of government bills, although in practice they are essentially similar to those in Sweden. From the government viewpoint, what is important is to keep in contact with the assembly via the Speaker's Council in order to give adequate notice of legislative intentions and so avoid charges of burdening parliament with an impossible workload. Criticism along precisely these lines in the annual reports of the Riksdag's Constitutional Committee is discussed more fully in chapter 9.

Before their final approval in cabinet, drafts of bills need to be reviewed on technical grounds to ensure that they conform to the conventional format and are not couched in terms which are ambiguous, misleading or even in violation of the constitution. In Denmark this task is undertaken by the Constitutional and Public Law Section of the Legal Division within the Ministry of Justice, which deals with every ministerial proposal. Suggested modifications to the wording of draft bills are mainly advanced on stylistic rather than substantive grounds and are effected speedily and informally via the appropriate minister. However, if the minister proves reluctant to acquiesce in the changes, as for example over a bill formulated by the trade union movement which puts him under great pressure, the ultimate sanction is the threat of the Minister of Justice subsequently opposing the measure in full cabinet.[43] In Finland arrangements are not dissimilar, except that there is a Chancellor of Justice, *oikeuskansleri,* a permanent civil servant appointed by the President, who is obliged to attend cabinet meetings and has responsibility for the legal supervision of the matters discussed there. The Chancellor vets the minutes of both Presidential and ordinary cabinet meetings, as well as providing written statements relating *inter alia* to matters of juridical interpretation. It has recently become standard practice to turn to the Chancellor of Justice at the pre-cabinet stage for guidance on legal matters.[44]

In addition to the technical review of draft legislation, there are various procedures throughout the region for examining constitutional proposals and indeed those bills the constitutionality of which may be in doubt. In none of the Nordic states, however, is there a special Constitutional Court along Austrian, Italian or West German lines which has the exclusive power to give an authoritative and binding interpretation of the constitutionality of laws and to which, as David Southern has observed in the West German context, 'all citizens prejudiced in their fundamental liberties by action of the state have direct access.'[45] The Danish constitution specifically prohibits the establishment of extraordinary courts with judicial authority.[46]

The Swedish Law Council, however, has a distinctive position. Appointed by the government and comprising judges from both the High Court, *högsta domstolen*, and Supreme Administrative Court, *regeringsrätten*, judgements from the Law Council are requested by the government when the content of bills is thought to affect basic individual freedoms.[47] A matter can also be referred to the Law Council by one-third of the members of a Riksdag standing committee.[48] The influence of the Law Council grew during the period of non-socialist government from 1976 to 1982, although it is imperative to note that it does not have the right to instigate an examination of a legislative proposal, nor can it deal with citizens' complaints, still less exercise punitive powers in respect of acts of unconstitutionality, in the manner of the West German Constitutional Court. There were Conservatives in Sweden and, indeed, Finland who advocated the adoption of a Constitutional Court during the constitutional debates in the two countries in the early

1970s.[49] Early in 1983 there were renewed calls in some quarters in Finland for a Constitutional Court following a controversial recommendation from the Chancellor of Justice to the Office of Parliament in which it was stated that daily allowances were being paid incorrectly to three delegates and should be stopped forthwith. Though the payments were discontinued, a furore grew over whether the Chancellor of Justice had the constitutional right to issue a reprimand to members of the Executive Board of the Office of Parliament, *eduskunnan kansliatoimikunta,* a prerogative which was rejected by a large majority (127–48) on the floor of the assembly. Some felt this to be an issue that could have been examined better in a Constitutional Court.[50] Pressure to found such a court has been resisted, as in Sweden, by the parties of the Left. In both countries there is an overwhelming consensus in favour of the traditional legal supremacy of the legislature and the deployment of *political* means to settle disputes on constitutionality. The Constitutional Committees of the Riksdag and the Eduskunta consequently bear primary responsibility for adjudicating on the constitutionality/legality of proposals.

The Norwegian and Danish cases are different again. In neither are there special procedures, parliamentary or judicial, for examining the constitutionality of bills. This seems ironic in Norway, where a procedural distinction is drawn between the consideration of 'laws' — viz. rules, usually of a permanent character, regulating citizens' rights and duties — which must be discussed in the Lagting, and ordinary legislation which is dealt with in the undivided Storting. There is, in short, no purpose-specific institution ruling on when a law is rightfully a 'law'. Unlike the Swedish and Finnish tradition, however, the constitutionality of Norwegian legislation can be challenged in the ordinary courts in connection with actions brought either by an individual citizen or by an organisation legally interested in having the dispute resolved.[51] In Denmark, the situation in this respect is somewhat unclear. The constitutions of 1849 and 1953 do not refer to the role of the ordinary courts in assessing the constitutionality of laws and in the Folketing debates in 1952 on a new form of government, there was much opposition in Social Democratic and Radical Party quarters to granting them such powers. Although the courts have repeatedly affirmed their right to pronounce on the constitutionality of legislation, they have in practice, as John Fitzmaurice has noted, sought to avoid conflict with the Folketing and government.[52] In Iceland, however, the courts also have the right to declare a statute unconstitutional, and this has been done on a few occasions.[53]

Having identified the main stages through which a draft bill passes before gaining collective ministerial assent and being submitted to parliament, we should now consider the overall impact of the cabinet in the legislative process. Is it realistic to refer to cabinet government in the Nordic states in the sense of meaningful collective discussion and policy direction by a ministerial team coming together at regular sittings of the full cabinet? Conversely, is it more appropriate to speak of the 'disintegration of the cabinet', in that power has increasingly devolved upon cabinet committees, leaving plenary cabinets simply to adopt decisions effectively taken elsewhere? Moreover, how important in the region is the policy role of the Prime Minister?

In the search for answers to these questions, a starting point might be Johan P. Olsen's statement in the Norwegian context that controversial decisions tend on the whole to be taken outside full cabinet. Olsen elaborates this view by presenting a picture of a political executive in which power is decentralised and policy-making involves a largely informal search for consensus at various levels below full cabinet.[54] Compromises are sought in cabinet committees, interdepartmental committees of under-secretaries or, most commonly, in *ad hoc* groups of one or two leading cabinet members. The whole approach is incrementalist: recommendations are made, discussions take place, support is canvassed and provisional agreements are reached. In this process of 'log-rolling' involving ministers, their advisers and departmental officials, it becomes extremely difficult to identify the key locus of decision-taking. In Norway, for example, Olsen notes that while there are a few important cabinet committees, 'they have become less rather than more crucial over the last two decades'.[55] However, in Denmark the tendency seems to have been the reverse: real decisions are increasingly taken in cabinet committees which, although not as powerful as in Britain, have become more institutionalised in recent years. Hence from the mid-1970s onwards each cabinet committee has had a civil servant attached to it as minutes secretary, with the result that minutes have been circulated to members of the committee and a copy of the agenda distributed to all cabinet ministers. Government departments have also been encouraged to operate as informal support agencies monitoring the activities of cabinet committees. As in the other Nordic states, the policy significance of particular Danish cabinet committees has of course varied over time. The cabinet committee on Economic Affairs, which earlier played a role comparable to that of an 'inner cabinet,' has declined in importance whereas the EC Market

Relations cabinet committee has developed into a significant organ of co-ordination, scrutinisation and decision-taking attended by a range of officials including a permanent secretary in the Prime Minister's Office.[56]

Yet if power has accrued to groups outside full cabinet — cabinet committees, parallel civil service committees, informal ministerial gatherings etc. — it would be a misleading simplification to suggest that cabinet government in the Nordic states has effectively collapsed. Herman and Alt's summation of British developments is relevant here: 'To argue that the nature of government has changed because the cabinet reaches decisions in committees rather than in plenary session is not necessarily to say the position of the cabinet has changed for the worse — simply that the status of plenary sessions has altered.[57] However, if, as seems to be true of the whole Nordic region, the status of plenary cabinet sessions has indeed altered, what functions, if any, does the full cabinet perform? Søren-Ole Olsen's observations on cabinet practice in Denmark can be taken as typical. He notes that full cabinets are important, 'but they are not the arena in which the real decisions are taken. Cabinet meetings are a valuable part of the work of the government because they bring ministers together and give them a sense of unity. A good deal is resolved when brought before the cabinet, but what takes place is in reality the final trial of policy recommendations agreed elsewhere and constitutes the ultimate guarantee that policy coordination takes place at the highest level.[58] Plenary cabinets, it is implied, are functional in so far as they invest members with a feeling of collective and partisan identity and provide a political High Court in which to reaffirm, or occasionally to reverse, verdicts reached lower down in the structures of government.

While it would hardly have dissociated from this view, the report of a commission investigating the workings of the Central Public Administration in Finland, *Valtion keskushallintokomitean II osamietintö*, in 1978 developed a different line of argument, using as its starting point the high workload faced by meetings of the plenary cabinet. Beginning by listing some of the structural factors underpinning the changing nature and context of government in Finland, the report states that 'the increase in the scale and scope of state activity, the growing complexity of social questions, the heightened activity of pressure groups and the enhanced salience of the international environment have conspired gradually, but fundamentally, to challenge the traditional *modus operandi* of full cabinet meetings'.[59] A great quantity of decisions are being taken in cabinet — on about 5,000 matters annually — but the commission report insists that it is essential for the cabinet to consider the broad principles and guidelines governing the preparation and planning of sectoral policies.

Two points in particular from the Finnish commission's report need emphasis. First, that in line with the Norwegian and Danish evidence, policy direction occurs largely outside the full cabinet, which in turn has been reduced to a mechanistic organ for adopting measures effectively decided elsewhere. In the written response of the Cabinet Office to the commission's recommendations, it was stated that the cabinet's Political Economy committee had developed into an 'inner cabinet' and that its decisions were merely being rubber-stamped at plenary sessions of the cabinet. The Political Economy cabinet committee, which was given legal status only in 1977, comprises the Prime Minister as chairman, a minister from the Finance Department, the Employment Minister, the Minister of Transport and at most four other ministers. Its formal powers include the preparation of matters relating to medium-term economic planning, the main lines of public sector development, the direction of investments and the consideration of other economic measures at the discretion of the Prime Minister.[60] Secondly, the Finnish commission held that policy direction should be regarded as the paramount task of governments and be undertaken by cabinets whose vision is not blinkered by a schedule of meetings called to approve routine matters. Indeed, the commission proceeded to recommend that broad planning decisions should be binding and not lapse with the advent of a new government, unless of course they are specifically amended or repealed.[61]

To be fair, the *capacity* of the Nordic cabinets effectively to direct and plan policy, especially economic policy, in the way prescribed by the Finnish commission, has been limited by outside factors largely beyond their control. For example, in the 1970s world trade increased two or three times faster than industrial production so making states, not least the export-oriented Nordic ones, vulnerable to the vicissitudes of the international economic system. In crude terms, party programmes and ideologies were less relevant in the making of economic decisions than the dictates of macro-economic forces. In 1979 Andrew Schonfield pointed to the dilemma of the non-socialist coalition in Sweden in 1976 which, having finally broken the Social Democrats' 44-year stranglehold on power, was prompted in the teeth of a serious world recession to take a number of traditional heavy industries into partial public ownership.[62] At the same time, of course, the *determination* of cabinets to grasp the the nettle and take broad policy decisions is largely a matter of political will and this has been affected by a variety of considerations including the size of the governing majority (if any), the party composition and ministerial experience of the cabinet, and the proximity of a general election.

As a rule, the higher the level of government cohesion, the greater the likelihood of at least some move towards policy planning. It was a single-party Social Democratic government led by Odvar Nordli that established a Ministry of Long-Range Planning in Norway in October 1979.[63] Policy direction during periods of coalition government presents its own problems. With the system of 'shadow ministers' employed in the historic Social Democratic-Liberal administration in Denmark in 1977–8 — similar arrangements prevailed in Sweden in 1976–82 — the official opposition seemed almost to be operating from within the government itself. The work of the Social Democratic Minister of Housing was thus overseen by the Liberal Minister of Education acting as a so-called 'contact minister', while education policy was monitored by the Housing Minister.[64] The network of 'contact ministers', often cynically referred to as 'control ministers', was scarcely conducive to building mutual trust and unity of purpose. The exceptional 4-party non-socialist coalition under Per Borten in Norway in 1965–9 proceeded differently. A network of deputy ministerial committees was developed, comprising the deputy (assistant) ministers from all the governing parties, and these constituted important forums of consensus-building. As Arve Solstad observed, 'the deputy ministerial system has in many ways succeeded in solving some of the problems of co-operation with which a coalition government of the Borten type is faced.[65]

The policy role of the Nordic prime ministers

In maintaining government morale and the cabinet's collective sense of purpose and direction, the Prime Minister has an extremely important role. Yet concerning the formal powers of the Prime Minister, the Nordic constitutions make only two things clear: first, that the Prime Minister is chairman of the ordinary session of the cabinet[66] and secondly that he/she is leader and spokesman of the government in parliament.[67] The Prime Minister is not indisputably second in line in the state hierarchy of the region. It is true that in the Finnish constitution explicitly, and in the Danish and Norwegian constitutions implicitly, the Prime Minister emerges as deputy Head of State: an amendment of 1956 to the Finnish constitution states that if the President is prevented from attending to his duties, the Prime Minister shall be responsible for them,[68] while the Danish monarch if prevented from attending the Council of State, can permit a matter to be handled at a special session of the cabinet held under the chairmanship of the Prime Minister; the vote of each minister shall then be recorded in the minutes, resolutions being taken by a majority decision.[69] In Norway in similar circumstances, the constitution provides the Prime Minister with a casting vote.[70] In Iceland and Sweden, the Prime Minister's position is constitutionally weaker. If the Icelandic President is temporarily unable to hold office because of residence abroad, illness etc, the Prime Minister, the Speaker of the United Althing and the Chief Justice of the Supreme Court exercise the presidential power conjointly; the Speaker of the United Althing presides.[71] In Sweden, it is the Speaker who nominates a Prime Ministerial candidate; his proposal is presented to the Riksdag, following consultations with a representative of every parliamentary group, and must be voted in the assembly without discussion in a parliamentary standing committee within four days. If more than half the total Riksdag members vote against, it is rejected and the Speaker must come up with another proposal.[72] Differences in their formal status are ultimately less important than the fact that despite the relatively sparse constitutional reference to their powers, the Nordic Prime Ministers participate extensively in the policy process at the cabinet stage, performing various important roles, which we will now briefly delineate.

First, Prime Ministers in the region integrate, co-ordinate and maintain the policy activities of their administration. A Nordic Prime Minister is a link man, a man in the middle, and he acts as the personal hub of much government activity. Through extensive daily contact with his cabinet team on the telephone, at lunch meetings, in parliamentary group meetings or in the Cabinet Office, the Prime Minister can construct a fairly comprehensive picture of what is going on throughout the various stages of the cabinet's adoption of policy. The crucial task of handling personal contacts with ministers is clearly an arduous one, which is made even more so in the case of coalition governments because the Prime Minister will be required to act as mediator and peacekeeper, seeking through compromises to preserve unity on the government's front and backbenches.

The willingness of the Finnish Prime Minister Mauno Koivisto in March 1980 to work out a compromise between his own Social Democratic Party and the farmer-oriented Centre Party on agricultural incomes — against the background of threats from the producers' organisation MTK to withhold meat supplies etc. — undoubtedly saved his left-centre government. Koivisto admitted to having learned the lesson of history and being mindful throughout the conflict of how ten years earlier a similar coalition led by Centre Prime Minister, Ahti Karjalainen, had fallen over a similar issue.

Obviously too, the smaller the coalition's majority, the greater the premium on an effective rapport with its backbench delegates. With a precarious majority of only a single member in 1979–81, the Swedish Prime Minister Thorbjörn Fälldin had to be especially alert to deal with possible rank-and-file revolts. On the eve of the opening of the 1980–1 Riksdag session, ten bourgeois delegates — six Centrists and four Liberals, all from Stockholm city and province — were poised ready to defeat their own government's proposal, albeit one associated with the Conservative Communications Minister, Ulf Adelsohn, over the question of noise control at the main domestic airport at Bromma near the capital. After initial attempts at reconciliation had broken down, the rebels were summoned to meet the Prime Minister himself only one hour before the opening of parliament on 7 October 1980, and he in turn was compelled to combine the roles of chief whip and general peacekeeper.[73]

With minority governments, such as most Danish ones are, it is of paramount importance that the Prime Minister negotiates a good climate of relations between his administration and the opposition parties backing it. In particular, it is essential to weigh his government's interests against the costs of any deterioration in relations with the co-operating groups in the legislature. This type of cost-benefit calculus is central to the Prime Minister's thinking in much of the region and obviously facilitates the presentation of views to his own parliamentary groups.

In orchestrating relations between the cabinet, the government's backbenches and the administration's legislative allies in the chamber, the Prime Minister invariably assumes the role of master-tactician — laying contingency plans, directing the campaign in the assembly and commanding his troops towards the achievement of short- and longer-term policy goals. Among the strategic weapons in the Prime Minister's arsenal (except in Norway) is the threat to resign and call a premature election, and so capitalise on support in the country. Alternatively, the threat to resign without having recourse to the polls may, when correctly deployed, expose divisions and weaknesses in the opposition camp. Yet another tactic is to turn an issue into one of confidence in the government in the hope of calling the opposition's bluff. The Danish Prime Minister Anker Jørgensen used a combination of these ploys during the first six months of his fifth minority administration which began inauspiciously in January 1982 following the Social Democratic Party's nine-seat defeat at the polls.

Eschewing the note of conciliation traditionally associated with the initial pronouncements of minority governments, Jørgensen stated in the Folketing that his cabinet proposed to tackle the nations's economic problems head-on and that if defeated he would resign, though without necessarily calling fresh elections. Moreover, when introducing the so-called 'March package' of measures to deal with the growing problem of youth unemployment, Jørgensen made it clear that their approval in the Folketing was a precondition of the government remaining in office.[74] The Prime Minister was thus able to threaten parliament with a double-edged sword: the 'March package' had been made a confidence issue, but a negative outcome for the government would not guarantee a dissolution and new elections. Clearly the highly-experienced Jørgensen was attempting to use the leverage created by an anticipation of the considerable difficulties in forming an alternative government to force his will upon the legislature, and in this he succeeded. The 'March package' was ultimately approved and Jørgensen achieved what he said he wanted — a Social Democratic administration in office when Denmark took over the chairmanship of the EC on 1 July 1982.[75]

To sum up, Nordic Prime Ministers are engaged in the elaborate and sometimes intricate task of maintaining a ministerial team, co-ordinating cabinet activities, interceding to settle disagreements among its members, and appraising general tactics both from an electoral as well as a more routinely parliamentary standpoint. Moreover, much of the political resolve and willpower of governments, not least when they lack the necessary plurality in the legislature, stems from the Prime Minister, who can impose an authority on colleagues and even dominate them in a way which challenges the British notion of the Prime Minister as *primus inter pares*. It seems that as the chief spokesman for the government in both parliament and the country, the Prime Minister can direct policy to a significant extent.

Through the vehicle of television and press interviews, the Prime Minister can fashion and lead public debate. Equally, the Prime Minister has the opportunity to react publicly to developments, to comment on the comment, and ultimately to pronounce on a discussion he/she may well have set in train. The Prime Minister is also called upon to answer members' questions in the assembly — most of which, of course, are reported in the newspapers — and this enhances the appearance of being the government's leading policy spokesman. In Sweden and Denmark the government's annual report to parliament is read by the Prime Minister at the opening session, although this is not a personal manifesto and in the Danish case has usually involved about five preparatory cabinet meetings. The Prime Minister thus appears to define, interpret and clarify the objectives of the administration and by using a suitable approach and/or possessing an appealing personality, is largely instrumental in its success or failure at the polls. It was noticeable how much the region's first female Prime Minister, Gro Harlem Bruntland, revived the flagging fortunes of the Norwegian Labour Party government in 1980–1, albeit not quite sufficiently to retain office after the general elections of September 1981.

In cabinet, moreover, the Prime Minister can use his position as chairman to challenge colleagues on policy. Indeed, a single-minded chairman can sometimes get things his own way. The former Eduskunta Speaker, Johannes Virolainen, has recalled the way in which Urho Kekkonen managed cabinet meetings in the early 1950s. 'Right', Kekkonen would say, 'we have a decision to make on the following item. I thought we'd do this, what do you think?' After the ensuing ministerial discussion, Kekkonen would invariably declare, 'Fine, that's decided then. We'll do it as I proposed!'[76] The Prime Minister also nominates, chairs or may be an ordinary member of cabinet committees. In Denmark in 1982 the Prime Minister was a member of eleven cabinet committees and chairman of four.[77] In Finland, the Prime Minister is chairman of all three of the influential permanent cabinet committees and although the decision to create extraordinary ad hoc committees is taken by the full cabinet, their members are appointed by the Prime Minister.[78] In Sweden where there are no cabinet committees, the Prime Minister may choose to play a co-ordinating role in the formulation of policy by chairing a preparatory committee himself. The aim here is not only to monitor progress in the generation of legislative proposals but, equally, to be seen to elevate the status of the substantive area in question. Palme's decision in February 1983 to chair a special committee to co-ordinate government policy in relation to Children and Young Persons, *barn-och ungdomsdelegation*—it included the Education Minister and several outside experts[79] — should be seen in this light. At a time of economic restraint and concern to cut costs in all areas the Prime Minister doubtless wished to associate his administration in the public eye with a forward-looking concern to promote and safeguard a reasonable environment (irrespective of income differentials) in which to bring up the future generation of Swedes.

Obviously, too, a Prime Minister can attempt to create and direct a small policy management team made up of a select party élite. In Denmark, for example, it is normal for a Prime Minister to establish an 'inner cabinet' or, more exactly, an inner policy circle — 'a government's government' in Søren-Ole Olsen's phrase — which will normally comprise two of the most influential ministers, the chairman of the government's Folketing group along with a representative from its parliamentary group and its party organisation respectively.[80] Clearly such a body constitutes an important planning and decision-making organ. In addition, a Prime Minister may bring to his office a particular competence as a trained economist, for instance, or with a specialist knowledge derived from long ministerial experience in a particular government department. In contrast to France, however, Nordic Prime Ministers are only rarely appointed as experts. What a Prime Minister really has to be expert in, as Johan P. Olsen has pertinently observed, is the political effects of policies.[81]

Finally, and as a corollary to the post-war evolution of the Nordic state towards economic management, the Prime Ministers in the region seek support and strive to exert influence by maintaining wide-ranging contacts with organised groups in the corporate sector. In a group of small democracies like the Nordic states, where decision-making is based largely on personal contacts between the relevant sectoral actors, it is hardly surprising that consultations between the Prime Minister and labour-market leaders have been characterised by informality. This has been so particularly during periods of stable Social Democratic cabinets, when relations between the government and trade union organisations have been close, with extensive collaboration on policy matters. When the Nordli cabinet in Norway was preparing its legislative programme for 1978–81 and a liaison committee was established to advise on proceedings, this was headed by the Prime Minister and comprised representatives from the Labour Party, its youth organisation and Storting group, and the labour federation LO.[82] Moreover, when the Labour Party has been in power, the employers' and farmers' organisations *inter alia* have enjoyed special contacts with the government. In Sweden there has been the country-house *politik* of Tage Erlander's 'Harpsund Democracy' — with pressure groups incorporated at the highest level. It must be emphasised that despite the easygoing atmosphere of such talks, the Prime Minister has operated as more than an honest broker. Although possessing no specific remit, he has tended to emerge as the leading economic spokesman of the government, a role enhanced and supported in Finland by the creation in the autumn of 1971 of a special incomes policy official in the Cabinet Office.[83]

True, the Prime Minister cannot monopolise the influence deriving from his network of extra-parliamentary contacts. Many interest groups prefer integration at the departmental level where contact is with the individual cabinet minister. The Prime Minister's capacity to direct the policy of his administration may well be limited too by the circumstances of his accession to office and/or his esteem among his party rank-and-file. In this latter context, Nordic Prime Ministers have in general been appointed on the basis of an established position in a political party, sometimes even as its chairman. Accordingly, their authority as Prime Minister has stemmed in no small measure from the legitimacy afforded to their performance by the various groups within the party — groups to which the Prime Minister is ultimately answerable, if only annually or bi-annually at party conferences. On the question of accession, there is a marked contrast between heading a single-party administration and leading a coalition. In a multi-party cabinet, the choice of Prime Minister is contingent upon wheeling and dealing, sometimes even balloting among members, and in extreme cases his subsequent influence outside the councils of his own party may be very limited. In coalition governments, the selection of ministers is not the Prime Minister's job, but that of the participant groups; an inner cabinet is less likely to emerge and will in any case remain effectively powerless; and cabinet committees are primarily concerned with conflict-resolution rather than acting as policy task forces. In such (admittedly extreme) circumstances, the role of the Prime Minister is confined to co-ordinating and maintaining a team of ministers. The reality of this situation was tersely described by a recent Norwegian Prime Minister: 'If you cannot get the ministers you love, you have to love the ones you get.'[84] Before concluding our present discussion of the roles of cabinet and Prime Minister in the Nordic policy process, the unique position of the Finnish Prime Minister should be briefly noted. Nowhere in the region does the real influence of the Prime Minister rest on constitutional prerogatives; in Finland, however, there are important formal limitations on the scope of the office. In Paavo Kastari's submission, the office of the Prime Minister in Finland has been overshadowed, far more than its counterpart in the French Fifth Republic, by the institution of the Presidency.[85] The Head of State has derived much of his heightened authority from the increased significance of his constitutional powers to direct foreign policy, and particularly the successful and personalised management of the crucial area of Fenno-Soviet relations by Presidents Paasikivi (1946–56) and Kekkonen (1956–81). Instead, before the Second World War the running of foreign policy was largely in the hands of the Foreign Secretary, who is by convention the personal nominee of the President.[86] Kastari emphasises the point: 'Foreign policy', he claims, 'constitutes the Archimedian point on the basis of which the President can direct Finnish internal affairs to a hitherto unknown degree.'[87] The validity of this view is elsewhere examined in some depth by the present author.[88] For present purposes, it is sufficient to note three main points.

First, during the long incumbency of Urho Kekkonen, there was an unquestionably high level of Presidential engagement in the domestic policy process, dictated not least by the need to mediate in the settlement of conflicts which Prime Ministerial exhortation had failed to resolve. In such cases, the President was clearly exercising the authority of his office in the direction of consensus-building. There were occasions, on the other hand, when the President seemed guilty of unsolicited interference in the internal affairs of governments: Kekkonen's warning to the Prime Minister, Ahti Karjalainen, in the summer of 1971 to take account of what the President saw as an impending international currency crisis in the preparation of the budget is a case in point.[89]

Secondly, the Finnish Prime Minister enjoys few formal powers beyond those of chairing the 301-seat Presidential electoral college and serving as acting Head of State when the occasion requires it. He is beholden to the President for his appointment and is personally responsible for keeping the President informed and in turn convinced of the continuing viability of his administration to proceed with its legislative programme. The Prime Minister is at once *rapporteur,* ambassador and negotiator on behalf of his government in dealings with the Head of State.

Yet — and this is the third point — it would be misleading to exaggerate the submissiveness and subordinate position of the Finnish Prime Minister to the Presidency or to minimise his autonomy of action. There have been strong Prime Ministers as well as weak ones and much has depended on circumstance and personal character. Certainly the single-mindedness and determination of Svinhufvud, the Prime Minister during the upsurge of the neo-Fascist Lapua movement in the late 1920s, contrived to elevate his office above that of Parliamentary Speaker as number two in the State hierarchy.[90] The charisma of the Social Democratic premier, Mauno Koivisto (1968–70, 1979–81) succeeded in raising the status of the office of Prime Minister to a level unprecedented in post-war times. Koivisto's successful defiance of a bid to oust him engineered by the Centre Party, a coalition partner, in a manoeuvre which almost certainly had the tacit backing of Urho Kekkonen further enhanced the reputation of a Prime Minister who had become heir apparent to the Presidency long before Kekkonen retired through ill-health in September 1981. Indeed, the Prime Ministership has been a stepping-stone to the Presidency: out of a total of nine Finnish Presidents, six have been former Prime Ministers, including the last three — Paasikivi, Kekkonen and Koivisto.[91]

In Finland, as elsewhere in the region, the administrative resources at the Prime Minister's disposal are limited. There is no

Prime Minister's Office, although the Finnish Social Democrats have favoured one,[92] and both reports of the commission on Central Public Administration have advocated the creation of a small Prime Ministerial section within the Cabinet Office.[93] However, in Norway, where a Prime Minister's Office was set up in the mid-1950s, there is at present a staff of barely 20, including secretaries and chauffeurs.[94] The Danish Prime Minister's Office, *statsministeriet*, has about 50 staff, and its Swedish counterpart, *statsrådsberedningen*, has 40, about 10 of whom have roles which are actually to support the Prime Minister.[95] With only small personal staffs, it is obvious that the energy and time at the disposal of Nordic Prime Ministers are strictly finite, while the physical demands of the office are extremely exacting. It is plain that the Prime Ministers in the region perform a range of influential roles including policy leadership, but that it would be ingenuous to speak of Prime Ministerial government if by the term is intended government by a single person. Nor would it be realistic to speak of cabinet government, at least in the Finnish commission's sense of collective policy direction and long-range planning. Rather, it has been a central assumption of our thesis that the extent to which a small and fluctuating group of partisans is able conjointly to direct and manage a central administration is necessarily limited, and that it is therefore both pointless and misleading to attempt to characterise a system as either cabinet government or Prime Ministerial government. Instead, it is imperative to examine the contribution of both cabinet and Prime Minister to the policy process.

Conclusions

Fully to understand that contribution, it is necessary to see the rôle of the cabinet and Prime Minister in the widest possible perspective, and in particular to view both in the context of an overall expansion in the scale and scope of government in the post-war period. It is a commonplace that the Nordic state has become increasingly interventionist in the last two or three decades and provides a comprehensive range of welfare services, i.e. womb-to-tomb protection for citizens as well as participating more in the central task of economic management. A corollary of the emergence of a welfare-managerial state[96] has been the heightened complexity of the formal structures of central administration with the creation of new departments (Energy and the Environment to name but two), the establishment of new sections within existing ministries, and the hiving off of the overseeing of particular policy areas (the implementation function) to *ad hoc* boards — a practice well established in Sweden and Finland and recently developing elsewhere in the region. In such a situation, there are bound to be conflicts of interest between, and sometimes even within, individual departments: issues increasingly cross-cut ministries, civil servants are divided among themselves and the state is characterised by high levels of internal pluralism.

Policy in consequence is surprisingly decentralised, being generated in relatively independent communities of actors recruited in the main from the corporate sector, professions and government ministries and conferring on commissions and committees operating not infrequently in a policy space outside the immediate orbit of a particular department. Two or three ministers may be involved and/or consulted in the process of examining a measure; provisional recommendations may even be taken up in a cabinet committee, but the plenary session of the cabinet will have little effective control, still less direction, over the course of developments. Its role will be to deliberate and scrutinise, but in the vast majority of cases ultimately to ratify recommendations and proposals emanating from the complex of shifting issue-communities operating within the central state machine. True, the cabinet will be concerned to produce a more efficient overall management structure, and this is likely to result in the periodic reorganisation of government departments — the recent abolition of the Ministry of Long-Range Planning in Norway and the creation there of a new Department of Culture and Science (separated off from the oldest ministry, Church and Education) was a case in point. So was the Swedish Social Democratic government's decision in 1983 to cut back on the commission of inquiry system. The creation in Finland in 1983 of a Department of the Environment formed from sections of the Ministry of the Interior, the Ministry of Agriculture and Forestry and the Central Water Board — and against the backdrop of long-standing opposition from a Centre Party fearing it would weaken the Department of Agriculture and Forestry which it had traditionally controlled — is yet another.[97] Also, the cabinet sets the agenda of politics, laying down its programme, defining its priorities and issuing, via its individual members, ministerial directives to commissions and committees. It is clear that government control over policy formulation will be differential: greatest on matters of 'high politics' and the constitution, smallest in the areas of social policy, finance and the economy. Moreover, some cabinets, because of their personnel, will obviously be stronger than others. Yet in practice recommendations made by the plethora of advisory groups and committees collated and drafted in a government department by civil servants and modified at *remiss* by the 'affected interests' are difficult to resist in full cabinet. In sum, the full cabinet is primarily engaged in policy adoption. Indeed, it may be that one of the foremost concerns of plenary sessions of the Nordic cabinets is with the timing of the presentation of its proposals to the legislature and with anticipating the likely reaction to them in the assembly — in other words, with the successful prioritisation and management of bills at the parliamentary stage of policy adoption, the subject of Part II of this book.

In concluding Part I, however, five main points need emphasis. First, extensive use is made of commissions of inquiry at the pre-legislative stage of policy-making and, accordingly, there is extensive government consultation with the range of affected interests. Secondly, civil servants play an extremely important part in the preparation of legislation, both in constituting the permanent secretariat of commissions — the bodies that effectively direct their proceedings — and in determining how problems are to be presented in the drafting of proposals in the government ministries. Thirdly, there is a distinctively high representation of parliamentarians on Swedish commissions of inquiry, although parliaments can exert an *indirect* influence at the formulation stage throughout the region, — *inter alia* by means of tabling interpellations and questions (see chapter 8) and putting pressure on the corporate interests on commissions. Next, it appears likely that the plenary meetings of the Nordic cabinets involve the adoption rather than direction of public policy. In theory decisions are taken in plenary session; in Sweden, however, perhaps 90% of decisions are in practice taken by the responsible minister in conjunction with the officials in his department. With the cabinet dealing annually with over 26,000 matters, this is hardly surprising.[98] Furthermore, as matters of 'high politics' tend to be discussed at *ad hoc* meetings of the parliamentary group leaders, broad discussion in full cabinets is largely confined to issues of secondary importance such as public appointments.

Finally, there seems to be widespread acceptance among Nordic parliamentarians of both the rationality of the existing policy formulation machinery and their reliance on elements in it, namely the information provided by interest groups. Not surprisingly, the perception by parliamentary delegates of where power lies at the pre-legislative stage depends largely upon whether they belong to the government side or the opposition. In Erik Damgaard's study of the parliamentary party groups in the Folketing, it emerged that members of the governing party's (parties') parliamentary group(s) were in no doubt that Denmark was governed first and foremost by the political parties in the cabinet and Folketing, whereas the opposition groups on both left and right pointed up the complementary — indeed greater — influence exercised by pressure groups and civil servants in the formulation of policy.[99] It cannot be doubted that his conclusions have a basic validity for the whole Nordic region.

REFERENCES

1. Erik Damgaard, 'Party Coalitions in Danish Law-Making 1953–1970'. *European Journal of Political Research* 1, 1973, p. 39.
2. Simo Juntunen, 'Tilinpäätös'. *Suomen Kuvalehti* 19.12.1980.
3. *Danmarks Riges Grundlov* (*DRG*) 1:3.
4. DRG 3:14.
5. Interview with the Prime Minister's Secretary, Søren-Ole Olsen 21.4.1982.
6. *Suomen Hallitusmuoto* (*HM*) 1:2.
7. David Arter, 'All-Party Government for Finland?' *Parliamentary Affairs* 31, 1, 1978, pp. 67–85.
8. Interview with Claes Eklundh 15.9.1982.
9. *Regeringsformen* (*RF*) 1:6.
10. *Protokoll och expeditioner i regeringskansliet*. Stockholm: Departementens offsetcentral, 1981.
11. *Norges Grundlov* (*NG*) 12.
12. Seppo Salminen, 'Toimintakykyinen hallitus'. *Kanava* 5, 1979, pp. 294–7.
13. Søren-Ole Olsen, *En oversigt over regeringsudvalg*. Til ministre, departementschefer og ministersekretærer. 19.3.1982.
14. Interview with Søren-Ole Olsen 21.4.1982.
15. Johan P. Olsen (1980), p. 211.
16. Interview with Søren-Ole Olsen 21.4.1982.
17. Olsen (1980), p. 209.
18. Svegfors (1981), p. 46.
19. Barbara Castle, *The Castle Diaries 1974–76*. London: Weidenfeld and Nicolson, 1980, p. 331.
20. RF 7:4. HM 4:40.
21. RF 6:9.
22. NG 12.
23. HM 4:36.
24. DRG 3:18.
25. Interview with Søren-Ole Olsen 21.4.1982.
26. Søren-Ole Olsen, 'Regeringsarbejdet og statsministeren'. *Nordisk Administrativt Tidsskrift* 59, 2, p. 58.
27. Ibid., p. 57.
28. NG 13.
29. NG 30.
30. NG 27.
31. Olsen (1980), p. 237.
32. 'Pientilojakin rangaistaan ylituotannosta'. *Kristityn Vastuu* 2.4.1981.
33. HM 4:43.
34. HM 4:44.
35. RF 7:6.
36. 'Rättschefen i Statsrådsberedningen', *Regeringen och Regeringsarbet*. 1.9.1982.
37. *Handelsdepartementet*. Sandvik AB 811 81 Sandviken. *Protokoll vid regeringssammanträde 1981.01.29*. Huvudprotokoll nr 5.
38. RF 7:7

39. Riksdagsordningen (RO) 3:1.
40. RO 3:2.
41. RO 3:3.
42. RO 3:5.
43. Interview with Michael Lunn, Head of the Legal Division in the Danish Ministry of Justice, 26.4.1982.
44. Jaakko Nousiainen, *The Finnish Political System*. Cambridge Mass.: Harvard University Press, 1971, p. 251.
45. David Southern, 'Germany', in F.F. Ridley (ed.), *Government and Administration in Western Europe*. Oxford: Martin Robertson, 1979, p. 149.
46. DRG 6:61.
47. RF 8:18.
48. RO 4:10.
49. Paavo Kastari, 'Pouluejohtajat sovittelukokoukseen'. *Suomen Kuvalehti* 15.2. 1980.
50. Esko Almgren, 'Kristillinen Liitto kannattaa perustuslakituomioistuinta'. *Kristityn Vastuu* 24.2.1983.
51. Erik Mo, 'The Norwegian Parliamentary System'. Unpubl. paper by the Secretary-General of the Storting, p. 14.
52. John Fitzmaurice, *Politics in Denmark*. London: Hurst, 1981, pp. 73–4.
53. Jóhannes Nordal and Valdimar Kristinsson (eds), *Iceland 874–1974*. Reyjavík: Central Bank of Iceland, 1975, p. 134.
54. Arve Solstad, 'The Norwegian Coalition System', in *Scandinavian Political Studies* 4, 1969, pp. 160–7.
55. Olsen (1980), p. 236.
56. Olsen (1978), p. 58.
57. V. Herman and J. Alt (eds), *Cabinet Studies: a Reader*. London: Macmillan, 1975, p. vii.
58. Olsen (1978), p. 57.
59. Valtion keskushallintokomitean 11 osamietintö (1978), Nide 1, p. 248.
60. Ibid., p. 369–72.
61. Ibid., pp. 250–1.
62. Andrew Schonfield, 'The Politics of the Mixed Economy of the International System of the 1970s' Stevenson Lecture. BBC Radio 3 29.11.1979.
63. Olsen (1980), p. 206.
64. Interview with Søren-Ole Olsen 21.4.1982.
65. Solstad (1969), p. 165.
66. HM 4:39. RF 7:4. Icelandic Constitution (IC) 17.
67. DRG 4:32:2.
68. HM 4:25.
69. DRG 3:18.
70. NG 13.
71. IC 8.
72. RF 6:1–5.
73. 'Fälldin låter partipiskan vina'. *Expressen* 5.10.1980.
74. 'Fem lovforslag om unge lediges beskæftigelse og uddannelse'. *Nordisk Kontakt* 6/82, pp. 437–8.
75. 'Formandskabet i EF spiller også en rolle i mine overvejelser'. *Weekendavisen* 28.5–3.6.1982.
76. Johannes Virolainen, *Pääministerinä Suomessa. Poliittisia ratkaisuja vaalikaudella 1962–66*. Helsinki: Kirjayhtymä, 1969, p. 127.
77. Søren-Ole Olsen, 'En oversigt over regeringsudvalg'. 19.3.1982.
78. Valtion keskushallintokomitean 11 osamietintö (1978) Nide 1, p. 356.

79. For the committee's terms of reference, see 'Bättre villkor för barn nödvändiga. Särskild delegation har tillsatts'. *Från Riksdag & Departement* 18.2.1983.
80. Olsen (1978), p. 61.
81. Olsen (1980), p. 210.
82. Ibid., pp. 211–12.
83. Jukka Gronow, Pertti Klemola and Juha Partanen, *Demokratian rajat ja rakenteet. Tutkimus suomalaisesta hallitsemistavasta ja sen taloudellisesta perustasta.* Porvoo-Helsinki-Juva: WSOY, 1977, pp. 423–4.
84. Olsen (1980), p. 218.
85. Paavo Kastari, *Suomen valtiosääntö.* Suomalaisen lakimiesyhdistyksen julkaisuja B-sarja, 179, 1977, pp. 179–84.
86. Seppo Laakso, *Hallituksen muodostaminen Suomessa.* Suomalaisen lakimiesyhdistyksen julkaisuja A-sarja, 110, 1975, p. 264.
87. Kastari (1977), p. 151.
88. David Arter, 'Kekkonen's Finland: Enlightened Despotism or Consensual Democracy?' *West European Politics* 4, 3, 1981, pp. 219–34.
89. Urho Kekkonen, *Kirjeitä myllystäni 2, 1968–1975.* Pääministeri Ahti Karjalainen 30.8.1971. Keuruu 1976.
90. Juha Korppi-Tommola (ed.), *Kansa kaikkivaltias—keskustelu valtiosäännön perusteista.* Helsinki: Tammi, 1975, p. 89.
91. Tapio Koskiaho, 'Näin tehdään ministereitä ja hallitusohjelmia — poliitikot kertovat' in Harto Hakovirta and Tapio Koskiaho, *Suomen hallitukset ja hallitusohjelmat* 1945–1973. Helsinki: Gaudeamus, 1973, pp. 54–5.
92. Valtion keskushallintokomitean 11 osamietintö 1978. Liiteosa. Helsinki 1979, p. 117.
93. Valtion keskushallintokomitean 11 osamietintö 1978. Nide 1, p. 276.
94. Olsen (1980), p. 216.
95. Interview with Marianne Eliason, a staff member in the Swedish Prime Minister's Office, 15.9.1982.
96. R.N. Berki and Jack Hayward, 'The State of European Society' in J.E.S. Hayward and R.N. Berki (eds), *State and Society in Contemporary Europe.* Oxford: Martin Robertson, 1979, pp. 253–264.
97. 'Nytt kulturdepartement i arbeid. Skal ta seg av saksområder innenfor kultur og vitenskap'. *Nordisk Kontakt* 1/82, pp. 53–54.
98. Interview with Claes Eklundh 15.9.1982.
99. Erik Damgaard (ed.), *Partigrupper, repræsentation og styring.* København: Schultz, 1982.

THE INVOLVEMENT OF THE NORDIC PARLIAMENTS IN POLICY ADOPTION: LEGISLATING OR DELIBERATING ASSEMBLY?

4

LEGISLATIVE CHAMBERS: ORGANISATION AND POLICY IMPACT

In legislating [illegible] major public [illegible] within the [illegible] arena for public policy [illegible] number of major [illegible] the main function of deliberative assemblies [illegible] legislative [illegible]

Samuel C. Patterson [illegible] Comparative Legislatures [illegible]

In the Nordic parliaments, legislative measures, whether formulated as government proposals or private members' bills, must be adopted by a majority vote in the legislature. [illegible] In common with [illegible] throughout Western Europe, the process of adoption or rejection takes place in arenas of contrasting size and importance — namely, full plenary sessions of the assembly and the small but influential standing parliamentary committees. In addition, the government [illegible] forms of decision-making and conflict resolution [illegible] outside the formal structures of the legislature. This second part of the book is concerned [illegible] day in the [illegible] procedural differences. More important [illegible] of general [illegible] of bills [illegible] policy adoption [illegible] the legislature [illegible]

Part II
THE INVOLVEMENT OF THE NORDIC PARLIAMENTS IN POLICY ADOPTION: LEGISLATING OR DELIBERATING ASSEMBLIES?

4

LEGISLATIVE PLENARIES: ORGANISATION AND POLICY IMPACT

> 'In legislating assemblies, major public policies are initiated within the legislature, proposals for public policy that come from outside are transformed by the parliament in major ways . . . the main function of deliberating assemblies in contrast is authorizing and approving proposals for law formulated outside the legislature proper, most often by the executive.'— Gerhard Loewenberg and Samuel C. Patterson (1979), 'Comparing Legislatures', p. 197

In the Nordic parliaments legislative measures, whether in the form of a government proposal or a private member's bill, must be adopted by a majority of the legislature in order to become law. In common with assemblies throughout Western Europe, this process of adopting or rejecting bills takes place in arenas of contrasting size and importance — namely full *plenary sessions* of the assembly and the small but influential *standing parliamentary committees*. In addition, *the parliamentary party groups* are significant forums of decision-making and conflict resolution, albeit strictly outside the formal structures of the legislature. This second section of the book is concerned to focus in detail on precisely how a bill becomes law in the five states of the region and on the significant procedural differences. More important, the section investigates a number of general questions arising out of the adoption and enactment of bills. How effective, for example, are the procedures for policy adoption at the parliamentary stage? Are bills subject to rigorous scrutiny and debate and, if so, at what point in the parliamentary process? How often do the parliaments of the region adopt legislative initiatives from their own members? Above all, can the Nordic assemblies be said to deliberate, to legislate or merely to legitimate government proposals?

The initial phase in the life of a bill is similar throughout the region: the bill is registered with the Office of Parliament and subsequently the Speaker's Council and is thereafter introduced by the Speaker — often, as in Sweden, at the plenary session following its distribution to members. There is therefore no formal 'ministerial' reading of bills as at Westminster where the responsible minister personally reads the text of a proposal before it is printed and circulated to members of parliament. Instead, the proposal is placed 'on the table' by a decision of the assembly and then either dispatched to a standing committee or discussed in a full plenary session of parliament. Nordic plenaries are of two main types. *Legislative plenaries* are designed to facilitate the engagement of parliamentarians in the consideration of proposals at complementary levels — that of generality and principle (the equivalent of the second reading debate at Westminster) and thereafter that of detail and practice (the report and amendment stage in the House of Commons). *Plenary account debates*, by contrast, involve the government in answering questions and interpellations tabled by members or, alternatively, reporting to parliament on the main lines of its policy or policy intentions. Plenary account debates are considered in detail in chapter 8, which deals specifically with plenary controls over the executive in respect of the implementation of policy.

Before we examine the main types of legislative plenary, the level of delegate participation at them and the policy impact of these full-reading debates, it is important first to consider the organisation of full sittings in the Nordic parliaments as well as procedures at them. This can be done by examining (1) how delegates are seated at plenaries, (2) the rules and conventions relating to speechmaking, (3) the role of the Speaker and parliamentary secretariat in legislative management, and (4) the extent of assembly control over the parliamentary agenda.

Seating arrangements

The seating of delegates in the semi-circular Nordic parliaments is arranged by region in Norway and Sweden and on the basis of party in Finland and Denmark. Iceland is the deviant case, eschewing both regional and partisan placement of delegates.

In the United Storting and Odelsting, members take their places in alphabetical order of electoral district.[1] Thus at the 'ordinary' opening of a new Storting session (cf. the official Royal Opening about a week later), it is the delegate polling the highest vote in alphabetically the first constituency Aust Agder (in October 1981 this was the Labour delegate Osmund Faremo[2]) who knocks on his desk and requests the Speaker of the previous Storting to lead proceedings until a new Speaker shall have been elected. The latter then holds a roll-call of attendance during which the top person on the electoral list of the leading party in each of the nineteen constituencies presents the details of the result in that constituency. Throughout the ordinary opening of parliament, the ministerial seats in the Storting remain empty when the new session follows a general election, since a fresh government will not have been formed. There are special seats in the Storting behind the Speaker for journalists, civil servants and high-court judges, though of course they are not allowed to participate in debates.

Like Storting delegates, members of the Riksdag are allocated numbered seats in accordance with their electoral district. Members for Stockholm occupy the lowest numbers to the Speaker's left, while delegates for Norrbotten are seated at the back of the assembly to the extreme right. There are special places set aside for members of the cabinet and they, as in Norway, are to the Speaker's right.[3] Officials and committee staff sit in chairs along the outer aisles.

There was a colourful consequence of the regional seating of delegates in the later part of the 1980–1 Riksdag session when Gösta Bohman, the leader of a Conservative Party which had withdrawn from Fälldin's bourgeois coalition, rubbed shoulders, so to speak, on the Stockholm constituency's front seats with Olof Palme, the leader of the main opposition party, the Social Democrats.

In accordance with the Eduskunta Standing Orders, when the Finnish parliament convenes after a general election, members are to be seated alphabetically until such time as a different arrangement is approved.[4] No mention is made of parties, although in practice seating has followed party lines throughout the Independence period with delegates who represent the Finnish People's Democratic League occupying the places on the extreme left and those of the Swedish People's Party the extreme right. The position of the Swedish People's Party, today very much a centre-based party, is something of an historic anachronism and dates back to a unanimous agreement of the Eduskunta on 4 April 1919[5] — a time when its demand for a separate Swedish-speaking province in Finland placed the Swedish People's Party to the right of the newly-formed Conservatives. Since then, tradition has dictated no change in the Swedish People's Party's parliamentary location, with the result that the party sat to the right of the neo-fascist Patriotic People's Movement (IKL) in the 1930s and the radical rightist Constitutional People's Party (PKP) in the 1970s! However, the party itself seems entirely happy with the seating arrangements. Distinctively in the region, seating provision in the Eduskunta is provided for interpreters: according to a parliamentary decision of March 1935, the main points of Swedish-language speeches at plenary sessions are to be rendered in Finnish directly afterwards.[6]

As in Finland, the seating of members in the Folketing is organised on a partisan basis although, in contrast to the rest of the region, the parliamentary standing orders make no reference to the matter. In the 1981–2 session, this meant that Mogens Glistrup occupied seat no. 94, which was the one furthest to the right in the assembly, while the seat furthest to the left, no. 132, belonged to Mette Groes of the Social Democrats. The only exception to the partisan allocation of places in the Folketing involves the two representatives for Greenland who have seats together behind the Social Democratic delegates. It is also the convention in Denmark that the parties themselves determine the arrangement of places in the section allocated to the group. The chairmen of the various parliamentary groups, together with the official party spokesmen, occupy the front seats and behind them sit the rank-and-file delegates in order of seniority according to the length of their membership of the Folketing — the most recently elected delegates located at the very back. As Gert Andersen notes wryly, 'it is characteristic of this classical agricultural country and of the great importance of the farming community in Danish political affairs that these rear seats in the assembly should be known earthily as the "dung channel", *grebningen* — that is, the gutter behind cattle in a cow-shed!'[7] This is where the newest and invariably least influential of the Folketing delegates are to be found. In addition to a special bloc of seats for cabinet ministers to the Speaker's left, and places for the various parliamentary officials and secretaries, there is the prestigious 'spokesmen's table', *ordførerbordet*, positioned just in front of the semi-circular curve formed by the front seats and so called because during debates it is used by party spokesmen whose distance from the Speaker's rostrum is thus reduced to the very minimum.

Iceland represents the exception to the arrangement of legislative seating by region or party, as in the other Nordic parliaments. Indeed, in keeping with the spirit of article 48 of the 1944 Constitution — which states that members of the Althing are bound solely by their consciences and not by any order from their constituents — seating both in the United Althing and its two divisions is fixed by lottery. Delegates, in short, draw a number which corresponds to a particular seat place. The only comparable practice to this is found in the Norwegian Lagting, despite the more formal provisions in the parliamentary standing orders.[8] True, long-serving Althing members like People's Alliance delegate Lúdvík Jósepsson, who was a member from 1942 to 1979, the Progressive Eysteinn Jónsson (1934–74) and Independence Party member Péter Ottesen (1916–59) were able to lay claim to their 'own' seats, and in such cases custom has required members on request to relinquish their seats to veteran parliamentarians.[9] This, of course, only serves further to underline the individualistic nature of seating in the Althing.

As to the broader significance of the ecology of the Nordic parliaments, two hypotheses suggest themselves: first, that the seating of delegates by region in Norway and Sweden serves to avoid inter-party conflict over the rightful positioning of groups in the assembly; and secondly, that to a greater extent than elsewhere in the Nordic states, the regional seating of delegates in Norway and Sweden predisposes members on occasions to place local interests ahead of partisan commitment. In practice, the former has the greater validity.

Conflict over seating arrangements has been particularly evident in Finland and at times has generated considerable friction. After the general election of March 1979, the Conservative Party leader, wishing to emphasise the growing moderation of his party following significant electoral gains, proposed that the Christian League be placed to the right of his party in the Eduskunta. Tactical discussions between the Conservatives and the other main non-socialist party, the Centre, lent weight to the case for re-locating the Christian League, and it was inferred that because they had run a candidate against President Kekkonen the previous year, they were to be regarded as an extreme party. However, when the Christian League threatened to support the Social Democrats' candidate for Speaker, the Centre Party backed down and the Christian League retained its place to the left of the Conservatives and alongside the Centre Party and Liberals.[10]

The Finnish Rural Party had no such good fortune in 1975 when, following a disastrous general election in which the party returned only two delegates, it was evicted from its place at the centre of the Eduskunta and obliged to occupy a position to the right of the Conservatives. This followed combined pressure from the Conservative and Centre parties — the latter being the party from which, as the Agrarians, the Rural Party had split away in 1957. The issue generated considerable animosity at the opening session of the

Eduskunta in October 1975, and the Rural Party leader even forced the matter to a vote.[11]

As it turned out, the Rural Party was by no means finished. At the general election in March 1983, it returned seventeen delegates, an increase of 10 over the result four years earlier and sufficient to hold the balance between the socialists (with 83 seats) and the non-socialist bloc (with 96). Had the Rural Party insisted on putting up its own slate at elections for standing committee places and eschewed an alliance with either bloc, the distribution of standing committee seats would have been 8 socialists, 8 non-socialists and 1 strategically well-placed Rural delegate. Instead, the deal which the Rural Party struck with the non-socialist groups (and which secured a Conservative Party Speaker and a comfortable 10:7 non-socialist majority on standing committees) gave the Rural Party — subsequently to enter government — a free hand to choose its seating location in the Eduskunta chamber.

The rules on plenary speeches

Plenary sessions of the Nordic parliaments are open to the public,[12] and proceedings may be followed from the public gallery or on radio and television.[13] Arrangements for broadcasting are made through the Speaker's Council, *talmanskonferensen*. In Sweden, a plenary session may be held behind closed doors if this is required in the interests of national security or if the matter concerns relations with another state or an international organisation.[14] But since the Second World War there has not been a single closed session under these provisions. The same has not been true in Norway, where a closed session was held on 7 June 1977 to discuss the Schei committee report on the navigational systems Loran C and Omega which had been installed in the early 1960s. The matter was to have dramatic consequences when two Left-Socialists contravened article 60 of the Standing Orders of the Storting pledging delegates to maintain silence on all matters discussed behind closed doors and used confidential parts of the Schei report in their election campaign the same year. This episode will be discussed at greater length in chapter 9.

In Denmark, either the Speaker, a cabinet minister or 17 Folketing delegates can demand the removal of all unauthorised persons from the public gallery and it is then decided without debate whether the matter should be considered at a secret sitting of the assembly.[15] Furthermore, if the audience which is admitted to the public galleries does not keep quiet, the Speaker has the power to order the removal of the culprits and if necessary to clear the public gallery altogether.[16] Ironically, when unknown onlookers let off a stink-bomb in the Folketing in October 1982 it was necessary for the Speaker to clear the assembly and not the public gallery, and to suspend the sitting for half an hour. Indeed, during a speech by the Centre Democrat, Erhard Jakobsen, three young demonstrators had removed their trousers and then displayed a banner before being ejected by Folketing staff![17]

In Finland if the Speaker regards a particular question as unsuitable for consideration in a public session, or if 25 Eduskunta delegates require a secret sitting, the public gallery is cleared and parliament proceeds to decide whether or not the matter should be dealt with behind closed doors.[18] Such occasions have been rare: during the Second World War, there were twenty-three closed or partly closed sittings although the majority dealt with cabinet statements on the war effort and progress towards peace.[19]

Members wishing to contribute at plenary sessions are to be dressed in a manner befitting public meetings of an assembly of elected representatives of the people: in other words, male delegates should wear a collar and tie. Recent breaches of these norms have produced some amusing incidents. In May 1980, the usually immaculate Christian League member, Esko Almgren, was informed by the Speaker of the Speaker's Council ruling that ties should be worn in the Eduskunta — this despite extremely hot weather and the fact that Almgren was not giving a speech but rather consulting a senior member of the parliamentary staff, and the curious fact too that a number of other delegates did not have ties on![20] With the temperature in Denmark around 30° centigrade in the shade at the beginning of June 1982 and other Folketing delegates sweltering in their conventional clothes, the Left-Socialist party spokesman Steen Tinning chose to appear to speak dressed in red shorts with white stripes. On receiving the expected reprimand from the Speaker he promptly returned clad this time in blue corduroy trousers. In Sweden, a Left-Communist delegate, John Andersson, was dressed in a 'Manchester suit' made at Norrkläder when he arrived for a plenary session of the Riksdag on 10 March 1981. He had, he claimed, bought the suit to support 'alternative production' at Norrkläder, but was discreetly asked to leave by the chief attendant, *vaktmästare*, for whom it fell short of the convention — established during the era of Speaker Henry Allard — of either a suit or a jacket. The Manchester suit, it was held, had neither collar nor lapels. An indignant Andersson claimed that he had worn the garment to several earlier plenary sessions and had even spoken in it at an interpellation debate without attracting censure.[21] Certainly the present Speaker, Ingemund Bengtsson, claimed that the incident should have been avoided.[22]

Members wishing to address a plenary meeting of one of the Nordic assemblies must also abide by the procedures for speaking laid down in the relevant standing orders and this has meant that throughout much of the region there is a time-lag of varying length between a delegate giving notice of intention to speak and gaining the opportunity to do so. Indeed, with the possible exception of Iceland, where the extremely small number of Althing delegates has invested plenary proceedings with a distinctive informality, and where members knock on their desks or raise their right hands if they want to speak, the intention to contribute at a full-sitting debate in the Nordic parliaments does not involve 'catching the Speaker's eye' in the British sense. True, the Storting Orders state that in the event of several delegates simultaneously requesting to speak, it is the Speaker's responsibility to determine the order of speeches.[23] But in practice the Speaker is not required to decide 'in the heat of the battle' whom to permit to speak and how best to balance contributions from both sides of the House as at Westminster. Rather, he simply enters the delegates' names on a list he keeps and calls them in turn. In Denmark the procedure is essentially the same, although the Speaker can give precedence to party spokesmen along with the movers of bills and resolutions, and may at his discretion change the ordering of speeches with a view to expediting a conclusion to a debate by ensuring a specific exchange of views.[24] In Finland, however, it is permitted[25] and in Sweden required of a delegate to register his intention to speak with the office of parliament, *kammarkansliet*, as soon as possible before the debate and give an approximation of how long the speech will last.[26] In Norway, too, the Speaker invariably has discussions with the parliamentary group leaders in advance of a topical or controversial debate — e.g. in the fields of foreign policy and finance — so as to be able to gauge the approximate length of time to be allocated to proceedings.

The procedures for the enlistment and prior registration of speeches have doubtless contributed to denying the parliaments in the region an excited, excitable or spontaneous atmosphere at major debates. Proceedings are rather stilted, and lack cut and thrust. Even the institution of short (and necessarily unrehearsed) 'reply speeches', *genmäle*, and hence a brief reply debate, *replikkdebatt*— lasting a maximum of 20 minutes in Norway[27] — has not succeeded in enlivening matters. Reply speeches — at most two of 2 minutes' duration in Norway and Finland[28] and 3 minutes in Sweden (10 minutes for a cabinet minister)[29] — are allowed, at the discretion of the Speaker. They are invariably granted for personal attacks, and usually too for spokesmen to respond to explicitly partisan criticism. In Denmark there is no reply debate as such, but in special circumstances the Speaker can call upon a delegate to make a short reply of up to five minutes in length.[30] In contrast to Westminster, the Standing Orders of the Storting and Eduskunta state that 'noisy heckling and other disruptive expressions' are prohibited — although it is not unusual for general laughter to greet a delegate's remark — while in the Folketing 'expressions of approval and disapproval are regarded as disorderly.'[31] Moderate and respecful language is also required of delegates at all times. The Eduskunta Standing Orders state that 'no delegate is permitted to employ hurtful and ridiculing rhetoric in respect of either the government or an individual member of parliament.'[32] Even so, towards the end of the 1973 Eduskunta session, with divisions in Vennamo's Finnish Rural Party coming to a head, there were almost ten instances of delegates being reprimanded and warned about their language, and on six occasions an offending member was suspended from parliament for the maximum period of two weeks.[33] However, on the whole the culture of plenary meetings in the Nordic assemblies is deferential and quietist: sessions are highly planned and time is carefully husbanded, but proceedings are essentially undemonstrative. Speeches are usually written and well-prepared, albeit rather flat and humourless: debates are debates in name only and the intoning of speech after speech creates an impression of aridity, which is a far remove from the 'baying of angry vocies' which, as George Thomas noted when Speaker of the House of Commons, tends to accompany major speeches at Westminster.[34]

The prevalence of written speeches is a notable feature. Erik Ninn-Hansen, the former Conservative Speaker, remarked that fewer speeches were merely read out in earlier times when there were more farmer and worker delegates in the Folketing.[35] The present Riksdag Speaker, Ingemund Bengtsson, has also expressed regret at the increased reliance by delegates on scripts since his first years as a parliamentarian more than thirty years ago. However, he commented sardonically that his practice has been to request a copy of plenary speeches, and while it often still remained difficult to follow them, he was at least able to know where members had got to![36] To be fair, there are examples of more or less extempore speakers. Ninn-Hansen could think of between ten and fifteen members of the Folketing who speak 'off the cuff', including himself contributing in his capacity of private member. Elsewhere in the region, a few names stand out: Olof Palme (Social Democrat),

Johan Svensson (Left Communist) and the Conservative Nils Carlshamre in Sweden, and the Conservative Jalmari Torikka and Centre delegate Väinö Raudaskoski in Finland. Above all, however, those who do without written speeches tend to be the party leaders or highly experienced parliamentarians like Veikko Vennamo, an Eduskunta delegate since 1945, who is said to adapt his contributions according to his appraisal of what type of people are occupying the public gallery.

Adding to the formality of Nordic parliamentary proceedings is the fact that until recently all plenary contributions, except in the Swedish Riksdag, had to be made from the Speaker's rostrum; in Norway and Iceland this is also the rule for reply speeches. Since 1982, however, with the technical modernisation of the audio equipment in the Folketing, Danish members have been able to speak from their places although, as in Sweden, they still tend to prefer the rostrum.[37] That said, the principle that every delegate wishing to speak should be permitted to do so is firmly established in the region — and explicitly stated in the Orders of the Storting[38] — although, except in Finland and Iceland, a series of time limits is imposed on speeches to prevent plenary debates lasting too long.

In this last context, the Swedish Constitutional Commission's report 'Partial Constitutional Reform' in 1967 held that it was essential in the new unicameral assembly not to have so many delegates as to make plenary sessions unreasonably long. However, the final figure of 350 members — only thirty-four less than in the old bicameral Riksdag — prompted a commission member to table a reservation expressing the fear that elongated debates would result. To counter this possibility, the majority underlined the need for careful planning of the Riksdag's work and *as a last resort* restrictions on debating time. This principle was ultimately incorporated into the new Riksdag Standing Orders.[39] Parliament has the right to limit both the number of speeches a delegate is allowed to make on any one topic, and the length of each contribution. A rank ordering of speeches was established: cabinet ministers, together with spokesmen on standing committees and for the party groups, were accorded the greatest time allowance. In contrast, those who do not register their intention to speak — this should be done at least one day in advance[40] — are restricted to a contribution of at most six minutes' duration, unless the Speaker sees fit to grant longer. Speeches at non-legislative account debates must not exceed fifteen minutes, or half an hour in the case of ministers and party group spokesmen.[41]

In Denmark and Norway[42] there is a similar hierarchical structuring of speech lengths. In Denmark ministers are given the most generous allowance: half an hour for a first speech at a Second Reading debate and ten minutes for following contributions. The various policy spokesmen are permitted ten and five minutes respectively for first and second speeches, while rank-and-file members get five and three minutes.[43] In the Storting's Budget Debate, party group spokesmen, the appropriate cabinet minister and the Prime Minister are permitted up to fifteen minutes and other delegates ten. In Denmark, Iceland and Norway no ordinary member may normally speak more than twice at each plenary reading of a bill (unless it is a 'law' proposal in Norway).

These rules on the number and length of plenary speeches cannot be regarded as particularly restrictive and moreover any decision to impose tighter limits than those prescribed usually rests with the assembly itself, albeit on the initiative of the Speaker. In any event, the regulations on speech-making should be viewed as a purely pragmatic device of legislative management. It is significant to note here that faced with a marked increase in the amount of time consumed annually by full-sitting debates, proposals have been made for the introduction of restrictions in Finland.

In 1951, the Kekkonen Committee proposed that article 57 of the Parliament Act be amended so that at the Speaker's initiative, and with the consent of a two-thirds majority in the assembly, a clôture could be imposed. In January 1976 the Centre Party Speaker, V.J. Sukselainen, suggested a delimitation of speech lengths, and the Speaker's Council was requested to set up a working group to look into the matter, A questionnaire was circulated to delegates and this revealed that precisely half were opposed to time restrictions while 47.5% were in favour. Of the latter 61.5% preferred curtailments by voluntary agreement and 38.5% inclined towards statutory provision.[44] The fact that nothing has been done so far has permitted opposition groups in Finland an ideal opportunity for tactical American-style filibustering.

The Speaker's role

Traditionally, the Speaker as the highest office-holder in the Nordic parliaments has ranked second in the political hierarchy to the Head of State — 'next in line', so to speak behind the monarch or President, although in reality this position has been usurped in recent years by the head of the cabinet — the Prime Minister. Only in Sweden, uniquely in Western Europe, has the position of the Speaker rivalled that of Prime Minister. Thus if the Swedish King is prevented from attending at the Riksdag, it is the Speaker who declares parliament open and who plays a central role in the formation of new governments. The niceties of status apart, the Speaker of a Nordic parliament is required, as the senior officer of the legislature, to perform a great number of ceremonial and symbolic duties. For example, he will often head a delegation of parliamentarians visiting fellow-assemblies in the region: in June 1982 at the invitation of the Speaker's Council of the Folketing, Jón Helgason, Speaker of the United Althing, led a group of Icelandic delegates to Denmark. Early the same autumn, the Riksdag Speaker in the simplest of ceremonies thanked the 47 delegates who were not seeking re-election at the September 1982 elections. Incidentally, the Nordic Speakers do not necessarily receive any extra emolument for their duties: the Eduskunta Speaker, for instance, does not receive a higher salary than an ordinary member.

As regards the recruitment of the Speaker, it has become conventional in Denmark, Norway, Sweden and Iceland for the chief Speaker and the Prime Minister to be of the same party. The tenure of office by the Social Democrat Ingemund Bengtsson during the 1979–82 period of bourgeois government was exceptional and is discussed shortly. In Iceland too, although the first Speaker is invariably drawn from the governing majority, it has become the practice since 1971 for the first deputy-Speaker of the United Althing, and indeed his counterpart in both chambers, to be a member of the opposition ranks. The same is true elsewhere in the region.

The only real exception to the rule of party consonance between Chief Speaker and Prime Minister has been Finland where tradition has dictated that the Speaker and Prime Minister should be from different parties, albeit not infrequently parties within the same coalition. A 'Red' (Social Democratic) Prime Minister and 'Green' (Agrarian-Centre) Speaker and *vice versa* have been typical since the last war. There was a rare exception during the period of two Agrarian premierships between 1962 and March 1965, throughout which time an Agrarian, Kauno Kleemola, was Speaker. Nonetheless, it should be borne in mind that for essentially foreign policy reasons[45] relations between President Kekkonen (a former Agrarian) and the Social Democrats were extremely poor, and even then it seems that a significant number of Agrarians expressed disquiet about the break with convention and favoured the nomination as Speaker of the former Social Democratic Prime Minister, K.A. Fagerholm.[46]

The office of Speaker in the Nordic parliaments is of course an elected one and, as with the deputy-Speakers, the ballot is secret. Denmark will serve to illustrate the typical procedure. At the first sitting after a general election, the senior or longest-serving member of the Folketing takes the chair and directs proceedings pending the scrutiny of the newly-elected delegates' mandates. Subsequently, and without any debate, the Folketing elects a Speaker's Council comprising the Speaker, at most 4 deputy-Speakers and 6 tellers — all to be elected annually. In January 1982, for example, the veteran member and former Foreign Minister K.B. Andersen — who did not seek re-election in December 1981 — was replaced as Speaker by the former Social Democratic Finance Minister Svend Jakobsen, who was supported by all the Folketing groups except the Progress Party. With no other candidates for the Speaker's position, a formal vote was not necessary.

In Norway in recent years the Speaker's Council has comprised a Speaker, deputy Speaker, secretary and vice-secretary elected for each of the three '*tings*' — that is twelve persons in all[47] (the Storting Standing Orders refer to a 'President', the Folketing Orders to a 'Chairman': the term 'Speaker' is used here to avoid confusion with the Finnish and Icelandic Heads of State). As in Finland, Denmark and Iceland, the Norwegian Speaker is elected annually (his renomination is invariably a formality) and if this is not achieved by an absolute majority at the first two attempts, a simple run-off at the third round is sufficient. However in more than twenty years, the proceedings have not progressed beyond the first round of voting. Since 1981 a vice-deputy Speaker has been elected in each division of the Norwegian legislature in addition to a Speaker and deputy Speaker.

In Finland, if no candidate for Speaker gains an absolute majority at the first round of balloting (as elsewhere, no prior plenary debate is permitted), a second vote follows and if an absolute majority is still not obtained, a simple plurality suffices at the third round. In the (unprecedented) event of a dead heat at the third round, the matter would be decided by lottery. The result of the election for Speaker is then conveyed in writing to the President. In contrast to the third round of electoral college voting for a new Head of State — where the original field of candidates is narrowed down to the two persons with the highest counts following the second electoral college vote — there are no restrictions on the number of eligible candidates at the third round of voting for the Speaker's position. Incidentally, in accordance with wide-ranging government proposals for reforming the 1928 Parliament Act which were placed before the Eduskunta in autumn 1982 and came into effect after the March 1983 general elections,[48] the Speaker and deputy Speaker continue to be elected on a yearly basis — precisely in the manner of Finland's delegation to the Nordic Council — despite the strenuous arguments of the former Speaker Johannes Virolainen that the

Speaker's mandate should run the full 4-year electoral term of parliament. A minor change approved was that in the event of the Speaker and deputy-Speakers being prevented from directing the proceedings of the Eduskunta, their responsibility should fall to the chairman of the Grand Committee or, failing that, the senior member of the Speaker's Council.[49]

Unlike the practice in the rest of the region, the Riksdag elects a Speaker along with a first, second and third deputy Speaker for the full 3-year term of parliament.[50] The election has on occasions been a close-run affair, and the 1979 ballot saw a wholly unprecedented series of events. As the largest single party in the Riksdag following the September general elections, the Social Democrats — although relegated to the opposition when the postal vote belatedly provided the non-socialist parties with the narrowest of majorities — claimed the right to the Speakership and prevailed upon the highly experienced Ingemund Bengtsson to stand. The gesture was largely symbolic, for convention ruled that the Speaker should be from the ranks of the governing parties. Indeed the Conservatives, who had made the most significant gains at the polls but failed to secure the Premiership, insisted on their right to the office even if, as Bengtsson was aware, the Social Democratic candidate had, initially at least, some support from the Liberals, the third and smallest member of the planned bourgeois coalition.

Bengtsson did not expect to be elected, although he confessed to the author that he returned to his room and donned a white shirt before the ballot — just in case![51] At the first ballot, the Conservative candidate defeated Bengtsson by one vote, but because he lacked an absolute majority, the issue was voted on a second time. Meanwhile, journalists watching from the public gallery had observed a mistake in the count (despite three scrutineers!) and it later appeared that Bengtsson had won by 167 votes to 166. In any event, the second ballot proved equally tight: Bengtsson won by two votes, but following a complaint the matter was referred to an independent body and Bengtsson was suspended for three days. Finally, on the third vote, Bengtsson was elected unanimously, as indeed he was in October 1982 when his own Social Democratic Party returned to power.

The wide-ranging internal duties of the Speaker are set out in the Standing Orders of the regional assemblies. In Denmark it is simply stated that he shall direct the proceedings of the Folketing and maintain order,[52] while in Sweden he is required to lead meetings of the Riksdag.[53] In the narrowest technical sense — cf. any possible political and/or partisan influence that may be exercised, — what does this direction and leadership involve? Four functions need emphasis.

First, the Speaker in all the Nordic assemblies convenes the first sitting of each session — in Denmark this involves a personal directive[54] and in Sweden the possibility of a telegram or telephone call to all members from the Speaker — and thereafter calls all full sittings. In Finland this has meant arranging for the posting of a notice regarding a forthcoming plenary on all the notice boards in the Eduskunta as well as in the main Helsinki newspapers in a form agreed with the Office of Parliament, *kansliatoimikunta*. If possible, this notice should be published by 1800 hours at the latest on the evening before the full-sitting debate and if a vote is to take place this should be mentioned in the notice.[55] Arrangements are identical in Sweden except that if, in the event of an unforeseen situation arising, the Speaker announces a plenary after 1800 hours the previous evening, this full sitting debate can take place only if more than half the Riksdag delegates consent to it.[56]

The right to convene sittings in the Nordic assemblies does not reside exclusively with the Speaker. In Denmark he is obliged to convene a sitting of the Folketing either at the request of the Prime Minister or following a petition undersigned by at least two fifths of all delegates.[57] In Sweden, too, he is obliged to call an extraordinary session of the Riksdag if no less than 150 members so request and explain the reason for their request. This shall be held within 20 days of the request being submitted and notice given of the extraordinary session in the press at least one day beforehand.[58] Moreover, the Riksdag can be convened in extraordinary session if the government so desires, and while it ordinarily meets in Stockholm, the assembly or Speaker may decide to remove elsewhere if this is in the interests of the legislature's security and freedom.[59] However, in the overwhelming majority of cases it is the Nordic Speakers who convene full-sitting meetings of the regional assemblies.

Secondly, the Speaker or his deputy (in Norway they alternate on a monthly basis)[60] presides over the plenary deliberations of the Nordic assemblies. This involves *inter alia* maintaining the norms regarding the standards of delegates' attire; ensuring that, when required, contributions are made from the rostrum (and in the order that requests have been received); allowing reply speeches where appropriate; and ensuring that the necessary decorum and protocol are maintained.

According to the Folketing Orders, delegates — excepting ministers — are to be addressed as 'Mr', 'Mrs' or 'Miss' along with their surnames, but without any title. However, it is permissible for delegates to be referred to as 'the honourable member' in the style of Westminster.[61] Furthermore, the Speaker must insist that members stick to the point: if a warning of this nature is ignored, the Speaker is empowered to forbid the delegate from continuing.[62] Adherence to prescribed time limits for contributions is also important. If a Folketing member exceeds the allotted time, the Speaker will ask him to withdraw after one reminder that his time is up. In this event, the delegate is not allowed to speak again on the same matter.[63] Above all, the Speakers of the Nordic parliaments are centrally engaged in planning the agenda and introducing matters for discussion. In Denmark, if at all possible, a provisional agenda is distributed to delegates on the last sitting day of each week setting out the Speaker's provisional arrangements for business in the following week.[64]

Up to a point, the priority given to issues on the agenda is beyond the Speaker's control in so far as it is set out in the Parliamentary Standing Orders. Article 2 of the Riksdag Standing Orders sets out the following ranking of issues:[65]

Table 4.1. THE ORDERING OF ISSUES ON THE RIKSDAG AGENDA

1. demands for referendums on constitutional questions;
2. a proposal for a new Prime Minister or a vote of no confidence;
3. internal elections;
4. government bills, reports and accounts of particular activities;
5. proposals and reports from Riksdag bodies other than standing parliamentary committees;
6. private members' bills;
7. standing parliamentary committee reports in the order set out in the Standing Orders,[66] i.e. starting with the report of the Constitutional Committee and finishing with the Civil Affairs Committee report.

In the vast majority of parliamentary sittings, however, the Speaker regulates the ordering of proceedings. Even items 3–7 listed above are at the Speaker's discretion, and in any event, though part of the Standing Orders, are subject as so-called 'supplementary stipulations,' *tilläggsbestämmelse*, to amendment (as with any ordinary law) by a simple majority of the Riksdag.

Looked at more from the delegate's viewpoint, as the Finnish Parliamentary Orders specify, the Speaker cannot prevent a matter from being debated and voted on unless he believes it contravenes the constitution, and then he must explain the reasons for his decision to proscribe deliberation of the matter.[67] If the Eduskunta is dissatisfied with the Speaker's ruling, the whole question is then referred for investigation to the standing parliamentary committee on the Constitution.[68] The procedure is identical in Sweden.[69] All in all, the Speaker is charged with managing the overall work of the assembly so as to facilitate and effect the necessary degree of continuity, coherence and progress in its activities.

To do this, the Speaker may, as in Denmark, change the order of business and remove an item from the Order Paper provided that he informs the Folketing of his reasons for doing so.[70] Moreover, although in Finland full-sitting debates normally terminate at 2300 hours, the Speaker may decide that a prolongation is necessary to complete an important item of business, while in Denmark, Norway and, in particular, Sweden Saturday sittings are by no means unknown particularly before Christmas and towards the summer recess. In Sweden, the Speaker in conjunction with the Speaker's Council, is responsible for ensuring that the Riksdag completes its annual business by June 15 at the latest (May 31 is the date prescribed in the constitution for the normal end of sittings).[71] When by May 1982 it became evident that the customary logjam of unfinished business exceeded even that of the previous year and could not be cleared by the end of the month, Speaker Bengtsson was compelled to exhort standing committees and parliamentary party groups alike to relegate some of the Riksdag's legislative programme to the autumn and substantially to truncate debates.[72]

Next, the Nordic Speakers, having ascertained that meetings are quorate for voting purposes, close debates or initiate moves to that end, and then organise the voting on proposals. In Denmark, if the Speaker considers that the debate is proceeding in an unduly dilatory fashion, he can propose a clôture which is then put to the Folketing without debate after the names of the delegates requesting to speak have been read out.[73] In Iceland the authority to move a closure motion is vested in the Speaker or a fixed number of delegates. If a majority of the quorum (half plus one) is in favour, the closure is carried. In both cases, although the initiative comes from the Speaker, majority consent in the assembly is imperative to the success of a closure motion. No less than a two-thirds majority is required in Norway.[74]

Whenever the result appears a foregone conclusion, the Speaker of the Folketing (there are similar provisions elsewhere in the region) has the right to resolve a matter without a ballot, provided that no member objects.[75] Otherwise the Speaker organises a formal vote, the various methods for which are discussed in more detail in chapter 7. However, as the Standing Orders of the Storting put it, if there are several motions to be voted upon, they must be organised in a logical sequence, this ordering being agreed beforehand by the assembly as a whole.[76]

Further miscellaneous duties of the Speaker in plenum include ensuring that delegates use citation only sparingly in their speeches,[77] dealing with questions and interpellations (see chapter

8), and determining in exceptional circumstances whether to hold sittings behind closed doors.[78]

Finally, the Nordic Speakers are required to deal with a considerable amount of routine administrative work. In Denmark alone, the Speaker makes recommendations to parliament regarding delegates' applications for leave of absence from the assembly (whatever the reason given) and the need to summon deputy-members (also in Sweden when the sabbatical period sought is less than one month).[79] The Danish Speaker receives all communications addressed to the Folketing; is in charge of letters and papers issued by it, and in collaboration with the deputy-Speakers is in charge of the Folketing's internal organisation, i.e. he appoints and dismisses Folketing officials and so on.[80]

Do the four functions of the Nordic Speakers which we have identified afford to this highest elected official a *political* or merely a *technical* influence? In Iceland, Norway and Sweden, the Speaker is able to participate in a plenary debate and cast a vote. In Norway, when the Speaker wants to take part in a debate, which is quite common, he must hand over his duties to one of the deputy-Speakers and is not permitted to resume as Speaker the same day.[81] Incidentally, unlike his Swedish counterpart, the Norwegian Speaker is replaced by a deputy delegate only when he is on official leave of absence from parliament. Moreover, although in Norway and Iceland the Parliamentary Orders state that the Speaker may be exempted from membership of a standing committee, there have been recent instances of Speakers serving on such committees. In Finland, in contrast, the Speaker cannot speak at full-sittings or vote at plenary divisions; neither the Speaker nor deputy-Speakers exercise their legal right to attend meetings of parliamentary standing committees;[82] and while the Speaker does possess a constitutional right of legislative initiative, he does not customarily use it. Precisely as elsewhere in the region, however, the Finnish Speaker is actively engaged in partisan activity both inside and outside the chamber. He is able simultaneously to hold down a range of party jobs — as party chairman, for example, and/or to participate in meetings of his parliamentary party group. When Johannes Virolainen was elected Speaker of the Eduskunta in 1979, he was chairman of the Centre Party, a position he had held for fifteen years.

Indeed, the irony would appear to be that in contrast to the Speaker of the House of Commons, who is strictly impartial and is returned automatically to parliament at elections, Nordic Speakers can and do exercise political influence, though not it seems in their capacities as Speakers. When acting as Speaker their influence is primarily technical: as Svenn Stray put it in Norway, 'the main skill and art of the office is setting up the voting.[83] In the same vein, the Social Democrat K.A. Fagerholm, a Speaker in no less than sixteen post-war Eduskunta sessions, and V.J. Sukselainen, an Agrarian-Centre Speaker in another ten, have both noted that the Speaker has only a limited opportunity to influence proceedings and then he can only do so by the force of his personality. True, the status of the Speaker has been bolstered by the parties putting up strong candidates, many of whom are re-elected to the office. Even so, Leinonen's conclusion seems apposite: 'The Speaker's position as number two in the State hierarchy immediately behind the President is based not on the Speaker's influence as such, but rather reflects the perceived centrality of parliament as a political institution.'[84] Indeed the convention has developed in recent years that in the event of a governmental crisis (common enough, though rather less so than in the 1950s), the Finnish Speaker initiates the so-called 'Presidential round', *Presidentin kierros*, i.e. the President listens to the Speaker's opinion on the most suitable basis for a new government. But his role is in no sense comparable to that of his Swedish counterpart: indeed, the new Swedish constitution significantly enhances the weight of the office by investing the Riksdag Speaker with a vital role in government-building.[85] To what extent has this given the Swedish Speaker political influence?

To answer this, we must briefly describe the process involved in forming a new administration. When a Prime Minister is to be elected, the Speaker consults extensively with the representatives of the various parliamentary party groups, along with the deputy-Speakers, and ultimately makes a proposal on the matter to the Riksdag. Within the space of four days and then without a recommendation from a standing committee, the Riksdag must then vote on the proposal. If more than half the Riksdag's delegates vote against, the proposal is rejected — otherwise it is approved. In the event of a rejection, the whole process is repeated: if the Riksdag rejects the Speaker's proposal on a Prime Ministerial candidate on four occasions, the process is discontinued and new elections are held. Although the constitutional position of the Speaker is unquestionably strengthened and the parliamentary basis of government-building enhanced, the Speaker's independent room for manoeuvre in the process of selecting a Prime Minister should not be exaggerated. After the withdrawal of the Conservatives from the three-party bourgeois coalition in the spring of 1981, when the alternative government options were very limited, an editorial in *Dagens Nyheter* went so far as to suggest that 'one escape route in the event of political deadlock would be the creation of a civil service administration,' *tjänstemannaregering*, although it conceded that from a parliamentary viewpoint this would be 'a fiasco'.[86] Certainly Bengtsson made it clear that he had never for a moment considered a government of officials, although with the main opposition Social Democratic Party threatening to table a vote of no confidence in the new Prime Minister, he admitted he had taken something of a chance. Above all, however, Bengtsson emphasised the fundamentally technical character of his role and the weight he gave to his extensive consultations with the various parliamentary groups.[87]

If the influence of the Nordic Speakers is primarily technical rather than political or partisan, this is not to say that they are necessarily uncontroversial figures. Several have been former Prime Ministers or senior cabinet ministers, while others have engaged in a range of much-discussed extra-curricular activities. Johannes Virolainen, the former Eduskunta Speaker, is a case in point. Having stood unsuccessfully as the Centre Party's Presidential candidate in January 1982, he appears to have regarded his re-election as Speaker the following month as a springboard from which to perform an 'elder statesman' role in Finnish politics in the style of Willy Brandt and Edward Heath — not from the backbenches, but as Speaker and at times overshadowing the new President with his pronouncements. No longer chairman of the Centre Party, Virolainen publicly reiterated in May his long-held belief in the need for Swiss-style all-party government in Finland and in a speech commemorating the seventy-fifth anniversary of the unicameral Eduskunta the same month, he urged the need to reduce the powers of the Presidency — something, incidentally, which the new incumbent Mauno Koivisto also seems to favour, at least in respect of Presidential involvement in coalition-building and the Head of State's right to dissolve the assembly. Virolainen even contrived in another well-publicised speech to argue the need for co-operation between the parties of the centre and right before the general election in March 1983 with a view to offsetting a possible repeat of the so-called 'Koivisto phenomenon' of January 1982 — i.e. a Social Democratic landslide leading to a leftist hegemony of power. Matters were to become still more heated. In his capacity as chairman-designate of the Inter-Parliamentary Union (apparently with the connivance of the Centre Party's left-wing government allies, but unknown to the bourgeois Swedish People's Party Foreign Secretary), Virolainen extended an invitation to the PLO leader, Yassir Arafat, to visit Finland. This was later withdrawn in the face of criticism from the President, among others, that it violated the principle of Finnish neutrality. But then in the autumn of 1982 Virolainen visited Poland and held personal talks with General Jaruzelski — a trip which he claimed had been arranged much earlier. Thus, anonymity can hardly be said to have been one of the attributes of the Finnish Speaker in 1982.

Parliamentary control over the agenda

By dint of representation of the party groups and standing committees on the Speaker's Council, the Nordic legislatures participate in the organisation of their parliamentary agendas. However, this should be seen in the context of the customary priority given to government bills and the discretion granted the Speaker to alter the Orders of the Day in the circumstances already described.

The Swedish situation is typical. The Speaker's Council comprises the Speaker, the deputy Speaker, a representative of every parliamentary group (nominated annually), the chairmen of the Riksdag standing committees and the vice-chairman of the Riksdag's administration board, *riksdagensförvaltningsstyrelse*. In addition, the secretary of parliament, *kammarsekreteraren*, and the director of parliamentary administration are also permitted to attend. Meetings of the Speaker's Council, which are convened by the Speaker, are held in secret, although minutes are kept and should the Council wish to obtain information from somebody who is not a member, that person can be called to attend. The principal function of the Speaker's Council is to consider ways of dealing with and expediting the overall workload of the Riksdag.[88] In practice, the Speaker works out the parliamentary agenda and this is quickly approved. The Speaker' s Council also authorises the broadcasting of plenary proceedings on radio and television.[89] Two further objectives should be particularly emphasised. First, the Speaker's Council serves as an informal channel of élite communication: the chairmen of the parliamentary standing committees are able to report on the progress of a particular measure in their committee and provide the Speaker with an invaluable briefing session. Secondly, towards the end of a busy parliamentary session, the Speaker's Council acts as something of a 'ginger group' by enforcing a limit on the number of hours devoted to a particular measure.[90]

The composition of the Speaker's Councils elsewhere in the region is fundamentally similar to that in Sweden. In Finland the Speaker, deputy Speakers and chairmen of the Eduskunta standing committees make up the Speaker's Council;[91] in Denmark the Speaker's Council involves the five largest parties plus six parliamentary secretaries elected on the basis of proportional representation.[92] In Norway, the Speaker's Council[93] and the chairmen of the standing parliamentary committees constitute a planning committee, *arbeidsorningskomitéen*, which meets directly after the

Storting is convened to work out a schedule for the handling of all legislative matters.[94] However, with members of the opposition parties invariably represented on all the Speaker's Councils in the region, the legislature is permitted a role in outlining the sessional scheme of work undertaken by the Nordic parliaments. Moreover, once the weekly agenda is fixed, procedures exist (although they are seldom used) to alter and/or disrupt the Orders of the Day at short notice. For example, in Iceland an urgency question, which is allowed at the Speaker's discretion, may be added to the agenda on the morning of a day's proceedings; it gives the minister concerned only a few hours notice in which to prepare a reply. Then, distinctively, in Denmark there is the motion for a resolution on the order of business, *motiverat dagsorden*, so-called because the resolution, if adopted, always contains a formal reference to the Folketing's Order of Business on the day in question.[95] Used as an opposition device, the resolution, if successful, amounts in effect to a vote of no confidence in the government and enforces its resignation. Both these issues will be taken up again in chapter 8, which deals with the question of government accountability to parliament. While on the subject of no confidence, it is essential to note that the Nordic Speakers and their deputies, as the highest elected officials of parliament, are ultimately responsible for the management of legislative matters and the overall cohesion of the assembly, and as such they may be removed at the behest of (usually) a qualified majority of parliamentarians. Stated less dramatically, the procedures for such action exist. The Speaker or a member of the Speaker's Council can be forced out of office by the written demand of sixty Folketing members submitted three days in advance.[96] In Norway, if at least one-fifth of the members of the Storting, Odelsting or Lagting submit a written demand to the Speaker concerning a new election for the post, such an election becomes obligatory in the appropriate division.[97] In both divisions of the Althing, a two-thirds majority is required for a successful motion of no confidence in the officers; in Finland, the majority needed in the Eduskunta is five-sixths.

So much for the theory. In reality, throughout the region, the Order Paper is issued by the Speaker, usually after consultation with the cabinet and chairmen of the governmental parliamentary groups. As Thorsteinn Magnusson has observed of Iceland, 'priority is given to government bills and in effect it is the cabinet which controls the time in the Althing.'[98] Indeed, it is significant that although it takes a qualified majority of three-quarters of Althing delegates to put a matter on the agenda which is not on the Order Paper of the day, this is frequently done with the consent of all the political parties — not to oppose the administration or disrupt proceedings but for precisely the opposite reason, namely to expedite government business, particularly so as to finish more than one reading per day.

The stage is now set to consider the policy role of legislative plenaries in the Nordic parliaments. The credentials of delegates have been vetted and seating arrangements settled; a Speaker's Council has been elected and the selection of delegates to the various parliamentary standing committees ratified by the House as a whole. It is worth noting that the various committees prescribed for the purpose of electing standing committees are nowadays merely a formality, for while the principle of proportionality is strictly observed, the nomination of standing committee personnel is left entirely in the hands of the various party groups. The opening of parliament and the inaugural address — the Speech from the Throne in Norway or Presidential statement in Finland (both discussed at length in chapter 8) have been completed and the Nordic parliaments are ready to begin their routine work of debating and deliberating legislative proposals. Newly-elected delegates, for their part, will have familiarised themselves with the procedures relating to speech-making and will be preparing assiduously for their first contribution at a legislative plenary.

Legislative plenaries

Table 4.2 outlines the main parliamentary stages through which a bill must pass before it can be enacted as law in each of the five Nordic states. The information presented is fundamental to an understanding of the legislative process in the region and will be drawn on extensively throughout Part II. As for the incidence of legislative plenaries, the evident differences between one country and the next plainly have a bearing on the extent of the parliamentary scrutiny of proposals.

In the most recent unicameral system in Sweden, for example, a very simple legislative procedure is deployed which gives bills in effect only one reading on the floor of the Riksdag, so denying members the opportunity collectively to debate the main principles of a proposal before it is referred to a standing committee. Only very rarely are government bills considered in plenary before their transmission to a standing committee. One such unanticipated instance occurred in November 1982, shortly after the advent of the Palme Social Democratic administration when, ironically in the absence of any government ministers in the House, the opposition bourgeois parties seized on the so-called 'promised bill', *löftespropositionen*, together with the recently-announced crisis package of

Table 4.2. AN OUTLINE OF THE LEGISLATIVE PROCESS IN THE NORDIC STATES

Denmark

1. The Speaker (*formand*) of the Folketing announces a bill in the assembly and when drafted in statutory form this is distributed to delegates.

2. *First Reading*. This can take place at the earliest 2 days after the distribution of the bill to delegates. At this plenary stage, debate is confined to principles and amendments may not be moved. There is then an optional committee stage, which is in fact usual.

3. *Second Reading*. This can take place, at the earliest, 2 days after the conclusion of the First Reading. There is a debate on the bill in general, its individual sections, plus any amendments moved in standing committee. At the close of the Second Reading, the various sections of the bill together with any amendments are put to the vote. Matters are very often referred back to a parliamentary standing committee.

4. *Third Reading*. This can take place at the earliest 2 days after the close of the Second Reading. Two-fifths of the delegates in the Folketing can request that the Third Reading be postponed until 12 days after the Second Reading. Amendments may still be moved at this stage and are debated first. The bill is then brought to a general debate and vote.

5. If adopted at Third Reading, the bill is signed by the Folketing Speaker and one of the elected tellers, and is sent to the Prime Minister.

(*Forretningsorden for Folketinget* Kap IV 10–14. Optrykt September 1981.)

Norway

1. The Speaker's Council (*Presidentskapet*) makes a proposal on how government bills (*Kongelige proposisjoner*) and private initiatives should be handled when they are registered in the appropriate division of the Storting. Government bills, which should normally be introduced at the beginning or end of a parliamentary session, are usually sent direct to a standing committee. 'Law proposals' from a member of the Odelsting are also sent to an appropriate standing committee for its report.

2. *Standing committee stage*. A committee report is duplicated and distributed, but cannot be debated for at least 2 days after its circulation. In special cases, however, the appropriate division may decide by a simple majority to take the matter up before that.

3. *Plenary debate*. According to the Parliamentary Orders, 'when more important matters are considered, the Speaker shall first give members of the appropriate division the opportunity to express themselves in general'. As elsewhere in the region, however, there are (fairly generous) restrictions on the lengths of members' speeches.

(*continued*)

Table 4.2 (*continued*)

4. *Voting in plenum*. When a matter is finally decided, it cannot be reintroduced or taken up again during the same parliamentary session. If this proves urgently to be necessary it may be again taken up provided that it is not again sent to a standing committee.

(*Stortingets Forretningsorden* Kap. V:29, 30, 32. Kap. VI:35. Kap. VII:43, 47. Ajourført pr 1 mars 1979.)

Finland

1. A government bill is registered with the Office of Parliament and subsequently introduced by the Speaker. There may then follow a *Preliminary Debate* (*lähetekeskustelu*). This is entirely optional and is not mentioned in the Parliamentary Standing Orders. However, it has become increasingly common and is always held in connection with the Budget.

2. *Standing Committee*. A standing committee report when first introduced is placed 'on the table'; it may be placed on the table a second time if two or more delegates so request. If a standing committee report relates to the approval and/or rejection of a proposal for a new law it must be given three readings on the floor of the Eduskunta.

3. *First Reading*. The standing committee report is discussed whence, without a decision being taken the matter is sent to the Grand Committee.

4. *Grand Committee (suuri valiokunta)*. The 45-strong Grand Committee produces a report and proposals.

5. *Second Reading*. The Grand Committee's report provides the basis for a detailed plenary reading of the proposal. If the Grand Committee's report is not approved in its entirety, the proposal goes back to the Grand Committee which can approve or reject the changes made at Second Reading. At this stage, the Eduskunta or, indeed, the Grand Committee can request further statements from a specialist standing committee. At the *Continued Second Reading*, parliament decides simply to accept or reject any changes suggested by the Grand Committee.

6. *Third Reading*. This can take place at the earliest on the third day after the completion of the Second Reading. There is no discussion. The Eduskunta simply accepts or rejects the bill in the form in which it has emerged from Second Reading.

(*Valtiopäiväjärjestys*, 5 luku:65–66. Annettu Helsingissä tammikuun 13 päivänä 1928.)

Sweden

1. A government proposal is registered with the Office of Parliament. Notice of the bill is given by the Speaker at the first plenary sitting following

(*continued*)

Table 4.2. (*continued*)

the bill's distribution to delegates. The bill is placed 'on the table' at a plenary Riksdag sitting (*bordläggningsplenum*) if the assembly does not decide to send it directly to a standing committee.

2. *Standing Committee Stage*. Consideration of the bill and related initiatives. The committee report distributed to delegates. Before the ensuing plenary debate, the standing committee report is placed 'on the table' at two plenary sessions, if the Riksdag, at the request of the standing committee, does not decide one is sufficient.

3. *Plenary Debate* (*arbetsplenum*). General discussion on the committee report and any reservations tabled to it. The Speaker then closes the discussion and puts the proposal as presented by the standing committee to the vote (*talmannens förslag till beslut*). The matter may, of course, be referred back to the standing committee.

(*Riksdagsordningen* 3 Kap: 1; 4 Kap: 1; 5 Kap 1, 1:1 *i lydelse 1 januari 1980*.)

Iceland

1. The bill is registered with the Office of Parliament. Thereafter it is given a *First Reading* at which the general principles are debated.

2. The bill is then transmitted to one of the *permanent standing committees of the Althing*. There are 9 in the Lower House (*Nethri Deild*) with 40 delegates in all; 9 in the Upper Division (*Efri Deild*) with a total composition of 20 delegates; and another 4 permanent committees in the United Althing.

3. *The Second Reading or Report Stage*. This involves clause by clause scrutiny of the bill, although general speeches are still possible.

4. *The Third Reading*. This does not usually involve any debate.

A bill may be introduced into either division of the Althing but must complete its passage through both in order to be enacted as law. The procedure outlined above is identical in both divisions.

political and economic measures which they criticised as evidence of the government betraying its electoral promises. It was argued in general terms that the government wanted to reduce the budget deficit but was indulging in expenditure that would actually increase it. The Conservative leader, Ulf Adelsohn, noted, for example, that the government's 'aggressive devaluation' (16%) represented a risky undertaking given the need to cut central and local costs and stimulate industry, while the former Prime Minister and Centre Party leader, Thorbjörn Fälldin, feared that the proposed measures would lead to rapidly rising inflation and unemployment. With the Liberal Party leader also joining in the offensive, the motive was clearly to demonstrate a tactical unity on the part of the three non-socialist opposition groups. However, the whole episode was exceptional: under normal circumstances, government bills, controversial or otherwise, are sent directly to the appropriate standing committee.[99]

The same is emphatically true also in Norway. Bills introduced into the Storting are submitted direct to a parliamentary standing committee. Elsewhere, a First Reading in Denmark and Iceland and increasingly too a Preliminary Debate, *lähetekeskustelu* in Finland permit broad discussion of the principles of a bill before its progression to a standing parliamentary committee. However, largely irrespective of the differential structure of the legislative process in the region — a matter which will be explored further in later chapters — the engagement of Nordic parliamentarians in full-sitting debates is extremely low when measured in terms of delegate attendance.

Not surprisingly, systematic data on participation at plenary debates do not exist. Interview evidence, on the other hand, suggests that the number of delegates present is very low and has in fact declined over the last twenty or thirty years. There are 'often below ten' members at Storting plenaries,[100] while in similar debates in the Riksdag the figure is also 'frequently as low as ten delegates' (out of 349!).[101] These were just two of the estimates cited to the author. Indeed, in Denmark, the spectacle of an empty chamber has prompted the assertion that anybody wishing to keep something secret need only announce it in the Folketing, for then nobody will hear it! Recent adverse press comment about the sparse attendances at full-sitting debates of the Finnish Eduskunta — 'twenty-five per cent at a typical autumn plenary' would be a generous estimate[102] — prompted Johannes Virolainen, then Speaker, to recall how in the 1930s a radical leftist minister actually had his salary stopped for two days for absence without due cause, although Virolainen hastened to add that he was not himself advocating a return to such stringency.[103] In Iceland, too, visitors to the public gallery of the Althing frequently comment on the large areas of empty space in the chamber even if the matter has not as yet attracted the media attention it has in Finland. Symptomatic of the conduct of members throughout the region is the dash along the underground tunnel connecting the Storting library and parliamentary offices to the chamber at the sound of the 5-minute-bell in order to achieve the 50% minimum attendance necessary at the start and close of debates for valid decisions to be taken.

Strictly, of course, delegates do not need to attend plenaries to hear what is going on: they are able to follow debates by internal radio from their own rooms (except in Iceland where proceedings are transmitted to the cafeteria). But this is to consider the matter at a superficial level. More fundamentally, is the low level of delegate participation at plenaries the product of distinctively Nordic factors? The short answer is that it is not, although in the region there are three particularly important causes. First, parliamentary involvement in the policy formulation process — especially on commissions of inquiry in Sweden, but also on various labour-market committees and through informal contacts with officials — has tended to debase the status of plenaries as arenas for legislative deliberation. The crucial wheeling and dealing, in short, has involved parliamentarians as members of particular issue-communities. This demotion of plenaries has been accentuated in Sweden and Norway, where the structure of the legislative process, in short-circuiting the initial consideration of the principles of a bill, has subordinated the collective consideration of proposals to their detailed scrutiny in the standing committee groups.

Next, Nordic parliamentarians tend to see their role as being essentially that of specialists — as articulators of particular interests — rather than generalists in the classical mould of Edmund Burke. Thus they view the subject-specific standing committees as more conducive an avenue for exerting policy influence than plenary sessions. The centrality of the standing committee systems, in turn, has minimised the opportunity for delegates not involved in the detailed examination of an issue to make a meaningful plenary contribution.

Finally, by far the most important general explanation of the low level of delegate involvement at Nordic plenaries has been their almost total party-politicisation. For most delegates, the party groups which consider bills throughout the process of their parliamentary adoption constitute a more important forum for expressing their views than full sittings of the assembly. It is significant that in Sören Holmberg's study of Riksdag members, four out of five delegates reported no difficulty in obtaining an audience for their views in their parliamentary group.[104]

If delegate participation has been low, what can be said to have been the functions of plenary speeches? At one level, the task of the party spokesmen who dominate plenary discussion, particularly at the report and amendment stage, is publicly to clarify their parties' standpoint, oppose that of the other parties and, notably in the case of small parties, attempt to gain some electoral *kudos*.

For rank-and-file delegates, the character of plenary speeches — which are carefully prepared, well-documented, but generally dull — reflects a realistic appraisal of their modern function: this is not so much to sway fellow-members or influence the outcome of a vote as to advertise the delegate's concern to promote and defend his constituency interests. For example, the former Speaker of the Storting (now Foreign Secretary), Svenn Stray, could recall only one instance in a parliamentary career dating back to 1957 when a plenary speech — on fishing policy — had affected the ultimate result of the vote.[105] Significantly, it has been the practice to submit manuscripts to the national and (often more important) local press at least half a day before the relevant debate, a fact which has meant that the press gallery is also largely empty. 'It would almost be necessary to announce the outbreak of a Third World War in the Storting,' according to Svenn Stray, 'before the press gallery would take any notice, if a speech had not been submitted earlier to the newspapers!'[106] Indeed although, in Sten Sparre Nilson's view, Storting debates play an important part in moulding public opinion, given their detailed coverage in the press,[107] it is ironic that because of the convention of submitting the text of speeches in advance to newspapers the same coverage could probably be obtained without the debates themselves taking place. In any event, what now requires little further substantiation is that the impact of plenaries on policy adoption at the parliamentary stage is small. As Jaakko Nousiainen shows in the Finnish case, whereas in 1920 only 58% of government bills, after consideration by a standing parliamentary committee, passed the plenary stage without modification, this figure had risen to 78% in 1937 and no less than 94% in 1964.[108]

One final point on plenaries. Although Nordic delegates spend markedly more time in their parliamentary groups or even in the parliamentary cafeteria — where in Norway the parties traditionally have their own tables — than in full-sitting debates, their presence on the floor of the chamber varies according to the season. Special Saturday plenaries are not uncommon before Christmas in Norway[109] and the end of March in Denmark — on both occasions to complete consideration of the national budget — and generally throughout the region towards the end of the parliamentary year in late May or June to clear up unfinished business. However, these Saturday plenaries are solely legislative plenaries: there is really no machinery in the Nordic states for debating topical issues whereby the first emergency debate was made possible at Westminster on the South Atlantic crisis in April 1982, the first Saturday session of the House of Commons since the Suez crisis in 1956.[110] Certainly the end of the parliamentary session is specified in the Standing Orders of the regional parliaments: e.g. May 31 or at the latest June 15 in Sweden.[111] Yet invariably the Nordic assemblies exceed their prescribed term so involving delegates in long and frantic days of voting to finalise outstanding matters.

In Finland the controversial bill on gravel and grit compensation payments, *soralaki* (see chapter 7) passed through the Eduskunta on Midsummer Eve in 1981, while 10 June 1981, the last scheduled day of the Riksdag session, saw parliament begin proceedings at 0900 hours and continue till midnight.[112] In the Swedish case, the government crisis prompted by the withdrawal of the Conservatives that spring meant that the Prime Minister, Fälldin, had not answered the customary number of members' questions and interpellations.

All the Nordic legislatures observe at least one meeting-free week in the parliamentary calendar (in addition to holiday recesses at Christmas and Easter) to accommodate the annual session of the Nordic Council in February and March. In Sweden, emulating West German practice, there is a second free week at the end of October when there are usually few government bills to discuss. When in September 1981 the Prime Minister's secretary suggested the cancellation of this early autumn break to facilitate the passage of a much-criticised government bill reducing VAT,[113] it produced a powerful speech on the Riksdag floor from the Social Democratic leader, Olof Palme, backed by the second main opposition party the Conservatives, and resulted in a government defeat in the very first plenary of the 1981–2 session of the Riksdag.

REFERENCES

1. *Stortingets Forretningsorden* (*SFO*) 1:2.
2. *1981–82. Den vanlige fremgangsmåte ved Stortingets sammentreden.* The agenda of the 'ordinary' opening of the 1981–2 sesion of the Storting kindly supplied by Erik Mo, the Secretary-General of the Storting.
3. RO 2:3:1.
4. *Eduskunnan Työjärjestys* (*ET*) 1
5. *Valtiopäivät 1919, pöytäkirjat 1*, p. 20.
6. ET 40.
7. Gert Andersen, *Folkestyrets arbejdsplads*. Folketingets Præsidium: Beckers Papirindustri, 1974, p. 5.
8. SFO 1:2.
9. Gröndal (1981), p. 12.
10. Interview with Esko Almgren (then party secretary and now) chairman of the Christian League and parliamentary delegate for the Kymi constituency, 9.7.1979.
11. *Vuoden 1975 toiset valtiopäivät, pöytäkirjat 1*, pp. 26–32.
12. IC 57.
13. RO 2:4:1, 2:5.
14. RO 2:4. SFO 12:60–1.
15. Forretningsorden for Folketinget (FOF) 14:37.
16. FOF 14:38.

17. 'Stinkebombe i Foketinget'. *Nordisk Kontakt* 13/82, p. 999.
18. ET 58.
19. Jaakko Nousiainen, 'Valiokuntalaitos', in *Suomen kansanedustuslaitoksen historia X*. Helsinki: Eduskunnan historia-komitea, 1977, pp. 437–8.
20. Interview with Esko Almgren 9.7.1980.
21. 'Utkörd ur Riksdagen'. *Aftonbladet* 12.3.1981.
22. Interview with Ingemund Bengtsson 10.9.1981.
23. SFO 7:35.
24. FOF 11:28:1.
25. ET 37
26. RO 2:14:1.
27. SFO 7:37.
28. ET 37. SFO 7:37.
29. RO 2:15:1, 3.
30. FOF 11:28:3.
31. FOF 11:30.
32. *Valtiopäiväjärjestys (VJ)* 5:58.
33. Nousiainen (1977), p. 457.
34. George Thomas, 'The Changing Face of Parliamentary Democracy? *The First Hansard Society Lecture* 17.5.1982.
35. Interview with the Conservative First Speaker of the Folketing, Erik Ninn-Hansen 21.4.1982. Ninn-Hansen is, at the time of writing, Minister of Justice.
36. Interview with the Riksdag Speaker, Ingemund Bengtsson 10.9.1981.
37. RO 2:15:4.
38. SFO 7:35.
39. RO 2:14.
40. RO 2:14:1.
41. RO 2:14:2
42. SFO 7:35.
43. FOF Bilag: Taletidsregler.
44. Kullervo Leinonen, *Puhemies eduskuntatyön johtajana Suomessa*. Projektiin — 'Edustuksellisen kansanvallan ja parlamentaarisen demokratian toimivuus Suomessa' kuuluva tutkimus (Pardem 3/1979). Tampereen yliopisto, politiikan tutkimuksen laitos, tutkimuksia 52, 1979.
45. David Arter, '*Social Democracy in a West European Outpost: The Case* of the Finnish SDP'. *Polity* 12, 3, 1980, pp. 373–5.
46. Leinonen (1979), p. 9.
47. SFO 2:4.
48. 'Författningsreformer aktualiseras på nytt'. *Nordisk Kontakt* 7/82, pp. 524–5.
49. 'Funktionsduglig riksdag under hela valperioden'. *Nordisk Kontakt* 14/82, pp. 1088–90.
50. RF 4:2.
51. Interview with Ingemund Bengtsson 10.9.1981.
52. FOF 2:4.
53. RO 1:7.
54. FOF 11:32:1.
55. ET 31.
56. RO 2:6.
57. FOF 11:32:4.
58. RO 1:3.
59. RF 4:1.
60. SFO 2:6.
61. FOF 11:26.
62. ET 39.
63. FOF 11:29.

64. FOF 11:32:5.
65. RO 2:7:1.
66. RO 4:2:1.
67. VJ 5:80.
68. ET 40.
69. RO 2:9.
70. FOF 11:32:3.
71. RO 6:4.
72. 'Febril aktivitet i riksdag och utskott'. *Nordisk Kontakt* 9/82, pp. 686–7.
73. FOF 11:31.
74. SFO 6:37.
75. FOF 12:35:1.
76. SFO 7:43.
77. SFO 6:40. FOF 11:27.
78. SFO 12:60–61.
79. RO 1:8:1.
80. FOF 18:44.
81. SFO 7:35.
82. VJ 4:52.
83. Interview with Svenn Stray 30.9.1981.
84. Leinonen (1979), p. 90.
85. RF 6:23.
86. 'Bohman krävs på besked om han stöder mittenregering'. *Dagens Nyheter* 14.5.1981.
87. Interview with Ingemund Bengtsson 10.9.1981.
88. RO 1:7:1, 2, 3.
89. RO 2:5.
90. Interview with Ingemund Bengtsson 10.9.1981.
91. VJ 4:54.
92. FOF 2:2:1.
93. SFO 2:4–6.
94. SFO 3:22.
95. FOF 9:24. 8:19:1. 8:21:4.
96. FOF 2:2:2.
97. SFO 2:4.
98. Interview with Thorsteinn Magnusson, a doctoral student at the University of Exeter doing research on the Althing standing committees.
99. 'Oväntad remissdebatt om krispaketet'. *Från Riksdag & Departement* 19.11.1982
100. Interview with Erik Mo 17.11 1981.
101. Discussion with John H. Hagard 10.11.1981.
102. Interview with Esko Almgren 9.7.1980
103. 'Minulta ei mene aika kapakoissa istumiseen'. *Uusi Suomi* 17.5.1981.
104. Sören Holmberg, *Riksdagen representerar Svenska folket. Empiriska studier i representativ demokrati.* Lund: Studentlitteratur, 1974, p. 245.
105. Interview with Svenn Stray 30.9.1981.
106. Ibid.
107. Sten Sparre Nilson, *Norway's National Assembly: The Storting.* Oslo: Norway Information UDA 132/77, p. 4.
108. Jaakko Nousiainen, 'Näkökohtia eduskunnan asemasta ja päätöksentekojärjestelmästä. *Politiikka* 2, 1977, pp. 113–131.
109. SFO 4:25.
110. 'MPs clamour for Carrington and Nott to quit'. *The Guardian* 5.4.1982.
111. RO 1:4.
112. 'Bråda dagar för riksdagen'. *Dagens Nyheter* 3.6.1981.
113. Göran Johansson, 'Inställ arbetsfria veckan'. *Dagens Nyheter* 27.9.1981.

5

PARLIAMENTARY STANDING COMMITTEES: THE CORPORATE OR PERMEABLE TYPE?

'In the corporate type of standing committee, members are orientated towards the legislature, emphasize their committee expertise and have a strong sense of identification with the committee. On the permeable type of committee, members lack a sense of group identity, de-emphasize committee expertise and indicate an orientation to political forces outside the legislature.' — Richard F. Fenno Jr, *Congressmen in Committees* (1973), pp. 278–9

All bills in the Nordic assemblies, whether government or private member's proposals, have to be scrutinised and reported on by a standing parliamentary committee before becoming law.[1] Despite some variation in the exact steps involved in the parliamentary approval of bills, a committee stage is compulsory throughout the region. It is at this juncture that every bill receives, as the Swedes put it, 'compulsory prep', *beredningstvång*. Throughout the region, too, as the Standing Orders of the Folketing state, 'a matter may be referred to a committee for examination at any stage of its consideration'.[2] At the discretion of parliament, in other words, a bill can be returned to a committee, or alternatively it can be directed to another for further consideration. As the Riksdag Standing Orders require, a matter on which a standing committee has reported can be returned to it for extra examination if at least one-third of those voting in plenary session so demand, although this can occur only once in connection with a particular measure.[3] Standing committees thus occupy a pivotal position in the parliamentary deliberation of proposals.

In this chapter we raise a number of central questions relating to the role of parliamentary standing committees in the Nordic legislative process. How important are the standing committees in the region as negotiating sites for the deliberation and adoption of public policy? What are the primary determinants of their legislative influence? Above all, are the Nordic standing committees essentially of the corporate or the permeable type? The discussion is inevitably set within the framework of the vastly increased workload facing parliamentary standing committees (a corollary of the general growth in the scale and scope of government). Having considered a number of fundamental practical questions — *inter alia* their membership and recruitment, work procedure, staffing etc., along with their impact on the vital matter of the annual Finance Bill — we will then seek to test a number of hypotheses related to the size, plurality and subject-specific character of the Nordic standing committees. Three primary conclusions are reached. The first is that the policy impact of standing parliamentary committees is not narrowly determined by fixed structural factors such as size and subject-specificity: rather, the extent and significance of their role is integrally tied to the dynamics of the contemporary political situation. Secondly the parliamentary party groups have *the decisive influence* at the assembly stage of policy adoption. Finally, although the Nordic standing committees differ considerably from the weak permeable committees of Westminster, the power of partisan alignments has offset the emergence of the predominantly corporate orientation of a number of Congressional standing committees.

Despite the unquestionably central part they play at the assembly phase of policy adoption, there is an almost total lack of constitutional prescription regarding the role of Nordic standing committees. In the two oldest documents in the region, Norway (1814) and Finland (1919), it is not surprising perhaps that there is no reference to standing committees, although the Finnish Parliament Act of 1928 — which has acquired the status of basic law — does authorise a small number of permanent legislative committees.[4] It is surprising, however, that the post-war constitutions of Iceland (1944) and Denmark (1953) do not mention parliamentary standing committees. In the former, the only provision relating to parliamentary committees concerns investigatory bodies operating outside the legislative process. Article 39 of the Icelandic Constitution states that each chamber of the Althing has the right to appoint committees of its members to investigate important matters of public interest, and proceeds to empower both chambers to grant these committees authority to demand oral and written reports from either government officials or private persons. The Danish constitution makes similar provisions for investigatory parliamentary commissions[5] (see chapter 9), but although it includes a surprisingly detailed section on Folketing procedure, it contains no reference to standing committees. Only in the most recent form of government in the region, the Swedish *Regeringsformen* are standing committees given constitutional status when it is stated that the Riksdag shall elect standing committees which should include a Constitutional Committee, a Finance Committee and a Committee on Taxation and that matters should be prepared in committee before a final decision in the assembly.[6]

The virtual absence of any constitutional recognition of the crucial role played by legislative committees in the Nordic region might well be regarded as little more than an historic curiosity. The Basic Law of the Federal German Republic (1949) and the Fifth French Republican Constitution (1958) contain sections on standing parliamentary committees (article 43 in each case), although in both France and West Germany the actual functioning of standing committees has been governed as much by conventional practice as by the letter of the constitution. Hence in France the aspirations of the constitution-makers to reduce the powers that were enjoyed by committees in the Fourth Republic — by creating a dual system in which the majority of bills would be considered by *ad hoc* committees while only a few would go before the significantly reduced number of specialist committees — were frustrated by a combination of the procedural rules of parliament and the traditions of French political life. Certainly the role of standing committees cannot be examined in France, any more than in the Nordic states, simply by reference to the constitution.

In the Nordic states, absence of constitutional recognition masks the well-institutionalised position of the standing committee system. In Sweden, the oldest standing committee, the Constitutional Committee, dates back to 1809, while in Denmark the strategic Finance Committee was effectively incorporated into the legislative process in 1888–9 Folketing session — to cite but two random examples. In Finland, moreover, a parliamentary standing committee system was operational with the transition to unicameralism, although before Independence a decade later the Russian Tsar's repeated dissolution of the Eduskunta meant that standing committees invariably failed to complete their consideration of proposals.

In the Standing Orders of the five national parliaments are regulations on the nature and procedure of standing committees and these will be drawn on throughout this chapter. Ultimately, however, any analysis of the role of standing committees at the parliamentary stage of policy adoption must view their activities in the context of the vastly increased legislative output of modern governments. Indeed, it is with considerable justice that standing committees have been described as the workhorses of the legislature.

The increased workload of standing committees

Some of the substantially heightened workload of Nordic standing committees has been caused by the enormous rise in the number of private initiatives to be considered; mostly, however, standing committees have been engaged in the time-consuming and increasingly technical task of examining government proposals, the number of which has grown significantly, albeit unevenly, in the region

Table 5.1. THE INCREASE IN GOVERNMENT BILLS IN THE ICELANDIC ALTHING, 1940–80

	Government bills	
Session	*No. introduced*	*No. passed*
1940–1	14	14
1950–1	61	53
1960–1	65	55
1970–1	79	61
1980–1	98	84

since the Second World War. In Iceland, as Table 5.1 illustrates, there has been a steady sevenfold increase in the number of government bills introduced into the Althing.

Elsewhere, the rate of the upward trend in government proposals has been subject to marked variation. In Sweden, where in contrast to the rest of the region the contours of the party system have remained stable, an average of 183 government bills introduced into the Riksdag annually in the period 1971–80 was exceeded by 15% in 1979 as Table 5.2 shows. Also, particular standing committees have experienced notable discrepancies in the volume of their legislative business: such heavily-worked standing committees as Industry, Finance and Taxation have contrasted sharply with the much lighter loads of, say, the committees on Defence and Social Insurance in Sweden or the Bank Committee in Finland. The sched-

Table 5.2. THE VARIATION IN THE NUMBER OF GOVERNMENT BILLS IN SWEDEN, 1971–80

	Government bills
Year	*No. introduced*
1971	181
1972	147
1973	204
1974	188
1975	190
1976	177
1977	172
1978	186
1979	210
1980	176

Source: Konstitutionsutskottets betänkande 1980/81:25 Granskningsbetänkande. Bilaga 3, p. 109.

ule of a number of committees, moreover, has been dominated by the examination of a single issue: without the 6 billion kronor Development Aid and Co-operation Budget (fixed at 1.014% of GNP), the agenda of the Riksdag Foreign Affairs Committee would be much lighter.[7] As Hellevik has observed in Norway, it has been largely the gentle workload of the Storting standing committee on Foreign Affairs that has attracted senior parliamentarians, particularly the leaders of the party groups, and lent the committee something of an upper chamber quality.[8] Notwithstanding such variations, it is clear that there has been a general increase in the amount of legislative business to be handled by the standing committees of the region commensurate with the growth in the post-war state.

At the most superficial level, evidence of this can be found in the frequency with which standing committee meetings are held, and in the practical difficulties of timing them to take place when a plenary session of parliament is not being held. The regional norm of making a clear distinction between the collective consideration of bills in plenaries and their detailed deliberation in standing committees, while at the same time emphasising the complementarity of both stages, is enshrined in the various parliamentary standing orders. In Sweden, a standing committee is allowed to meet concurrently with a plenary session only when the latter is not taking a decision on a legislative proposal (i.e. it is dealing with questions and interpellations) and when the intention to convene a committee meeting is notified in advance to the Riksdag as a unanimous decision of the standing committee.[9]

In Denmark, the Folketing Standing Orders state more briefly that normally standing committee work shall not coincide with full sittings of parliament.[10] Despite this last ruling, it is symptomatic of the overall growth in legislative output, as well as parliamentary concern effectively to cope with the wide range of government proposals through a modernised committee system,[11] that of the thirty-two times specified for weekly meetings of the permanent standing committees in the second session of the 1981–2 Folketing, only fourteen such meetings were scheduled to begin earlier than the 1 o'clock start for plenary sessions.[12] Moreover, a number of these, in particular the Friday meetings of the Market Relations Committee which start at noon, actually extend into time allocated for plenary meetings of the assembly. With some standing committees convening as often as thrice weekly (the Justice Committee always in the afternoon) it is small wonder that a female delegate elected for Sjælland in 1977 was prompted to comment: 'I have three committee meetings today and shall be able to visit the plenary session only to vote.[13] About two-thirds of Danish standing committee meetings coincide with Folketing plenaries. It is, of course, not only the frequency of standing committee meetings which serves to indicate their increased workload; so too does the existence of a few standing committees designed to deal with the overspill of proposals from the other committees. In Finland, for example, the Second Legal Affairs Committee, *toinen lakivaliokunta*, has functioned as a type of relief committee alleviating some of the burden on the other standing committees.[14] The General Affairs Committee in the United Althing has performed a somewhat similar role.

However, the increase in the amount of legislative business has not always been reflected in a growth in the number of standing committee reports. In Sweden, there has been a tendency for committees to group together private initiatives on related topics for common consideration: in the 1980–1 session of the Riksdag, the Foreign Affairs Committee undertook conjoint examination of separate motions from non-socialist delegates, all of whom were requesting in slightly differing ways that Sweden establish diplomatic relations with the Vatican — Sweden, Norway and Denmark are the only West European states not to have such relations. These requests were turned down on the grounds that informal channels worked well enough.[15]

This type of common treatment of measures covering similar areas has meant that despite a significant rise in the number of private initiatives, the number of standing committee reports has actually fallen in Sweden[16] — from 270 in 1973 to 251 in 1981 (see Table 5.3). Many of the private initiatives can in any event be fairly summarily dispatched: the Swedish Foreign Affairs Committee took little time to reject as simply impracticable a motion from two Conservatives that the Riksdag request the government to persuade the United Nations to work to give Soviet citizens access to Bibles and Christian literature.[17]

Committees can also rationalise their workload by relegating measures where necessary. In Sweden, standing committees have considerable licence over the timing of reports, the only formal requirement being that this must be done at the latest by the close of the year following that in which the proposal was introduced; this has allowed Riksdag committees (sometimes tactically) to postpone consideration of proposals and initiatives from the spring, when the majority are introduced, till the much quieter autumn session of parliament.

Notwithstanding these expedients — meeting during time set aside for plenaries, grouping together related proposals for common consideration, relegating the examination of bills from one session

Table 5.3. THE ANNUAL NUMBER OF STANDING COMMITTEE REPORTS IN THE SWEDISH RIKSDAG, 1973–81

	No. of committee reports
1973	270
1974	251
1975	295
1976	216
1977	238
1978	248
1979	272
1980	247
1981	251

Source: Statistik rörande Riksdagsarbetet. Kammarkansliet 1981-12-17, p. 3.

to the next — the capacity of standing parliamentary committees in the region to withstand the increased legislative workload has been strictly limited, and many measures, — mostly private initiatives — are simply not dealt with and thereby lost. In Finland in 1970, 323 out of a total of 415 private members' bills were not scrutinised in parliamentary standing committee, while in 1979, the respective figures were 353 out of 389; yet only 34 of the 199 government bills in 1970 and 20 out of 233 a decade later were not handled in standing committee.[18] Uniquely in Finland, the work procedure of standing committees gives pride of place to government bills and lowest priority to the three main types of private initiative as Table 5.4 demonstrates. But elsewhere in the region, private initiatives have mostly suffered from an inferior status *vis-à-vis*

Table 5.4. THE WORK PROGRAMME OF FINNISH PARLIAMENTARY STANDING COMMITTEES

Matters are generally considered in the following order:

1. statements to other standing committees regarding bills and reports;
2. government proposals;
3. government reports to parliament;
4. government information, orders (*asetukset*) and general cabinet decisions;
5. statements to other standing committees regarding parliamentary initiatives;
6. private members' bills;
7. members' request proposals;
8. connected parliamentary bills.

Source: Eduskuntamuistio 1979, p. 21.

government bills, albeit without the same degree of formalisation as in Finland.

Government proposals also fare much better because in a number of the Nordic states standing committees are authorised to meet during the parliamentary recess to deal with new or outstanding matters. In Sweden the Finance and Taxation committees working together can deal with matters relating to indirect taxation when the Riksdag is not in session, while other standing committees can also call meetings out of session when the situation so requires.[19] It was the conjoint Finance and Taxation committee handling of controversial government proposals on VAT increases over the summer of 1980 which prompted the Opposition, with the necessary 150 delegates,[20] to force the Speaker to call the only extraordinary session of the Riksdag since the war. In Finland, following an amendment to the Eduskunta Standing Orders in 1969,[21] standing committees have also been able to convene during parliamentary vacations.[22] Even in Denmark the Finance Committee meets out of session to expedite its handling of the budget, although it does so without a legal remit. The finance bill is usually distributed to committee members in August and they then discuss it at a type of report stage in mid-September before the opening of the new parliamentary session.[23] In practice, therefore, and in this instance only, the Danish finance bill, in the manner of all government proposals in Sweden and Norway, is discussed in standing parliamentary committee *before* its first reading on the floor of the Folketing.

Even though our analysis of the regional standing committees is set in the context of the general growth in the amount and complexity of government activity since World War II, and we have established the limited capacity of a number of parliamentary committees to cope with the increased volume of business, at least in respect of private members' bills, this is not to suggest that standing committees have declined in importance. Although all proposals have to be vetted by a standing committee, the managerial problems delineated earlier should not be exaggerated: the vast majority of government bills are dealt with, the committee systems themselves have adapted and expanded, while individual committees are only rarely called upon to convene outside parliamentary sessions. Rather our discussion so far has been designed as a framework for our next task, which will be to examine the major determinants of the legislative influence of standing committees in the region. This in turn will lead us to the fundamental question of this chapter: how important are regional standing committees as negotiating sites in the deliberation and adoption of policy? Putting this same question in the terms of Hernes' analysis in Norway, how valid is it to say that standing 'committees are the crucial stage in the decision-making process in parliament because most control over the outcome of decisions is bestowed on the committees'?[24]

The major determinants of the policy influence of parliamentary standing committees

In the broadest terms, the policy impact of legislative committees in the region may be said to derive from two mutually reinforcing factors: their *size and plurality* and their *specialist nature*. The Nordic parliaments are characterised by a large number of relatively small permanent or regular *ad hoc* standing committees which would tend, all other things being equal, to reduce the amenability of the committee system to government control. In this context it is worth recalling Jean Blondel's hypothesis that 'the maximum effectiveness of assemblies is obtained if small groups are created'.[25]

The precise number and composition of the standing committee systems in the region are set out in Table 5.5. As can be seen, the number of regular standing committees ranges from thirteen in Finland to no less than twenty-two in Iceland and their membership varies from 7 delegates in Iceland to 21 in Denmark and Finland. This situation is directly comparable to that in West Germany, where there are 19 Bundestag committees ranging in strength from 13 to 33 members and where, according to Loewenberg and Patterson, committees are of great importance in legislative policy-making.[26] Indeed, the West German standing parliamentary committees tend to be rather larger than those in the Nordic region: e.g. the smallest two Bundestag committees (on Sport and Research and Technology respectively) have 17 members, more than any Swedish committees.

Not surprisingly perhaps, the number of standing committees has varied over the years within the Nordic states. Before 1930, the Storting had an average of 17/18 standing committees; this dropped

Table 5.5. THE NUMBER AND COMPOSITION OF STANDING COMMITTEES IN THE NORDIC STATES

	No. of permanent committees	*Ad hoc committees*	*Membership*
Denmark	21	1	17–21
Norway	12	—	9–18
Finland	5	8	11–21
Iceland	22	—	7–9
Sweden	16	—	15

to 16 between 1931 and 1949 and to 13 between 1949 and 1973. Since 1973 Norway has had only twelve permanent standing committees. Occasional measures of structural rationalisation have also been evident: the present 13-member Storting Communications Committee was formed by a merger of two previous committees — those of Post, Telegraphs and Coastal Traffic and of Roads and Railways.

The least institutionalised standing committee system in the region — at least, in the strict legal sense — is that in Finland, where, until an amendment in 1983, the Parliament Act required only five permanent committees to be elected within 5 days of the opening of a new parliamentary session and where, even today, the number of permanent standing committees in the Eduskunta is exceeded by the eight specialist but 'extraordinary' *ylimääräisiä*, committees. Before a major reform in the committee system in 1971, the situation in Denmark was similar in kind if not detail — there were only four permanent Folketing committees, the others being temporary, *ad hoc* and bill-specific along the lines of standing committees at Westminster. Even after the constitutional reforms of 1969–74 in Sweden, the revised Parliamentary Standing Orders required the appointment at the beginning of each electoral period of no more than three *regular* standing committees — on the Constitution, Finance and Taxation — along with at least twelve others whose substantive competence was not laid down.[27] Since then the number of permanent and regular Riksdag committees has increased greatly with the approval of an amendment to the Standing Orders stipulating that by the eighth day of the new session at the latest, parliament shall nominate sixteen policy-specific standing committees for the full period till the next general election.[28]

Outside Finland, and despite facilitating provisions in the Parliamentary Standing Orders, the creation of *ad hoc* standing committees has been relatively infrequent. In Norway, the Storting did set up an *ad hoc* committee during the 1955–6 session to deal with the question of State companies,[29] and another was formed in 1963 in connection with the Svalbard affair. In Denmark an *ad hoc* committee on Youth Employment was created on 11 February 1982 following pressure from the Radical Liberals, *Radikale Venstre*;[30] the Radicals had wanted a specific ministry created to deal with the growing problem of youth unemployment, but the compromise proposal for an *ad hoc* standing committee — operational for a single Folketing session only — came from the Social Democratic Minister of Labour.[31]

The rules on the size of standing committees in the region can be summarised briefly. All legislative committees in Denmark, including special *ad hoc* committees, shall contain seventeen delegates except the 21-member Energy Committee; in Sweden, all the Riksdag's committees have 15 members; while in Iceland every standing committee has 7 members, except the Budget Committee in the United Althing with 9. The size of Norwegian standing committees varies, from the nine-member Justice Committee to the eighteen-member Finance Committee. In Finland alone, it is only the *minimum size* of standing committees which is prescribed in the Parliamentary Standing Orders: namely at least 21 for the Finance Committee and 17 in the other permanent committees except the eleven-member Bank Committee — the same minimum number as for any *ad hoc* legislative committees that are created.

The size of Nordic standing committees is relatively low when compared with the rest of Western Europe, cf. the 125 members in a number of committees created by the French Fifth Republican constitution, while the number of committees remains relatively high — in France, only six legislative committees are legally required. Moreover, the structure of the Nordic standing committee systems has proved adaptive, and as the new Storting committee on Energy and Industry set up in October 1981 and the Folketing committee on Youth Unemployment illustrate, there has been no tendency for a reduction in the plurality of standing committees — if anything, the reverse. Although too much should not be made of numbers alone, the large number of relatively small permanent or regular *ad hoc* standing committees in the Nordic parliaments needs re-emphasis. Gordon Smith suggests the existence of 'an inverse relationship between the number of assembly committees and the power of the government. It is not difficult to see why: the greater the number of small groups, the less amenable to government control they are than a single, large one.'[32]

There is already a problem of government control created by the existence of a relatively large number of small standing committee groups. This is compounded, potentially at least, by the subject-specific nature of Nordic standing parliamentary committees, which has tended to encourage member-expertise and development of a common interest orientation. The potency of small, substantive parliamentary groups can best be illustrated in a broader West European perspective. In France in 1958, the constitution-makers were concerned *inter alia* to avoid the proliferation of standing committees, comprising small numbers of highly expert members, which had existed under the Fourth Republic. This had resulted in pressure groups and more generally sectional interests exerting a considerable and direct influence on the parliamentary scrutinisation of proposed legislation. This type of specialist standing committee system, in short, represented a significant brake on the executive: indeed, the fact that limitations on its use have been thought necessary during the Fifth Republic indicates just how important the control function of specialist standing committees can be when deployed to the full.[33] Just as in West Germany today, there is a relatively high number of standing committees in the Nordic region, each focusing on a substantive legislative area normally corresponding to the competence of a single government department; and each involves a stable membership recruited essentially on the basis of known interest or training and is supported by a parliamentary secretariat of varying size. But this is *not* to say that Nordic standing committees enjoy comparable powers to those in the French Fourth Republic.

Before elaborating on these characteristics, it is worth recalling that, by contrast, British standing committees are characterised by neither subject specialism nor departmental anchorage; instead, they are 'bill-related' institutions, every one a purpose-specific creation extant only for as long as a single bill is being considered. A reminder of this is the alphabetical ordering of committees, so that in any parliamentary session a number of separate and sequentially-formed bodies, all known as Standing Committee A, will deliberate on government proposals spanning the entire policy spectrum. As already mentioned, this was the system which, in its essentials, operated in Denmark before the committee reform of 1971: each bill had its own committee and in addition there were between three and five permanent committees. The increasingly specialised nature of government, combined with more immediate pragmatic considerations of work schemes and facilitating the planning of deliberation in the legislature, prompted a transition to the type of subject-specific standing committees which Sweden had adopted at the same time in connection with the move to unicameralism, and which Norway and Finland had developed (albeit less comprehensively) much earlier.

The policy range of the standing committee systems in the region is set out in Tables 5.6–5.10. It can be seen that the degree of substantive differentiation is highest in Denmark where, uniquely in the region, there are standing committees concerned with Science and Technology, Immigration and the Environment. It is lowest in Finland, which lacks *inter alia* the standing committees on Education and Industry which are found almost everywhere else in the region. Norway and Sweden exhibit medium levels of functional differentiation within their standing committee systems. Sweden, for example, has no Immigration-Naturalisation committee such as Denmark has, although there has been an Immigration Minister, and although a number of controversial issues affecting aliens — e.g. the fate of Turkish refugees seeking political asylum — have attracted considerable parliamentary interest in recent years.[34] In Norway a number of standing committees (e.g. Energy and Industry, Church and Education) cover policy areas which in Denmark enjoy separate committee status.

Throughout the region, of course, standing committees reflect traditional economic interests, viz. Fisheries in Iceland, Shipping and Fisheries in Norway, and Agriculture and Forestry in Finland; much newer economic commitments and alignments as with the Market Relations Committee in Denmark; and contemporary concerns and issues such as the Youth Employment Committee in Denmark. Most Nordic standing committees deal with legislative proposals which come within the orbit of a particular department

Table 5.6. DENMARK: LEGISLATIVE STANDING COMMITTEES IN THE FOLKETING

Permanent committees

Labour Market
Housing
Energy
Labour Force (*erhvervsudvalget*)
Finance
Defence
Immigration and Naturalisation
Ecclesiastical Affairs
Municipal Affairs
Cultural Affairs
Agricultural and Fisheries
Market Relations (EC)
Environment and Regional Planning
Public Works
Political Economy
Justice (*retsudvalget*)
Taxes and Duties
Social Affairs
Education
Foreign Affairs
Science and Technology

Ad hoc standing committees

Youth Employment

Forretningsorden for Folketinget Kapitel III: 7. Stk 3–23. J.H. Schultz A/S, København, September 1981, pp. 11–16. *Oversigt over stående udvalg 1981–82* (2. samling), Folketingssekretariatet, Januar 1982. The Standing Orders Committee (*Udvalget for forretningsorden*) and the Credentials Committee (*Udvalget til valgs provelse*) are excluded from the above list.

Table 5.7. FINLAND: LEGISLATIVE STANDING COMMITTEES IN THE EDUSKUNTA

Permanent Committees

Constitutional
Legal Affairs
Foreign Affairs
Finance
Bank

Regular ad hoc committees

Economy
Law and Economy
Cultural Affairs
Agricultural and Forestry
Social Affairs
Traffic
Defence
Second Legal Affairs (*toinen lakivaliokunta*)

Valtiopäiväjärjestys (annettu Helsingissä tammikuun 13 päivänä 1928), 4 luku: 40–53. *Eduskuntamuistio 1979*. Valtion painatuskeskus, Helsinki 1979, p. 10. The legislative, but non-specialist Grand Committee, *suuri valiokunta*, is not included above. Every bill, however, must be considered in the Grand Committee between its First and Second Readings.

Table 5.8. ICELAND: STRUCTURE OF THE LEGISLATIVE COMMITTEE SYSTEM IN PARLIAMENT

Permanent committees in both chambers

Finance and Trade
Communications
Agriculture
Fishery
Industry
Social Affairs
Health and Insurance
Education
General Affairs

Permanent committees in the United Althing

Budget
Foreign Affairs
Industrial Affairs
General Affairs

Thingsköp Althingis. Prentvo i október 1976 að tilhlutun skriftstofu Althingis, pp. 33–4.

Table 5.9. NORWAY: LEGISLATIVE STANDING COMMITTEES IN THE STORTING

Permanent committees
Energy and Industry
Finance
Consumer Affairs and Administration (*forbruker og administrasjonskomitéen*)
Defence
Justice
Church and Education
Municipal Affairs and the Environment
Agriculture
Communications (*samferdsels komitéen*)
Shipping and Fisheries
Social Affairs
Foreign Affairs and the Constitution

Stortingets Forretningsorden, Kapittel 10–12. A/S O. Fredr. Arnesen, Oslo 1979, pp. 8-11. *Stortinget 1981–85*. Arnesen, Oslo 1981, pp. 24–30. The Extended Foreign and Constitutional Affairs Committee (see chapter 9), the Election Committee and the Scrutiny Committee which are not concerned with ongoing proposals are excluded from the list above. So, too, is the Credentials Committee (*fullmaktkomité*). It is worth noting, however, that in unique circumstances following electoral irregularities in the constituencies of Troms and Buskerud at the general elections of September 1981, the Credentials Committee decided unanimously that the poll in these two areas should be re-run. 'To fylker får omvalg'. *Aftenposten* 3.10.1981, p. 8.

Table 5.10. SWEDEN: LEGISLATIVE STANDING COMMITTEES IN THE RIKSDAG

Permanent committees
Constitutional
Finance
Taxation
Justice
Legal Affairs
Foreign Affairs
Defence
National Insurance (*socialförsäkringsutskott*)
Social Affairs
Cultural Affairs
Traffic
Agriculture
Industry
Labour Market
Public Works (*civilutskott*)
Education

Riksdagsordningen 4 Kap: 2:1. Gotab Stockholm 1980, pp. 39–43. *Riksdagen 1981/82* Norstedts Tryckeri, Stockholm 1981, pp. 49–64.

or section within it — the Agricultural committees naturally scrutinise the output of the Agriculture ministries etc. However, this is less true in Finland where the Committee on the Economy, *talousvaliokunta*, is required to serve several departments.

Finally, it should be remembered that the structure of the standing committee system is also shaped by the internal organisation of the assembly itself: where parliament contains formal Divisions for the purposes of considering routine legislative proposals, as in Iceland, the standing committee system appears in duplicated form. There are nine permanent legislative committees in each of the two chambers of the Althing, and four others are concerned with bills tabled in the United Althing. Occasionally committees of both chambers can join together for specific purposes; more particularly the standing committees on Communication annually form a Joint Committee to allocate monies to ferry boats and other kinds of rural transportation.[35]

Delegate recruitment to standing committees

As regards the composition of the parliamentary standing committees in the region, membership is stable and recruitment proceeds largely on the basis of a delegate's expressed preference and known interest. The stable nature of committee membership — a potentially important factor in permitting the development of a common interest orientation — has two primary sources. The first consists of the rules prescribed by the Standing Parliamentary Orders, which state that standing committees are generally appointed for the full parliamentary term, rather than members having to submit themselves for re-election at the beginning of each new annual session. The chairman and vice-chairmen of Norwegian committees are elected annually,[36] although in practice this has become a mere formality and without further significance. Secondly, the norm in the region is for members to be returned to their previous committee unless they specifically request a move. Hence long-serving parliamentarians invariably become veterans on particular standing committees, and there is much continuity in the membership of particular committees over time.

On the Riksdag Constitutional Committee before September 1982, to cite a random example, there were those who had been members since before the reform of the standing committee system in 1971: men like the Centre Party chairman Bertil Fiskesjö, a former academic from Lund; the Social Democratic deputy chairman Hilding Johansson;[37] and a senior Conservative, Anders Björck.[38]

In the Storting Asbjørn Sjøthun, a farmer, first elected as a full Labour delegate for the Troms constituency in 1969/70, has served on the Agricultural Committee throughout his parliamentary career to date. How typical his case is can be seen from Table 5.11 which examines the standing committeeships of those Storting delegates who, like Sjøthun, have served continuously from 1969 to the current electoral period 1981–5. A number of delegates had to be excluded from the reckoning on the grounds that they did not hold committeeships at both the beginning and end of the period in question: the positions of three members of the 1981–3 Conservative minority government under Kåre Willoch, and of a former Labour Party minister in 1965, Odvar Nordli, have obviously been affected by the incompatibility rule. As for the remaining delegates, there are problems of comparability in the case of Liberal Party teacher Hans Rossbach, who in 1969 sat on a Protocol Committee that was abolished in 1972. However, where committees have extended their policy competence over the period — eg. the standing committee on Industry which in 1981 became Energy and Industry, and the standing committee on Administration which in the same year became Consumer Affairs and Administration — they have been regarded as essentially the same committee.

It can be seen that of those twenty-four veteran Storting delegates whose standing committeeships can be compared in 1969–73 and 1981–5 (*c*. 66% of them Labour delegates) five served in both periods on the same standing committee — some like Sjøthun and Bjarne Eidem, a Labour Party school teacher, rising in the process to become secretary of that committee. Sjøthun, Eidem and a third delegate Arnold Weiberg-Aurdal, a farmer on the Communications Committee, have indeed spent the whole of their parliamentary careers since becoming full members of the Storting in 1969 on the same standing committee. There is an even higher degree of committee continuity among Storting veterans if only the 8-year period 1977–85 is considered — 44% of the group have served the last two parliamentary terms on the same standing committee.

There seems to have been a particular readiness to remain on committees dealing with questions of economic management such as Finance and Energy/Industry. It also appears that long committee service can do one of two things: either leading a delegate to become an office-holder on a standing committee, thereby enjoying individual influence as well as a position of partisan responsibility or alternatively creating the leverage with which a delegate can move up the informal prestige hierarchy of the standing committee system. Certainly a number of those members who have moved from one committee to another in the period under scrutiny have

Table 5.11. STANDING COMMITTEES SERVED BY STORTING VETERANS, 1969–85

Name	Party	Committee		
		1969–73	*1977–81*	*1981–5*
Faremo	L	Municipal Affairs	Municipal Affairs & Environment	Defence
Benkow	C	Social Affairs	Justice	Foreign Affairs & Constitution
Førde	L	Church & Education	Finance	Foreign Affairs & Constitution
Fredheim	L	Foreign Affairs & Constitution	Church & Education	Foreign Affairs & Constitution
Hysing-Dahl	C	Industry	Defence	Shipping & Fisheries
Nilsen	L	Municipal Affairs	— (cabinet minister)	Consumer Affairs & Administration
Haugstvedt	CP	Justice	Defence	Energy & Industry
Fassen	L	Administration	Industry	Energy & Industry
Helland	CE	Industry	Finance	Finance
Weiberg-Aurdal	CE	Communications	Communications	Communications
Rossbach	LIB	Protocol	Industry	Foreign Affairs & Constitution
Eidem	L	Finance	Finance	Finance (secretary)
Andersen	L	Church & Education	Finance	Consumer Affairs & Administration
Berntsen	L	Industry	Municipal Affairs & Environment	Municipal Affairs & Environment
Frydenlund	L	Foreign Affairs & Constitution	— (cabinet minister)	Defence (chairman)
Berge	L	Municipal Affairs	Finance	Finance (deputy-chairman)
Kristensen	L	Defence	Industry	Energy & Industry (deputy-chairman)
Tynning	C	Municipal Affairs	Municipal Affairs & Environment	Foreign Affairs & Constitution

(continued)

Table 5.11 (*continued*)

Name	*Party*	*Committee*		
		1969–73	*1977–81*	*1981–5*
Sjøthun	L	Agriculture	Agriculture	Agriculture (secretary)
Hansen	L	Foreign Affairs & Constitution	Justice	Foreign Affairs & Constitution (deputy-chairman)
Eian	C	Agriculture	Shipping & Fisheries	Shipping & Fisheries
Martinsen	L	Church & Education	Social Affairs	Consumer Affairs & Administration (deputy-chairman)
Bakken	L	Agriculture	Agriculture	Justice
Skaug	L	Administration	— (not elected)	Social Affairs

Key: L = Labour Party, C = Conservatives, CP = Christian People's Party, CE = Centre Party, LIB = Liberals (*Venstre*).

Sources: Olaf Chr. Torp. *Stortinget, Høsten 1969–Våren 1973*. Universitetsforlaget, Oslo-Bergen-Tromsø 1972; Olaf Chr. Torp, *Stortinget i navn og tall, Høsten 1977—Våren 1981*, Universitetsforlaget, Oslo-Bergen-Tromsø 1978; *Stortinget 1981–85*, Fred Arnesen, Oslo 1981.

ended up on the high-status Foreign Affairs and Constitution Committee. Still, the fact remains that nearly half the Storting veterans had not changed their standing committee since 1977.

Clearly it is reasonable to presume that the longer a delegate serves on a particular standing committee, the greater will be his substantive competence in that policy area, not least because in most cases members bring to their committee work, a previous knowledge of the relevant field. A few committee members may be experts by dint of academic training: Kjell-Olof Feldt, the Social Democratic vice-chairman of the Swedish Finance Committee before September 1982, was a graduate economist, a former Minister of Trade and had experience in the Ministry of Finance. He is, at the time of writing, Minister of Finance. Many more will possess a professional or vocational grasp of a policy area. On the 17-strong standing committee on Agriculture and Forestry in the 1979–83 session of the Eduskunta, all but one in the narrow bourgeois party majority — Erkki Korhonen, a schoolteacher representing the Finnish Christian League — were either agronomists, farmers or had previously been employed in forestry.[39] The position was almost identical on the Riksdag Agricultural Committee between 1979 and 1982 where the only members of the non-socialist majority not to have had employment in farming or a related activity were the Liberal delegate Börje Stensson, a senior education officer, *skolchef*, and a housewife Märta Fredrikson representing the Centre Party.[40]

Above all, as Hernes has observed in Norway, 'representatives end up on the standing committee they are interested in.'[41] Not only that, but in Sweden delegates also tend to serve on pre-legislative commissions of inquiry so bringing to their participation at the formulative stage of policy-making a knowledge deepened by service, frequently over a long period, on a relevant standing committee, while in turn profiting in substantive terms from the consultations and discussions on the commission with policy experts outside the legislature.

Obviously it is important not to give an impression that is too black-and-white. While Nordic parliamentarians generally regard themselves as specialists in a particular legislative area and play an active role in standing committee work, not all of them get the committees they want or involve themselves in committee work as assiduously as some others do. A number, moreover, move from one committee to the next with some regularity: of the Storting veterans included in Table 5.11 approximately 33% served on at least three different standing committees in the four electoral periods between 1969 and 1985. It should also be noted that committee chairmen are first and foremost partisan appointments and need not possess any technical qualifications: Eric Enlund, the chairman of the Riksdag Finance Committee in 1979–82, was a farmer, his Danish counterpart Henning Jensen was a cigar-maker,[42] and the Norwegian Finance Committee chairman, Jan Syse, is an Administrative Director. Enlund in fact emphasised that he was not an expert and occasionally found difficulty in following the niceties of the terminology used by members of the Finance Committee. In any event, he claimed to prefer to try and see things as the ordinary man-in-the-street might and to adopt a generalist's perspective on proceedings.[43]

Yet if the expert qualifications of individual committee members should not be exaggerated, it is at least arguable that one consequence of the subject-specific nature of the Nordic standing committee systems is that committee members have had a much greater control over that policy area than non-members. This is reinforced by the preference given in parliamentary debates to committee spokesmen, who thus come into daily contact with the government department corresponding to their committee area. The differences with Britain, for example, may be more of degree than kind: members of the House of Commons do specialise on backbench committees within their parliamentary group, and MPs also tend to develop a particular policy interest. However, the structure of the standing committee system at Westminster has plainly not fostered the emergence of specialist sub-systems within the legislature to anything like the same extent as in the Nordic states. Certainly it appears that in the House of Commons the bill-specific standing committees involve individual MPs in scrutinising proposals that cover a much wider range of policy than is usual in Scandinavia, and that the ephemeral nature of British standing committees has militated against the kind of entrenched interest orientation which some commentators regard as endemic to the permanent specialist committees in the Nordic region.

The Nordic standing committee systems are underpinned by a permanent parliamentary staff, although its size varies considerably from one country to the next; this enhances the autonomy of these legislative sub-systems. Sweden and Norway have the most comprehensive support arrangements. All Riksdag standing committees are backed by a full-time secretary, *kanslichef*, a six-year nonpartisan appointment.[44] In addition to a full-time secretary, all committees have at least one other regular staff member. Most Riksdag standing committees have a secretariat of three, namely a secretary and two assistants, although the Labour Market and Constitutional Committee have four and five respectively.[45] In Norway, too, all standing committees have a permanent secretary who is on the staff of the Storting and usually at least one other assistant.[46] In Denmark and Finland only the Finance Committees have a full-time secretary, while the only Icelandic standing committee with its own secretariat is the Budget Committee in the United Althing. It is perhaps to be expected that in Finland, which has the least institutionalised standing committee system in the region, the understaffing of the committee secretariat should be most glaring. The thirteen standing committees are served by only 6 full-time and 3 part-time staff.[47] More surprisingly, the Danish situation is similar, despite the standing committee reform of 1971: one secretary serves the committees on Public Works, Political Economy and Ecclesiastical Affairs, although the last two have a relatively light workload and meet only once or twice a month.[48] The Standing Orders of the Folketing require parliamentary committee staff to be graduates in law or economics or to have a comparable training[49] — a few recently have had a grounding in political science. There has even been discussion in Denmark of the deployment of expert committee secretaries — i.e. with a substantive competence in the committee area in question. There have been objections to this primarily on financial grounds, but it must be allowed that this would certainly complement the functional subject-specific nature of the committees.

Nordic standing committees, then, are small, stable and subject-specific, involving members often with a known interest and/or competence in the relevant policy field, supported by a permanent parliamentary staff of variable size. It might be thought that, as permanent and specialist organs, they tend to promote a common interest orientation among members which, in so far as it does so, strengthens the deliberative function of parliament at the expense of complicating the government's management of bills in the assembly. It might further be suggested that this is more likely to happen in Norway and Sweden — where the principle of the specialist consideration of bills in standing committee has been most developed — than elsewhere in the region where it is rather less systematically applied.

Problems for the government in standing committee can arise in two main ways. The first is when a standing committee takes a united or majority stance either against, or involving significant modification to, a government proposal. This, of course, is most likely to occur when the government commands only minority support in the legislature, although the dilemma then is to determine whether a convergence of interests or rather partisan considerations have been at work. It can occasionally happen too when the government has a majority, with government backbenchers using the committee arena to express disquiet at a piece of their own administration's proposed legislation — as in Iceland in the spring of 1982 when notable changes were incorporated into the Tax Bill by the Economic Affairs Committee.[50]

The progress of a government bill can be jeopardised in another way: when two or more standing committees engaged in the conjoint examination of a proposal produce recommendations or informally apply pressure to further their substantive interests which threaten to undermine the original government measure. Normally a bill is allocated to a single standing committee and the problem does not arise. However, in the case of the Finance Bill (budget), procedures can differ and as such are worth considering in some detail.

The Budget in standing committee(s)

In Iceland, Denmark and Finland the detailed examination of the budget is the exclusive responsibility of a single Budget or Finance Committee. Dominated by this one task, this committee is without doubt the hardest-worked of all the national standing committees.

The Danish Finance Committee has been described by its secretary as 'a little Folketing' on account of the scale of its workload[51]: in the 1977–8 session of the Folketing, it held 55 (often protracted) meetings and had 66 consultations with ministers, to whom no less than 456 written questions were tabled.[52] Moreover, in addition to dealing with the budget itself — which is prepared in the ministries at least nine months before implementation and therefore cannot take economic trends and price rises into account — the Danish Finance Committee is also required to examine the (strictly unconstitutional) spring supplementary budget, together with a vast number of party motions connected with the budget. In 1982 there were more than 1,400 of these from the Progress Party alone![53] Anticipating the committee's heavy work schedule, it is significant that as early as 1928 a provision was incorporated into the Finnish Parliament Act enabling the Finance Committee to continue to meet out of session at the discretion of the Eduskunta.[54]

Various internal committee procedures have evolved for coping with the great volume of business. With the Budget Committee in Iceland and the Finance Committee in Finland, the practice has been to form working groups within the committee to deal with the different sections of the budget. In Finland the 21-strong Finance Committee is subdivided into nine sections, each of which may call on experts for advice in connection with its particular remit.[55] In contrast to procedure for other legislative proposals, the Finance Bill (along with connected finance motions) is subject to only a single reading on the floor of the Eduskunta. The budget is thus given a preliminary debate — usually lengthy and dominated by 'party group speeches', *ryhmäpuheenvuorot* — before being sent to the Finance Committee, whose report then provides the basis for a single plenary reading where general discussion is followed by detailed collective scrutiny of proposed expenditures and revenues. The Finance Committee is invariably called on to deal with the Finance Bill and parliamentary amendments to it a second time before it gains the approval of the assembly.[56] In an attempt to expedite matters at the preliminary debate stage in September/October, the government experimented in 1980 by presenting the Eduskunta with the main guidelines of the budget in the spring before a detailed proposal had been finalised.[57]

In Denmark, where the constitution states that the Finance Bill be submitted to the Folketing at least four months before the beginning of the financial year on January 1,[58] the 3-volume budget bill requires informal parliamentary preparation even earlier than that. In accordance with a practice dating from 1894, it has been conventional in mid-August for the business of every government department included in the Finance Bill to be divided among members of the committee on the basis of the numbered paragraphs in the bill (paragraph 10 relating to foreign affairs ect.). Via the committee secretary, each member is then put in touch with a designated budget expert in the appropriate ministry whom he is able to contact for further information and/or technical clarification. By the middle of September, individual members convene at a 'report stage' of the Finance Bill after which written questions are tabled to the minister or, if the matter has more of a political than a technical character, ministers can be called for personal consultations, *samrådsformen.*[59] A formal report is then produced in which the Finance Committee lists the questions tabled to ministers, ministers' replies, and the topics involving the minister in consultation with the committee. The report does not usually contain any indication of the extent to which contacts with the government might have proved effective or whether amendments to the Finance Bill are to be expected. At about the same time as this initial Finance Committee report is being given a Second Reading in the Folketing, the government's amended budget comes before the Finance Committee. The whole procedure of ministerial questions etc. is set in train again and a supplementary committee report is produced normally 14–16 days before the Third Reading stage.[60]

Two points need emphasis. First, in Iceland, Denmark and Finland, the various sections of the budget are considered by individual delegates or small working groups nominated on a more or less arbitrary basis from within a single standing committee. Secondly — a vitally important corollary to the first point — the competence of the other specialist committees is not used during consideration of the budget. In Finland particularly, most of the other standing committees are more or less underemployed during the handling of the budget, and this has not appeared to some a very efficient division of labour or use of member expertise.

Before the reform of their committee systems in the early 1970s, parliamentary consideration of the budget in Norway and Sweden was similar to that elsewhere in the region. Nowadays, however, the principle applied is that each standing committee is responsible for scrutinising that area of the budget which falls within its particular area of competence, *fackutskottsprincipen*. This has meant that the primary task of the Finance Committee in both countries is to coordinate overall scrutiny of the budget and ultimately to collect and present the result.[61]

In Norway the Finance Bill, *Kongens forslag til budsjett*, is presented to the Storting within four days of the opening of the new parliamentary session[62] at the beginning of October, and by the end of the same month the Finance Committee is expected to give a provisional Budget Report reviewing the overall shape and adequacy of the proposal. This is debated in a Finance Debate on the floor of the assembly which lasts until about November 5.[63] The Norwegian Finance Committee, unlike its counterparts in Finland and Iceland, is not divided in sections or working groups: instead, a general parliamentary planning committee, *arbeidsordningskomitéen*, allocates the various parts of the budget to the individual specialist committees and sets deadlines for their reports — they are generally ready from November 7 and are presented as a collective document.[64] The Finance Committee, which has authority to propose amendments to the special standing committees' estimates, then produces a final Budget Report about December 12.

In Sweden, the procedure is basically the same as in Norway, although the timetable for the parliamentary handling of the budget differs from that in the rest of the region. In Denmark, Finland, Iceland and Norway, the financial year begins on January 1 and the budget is considered as the main item on parliament's autumn agenda. In Sweden, the financial year runs from July 1 to June 30 and the government introduces its Finance Bill on January 10 and produces a revised and finalised draft by the end of April in the so-called 'completion proposal', *kompletteringsproposition.*[65] According to the Riksdag Standing Orders, the Finance Committee should consider the broad outlines of economic policy, including the budget and technical matters relating to it,[66] but not the detailed work of scrutinising the Finance Bill which should be undertaken in the specialist standing committees.[67] This has meant that although the Spring business of the Finance Committee is dominated by the budget,[68] some time remains to deal with one or two other matters. There are Swedish delegates who would prefer to bring their national practice into line with that in the rest of the Nordic region and consider the budget in the autumn session of parliament with the financial year starting on January 1. The Centre Party chairman of the Constitutional Committee, Bertil Fiskesjö, tabled a member's request proposal along these lines in January 1982,[69] although no change is likely in the immediate future.

The Norwegian and Swedish method of the specialist consideration of the budget in subject-specific standing committees appears to have a number of advantages. First, it maximises delegate participation in the consideration of probably the single most important government proposal — the annual Finance Bill — perusal of which is not confined to the small number of parliamentarians that happen to have seats on the Finance Committee. As a result, the overall workload is distributed more equitably and perhaps more democratically. Second and related, there is a much greater use of member expertise than in Denmark, Finland and Iceland: all standing committees are engaged in the budget examination process, and particular committees do not become all but redundant while scrutiny is in progress. The approach seems both rational and efficient.

Paradoxically, the practice of delegating the various parts of the budget to specialist standing committees can complicate the task of the governmental management of the Finance Bill in the assembly. Put another way, the entrenched self-interest of a stable subject-specific standing committee (its inevitable function?) can at times jeopardise the original level of the government's budget proposal. To illustrate the point, it is pertinent to recall how with the advent of recession in Sweden in the late 1970s, the task of keeping the budget within the terms of the non-socialist governments' proposal and adhering to planned cuts and stringencies proved extremely problematical in view of each standing committee's tendency to demand that more should be spent in its own area of concern. The minority position of the administration by 1981 made matters no easier; it meant that the chairman of the Finance Committee, as the government's right-hand man in the Riksdag, was compelled to strive for a moderation in the position of the recalcitrant standing committees by personal negotiation in the various parliamentary groups.[70]

In variation of this managerial dilemma — which applies more to Norway than to Sweden — a trial of strength over the distribution of resources in the budget has been fought out between the standing committees representing the strategic sectors of the economy. Hernes has described how in Norway this struggle has involved a three-cornered contest between the Finance Committee — largely defending the government's budget proposal — and, on the one hand, the standing committee on Industry and, on the other, the labour-oriented committee on Social Affairs.

Conflict between specialist standing committees — e.g. the Taxation Committee and the Finance Committee in Sweden — can be a threat to government finance proposals other than the budget. It will be recalled that the two committees are conjointly empowered to deal with matters involving indirect taxation when the Riksdag is not in session, but otherwise their functions differ: the Taxation committee is primarily concerned with the detailed implementation of proposed tax legislation, whereas the Finance Committee is broadly engaged in adjudicating on the desirability and feasibility of such proposals. Nevertheless, strains have been evident between them. As Bengt Johansson, the secretary of the Finance Committee put it in the context of the government proposal to raise VAT in the autumn of 1980: 'It is conceivable that the Riksdag could have been faced with two proposals — a detailed one from the Taxation Committee raising VAT and another from the Finance Committee imposing import controls!'[71]

The difficulties of steering the Finance Bill (and other matters of 'high economics') through twelve standing committees in Norway and sixteen in Sweden should not be exaggerated. From a parliamentary viewpoint, the capacity to enforce amendments to a government's budget proposal should doubtless be seen as beneficial. As a Liberal delegate in Sweden noted, modifications to the Finance Bill resulting from action in the assembly have helped to prevent the Riksdag from becoming merely a rubber-stamp for government proposals.[72]

All this is not to say that in Denmark, Finland[73] and Iceland the government has not had to accept compromises over the budget.[74] However, in Norway and Sweden the referral of sections of the budget to the appropriate standing committees has introduced an element of what Blondel referred to as 'viscosity' into the structure of policy-making at the parliamentary adoption stage.[75] Ephemeral talk of reforming the budget deliberation in Finland has revealed a critical awareness of the limitations of the Swedish and Norwegian approach. Finnish delegations have visited Stockholm and carefully observed the Riksdag standing committees over the years since their reform, but up till now the Finns have hesitated to follow their neighbours' example.

Throughout the region the government's management of bills at the committee stage is not expedited, and may indeed be complicated, by the preclusion of cabinet ministers from committee proceedings. Relations between ministers and parliament are not as close in the Nordic countries as they are at Westminster, nor are ministers personally involved in steering government proposals through standing committee like their British counterparts. This is explained by the continuing tradition of a separation of powers, whether expressed formally in an incompatibility rule (Norway and Sweden), whereby ministers on appointment give up their seats in the assembly and are replaced by deputies from the same party (parties), or simply by a conventional demarcation between legislature and executive expressed in the informal rule that ministers, although remaining members of parliament, may not be members of standing committees (Denmark and Finland).

In Anker Jørgensen's fifth Social Democratic minority government in Denmark in 1982 only the Minister of Social Affairs, Bent Hansen, was not a member of the Folketing,[76] although, as in

Finland, cabinet ministers do not participate in routine committee work — this despite the statement in the Eduskunta Standing Orders that ministers are eligible to participate in standing committee meetings unless the committee decides to the contrary.[77] Only in Iceland, and then very exceptionally, are ministers members of parliamentary standing committees: before the April 1983 general election, an Independence Party minister representing the minority governmental wing of the party had a standing committee place.

Denied access to regular committee deliberations, ministers need to develop a series of informal contacts so as to be able to monitor the progress of government bills in standing committee. That they are able to do so is evident from an interview survey covering the entire Norwegian cabinet of Trygve Bratteli in 1975 in which all the ministers reported either daily or weekly contact with 'their' committee in the Storting, though very much less contact with the other standing parliamentary committees.[78] Clearly it is imperative for ministers to be in touch with the chairman or senior party members on the appropriate standing committee — or indeed standing *committees*, as in Iceland where traditionally ministers have been responsible for two government departments and therefore two distinct policy communities.

The policy impact of Nordic standing parliamentary committees is not narrowly determined by fixed structural factors such as size and subject-specificity; rather the extent and significance of the role of standing committees is integrally tied to the dynamics of the contemporary political situation.

Clearly, the nature of the party system in the legislature can have important implications for the overall level of inter-group cohesion on standing committee. Before the era of party proliferation and the rise of Glistrup's Progress Party in 1973, for example, the Political Economy Committee in Denmark had been the arena for several 5-party agreements on economy-related packages. Since then, this type of bargaining has been conducted away from the Folketing and in the relative tranquillity of the Prime Minister's Office.[79]

Equally, the parliamentary balance between legislature and executive will affect partisan relations on standing committee. When governments possess only minority support in the assembly, the probability of *legislative coalitions* (agreements between one or more parties in government and one or more parties in opposition) of an *ad hoc* kind on standing committee is obviously increased. In Denmark this has become almost standard practice. In the course of the spring of 1982, the minority Social Democratic administration struck (rather unlikely) deals with the radical right-wing Progress

Party on petroleum tax and index bond proposals — in the first instance the policy coalition also included the radical leftist Socialist People's Party and centre-based Radicals, whilst in the latter it was joined only by the centre-aligned Christian Democrats.

In Sweden inter-party deals in standing committee characterised the distinctive parliamentary situation of 1973–6. In a real sense, the voters twisted the government's arm, for after the general election in 1973 — an election at which, incidentally, the turnout of voters exceeded 90% for the first time — a unique situation resulted, in which there was a dead heat between the socialist and non-socialist parties in the Riksdag. On the left, the Social Democrats, who opted to stay in office with only 156 seats, relied mainly on support from the 19 Left-Communists; in the bourgeois camp, the Centre, Liberals and Conservatives also had 175 seats between them. Legislative coalitions where inevitable:[80] indeed, in the words of Birgersson *et al.*, 'the centre of power shifted a good deal in the direction of the Riksdag . . . and, in particular, towards the standing committees where many agreements were worked out.'[81] Even then, the Social Democratic Speaker Henry Allard had to use lottery methods to resolve tied results on the floor of the assembly, the more so as the 1976 election approached. During the spring of 1973, 18 matters were decided by lottery in the Riksdag; in the spring of 1975, this had risen to 42, while in the course of the final pre-election Riksdag session in 1975–6, there was recourse to a lottery on no less than 79 occasions. The so-called 'Lottery Riksdag' had become a reality.

Having considered the primary determinants of the legislative influence of standing committees at some length, what can we conclude about their participation in the policy adoption process? How important are the Nordic standing committees as negotiating sites for the scrutinisation of executive proposals, and is it feasible to compare the role of standing committees in the region to those in the United States where, as Loewenberg and Patterson have argued, 'the specialised standing committees and subcommittees of Congress are the most important sites' in the policy deliberation process?[82] Certainly Gudmund Hernes has referred to the existence of 'committee government' in Norway in the sense that it is rare for the Storting not to follow the recommendations of a united standing committee. But how valid is his view? What are the mechanics of achieving a possible consensus at the standing committee stage? And can such broad agreement be said to be the exception or the rule? In sum, how effectively do the Nordic standing committee systems perform their deliberative function?

The deliberative role of standing committees

On the face of it the parliamentary standing committees in the region are mostly well-attended, and despite a heightened workload they perform a thorough examination of legislative proposals. True, the existence of rules on quorums for parliamentary standing committee meetings in several of the countries has ensured a higher attendance than might otherwise have been the case.

In order for standing committee resolutions to be valid in Denmark, half the full members of the committee must have been present and voted,[83] while in Norway at least three-fifths[84] and in Finland at least two-thirds of a standing committee's membership must be in attendance for a meeting to be quorate.[85] In Sweden and Iceland, no quorums are formally specified in the parliamentary standing orders, although as elsewhere in the region provision is made for deputies to attend standing committee meetings when full members are unable to do so. In Denmark, for example, deputies or alternate members, *stedfortrædere*, are nominated by the parliamentary groups to all standing committees except the Standing Orders Committee, the Credentials Committee and the specialist committees on Energy, Finance and Immigration — although the number of deputies must not of course exceed the number of full places allocated to a party on a particular committee.[86] In general, deputy members can, and do, play an active part in committee deliberations even if they are not always allowed to vote or table reservations to a committee's final report. That said, the rules on committee quorums have proved largely academic: the norm in the Nordic region is full attendance at standing committee meetings, and because of the high importance attached to this type of specialist legislative activity, the problems of recruitment experienced on the shifting 'generalist' committees in Britain have been absent. In short, almost all parliamentarians are full members of at least one standing committee, participate regularly at its meetings, and devote a good deal of weekly time to its work.

If most delegates belong to at least one standing committee, many are members of several. Potentially, this is of the utmost importance, for the higher the number of standing committeeships per delegate, the greater the implications both for a parliamentarian's personal efficacy and possibly, by extension, the overall efficiency of legislative scrutiny at the committee stage as well. In Norway, delegates have traditionally been members of only one standing committee: at present, there are 155 places on the twelve specialist standing committees and precisely 155 Storting delegates to fill them. In Sweden, however, there are more than 100 more delegates than there are standing committee seats, with the result that some have had to be content with being no more than deputy members of one or more committees. In Iceland, Finland and Denmark, in contrast, a plurality of committee places has been the inevitable corollary of the supply of committee places exceeding the available manpower in parliament. Table 5.12 shows the variance in committee obligations in the region by comparing the number of available parliamentarians with the aggregate number of committee places. In Denmark, Iceland and Finland, totals on the supply side of the equation are reduced by the rule that the Parliamentary Speaker and cabinet ministers are precluded from holding positions on standing committee, while in Finland, full and deputy members of the Finance Committee are also conventionally regarded as ineligible for seats on other committees.[87] In Norway, the Speaker and deputy Speakers of the Storting are members of standing committees — the Storting Speaker at the time of writing, Per Hysing-Dahl, sits on the Shipping and Fisheries Committee — whereas Riksdag Speakers are only seldom involved with standing committee work (the first deputy Speaker, *förste vice talman*, in 1979–82 was a member of the committee on Taxation). In both countries deputy members serve in place of cabinet ministers — and in Sweden Speakers too — so avoiding any reduction in the number of parliamentarians available for standing committee places.

It can be seen from Table 5.12 that notwithstanding minor variation caused by fluctuating cabinet sizes etc., the plurality of committee membership is highest in Iceland, where delegates are members of between three and five standing committees, but it is also high in Denmark and Finland where three committee places per delegate is usual. In each of these countries, only the specialist policy committees have been included in the calculations, although delegates also belong to non-legislative committees such as the various Credentials Committees and in Finland the legislative 'upper tier' Grand Committee. The same is true in Sweden and Norway: indeed,

Table 5.12. STANDING COMMITTEE COMMITMENTS OF NORDIC PARLIAMENTARIANS

	Total in legislature	*Available parliamentarians*	*Policy committees*	*Committee places*
Denmark	179	155	22	378
Norway	155	155	12	155
Finland	200	180	13	245[88]
Iceland	60	50	22	156
Sweden	349	349	16	240

in Norway a few delegates in the 1981–2 Storting session became for the first time members of a second standing committee with the creation of the Scrutiny Committee, *kontrollkomitéen.* Obviously, when there are more committee places than delegates to fill them, it is reasonable to speculate on some weakening of the deliberative function of the legislature: members' time is clearly limited, they cannot attend two meetings at the same time, nor realistically are they likely to be equally interested and/or industrious in the policy area of each of their three or four committees. Yet in Sweden many deputy committee members can play as active a part in committee work as full members, with the result that there is little apparent dissatisfaction with the way things presently operate; and elsewhere in the region, the anticipated problem of members tending to neglect their second, third or even fourth committees should not be exaggerated. We should comment further on both these points.

Particularly among the larger Swedish parties, delegates are normally deputies in only one standing committee and are so able to work assiduously in that capacity, sometimes appearing as often, as regular members, or even more frequently. Exceptionally, for example, the deputy for the Social Democratic chairman of the Riksdag Constitutional Committee was present — in the continued absence of the chairman himself — at every meeting but one from the mid-1970s till 1982. True, this would have been appreciably harder to arrange in the small parliamentary groups, where delegates tend to be deputy-members of several standing committees: a Liberal delegate commented on how it had proved extremely difficult to get cover on the occasions when he or his party colleague on the Constitutional Committee had been unable to attend.[89] But there were no general complaints about the restricted availability of committee places. A hard-pressed party leader may well eschew a regular position on a standing committee, so creating more full committee places to distribute among backbenchers. Between 1979 and 1982, the leader of the Social Democratic Opposition, Olof Palme, did not occupy a full committee place and was a deputy-member on only one committee. Cultural Affairs, although he was a member of the Foreign Affairs Council, *utrikesnämnden* throughout the period, and for a time President of the Nordic Council. All in all, the absence of multiple committee placements in Sweden has had a dual impact. At a pragmatic level, it has facilitated the concentration of standing committee meetings on two mornings a week, Tuesday and Thursday, so that although the number of hours per session spent in committees has varied appreciably — ranging in Birgersson's work on the 1974–5 Riksdag from 99 hours in the Education Committee to 33 in the National Insurance Committee[90] —

committee meetings are normally fully attended. In a wider legislative perspective, the limited supply of full committee places in Sweden may well have contributed to enhancing the value members attribute to standing committee work and hence their willingness, where necessary, to wait for full committee status.

Elsewhere in the region, the difficulties faced by parliamentarians in sitting on a number of committees at the same time are not excessive. In Iceland, standing committee meetings are timed so as not to be simultaneous, and are anyway short and infrequent. Only at the hectic end of the Althing year is a coincidence of several committee meetings possible. In Denmark, as we have seen, a number of standing committees convene only once or twice a month, while to avoid concurrent meetings the committee programme is timetabled so that it runs into periods which, strictly, are scheduled for plenary sessions. In short, despite multiple commitments and a certain propensity on the part of delegates to concentrate on one committee more than the others, standing committees are well attended in both Iceland and Denmark.

The same certainly cannot be said of Finland, where in a recent study by Kari Valtonen the following depressing statistics came to light: the typical delegate was absent from every fourth sitting of a standing committee during the 1979–80 session of the Eduskunta, every tenth committee sitting was inquorate, and there was no significant discrepancy in participation levels on the more influential committees compared with the less prestigious ones.[91] Among the political parties, members of the Centre Party were most prone to absenteeism: as Table 5.13 shows, only about a third of its members missed less than 20% of standing committee meetings, while almost half of the Centre Party's delegates missed between a third and three-quarters of all meetings.

Explanations of this apparently sorry state of affairs can be sketched only very summarily. The differential workload of committees may be a minor contributory factor in accounting for low levels of attendance: while standing committee meetings take on average rather less than an hour each, and delegates generally devote perhaps two hours weekly to them,[92] particular committees can deliberate much longer. According to a member of the Social Affairs Committee, proceedings may take as long as six or even eight hours per week.[93] The nature of committee discussions could well be pertinent too, for in Matti Oksanen's study of Finnish parliamentarians (admittedly conducted in the late 1960s) it is contended that instead of adhering to broad issues, delegates tend to get embroiled in wrangling about insignificant details.[94] In the media debate which followed publication of Valtonen's findings,

Table 5.13. ABSENTEEISM OF DELEGATES IN FINNISH STANDING COMMITTEES BY PARTY

Party	*Seldom absent (0–20% of meetings)*	*Quite often absent (21–30%)*	*Often absent (32–75%)*	*No. of delegates*
Conservatives	61.9	21.4	16.7	42
Swedish People's	42.9	28.6	28.6	7
Liberals	33.3	0.0	66.7	3
Centre	32.1	25.0	42.9	28
Christian League	71.4	0.0	28.6	7
Rural Party	75.0	25.0	0.0	4
Social Democrats	43.5	32.5	23.9	46
People's Democratic League	50.0	37.5	12.5	32
Average	49.1	27.2	23.7	169
n=	83	46	40	

Source: Kari Valtonen, *Kansanedustajien osallistuminen valiokuntiensa kokouksiin vuosien 1973 ja 1979 valtiopäivillä.* Helsinki 1981, p. 52.

however, delegates themselves pointed to a number of purely practical reasons for their absence from standing committee meetings — these included multiple committee membership and the impossibility of being in two places at the same time; the fact that standing committees *en masse* can make trips abroad or within Finland during the parliamentary session, thus reducing the average attendance figures; and a range of personal circumstances including occasional illness. In any event, the problem should not be inflated: Jorma Fred, a Christian League deputy, did not miss a single sitting of the Second Legal Affairs committee in the 1979–80 session of the Eduskunta,[95] and several other delegates were only fractionally less punctilious.

However, except for Finland, Nordic standing committees are well-attended, and throughout the region procedures for the deliberation of legislative proposals in committee are thorough. Danish committee rules permit the assembling of perhaps the most 'bill-related' clientele. Political parties are entitled to replace committee members by others who, for example, have a particular regional interest in a measure, and uniquely since the 1964–5 session of the Folketing, the authors of private initiatives have been permitted to attend a standing committee meeting and participate in discussion when their proposal is being considered. Although they do not have the right to vote or table reservations to a committee report,[96] private members have generally availed themselves of this facility. The same right applies to Folketing delegates elected for the Faeroe Islands and Greenland when measures concerning the Faeroes and Greenland are being debated in standing committee.[97]

Furthermore, although the Standing Orders of the Nordic parliaments are not at all expansive about the internal work procedures to be adopted in the specialist standing committees, it is evident that most bills are considered at length, often in small sub-groups within the committee itself. In Norway there is provision in the Storting Orders for the creation of working groups within standing committees and requiring each section to elect its own chairman or spokesman.[98] In Finland, the onus is placed on systematic deliberation: every measure is subject to two readings in standing committee, the first devoted to the principles contained in the bill and the general content of the committee's response, and the second to a detailed appraisal of the secretary's draft of the final committee report.[99]

Internal working methods aside, standing committees in the region possess a variety of 'external' means whereby they can enhance their scrutiny of government proposals. First, they can request further information from, and/or cross-examine, the government on bill-related matters and thus attempt to limit and control the executive within the legislative process (control outside the legislative process is discussed in chapter 9). Typically, this has taken the form of questions to ministers — either written ones, (the majority) or oral questions which may also serve as supplementaries to the written ones. In Denmark, Finland and Norway the practice is for ministers to attend in person — although they are not legally required to do so — and they can be given a rough ride by committee members. In Denmark, particularly, it has been known for a determined opposition party on a standing committee tactically to table a large number of written questions, partly to embarrass the minister, but more to slow down consideration of an unpopular proposal. It is then for the chairman as the minister's agent in committee to be firm in his handling of proceedings. Indeed, the Standing Orders of the Folketing state that it is the responsibility of the chairman of a standing committee to expedite the committee's work as much as possible and to keep the Speaker of the Folketing informed of the progress of the work and the prospects for its completion. These progress reports are to be submitted in writing at the request of the Speaker.[100] In Norway ministers and officials from the ministries are often present in standing committees to supply information and answer questions, and this may be the result of an initiative on the ministerial side as well as from the committee in question.[101] In Sweden, however, where ministers are also not required to answer questions in standing committee,[102] they hardly ever do so, except occasionally in the Constitutional Committee. Instead the under-secretary of state, as the minister's personal assistant, appears in order to respond to members' questions.

Secondly, standing committees can seek advice and guidance on a proposal by holding talks with interest group representatives. Not until December 1974 did an amendment to the Eduskunta Standing Orders give Finnish standing committees the right to hear experts and empower them to take part in discussions.[103] However, this has been common practice throughout the region for decades.

Next, government departments, central boards and authorities in the private sector can be approached in connection with committee scrutiny of a proposal. In Sweden, a government body is required to provide information and/or give a report when a standing committee so requests, although authorities not under the jurisdiction of the Riksdag are allow to refer such a request to the government for adjudication. Even so, if at least one-third of the members of a standing committee desire information from a body in connection with the handling of a measure, the committee shall be entitled to proceed to make the necessary arrangements to obtain it, unless this causes considerably delay and disruption to the legislative process.[104]

Fourthly, although the deliberations of standing committees are secret, subsequent statements to the press may be designed to invoke media support for a particular objective: the Folketing Standing Orders make provision for the selective dissemination of information regarding committee proceedings by stating that 'at its own discretion, a standing committe may decide to issue statements to the public at the end of a committee meeting.'[105] Such statements may be designed indirectly to elicit a government response on a matter under discussion, e.g. an official response to a committee report, or alternatively to criticise the government for its attitude or actions in respect of the committee. Firmly in the latter category was the Finance Committee's rebuke to the Employment Minister, Svend Auken, which concerned the creation of an inquiry in the spring of 1982 into the nation's work practices, *folks arbejdsvaner*, that had not been discussed in committee, as members hastened to tell journalists. According to one member, the Danish government was treating the Finance Committee as an 'afterthought', notifying it of the expenditure of public monies before the rightful permission had been granted.[106]

Finally, a Nordic standing committee is entitled to seek legal advice in the course of the scrutiny of a proposal, or indeed in con-

contemplation of an envisaged amendment to it. According to the Riksdag Standing Orders, one-third of the members of a parliamentary standing committee may refer a matter connected with the handling of a bill to the Law Council, unless the committee majority believes that this will cause undue delay in producing a final report.[107] Though used quite extensively, this right does not appear to have been abused. In Denmark a standing committee attempting to amend a bill can appeal to the Constitutional and Public Law Section within the Legal Division of the Department of Justice for a statement on the constitutionality of the original proposal. From the limited evidence available, this appears to happen about twice a year.[108] It should not be forgotten either that a standing committee can transfer a matter to another committee with the latter's consent or agree to prepare a matter conjointly.[109] The Storting can also request that standing committees be reinforced by the addition of members from other committees when matters of special importance are being considered.[110]

Thus Nordic standing committees possess a considerable array of devices with which to further the scrutiny of public policy. Yet we should make one important caveat. In the words of Sten Sparre Nilson when referring to the Storting committees, 'standing committees [in the region] are not to be compared with committees in the American Congress . . . They do not have any lines of communication with public opinion such as those which follow from public hearings, nor do they occupy an independent position as regards the matters which are to be put aside and which are to be proceeded upon.'[111]

Moreover, any attempt accurately to measure the efficiency with which the deliberative function is performed by standing committees in the region, i.e. to analyse their legislative 'output', is fraught with difficulties. First, although the obvious tangible product of committee deliberations is a report, the actual length of committee reports varies appreciably between the Nordic countries. On this basis, Norwegian standing committees would perhaps rank as the most thoroughgoing. Certainly Norwegian committees appear to debate longer and investigate a topic in greater depth than their Danish counterparts: Norwegian committee reports are voluminous and involve Storting delegates in spending more than one-third of their weekly working time on standing committee work.[112] The difference in length between the Norwegian Energy and Industry Committee's report on petroleum legislation in the 1981–2 Storting session and the slender document on the same subject by the Folketing's standing committee on the Environment and Regional Planning is typical. This is not to say that Danish standing committee meetings are desultory and serve as mere rubber-stamps for government proposals. On the contrary, as the Folketing Information Secretary noted of a meeting of the Committee on Taxation and Duties, not only are members' contributions well-prepared and highly practical, but there was also a genuine attempt at accommodation between the majority and minority on the committee over the details of legislation, and this led to some modification in attitudes to the bill across the board.[113]

Anyway, the length of committee documents in itself is of limited utility in policy terms if the reports are simply ignored by the government of the day. To gauge the policy impact of the committee scrutinisation process accurately, it would be necessary to consider the executive response to committee reports. The highly circumstantial nature of this response prevents generalisation; but suffice it to note that since the reform of the standing committee system in Sweden and the employment of a committee-based secretariat, the evidence points to ministers genuinely taking note of the content of committee reports.[114] A further test of the direct effect of committee activity on legislation is the number of committee amendments to a government bill and the number of reservations tabled to a committee report. Throughout the region, a delegate who has lost a vote in standing committee can table a reservation so long as the majority report is not unduly held up in the process.[115] A last indicator, perhaps, of the policy salience of committees is the preparedness of plenary meetings of parliament to follow the recommendations of specialist standing committees. In this context Hernes has asserted the existence of 'committee government' in Norway in the sense that it is extremely rare for the Storting not to follow the recommendation of a united standing committee. While the same might doubtless be said to be the case elsewhere in the region, it is equally obvious that the likelihood that a committee report will be unanimous, the number of reservations tabled where unanimity is not achieved, and indeed the ministerial response to committee reports are all tied to the partisan balance in the legislature as a whole. Even when standing committees are unanimous, the notion of committee government as applied to the Nordic region is rather superficial and misleading, for it belies the considerable deliberative influence of the parliamentary party groups.

Policy deliberation in the parliamentary party groups

Briefly stated, the argument advanced here is that the parliamentary party groups have *the decisive influence* at the assembly stage of policy adoption, limiting the deliberative function of standing committees in a significant sense. In pressing political situations, the parliamentary group may even determine what the standing committee will be called upon to debate or, more exactly, whether it will be called upon to debate it. Søren-Ole Olsen has observed that although most government bills in Denmark are considered in cabinet before their introduction into the Folketing, this is not exclusively so. Occasionally in urgent circumstances, when a hastily-prepared piece of legislation needs to be introduced quickly, there have been times when it has been considered only at a meeting of the governing party's parliamentary group, at which of course ministers can participate.[116] If this is exceptional, it has become widespread practice in the region for the parliamentary party caucuses to convene before standing committee meetings to determine their stance in committee. Indeed, it seems legitimate to speak of the wholesale party-policisation of Nordic standing committees and the reduction of their independent role as substantive arenas of legislative discussion. However, such strong claims obviously call for elaboration.

From the very outset of a new parliament, the parties control the process of nominating and selecting the personnel of standing committees, so reducing the role of Election Committees to the purely formalistic. Norwegian practice is typical. The Storting Standing Orders specify that when a new legislature is constituted, an Election Committee, *valgkomité*, of 37 members shall be chosen on which the parties are to be represented as far as possible in proportion to their strength in the legislature and on which the division by electoral districts is also to be taken into account.[117] Members of this Election Committee, who are validated for the full four-year term, then decide on the composition of the various standing committees. That, at least, is the theory. In practice, the Speaker and party group leaders simply get together and produce recommendations on committee membership which are then submitted by the Election Committee and formally approved by the assembly as a whole. The Election Committee is in fact greatly beholden to the party machinery. In Sweden, where there is no special election body in parliament, the procedure is effectively the same: horse-trading takes place between the party groups and a Riksdag plenary then acquiesces in the agreed lists of nominees.

The particular criteria used by the parties in selecting standing committee members need not detain us: as mentioned earlier, a member's known competence and/or expressed interest count for a good deal, although when partisan considerations so dictate, delegates can find themselves on committees involved with unknown and even alien areas of policy. Significantly, only one of the Broad

Left opposition delegates on the Eduskunta standing committee on Agriculture and Forestry in 1979–83 had an occupational background in either agriculture or forestry.[118]

Regional considerations also play a part in the party's reckoning. In approaching nominations to the Storting committee on Communications, for example, the parties are forced to confront the extremely difficult task of attempting to reconcile the range of (sometimes) conflicting regional interests they represent in the constituencies.[119] In Denmark this problem is largely obviated by the fact that the political parties can and do change members of standing committees, drafting in local and regional delegates as the occasion demands.

The informal status ranking of the parliamentary committees is also clearly a factor in the selection equation. This applies less in the small parties where there are fewer delegates to go round. But junior delegates of the larger parties are likely to be allocated a first committee place on one of the least prestigious committees[120] — e.g. the Ecclesiastical Affairs and Immigration committees in Denmark, the Legal Affairs Committee, *lagutskottet,* in Sweden or the General Affairs Committee in the United Althing in Iceland.[121] Women, moreover, have traditionally been given positions on the 'lightweight' committees like the Finnish Grand Committee. Over the years, about 40% of the female representation in the Storting has been concentrated on only two committees — Social Affairs and Church and Education. Until the 1960s, there had not been a single woman delegate on either the Industry or the Defence Committee and it was only in the 1977–81 session of the Storting that women had representation on all the standing parliamentary committees simultaneously.[122]

A measure of the influence of the parties in standing committee recruitment is indicated by the comment of Lars Nerheim, secretary of the Norwegian Christian People's Party's parliamentary group: 'It should be remembered that most Storting delegates end up in a standing committee which they did not originally want.'[123] Making essentially the same point, the secretary to the Finnish Social Democratic Party's parliamentary group went on to emphasise the unpopularity of two standing committees in particular — those dealing respectively with Agriculture and Forestry and with Law and the Economy.[124]

Party control is not restricted to the selection of committee members: the fact that throughout the region standing committee meetings are invariably preceded by meetings of the parliamentary groups or group policy committees is an indication that committee members function first and foremost as partisan actors. It is true that in general the substantive competence and experience of representatives on standing committees gives them an influential role in their parliamentary group: they are recognised as spokesmen in a particular policy area and as such they may significantly affect the party's standpoint in that area. The way the Report or Second Reading stage of a bill is dominated by committee spokesmen is evidence that the power structure in the parliamentary party groups tends to be diffuse and subject-specific, rather than comprising a vertical hierarchy based narrowly on seniority or patronage.

In this connection, the existence in the Nordic states of parliamentary group policy committees further underlines the relationship between specialist knowledge and delegate influence within the party groups. Nowhere in the region are the parliamentary group policy committees comparable with the backbench subject committees of the Labour and Conservative Parties in the House of Commons; they are necessarily smaller — the largest Nordic parliament contains only about half the total number of British MPs — and where, as in Norway, specialist parliamentary standing committees have long existed, they are less well established than at Westminster.

The most institutionalised systems of internal group policy committees are found in Finland and Sweden; Denmark and Norway represent a middle phase of development — the larger groups, particularly the Social Democrats, possessing internal policy committees while in the smaller parties they have been of a more *ad hoc* and flexible character; and in Iceland group policy committees do not exist at all at least as permanent bodies.

Although the existence of subject-specific parliamentary standing committees has perhaps made the specialist party group committees less functionally necessary than at Westminster, the full parliamentary group meetings nonetheless have neither the time nor substantive competence to give adequate consideration to the wide range of legislative proposals that come before them. Instead, there is considerable reliance on the advice of the relevant policy group spokesman. Inevitably too there is a considerable overlap in membership between the parliamentary standing committees and the internal policy committees of the party groups. In Finland, where the constitution prescribes only five permanent Eduskunta committees, party group policy committees are of comparatively long standing. In the Social Democratic Party they date back to the early years of Independence and in the Agrarian-Centre Party at least to the 1950s when their position was formalised in the rules of the parliamentary group. In both cases, their membership is the same as for the parliamentary standing committee groups. The Centre Party's policy committees are open to all parliamentary group members, although in practice other delegates very rarely attend. An occasional exception might be the situation in which, for example, the Eduskunta's Social Affairs Committee has requested a statement from the Constitutional Committee and this has prompted joint consultations between the two group policy committees concerned. According to the Centre Party's parliamentary group rules, policy committees are required to report back to the full group when controversial matters arise in standing committee, and the same is true in the other parliamentary groups although in the Finnish People's Democratic League the cohesion of group policy committees has been reduced by the need to mirror the balance between the reformist majority wing in the party and the hardline Sinisalo minority. In the 1979–83 Eduskunta session, the three-member policy committees were constituted on a 2:1 basis in the reformists' favour.

In Sweden there is a well-established system of policy committees within all the Riksdag's parliamentary groups. However, it was not until 1976, when after over four decades in office the party moved into opposition, that the need arose for policy committees in the Social Democratic Party. In the Liberal and Social Democratic Parties, the personnel is the same for standing parliamentary committees and group policy committees; in the Centre and Conservatives and Left-Communists however, the group policy committees are larger, comprising two or three standing committee groups. In consequence, there are only nine internal policy committees in the Conservatives' parliamentary group, eight in the Centre Party and seven in the Left-Communists. The three non-socialist Riksdag parties possessed permanent policy committees long before the reform of the parliamentary standing committee system in 1971. Accordingly, the network of internal group policy committees should be seen more as the result of a gradual process of evolution than reflecting the new system of Riksdag standing committees. As Magnus Isberg has argued, the existing structure of parliamentary group policy committees probably had a significant impact on the reform of the parliamentary standing committee system in 1971.[125]

In Norway, by contrast, where a specialist standing committee system has existed in the Storting since soon after the 1814 constitution, parliamentary conditions have not militated towards the organisation of intra-group policy committees to anything like the same extent as in Finland and Sweden. Certainly as Erik Mo has indicated in a wider perspective, there has been plainly less need to form policy committees in the parliamentary groups than in the House of Commons.[126] In the larger groups with three or four members in each of the Storting standing committees, the members of a standing committee group do indeed constitute a section which meets separately, and it is very rare for other members of the parliamentary group to participate at these meetings. Occasionally too, the parliamentary party may appoint special internal policy committees containing a number of its Storting standing committee groups. But in some of the smaller party groups which have only one or two members on parliamentary standing committees, internal policy committees may be created only for special subjects.

Unlike Norway, Danish policy committees have tended to be located inside the party organisation rather than the parliamentary group. In the Danish Social Democratic Party, for instance, there are fourteen subject committees comprising 20 members each within the party machine, although relatively few parliamentarians are involved on them. Alone of the Danish parties, however, the Social Democrats also have a formalised network of parliamentary group policy committees with 7–10 members each.[127]

Finally, there are no parliamentary group policy committttees as such in the Icelandic Althing, although temporary organs are frequently created within the groups to deliberate on particular matters including of course government bills. As Thorsteinn Magnusson has noted, if a proposal deals with an industrial matter, it will very probably be examined by delegates drawn from the standing committees on Industry in both divisions of the Althing.[128]

Informality and a certain amount of fluidity in their working arrangements have characterised the activities of parliamentary group policy committees outside Iceland too. This has been true even when, as with the Finnish Conservatives, the rules of the parliamentary group make explicit provision for internal policy committees. According to article 16 of the Finnish Conservatives' revised group regulations of 1979,[129] policy committees shall meet as the occasion demands and are open to all members of the parliamentary group: in practice, however, their operation has not been prominent and their importance is limited.[130] In Denmark the policy groups of the Liberals and Conservatives have been notably flexible in terms of their composition. When, for example, agricultural matters are under consideration in the Liberal Party (one of the parties represented in Schlüter's non-socialist cabinet), the Minister of Agriculture will invariably attend in a consultative capacity and there are also likely to be experts and advisers drawn from outside the Folketing. The fact that distinctively Danish parliamentary groups meet daily when parliament is in session tends to enhance the contacts and interaction between policy committees and the full group meetings of a party's parliamentary members. Lastly, it is commonplace in the smaller Storting groups also for party representatives from outside parliament to attend meetings of the group policy committees. This is largely a function of size: without external members, the one- or two-man policy committees would be too small to work effectively.

Assessing the importance of parliamentary group policy committees is a far from simple matter which does not lend itself to ready generalisation. Interviews with group staff members and parliamentarians in Finland point to the nature of the problem. In the second largest parliamentary party, the Conservatives, at the time of writing with 44 Eduskunta members, it became apparent that the 7-member group executive committee, *eduskuntaryhmäntyövaliokunta*, far outweighed the policy committees in importance, and the same was true in the radical leftist Finnish People's Democratic League with 27 members of parliament. According to the Communist delegate, Inger Hirvelä, the power exercised by the policy groups is very much dependent on the energy of the group rapporteur, *ryhmän vastaava* (the word chairman is not used in the party). When a party is in government, moreover, group policy committees tend to be less important. Members are not infrequently called upon to defend their ministers when technical shortcomings in proposals become apparent in standing committee discussions. In such circumstances, as Hirvelä insisted, the parliamentary group policy committees could reasonably be entrusted with more independent authority to amend bills.[131]

At the same time it is evident that in the two 'anchor' parties of Finnish governments, the Centre and the Social Democrats, group policy committees are becoming 'more and more important',[132] particularly in the Social Democratic Party's parliamentary group where, according to its secretary Erkki Meriläinen, policy groups have 'a good deal of power' and do 'all the significant work'.[133] If a policy group is unanimous, the matter will only rarely be taken up in the parliamentary group as a whole. This is mainly because the attention which the Social Democratic policy groups devote to topics is thorough and wide-ranging.

The SDP group policy committees enjoy a good deal of autonomy. Once selected at the first meeting of the parliamentary group each session, they immediately begin work devising and vetting private initiatives. They also hold 'hearings' connected with their consideration of proposals, which usually involve officials in the central administration who have been concerned with the preparation of the matter under scrutiny (these civil servants may, but do not always, have a background in the Social Democratic Party). Indeed, the ministry not infrequently has informal contacts with the corresponding SDP policy group during the formulation of legislation. In sum, the Finnish SDP parliamentary group policy committees are vital decision-taking organs.

The full parliamentary group, by contrast, is more of a deliberative forum: the Prime Minister may report to it on a topical question, progress on negotiations with the strategic labour-market organisations on incomes policy agreements etc. may also be discussed, and other controversial matters are liable to be raised. But the plenary meetings of the parliamentary group invariably ratify decisions taken by the party's ministers and comprehensively examined in one of the parliamentary group policy committees. Above all, the authority structure in the SDP group is neither narrowly hierarchical nor based exclusively on seniority. True, selection to the prestigious Eduskunta standing committees on Finance and Foreign Affairs proceeds purely in terms of seniority (as it does in all parties). But the chairmen of the influential parliamentary group policy committees in the SDP are chosen because they are known as the party's experts in a particular field and as such exert considerable influence. The same is true to varying degrees elsewhere in the region.

If the increasingly specialised and time-consuming nature of the task of legislative deliberation has made the parliamentary group policy committees more important than before as decision-taking organs (in line with the foregoing argument), it would still be misleading to underestimate the significance of the full parliamentary group and, particularly, of the group executive committee — the latter frequently possessing a direct link to the executive when the party in question is in government. A party's spokesman on a parliamentary standing committee (he is frequently chairman of the corresponding internal policy group also) must occasionally function as a rapporteur, reviewing controversial developments in standing committee at full meetings of the parliamentary group in non-technical language and in turn abiding by any collective decisions taken in the group. Invariably, he is mandated to act in a certain way and when unsure to refer matters back. In this way, representatives on standing committees are mouthpieces of their parliamentary group even if, as members of small policy communities deliberating in secret, the need for party posturing on standing committees is reduced.

In Norway particularly, the size and secrecy of standing committee meetings has encouraged an informality in proceedings which finds expression *inter alia* in the fact that, unlike in Sweden, meetings are not announced in the newspapers and can be called impromptu by the chairman at two or three hours' notice. The easy-going manner of standing committee deliberations is a distinctive trait of the parliamentary culture in Norway:[134] as the Secretary-General of the Storting put it, 'there is no real debate; they are more like round-table gatherings.'[135] In Denmark too the deliberations of standing committees are relatively informal, although it is a timely reminder of the partisan anchorage of delegates that in many cases seating in committee is arranged by party. In the Finance Committee, for example, seats are allocated on the basis of the size of the party: to the chairman's right is the place for the minister (when invited), followed in order by the committee secretary, the largest Folketing group, the Social Democrats, and then the other parliamentary party groups in diminishing order of strength in the assembly. Tradition dictates, however, that the deputy chairman and the other delegates from his party sit 'out of order' to the chairman's left.

Partisan considerations are not always paramount when the details of legislation are under scrutiny in standing committee; technical changes to a proposal may reflect a convergence of interests across parliamentary groups, and compromises over the 'small print' are achieved. Nonetheless it is crucial to note that standing committees mainly act as signalling devices pointing to any significant areas of partisan disagreement — which are then resolved through consultations at the inter-group level or in discussions outside parliament altogether. Important compromises and deals, in short, are only very rarely worked out in standing committee; rather, conflict is resolved within and between the parliamentary groups and the ensuing arrangements are merely given formal ratification in standing committee.

Particularly in light of earlier discussions of the role of the committees during the 1973–6 *lotteririksdag* in Sweden, it needs emphasis that even during minority administrations in the Nordic states, the centre of gravity has shifted to the parliamentary standing committees only in the superficial sense that *ad hoc* policy coalitions agreed beforehand between the government and members of the opposition are given formal expression in standing committee. True, when the Swedish Social Democrats opted to stay in office in 1973 they were faced with the challenge of achieving broad-based consensual solutions to problems. Indeed, despite demands from the Conservatives that the government 'go to the country' to resolve the parliamentary deadlock resulting from the election of 175 socialists and precisely the same number of non-socialists, the Social Democrats were able at the beginning of 1974 to get the support of the two 'middle parties', the Centre and Liberals, for a package of measures designed to stimulate the economy and in May the same year to do a deal with the Liberals on tax reforms and a flexible pensions scheme. The important point about this deal — the Haga agreement, *Hagaöverenskommelsen*, so-called after the venue of the talks (which included labour-market leaders) — is that it was concluded in Haga castle and not in the Riksdag standing committee. The same was true of the second Haga agreement between the government and the two middle parties in 1975, relating to adjustments in the tax scale. Haga became the watchword for talks between the government and opposition, whether they took place in the old castle or not. Only rarely did they take place in the Riksdag.

All in all, then, Nordic parliamentary standing committees are not important negotiating sites, as might at first appear: much of the real bargaining takes place elsewhere, either in the parliamentary party groups or outside the legislature altogether. However, the standing committees of the region are not at all easy to locate in comparative perspective at least on the basis of existing typologies. Certainly they do not conform neatly to either of the two ideal-types identified by Richard F. Fenno Jr in his study *Congressmen in Committees*. Fenno contrasts the *corporate* type of standing committee — for example, the committees of Ways and Means and Appropriations in the US House of Representatives, where members are oriented towards the House, emphasise their committee expertise, and have a strong sense of identification with the committee — and the *permeable* type of committee on which members lack a sense of group identity and play down committee expertise, and where the rules about decision-making indicate an orientation to political forces outside the House.[136]

Clearly one would have to begin any search for a wider perspective in which to define the place of Nordic standing committees by stressing their two main characteristics: substantive specialisation and effective party leadership. As to the former, there appear to be strong resemblances to the corporate type of committee. As we have seen, members are often recruited with, and invariably develop, a substantive expertise; they emphasise the importance of committee work, not least by regular attendance at meetings, cf. their absence from plenary debates; and not infrequently they build up an identification with a standing committee through long years of service. However, it is equally true that issues engender partisan controversies in committees, and that standing committees are highly susceptible to the influence of the government especially during periods of majority administration. In sum, if Nordic standing committees are to be located on a spectrum some distance away from the weak, permeable committees of Westminster, so too the power of partisan alignments has prevented the development of the predominantly corporate orientation found in a number of the standing committees in the US Congress.

REFERENCES

1. RF 4:3.
2. FOF 3:9.
3. RO 4:9.
4. VJ 40–53.
5. DRG 5:51.
6. RF 4:3.
7. Interview with Arnold Willén, Secretary of the Riksdag Foreign Affairs Committee 5.10.1981.
8. Ottar Hellevik, 'Stortingets rolle i den utenrikspolitiske avgjørelsesprosessen'. *Internasjonal Politikk* 6, 1969, pp. 691–713. In contrast to Sweden, the Storting's standing committee dealing with foreign and commercial affairs also incorporates responsibility for constitutional questions (*Utenriks- og konstitusjonskomitéen*)
9. RO 4:11:2.
10. FOF 3:8:5.
11. *Folketingets udvalg 1950–1975*. Århus: Danmarks Journalisthøjskole, Institut for Presseforskning, 1977.
12. *Oversigt over stående udvalg 1981–82* (2 samling) Folketingssekretariatet, Januar 1982.
13. Hanne Engstrøm & Ib O. Pedersen, *Folketinget*. København: Schultz, 1978, p. 31.
14. *Eduskuntamuistio 1979*. Helsinki: valtion painatuskeskus, 1979, p. 17.
15. *Motioner 1978/79*. 1779 Bo Turesson (mod.). 1979/80. 157 Bertil Hansson/Kerstin Anér (fp). *Utrikesutskottets betänkande 1980/81:9* om Vatikanstaten.
16. Birgersson (1976), p. 58.
17. *Utrikesutskottets betänkande 1980/81:4* om biblar till Sovjetunionen.
18. *Asiat vuoden 1970 ja 1980 valtiopäivillä*. Information supplied by the senior Eduskunta secretary Jouni Vainio.
19. RO 4:11.
20. RO 1:3.
21. VJ 4:43.
22. 'Eläkeuudistus eteni tiistaihin'. *Uusi Suomi* 30.12.1981.
23. Interview with Henning Vecht, secretary to the Folketing Finance Committee 22.4.1982.
24. Cited in Hilmar Rommetvedt, *Partiavstander i Stortinget som Grunnlag for Borgerlig Samarbeid 1945–1977*. Paper presented to the Nordic Political Science congress, Åbo, Finland, 17–19.8.1981, p. 26.
25. Jean Blondel, *An Introduction to Comparative Government*. London: Weidenfeld & Nicolson, 1969, p. 362.
26. Loewenberg & Patterson (1979), p. 205.
27. RO 4:2.
28. RO 4:2:1.
29. SFO 3:14.
30. Interview with Jens Adser Sørensen, secretary to the *ad hoc* Folketing committee on Youth Employment 26.4.1982.
31. FOF 3:23:5.

32. Gordon Smith, *Politics in Western Europe*. London: Heinemann, 1980, p. 167.
33. See the section by the *Groupe des spécialistes des études parlementaires françaises*, in Coombes & Walkland (1980), pp. 135–6.
34. 'Allt tveksamt skall prövas'. *Dagens Nyheter* 17.2.1981. There was an Immigration Minister, Karin Andersson, in Fälldin's Centre-Liberal minority in 1981–2 (as there had been in Fälldin's non-socialist majority coalition from 1979–81). Olof Palme's Social Democratic minority government (1982–) does not, however, contain such a post.
35. Information provided by Thorsteinn Magnússon 1.9.1981.
36. SFO 3:16.
37. Hilding Johansson, 'Grundlagsfrågan i riksdagen — några avsnitt'. *Statsvetenskapliga Tidskrift* 1, 1976, pp. 27–31.
38. Gösta Söderlund, 'Politikerna vår tids frälse'. *Svenska Dagbladet* 7.9.1981.
39. *Eduskunnan kalenteri vuoden 1981 varsinaisilla valtiopäivillä*. Helsinki: Valtion painatuskeskus, 1981.
40. *Riksdagen 1981/82*. Uppgifter om ledamöter och riksdagsorgan. Stockholm: Riksdagens förvaltningskontor: 1981.
41. Gudmund Hernes, 'Interest, Influence and Co-operation: A Study of the Norwegian Parliament'. Ph.D. thesis, Johns Hopkins University, 1971, p. 352.
42. Oversigt over stående udvalg 1981–82.
43. Interview with the Chairman of the Riksdag Finance Committee (1979–82), Eric Enlund 18.9.1981.
44. RO 9:2.
45. Riksdagen 1981/82, pp. 49–64.
46. Interview with Per-Christian Pedersen, deputy secretary to the Storting committee on Foreign Affairs and the Constitution 30.9.1981.
47. Interview with senior Eduskunta secretary (*vanhempi sihteeri*) Jouni Vainio 22.12.1981.
48. Interview with Peter Juul Larsen, secretary to the Folketing committees on Public Works, Political Economy and Ecclesiastical Affairs 20.4.1982.
49. FOF 3:8:4.
50. Discussion with Thorsteinn Magnússon 15.7.1982.
51. Interview with Henning Vecht 22.4.1982.
52. Finansudvalgets Sekretariat, *Redegørelse, vedrørende finansudvalget, dettes kompetence, funktioner og arbejdsmåde*. March 1979, p. 2.
53. Interview with Henning Vecht 22.4.1982.
54. VJ 4:43.
55. Olavi Salvervo, 'Eduskunnan valiokuntalaitoksen kehittämisestä'. *Politiikka* 2, 1976, pp. 105–18.
56. VJ 5:66–70, 76.
57. Pertti Ahonen, 'Eduskunnan saama julkista hallintoa koskeva informaatio: ongelmanmäärittelyä'. *Politiikka* 1, 1980, pp. 59–70.
58. DRG 5:45:1.
59. Redegørelse vedrørende finansudvalget, p. 3.
60. Ibid., p. 4.
61. RO 4:6:2.
62. *Bevilgningsreglement 2*.
63. SFO 3:19.
64. SFO 3:12, 15, 22.
65. RO 3:2.
66. RO 4:5, 6:2.
67. RO 4:6.
68. *Finansutskottets betänkande 1980/81:20* om riktlinjer för den ekonomiska politiken och budgetregleringen.

69. Riksdagen. *Från Riksdag och Departement* 5.2.1982.
70. Interview with Eric Enlund 18.9.1981.
71. Interview with Bengt Johansson, secretary of the Riksdag Finance Committee 18.9.1981.
72. Interview with (former) Riksdag delegate Daniel Tarschys 21.9.1981.
73. 'Kristityt avainasemassa'. *Kristityn Vastuu* 3.9.1976.
74. Interview with Henning Vecht 22.4.1982.
75. Loewenberg & Patterson (1979), p. 256.
76. *Bopælsliste for folketingets medlemmer*. Folketingsåret 1981–82.
77. VJ 4:52.
78. Olsen (1980), p. 229.
79. Interview with Peter Juul Larsen 20.4.1982.
80. Olle Wästberg, 'Politiker, sluta upp med hemlighetsmakeriet'. *Dagens Nyheter* 11.9.1981.
81. Bengt Owe Birgersson, Stig Hadenius, Björn Molin & Hans Wieslander, *Sverige efter 1900. En modern politisk historia*. Stockholm: Bonniers, 1981, pp. 284–6.
82. Loewenberg & Patterson (1979), p. 253.
83. FOF 3:8:5.
84. SFO 3:16.
85. VJ 4:51.
86. FOF 3:7:3.
87. Salervo (1976), pp. 109–10.
88. The eight *ad hoc* standing committees at present comprise 19 members each.
89. Interview with Daniel Tarschys 21.9.1981.
90. Birgersson (1976), p. 58.
91. Kari Valtonen, *Kansanedustajien osallistuminen valiokuntiensa kokouksiin vuosien 1973 ja 1979 valtiopäivillä*. Yleisen valtio-opin yleisen linjan pro-gradu tutkielma. Helsinki 1981, p. 91.
92. 'Kansanedustajain leväperäisyys aika ottaa esille'. *Helsingin Sanomat* 29.5.1981.
93. Antero Juntumaa, 'Nollatutkimusta'. *Kristityn Vastuu* 11.6.1981.
94. Matti Oksanen, *Kansanedustajan rooli. Tutkimus kansanedustajien suhtautumisesta edustajantoimeensa vuoden 1969 valtiopäivillä*. Helsinki: Gaudeamus, 1972, p. 108.
95. 'Fred ahkerin rivikansanedustaja'. *Kristityn Vastuu* 28.5.1981.
96. FOF 3:8:6.
97. FOF 3:8:7.
98. SFO 3:21.
99. ET 19 (edusk. päätös 5.12.1974).
100. FOF 3:8:8.
101. Information supplied by Erik Mo 24.2.1982.
102. RO 4:10.
103. ET 16.
104. RO 4:10.
105. FOF 3:8:5.
106. 'Arbejdsministeren bryder reglerne'. *Jyllands-Posten* 25.4.1982.
107. RF 8:18.
108. Interview with Michael Lunn 26.4.1982.
109. RO 4:8.
110. SFO 3:15.
111. Nilson (1977), p. 6.
112. Hernes (1971), p. 352.
113. Elise Stenbæk, *Til formanden for folketingets skatte og afgiftsudvalg Bernhardt Tastesen* 21.4.1982.

114. Interview with John H. Hagard 18.12.1981.
115. RO 4:14. VJ 4:51.
116. Søren-Ole Olsen (1978), p. 56.
117. SFO 3:8.
118. Eduskunnan kalenteri (1981), p. 45.
119. Nilson (1977), p. 6.
120. Interview with Arne Marquard (*Folketingets Protokolsekretær*), a senior member of the Speaker's Office in the Folketing 20.4.1982.
121. Information provided by Thorsteinn Magnússon 15.7.1982.
122. Torild Skard, *Utvalgt til Stortinget. En studie i kvinners frammarsj og menns makt*. Oslo: Gyldendal Norsk Forlag, 1980, pp. 135–139.
123. Interview with Lars Nerheim, secretary of the Norwegian Christian People's Party's parliamentary group 2.10.1981.
124. Interview with Erkki Meriläinen, secretary of the Social Democratic Party group in the Eduskunta 21.3.1983.
125. Isberg (1982), pp. 4, 10, 16–17.
126. Information from Erik Mo 21.3.1983.
127. Discussion with Kurt Andersen, Information Secretary in the Folketing 28.3.1983.
128. Information provided by Thorsteinn Magnússon 8.3.1983.
129. *Kansallinen Kokoomus, Eduskuntaryhmä — Säännöt*. Hyväksytty ryhmäkokouksessa 30.9.1976, 4 ja 8§ muuttettu 16.3.1978 sekä 4§ 3.4.1979.
130. Interview with Conservative Party Information Secretary Jari Erholm 21.3.1983.
131. Interview with Inger Hirvelä 23.3.1983.
132. Interview with Tapani Katila of the Finnish Centre Party's parliamentary group staff 23.3.1983.
133. Interview with Erkki Meriläinen 21.3.1983.
134. Interview with Henry Valen 1.10.1981.
135. Interview with Erik Mo 1.10.1981.
136. Cited in Loewenberg and Patterson (1979), pp. 204–5.

6

'UPPER TIER' COMMITTEES

> 'The Grand Committee represented a compromise solution designed to safeguard the "civilised classes" against "ill-considered decisions" once the principle of bicameralism had been lost. Its name was devised by Felix Heikel, a staunch bicameralist, but the Grand Committee was a hybrid rolling into one several earlier proposals for implementing "checks and balances".' — Tapani Turkka, *Parlamentaarisen hallitus järjestelmän muotoutumisesta Suomessa, Tampere*, 48, 1978 Pardem 1, p. 53.

This chapter is made up of two self-contained parts. The first continues the detailed examination of the scrutiny of proposals in the assembly and focuses in particular on the handling of specialist standing committee reports in the two distinctive 'upper tier' committees in the region — the Finnish Grand Committee and the Norwegian Lagting. The second part concentrates on the Nordic Council, an 'upper tier' assembly inasmuch as it deals with supranational matters, while operating as a type of Consolidated Committee of the national and devolved legislatures — appointed by them and ultimately subordinate to them.

The central issue in the first part, which highlights the modified unicameralist elements in the parliamentary adoption process in parts of the region, is why the Grand Committee and Lagting were set up and the extent to which they have consolidated and strengthened the deliberative function of the Eduskunta and Storting. Two conclusions on the modern role of these 'upper tier' committees, relics of a bygone era of constitution-building and spawned by conservative forces thwarted in their desire for full bicameralism, seem irresistible. First, the existence of the Grand Committee has contributed to making the Finnish legislative process one of the most complicated in the Nordic region without significantly reinforcing the Eduskunta's contribution in respect of policy adoption. The Grand Committee, in short, has not been the Council of Elders it was designed to be. Secondly and in a similar vein, there is the reality that, without a corporate identity either in the sense of comprising an 'estate' of lawyers or in avoiding the stirring-up of partisan conflict, the Lagting has lacked high status and, in many ways too, a sufficiently purposive role in the legislative process.

Consideration is also given to the emergence and growth of the Icelandic Upper Chamber, Efri Deild — though not here its modern role — in the national policy process. It is shown that historically the adoption of a two-divisional Althing in 1874 (as with the Finnish

Grand Committee) reflected the influence of the Norwegian constitution of 1814 and initially appeared to represent a victory for the independence movement, although its leader, Jón Sigurðsson, quickly saw that the Danish King's prerogative of appointing personnel to the Upper Chamber gave him the power to block unwanted proposals. Efri Deild is not an 'upper tier' committee in the sense of the Grand Committee and Lagting: it enjoys parity of status with the Lower Chamber *Nethri Deild* in so far as it is an arena where new proposals can be initiated rather than one to which ongoing measures are referred for possible amendment. However, as with the Norwegian Lagting but not the Finnish Grand Committee, there have been increasing calls in recent years for the abolition of Efri Deild.

Finally, and underlining the salience of institutional diffusion in moulding the modified unicameralist systems in the region, there is a brief note on the Grand Committee in the Åland Landsting. However, it is necessary first to resume our consideration of the adoption process at the point where bills have been handled by a specialist standing committee.

The handling of the reports of parliamentary standing committees

After sometimes lengthy consideration in standing committee, a bill in the Nordic parliaments is subject to one or more readings on the floor of the assembly. In Norway and Sweden a proposal generally receives only one plenary reading before it becomes law; elsewhere in the region, three readings are the rule. However, in Finland approval of the budget, and in Finland and Iceland private initiatives connected with the budget, along with members' request proposals (see chapter 7), require only a single reading. Otherwise, the Finnish Parliament Act states that if a committee report relates to the acceptance or rejection of a proposal for a new law, it must be subject to three plenary readings.[1]

A clear differentiation within the regional legislative processes is evident on the basis of the timing of the standing committee stage in relation to the plenary consideration of proposals. In Denmark and Iceland the First Reading debate, which is confined to a discussion of principles and does not involve the moving of amendments, *precedes* deliberation of bills in standing committee. In both these countries standing committee discussion separates the First and Second, and the Second and Third Reading stages. In Finland, the First Reading and in Norway and Sweden single plenary reading take place after scrutiny of bills in specialist standing committee.

Not infrequently, however, there is a pre-committee 'preliminary debate' in Finland, although this is entirely a matter of convention and is not mentioned in the Parliament Act. After the preliminary debate, a bill goes to standing committee whose report is discussed at the First Reading — from which, without a decision being taken, the matter is sent to the Grand Committee.

Throughout the region a short minimum period must elapse between the completion of a standing committee report and its discussion in the assembly so that delegates can receive the report and digest its contents. When a standing committee report is first introduced in Finland, it is placed 'on the table', a procedure which can be repeated when the Speaker introduces it a second time if two or more delegates so desire. In Sweden the standing committee report is placed on the table at two plenary meetings unless, at the request of the standing committee in question, the Riksdag decides that one is sufficient. When a Danish standing committee has considered a matter, it is required to submit a report — or, if it has previously submitted one, a supplementary report, *tillægsbetænkning* — which is then distributed to members of the Folketing and may not be debated in the chamber until two days thereafter. Exactly the same rule applies in Norway. Incidentally, when a Danish committee has submitted a report for Second Reading debate, it may make only an oral recommendation, *mundtlig indstilling*, at the Third Reading, provided that no reservations are tabled and no committee members request a supplementary report.[2] If the committee decides in favour of an oral recommendation, the Speaker of the Folketing should be notified through the Secretariat and the recommendation submitted to the assembly either by the chairman or by a specially-appointed rapporteur.[3]

'Report stage' plenaries in the Nordic states tend to be dominated by party leaders and specialist committee spokesmen. In Sweden many matters are decided without any real general debate, so reducing the post-committee 'working plenary', *arbetsplenum*, to something of a formality.[4] As elsewhere, however, amendments to a proposal can be moved on the floor of the Riksdag and the matter returned to a standing committee. In Denmark, for example, the Second Reading Debate examines the bill in general terms, its individual sections in detail and then the reservations tabled to it in standing committee. At the close of the debate, the substance of the bill and any amendments tabled in full sitting are put to the vote and the matter is invariably referred back to standing committee. Whatever the outcome, a standing committee which has examined a matter between First and Second Reading is not precluded from taking it up for renewed examination between Second and Third Reading provided the Speaker of the Folketing is notified.[5]

Uniquely in the region, though precisely as in the West German Bundestag, legislative amendments can even be moved at the Third Reading of a bill in the Folketing: in Finland and Iceland, however, no discussion is allowed at Third Reading and bills are simply accepted or rejected, although in Iceland a bill is required to pass through the same three stages in the Upper Division of the Althing.

The legislative process in Iceland is long but symmetrical: three readings and the corresponding standing committee stages in both divisions before a bill becomes law. However, in Finland all proposals, except the very small category which are subject only to a single reading, must pass after a First Reading through the 45-member Grand Committee whose report then provides the basis for a detailed Second Reading discussion. If the Grand Committee's report is not approved in its entirety, the bill is referred back to it and the Grand Committee can then approve, modify or indeed reject the changes made at Second Reading. At this stage, the Eduskunta or Grand Committee can request further statements from a specialist standing committee whence, at the so-called Continued Second Reading, parliament is called upon either to accept or reject the changes suggested by the Grand Committee.

The Finnish Grand Committee has no counterpart in the region: it is the largest standing parliamentary committee in the Nordic states and one of the oldest, originating with the transition to unicameralism in 1907. In the manner of parliamentary committees in Britain and France (in the Fifth Republic) it is a specifically non-specialist body which is simultaneously an integral part of the legislative process, and while not enjoying the 'divisional' status of the Norwegian Lagting or Icelandic Efri Deild, it is larger than both and far more centrally involved in policy adoption than the Lagting, which is restricted to the consideration of 'laws'. In our present discussion, two questions seem of paramount importance: why was the Grand Committee set up and to what extent has it strengthened the deliberative function of the Eduskunta in respect of policy adoption? In short, has it succeeded in ensuring a sufficiently careful examination of measures by, in Jaakko Nousiainen's words, preserving 'in the unicameral legislature some of the advantages of a two-chamber system'?[6]

The Grand Committee

Historically, the Grand Committee emerged as a compromise solution designed to safeguard the position of the 'civilised classes', *sivistyneistö*, against hasty and 'ill-considered decisions' on the part of the masses (see the citation at the beginning of this chapter) once the principle of a bicameral assembly had been rejected by a parliamentary reform committee created in the Grand Duchy following the Tsar's October Manifesto in 1905.

The name Grand Committee was coined by a Swedish-speaking bicameralist, Felix Heikel, who was plainly seeking safeguards against what he saw as the alarming prospect of the traditionally educated and influential groups in society — mainly, though not exclusively Swedish-speaking — being swamped politically by the newly-enfranchised workers in town and country. Various checks and balances were considered by the committee; here the Norwegian model of modified unicameralism with its 'three-*ting*' division was influential throughout. There was also a proposal from another supporter of a bicameral assembly for the creation of a 45-man review organ elected on corporate lines and involving representatives of the legal profession, higher education, agricultural societies and urban and rural district councils, but significantly not members of parliament.[7] It would have elected its own chairman and had the right to nominate three of its members to every parliamentary standing committee. In the event, although this blueprint received little support on the reform committee, the Grand Committee solution constituted a uniquely Finnish amalgam of the essence of both Norwegian and native practice: a general review 'division' at one stage removed from the specialist standing committees, but firmly located within a unicameral legislature and comprising sixty parliamentarians — precisely the number laid down for the 'augmented committees', *lisättyjen valiokuntien instituutio*, in the 1869 Standing Orders of the old Diet of Estates.[8]

In one sense, the end-product of the committee's deliberations was more radical than the Norwegian system of legislative divisions, for while the Lagting is required only to vet 'law proposals', i.e. a relatively small proportion of the government's total policy output, the Grand Committee was designed to examine all proposals except the very small category of measures subject only to a single reading, e.g. the annual Finance Bill. However, at a time of strikingly radical political reform, which witnessed the abolition at a stroke of the quadricameral Diet of Estates — in its day one of the most antiquated legislatures in Europe — along with the enactment of universal suffrage, making Finland the first European nation to give women the vote, the Grand Committee was an institution born in a conservative spirit from the establishment of the day. The latter's primary concern was to build safeguards into the political system to defend the minorities that made up the old order. The introduction of proportional representation, as well as the highly distinctive system of qualified majorities for the enactment of laws 'at the constitutional level' were part of this same concern to erect floodgates that would stem the rising tide of radical change.

Against this background, it was to be expected that the Social Democrats, as spokesmen of large sections of the newly-enfranchised population, would oppose the idea of the Grand Committee. One of their number on the reform committee tabled a dissenting reservation to its final report, while others subsequently likened the Grand Committee approach to what they saw as the high-handedness of the House of Lords in Britain! It was also to be anticipated that the Grand Committee would be accepted on 19 January, 1906 without discussion in the exclusively bourgeois Diet of Estates (the Social Democrats refused to run candidates) although in order that the new organ should not appear too much like a Second Chamber, its sittings were not to be made public.[9] At this juncture, a system of deputies was not considered for members of the Grand Committee nor were any quorums fixed for the taking of valid decisions.

For the first four years of its existence, the legitimacy of the Grand Committee continued to be challenged by the Social Democrats. Between 1908 and 1911, individual Social Democratic delegates tabled several members' request proposals pressing for its abolition and pointing to the way it could tactically protract the consideration of proposals. The handling of these Social Democratic initiatives was not completed because of the Tsar's frequent dissolution of the Eduskunta — an expression of his undoubted desire to snuff out the fledgling parliamentary democracy in Finland. The fall of Tsarism and the achievement of Finnish independence in 1917 moderated Social Democratic attitudes towards the Grand Committee, however. It was now argued that the size of the committee should be reduced so as not to prevent a sufficient pool of delegates from being available to attend other parliamentary committees meeting concurrently with the Grand Committee. In 1918 this was done, and the reduction was confirmed in the (still operational) Parliament Act of 1928; according to which the Grand Committee is to comprise a minimum of 45 members along with a necessary number of deputy-members.[10] The quorum for valid decisions set in 1918 at four-fifths of its membership was amended to two-thirds; parliamentary officials, in addition to delegates and cabinet ministers were permitted to attend meetings with the Grand Committee's consent;[11] and a norm of a single reading of bills replaced the previous two readings. Since 1928 the position of the Grand Committee has not seriously been questioned.

Its detailed work procedures, originally set out in a statute of 1927, were revised in 1976, but this mainly involved confirmation of a number of established conventions. In particular, the 1976 rubric ratified the practice, which had first appeared in the late 1920s and developed rapidly in the 1950s,[12] of creating sections or working groups within the Grand Committee with a view to preparing matters which are to come before it and producing a report for review by the full committee.[13] Formally, the decision to institute a bill-specific and temporary section is taken in full committee, by vote if necessary, and the Grand Committee then determines the size of the section's membership. An attempt is made in the sections, as in the committee as a whole, to reflect the relative socialist-non-socialist strength in the assembly, although representatives of the smaller parties have necessarily been excluded on some occasions. Perhaps in order to accommodate the smaller parliamentary groups, a growth in the size of sections has recently been evident: they can range from two to as many as eleven persons. The chairman of the Grand Committee serves as the chairman of sections — which, it should be added, often have recourse to the views of outside experts in the course of preparing a measure.

Having delved into the detailed *modus operandi* of the Grand Committee, we should briefly summarise its other main internal procedures. *All delegates* have the right to attend deliberations of the Grand Committee: the agendas of its meetings, which are fixed by the chairman, are posted on the main Eduskunta noticeboard.[14] All delegates, incidentally, can decline to serve on more than two parliamentary committees, except by convention when membership of the Grand Committee is at issue. This has meant that every parliamentarian — except, of course, cabinet ministers and members of the Speaker's Council — is eligible for recruitment to the Grand Committee. Recruitment itself is entirely in the hands of the political parties, which have a completely free hand in nominations. Full members are allocated their own seat places in the Grand Committee: if they are prevented from attending, they should notify an appointed deputy who is permitted to occupy the regular member's place and take a full part in the committee's work.[15] The chairman has the right to deviate from the order of business set out in the Grand Committee agenda or, indeed, take up matters not included on the agenda at all.[16] While the chairman is himself entitled to participate in the discussions of the committee, as well as to vote on its decisions, he confines himself in practice to casting his ballot. As a rule, the chairman and deputy-chairman are selected to represent the socialist and non-socialist sides of the House respectively.

Every matter is given a single reading in the Grand Committee unless the committee decides on two readings. As the basis for its discussions, the Grand Committee has one of three possible items before it: the report of one of the specialist standing committees, modifications to that report formulated in one of its own sections, or plenary amendments to the Grand Committee report tabled at Second Reading. When the Grand Committee decides to give a matter a second 'internal' reading, it will take the draft proposal agreed at first reading (and produced by the committee secretary) as the basis for a detailed reading stage.[17] Any decision to hear experts or request further statements from a specialist standing committee should be taken before this second reading. Finally, Grand Committee reports are short: there is no elaboration of the grounds for the recommendations made and, unlike specialist standing committees, no reservations to reports are permitted.[18] Although the workload of the Grand Committee has increased substantially in the post-war era, the number of its weekly meetings has declined: between 1920 and 1954 the committee met twice a week, whereas nowadays it usually does so only once, except towards the end of the parliamentary session when extra meetings are necessary to clear unfinished government business.

In the context of our primary task of considering the legislative role of the Grand Committee, it is an important though by no means decisive fact that whereas the bourgeois parties originally envisaged the creation of something approximating a Council of Elders,[19] the Grand Committee has in reality fallen far short of being an upper chamber both in terms of the seniority and prestige of its members and the stability of its membership. Indeed in its early years it appeared the very opposite to a Council of Elders, for in 1919 no less than two-thirds of its members were parliamentary newcomers — a significantly large proportion even allowing for the considerable renewal of Eduskunta members which took place in the aftermath of the 1918 civil war and the split on the Left. Voitto Helander has even suggested that one of the functions of the Grand Committee in the early independence period was to serve as a training ground for new delegates, allowing them a useful overview of the legislative process.[20] Even in later years, parliamentary party leaders have tended to steer clear of the Grand Committee: between the last war and the early 1970s, only three chairmen of parliamentary groups were members of the Grand Committee, two Conservatives and one Agrarian, V.J. Sukselainen, who was its chairman.[21] Not a single Social Democrat or Radical Leftist group chairman has sat on the Grand Committee. Furthermore, except for one or two veterans like Urho Kulovaara who sat for over thirty years, the turnover of personnel on the Grand Committee has been higher than on many specialist standing committees. The status of a committee — which is clearly middle-ranking in the case of the

Grand Committee — is not necessarily a reliable gauge of its legislative importance: for example, the policy significance of the prestigious Foreign Affairs committees in the region is small by any standards. Rather, to attempt a reasonably sensitive measure of the policy impact of the Grand Committee two indicators seem appropriate: first the changes the Grand Committee makes to the reports of specialist standing committees, and secondly the changes made to bills returned to the Grand Committee after their Second Reading on the floor of the assembly.

On the first count, the Grand Committee's propensity to change specialist committee reports has declined, as has the number of clauses in bills that it has modified. Before Independence, the Grand Committee amended on average every second standing committee report, during the inter-war period every fourth, and thereafter every eighth.[22] Moreover, while before Independence the Grand Committee changed more than ten clauses in over 18% of all bills and between the wars in over 10%, since then only about 4% have been substantially modified.[23] As Helander has pointed out, there has been a tendency in recent decades for bills to be accepted in the Grand Committee without either discussion or a vote.[24] The heightened workload of the Grand Committee, the increasingly technical nature of many of the proposals that come before it, the central role of partisan cohesion, and not least the effective resolution of the more controversial issues at the pre-legislative stage — often in conjunction with the labour-market leaders — are all factors accounting for the limited and declining impact of the Grand Committee. Significantly too, as Helander shows, most amendments are made to the reports of the Finance Committee and these are invariably of a minor non-political character.

There have been occasions when the Grand Committee has functioned as it was originally intended to do — to create checks and balances in the legislative process and to act as a brake on an ill-considered or controversial government proposal as it emerges from a specialist standing committee. Before the general election in March 1983, for example, divisions in three of the four major parties (the radical leftist SKDL was the exception) over a contentious government bill liberalising the existing legislation on surnames, *sukunimilaki* — the intention was to maximise individual self-determination over the surname used after marriage — enabled opponents of the bill in the Grand Committee to modify the Legal Affairs Committee proposal sufficiently for the House to decide by 88 votes to 81 at a Second Reading ballot to return the bill to standing committee. In accordance with the Eduskunta's Standing Orders, the Legal Affairs Committee was not permitted to alter the

Grand Committee's amendments to the bill, but was requested merely to comment having sounded out the unofficial positions of the parliamentary party groups.

The issue raises a number of general points. First, the bill, which took as its point of departure the need to realise the United Nation's declared goal of equality between the sexes, was undoubtedly controversial and had been under consideration in the Eduskunta for no less than one year and a half before coming to the Grand Committee.[25] Secondly, the question aroused notably strong feelings both in parliament and in the country: in a letter to the organ of the Finnish Christian League, *Kristityn Vastuu*, in January 1983, twenty-two public figures including the internationally-acclaimed opera singer Martti Talvela and the popular columnist on the current affairs weekly *Suomen Kuvalehti*, Elina Karjalainen, expressed their strong opposition to the bill and their fear that it would damage the solidarity and unity of the family in Finland.[26] Finally, and most important, the defeat of the Legal Affairs Committee's proposal in the Grand Committee was the result of a relatively rare incidence of cross-party voting. In fact the Centre and Conservative parties were internally divided into a men's and women's faction over the surname bill.

In the case of bills returned to it after Second Reading, the Grand Committee's position is formally quite strong. It is not confined to approving or rejecting the Second Reading proposal, but can make wide-ranging modifications to it. In practice, however, as Table 6.1 shows, this does not often happen: indeed, bills returned to the Grand Committee after Second Reading are only rarely amended substantially. It can be seen that of over 500 bills returned to the

Table 6.1. THE EXTENT OF GRAND COMMITTEE AMENDMENTS TO BILLS RETURNED AFTER SECOND READING (%)

	1907–14	*1917–44*	*1945–71*	*1907–71*
Accepted Second Reading Proposal	40	43.8	57.0	48.3
Partly accepted Second Reading proposal	37.2	32.6	22.8	29.3
Adhered to original Grand Committee report	17.1	22.4	18.1	20.5
Other	5.7	1.3	1.7	1.9
	100.0	100.0	100.0	100.0
n =	35	304	193	532

Source: Voitto Helander, *Kamari vai kirjaamo*? Turun yliopiston valtio-opillisia tutkimuksia 32, 1976, p.117.

Grand Committee after Second Reading between 1907 and 1971, almost half were approved unchanged by the Grand Committee, less than one third were approved with minor amendments, and in only a little over a fifth of all cases did the committee make major modifications to the Second Reading proposals or adhere to its original response to the standing committee report on the bill. In short, the obvious response to the rhetorical question in the title of Helander's study — 'Chamber or Registry?', *Kamari vai kirjaamo*? — is that the Grand Committee is essentially a registry, giving a legal stamp of approval and recording policy amendments mooted elsewhere, especially in a specialist standing committee.

This is not to say that conflict between the government and Grand Committee has not occurred or that ministers have not at times been prompted to visit Grand Committee meetings to expedite the handling of a matter or to prepare the ground for the smooth consideration of a forthcoming proposal. Moreover, while American-style filibustering does not form part of the culture of the Grand Committee, bills can be tactically delayed by referring them to one of the committee's internal sections, a device used particularly when general elections are approaching. Also, the Grand Committee's role in modifying legislation should not be underestimated. Jaakko Nousiainen writes: 'The Grand Committee serves a limited, albeit useful, control function, examining inadequately-considered Second Reading proposals and, above all, those amendments incorporated into bills almost accidentally during hectic plenary voting sessions. In such cases, the Grand Committee is invaluable in appraising the internal consistency of measures and the overall feasibility of implementing them.'[27] This is a pertinent point, especially because, although the right of Eduskunta delegates to initiate and amend proposals is relatively limited, they are entitled at the detailed Second Reading stage verbally to move amendments which, of course, have not been considered in a specialist standing committee and which are voted on there and then. Yet the existence of the Grand Committee has contributed to making the Finnish legislative process one of the most complicated in the Nordic region without significantly strengthening the deliberative powers of the Eduskunta over policy adoption.

The position of the Grand Committee is no longer controversial — its role was not considered in the discussion of rationalising the work of the Eduskunta in the 1950s or by the Constitutional Reform Committee in the 1970s. From a governmental viewpoint, obviously, it has provided an arena within which to attempt to redress changes to proposals made by a specialist standing committee; and at the level of amending the details of legislation, it has at times generated a cross-party consensus which, if anything, has served to legitimise the process of parliamentary scrutiny. However, Grand Committee meetings are not well attended despite the system of deputy-members; non-committee members only rarely avail themselves of the right to follow its proceedings; and any significant conflict that arises invariably follows partisan lines. Thus, although it occupies a strategic position between the considerations of a specialist standing committee and the detailed discussions of the Second Reading plenary, the Grand Committee has lacked both a specific role and a genuine identity and despite the aspirations held out for it at its inception, it remains definitely a permeable rather than a corporate type of committee.

The Lagting

Is this equally true of the Norwegian Lagting? Norway's version of unicameralism, although plainly influential in the decision to create the Grand Committee, has not involved the same extensive 'second-stage committee handling' of legislative proposals as in Finland. The Lagting's participation in the legislative process has been necessarily intermittent and confined to the relatively small category of 'laws'. At the same time, the Lagting and the Grand Committee had a very similar underlying rationale and, particularly in the context of the handling of specialist standing committee reports, the Lagting may be regarded (admittedly stretching the point a little) as an 'upper tier' standing committee of the Storting, albeit with a limited remit. As in our consideration of the Grand Committee, there are two basic questions: why was the Lagting originally set up and has its presence strengthened parliament's role as a deliberative body *vis-à-vis* the executive?

There was strong initial support for full unicameralism among the officials, peasants and merchants who made up the 112 members of the Eidsvoll National Assembly, *Riksforsamlingen*, convened by Prince Christian Frederik in April 1814 to formulate a new constitution and elect a monarch in the wake of the country's separation from Denmark — a break precipitated by the Napoleonic wars. That a modified form of unicameralism ultimately prevailed was due to a combination of ideological, pragmatic and plainly prosaic factors. At the ideological level, it was pointed out that a separation of powers was inscribed into the best forms of government — the English and American forms were cited during the debates of the 'Eidsvoll men' — and that the institution of 'checks and balances' was a *sine qua non* for the adequate scrutiny of measures in parliament as well as the sound working of the policy process as a whole. At a pragmatic level, it was widely felt that the typical contemporary division of legislatures into distinct Upper and Lower Houses would be unpopular and expensive: after all, the Nobility had only recently been abolished, while it was argued that a poor country like Norway, in contrast to Sweden, did not possess the social structure to sustain an upper chamber as an efficient and legitimate political organ. In a bicameral system, moreover, there was the inherent risk of the legislative process being impaired and even impeded altogether. More prosaically, the fear was also expressed that the number of farmers and peasants in subsequent sessions of an undivided Storting would be so great as to create 'an estate of the most foolish', *narragtigste ting*, within the assembly itself. There were those who, to offset this possibility, envisaged a Lagting drawing on the more educated classes, particularly lawyers, and comprising men past thirty years of age who would sit for a six-year term — twice that proposed for the Odelsting.[28] In its early years at least, these fears proved unfounded and the number of farmers in the Lagting was extremely small, as Table 6.2 shows. By the time the matter had been discussed in the Constitutional Committee of the Eidsvoll Assembly there was an overwhelming consensus favouring the principle of internal legislative divisions and the need to empower the Lagting *inter alia* to reject proposals from the Odelsting. This last recommendation was withdrawn, however, following a powerful and persuasive speech from Peter Motzfeldt when the Constitutional Committee's report was debated in plenary session: he maintained that a division into two chambers would be both futile and harmful — futile because a group with a majority in the full legislature, the Storting, would clearly possess a plurality in both divisions, and harmful since he felt that the Lagting would anyway tend to attract the most able parliamentarians. Although a majority in the Eidsvoll Assembly concurred with the main lines of the Constitutional Committee's proposal, the force of Motzfeldt's arguments

Table 6.2. THE COMPOSITION OF THE LAGTING, 1818–30

	Educated persons and officials	*Merchants*	*Farmers*
1818	18	—	—
1827	19	1	—
1830	16	2	2

Source: Sverre Steen, 'Hvordan Norges Storting ble til' in *Det Norske Storting Gjennom 150 år*. Gyldendal Norsk Forlag, Oslo 1964, p. 187.

nonetheless ensured that a free-standing Lagting with a veto right over the Odelsting never emerged. It was in the Storting that the full radical potential of parliamentary reform was most likely to be felt for, as T.K. Derry has observed, 'there was no legal obstacle to the domination of the Norwegian legislature by the peasantry, whereas their fellows in Sweden still constituted only one of the four Estates.[29]

The sections of the Eidsvoll constitution (articles 73–76) relating to the powers of the Lagting have remained unchanged since 1814. Accordingly, the people shall exercise the legislative power through the Storting which shall consist of two divisions, the Odelsting and Lagting. The Storting shall nominate from among its members one quarter to constitute the Lagting and the remaining three quarters to make up the Odelsting. The selection of delegates to both divisions shall take place at the first ordinary session of the Storting after a new general election, and thereafter the Lagting shall remain unchanged until the next election. Each *Ting* shall hold its meetings separately and nominate its own Speaker and Secretary. Neither division may hold a meeting unless at least half its members are present.

Every 'law' proposal must be introduced into the Odelsting either by the government[30] or by a member of that division. When law proposals have completed their committee stage and gained the assent of the Odelsting, they pass to the Lagting which will either approve or reject them. If a law proposal is rejected, it is returned to the Odelsting with comments appended. With these in mind, the Odelsting can either let the matter rest or alternatively send it back to the Lagting with or without amendment. When a law proposal from the Odelsting has twice been put before the Lagting and on both occasions rejected by it the United Storting, i.e. a joint session of Odelsting and Lagting, shall decide the matter by a two-thirds majority.

Although not explicitly stated in the constitution, it is clear that in its original conception the Lagting was envisaged as an organ on which those with the necessary technical knowledge, notably lawyers, would be able to utilise their professional competence to scrutinise the special and limited category of law proposals. It was designed, in short, to be a professional 'estate', its members boasting a corporate identity and operating like a subject-specific legislative committee at a time when the Eidsvoll constitution made no mention of parliamentary standing committees. The notion of functional representation embodied in the Lagting contrasted sharply with the emphasis on territorial representation which was reflected in the regional placement of delegates in the Storting assembly. However, intentions and reality often prove to be at odds, and the composition of the Lagting has borne this out: in short, it has not been a body of lawyers for over 100 years. The membership of three recent Lagtings is typical enough. The 1981–5 Storting contains only two full delegates with a legal background or training — Knut Frydenlund, a former Labour Party Foreign Secretary, and Morten Steenstrup, a barrister's clerk, *advocatfullmektig*, on the Conservative side — and neither is a member of the Lagting. In the previous Storting of 1977–81, three delegates, all Conservatives, listed the law as their profession but only the veteran, Svenn Stray, currently Foreign Secretary and a parliamentarian since 1958, was a member of the Lagting. The situation was precisely the same in 1969–73 when there were five lawyers in the Storting, not one of whom was a member of the Lagting. Obviously, then, the number of parliamentary delegates from the legal profession is very low, at least when compared with the House of Commons, and if there is any observable trend in their committee preferences, it seems to be that those with a legal training prefer the Justice Committee or even the Finance Committee (if tax lawyers) to membership of the Lagting.

In any event recruitment to the Lagting, as with the Storting's standing committees, is exclusively determined by the political parties. The partisan composition of the 1981–5 Lagting follows convention in being as close to a microcosm of the balance of power in the Storting as a whole as is mathematically possible (see Table 6.3). The two-strong Liberal parliamentary group, *Venstre*, found itself without representation in the Lagting. As to the criteria used by the parties in their nomination of group members to the Lagting, the matter is not one on which it is easy to generalise. However, two hypotheses at least seem defensible. First, it is likely that members who sit on a prestigious committee in the Storting will find this counter-balanced by a term of service in the Lagting. Just over 20% of Lagting members in the 1981–5 session sat on three prestigious Storting committees — Finance; Energy and Industry; and Foreign Affairs and the Constitution — and they included Reidar Due, who was the Centre Party chairman of the Energy and Industry Committee. These three committees are not, of course, the only ones in demand among delegates. For parliamentarians of the Christian People's Party the middle-status or even low-ranking committees on Social Affairs and Church and Education are generally regarded highly, although with a combined allocation of only three seats in 1981–5, competition within the party's parliamentary group for places on them was considerable. In such circumstances, membership of the Lagting may well be viewed as a *quid pro quo* for

Table 6.3(*a*). MEMBERSHIP OF THE LAGTING BY PARTY, 1981–85

Socialists		*Non-socialists*	
Labour	16	Conservatives	14
Left Socialists	1	Christians	4
		Centre	3
		Progressives	1
Total	17		22

Table 6.3(*b*). MEMBERSHIP OF THE STORTING BY PARTY, 1981–85

Socialists		*Non-socialists*	
Labour	65	Conservatives	54
Left Socialists	4	Christians	15
		Centre	11
		Progressives	4
		Liberals	2
	69		86

gaining or indeed retaining a seat on the Storting committee of a delegate's choice.

It also seems reasonable to suggest that in the absence of enough willing, experienced delegates, the most junior members of parliament are likely to be assigned to sit in the Lagting. Exactly one third of the 1981–5 Lagting members were newcomers to the Storting, and five of these were only deputy-members serving in lieu of Conservative cabinet ministers. Not surprisingly, perhaps, the newcomers mostly occupied places in the less prestigious Storting standing committees. Exceptionally, however, two new parliamentarians from the bourgeois ranks also became members of the important Finance Committee, while a third was appointed to the Foreign Affairs and Constitution Committee, a situation admittedly facilitated by the depletion in the ranks of the more experienced Conservative committee members caused by the demands of forming a minority government single-handed (by the summer of 1983 the Conservatives had formed a coalition with the Christian People's and Centre parties). There is certainly a good chance that new delegates who gain a seat on an influential Storting committee will find this offset by a place in the Lagting.

Yet if it is true that a majority of delegates would ideally wish not to be nominated to the Lagting, the point should not be exaggerated. Certainly this is not reflected in its recent composition,

Table 6.4. PERSONNEL CONTINUITY IN THE 1981–85 LAGTING

New Parliamentarians	13
Lagting members, 1977–81	13
Odelsting members, 1977–81	11
Cabinet Ministers, 1977–81	2
Total	39

which has revealed a relatively high continuity in personnel. As Table 6.4 bears out, precisely one third of the members of the 1981–5 Lagting also served in it in 1977–81, and of these more than half sat on the same Storting standing committee throughout the whole period 1977–85. Moreover, some delegates with official responsibilities in the Storting favour the Lagting in preference to the Odelsting: both Storting Speakers and one of its deputy Speakers were members of the 1981–5 Lagting as they had been in the previous parliamentary session.

Although the relatively light workload of the Lagting obviously appeals to hard-pressed members like the Storting Speakers, who also have standing committees to attend to, a general (if not always openly admitted) desire to avoid the Lagting is plainly a reflection of its perceived lack of influence among Storting delegates — an ironic state of affairs in view of the considerable powers vested in it by the constitution. A sufficiently resolute show of defiance by the Lagting towards law proposals from the Odelsting can enforce greater support in the United Storting (i.e. a two-thirds majority for their enactment) than is required for the approval of ordinary government or private members' proposals, although the ratio of members in the two divisions is such that the will of the Odelsting can normally be expected to prevail. Only twice in the twenty-year span, 1962–82, has a 'law' come before the United Storting for resolution as a result of repeated opposition in the Lagting to an Odelsting decision — once in 1963 over a Road Act, *veiloven*, and again ten years later over a Secondary Education Act, *gymnasloven*. In the former case, the Odelsting's second decision on the matter was unanimously carried in the Storting: disagreement between the two divisions and between the majority and minority in both Odelsting and Lagting centred on only two of the law's sixty-seven sections and it was ultimately felt that a Road Act with some imperfections was preferable to no Road Act at all.[31] With the Secondary Education Bill of 1973, the Odelsting resolution gained the support of only a simple majority in the United Storting — 70 votes against

68 — and was therefore lost. This rare 'victory' for the Lagting warrants brief elaboration.

The Secondary Education Bill had been in preparation for a long time: a commission of inquiry, the so-called Schools Committee, which laid the foundation for the government's proposal, had been set up as early as 1965 when it was called on to produce a scheme enabling young persons aged 16–19 to pursue an advanced course of general and vocational training.[32] The emphasis was to be on meeting the future occupational and social requirements of students, and as soon as Lars Korvald's Christian People's-Centre party coalition introduced the measure it was clear that there was broad cross-party consensus in favour of its aims. Liv Andersen, the Social Democratic spokesman in the Lagting, noted approvingly that the abolition of the artificial distinction between grammar schools, *teoretiskegymnas*, and the more vocational secondary modern schools, *praktisk yrkesorienterte skoler*, and the integration of practical and more strictly academic skills into a single 3-year advanced course of education involved nothing less than a 'social equalisation of the school milieu'.[33] There were some differences over how the principle of 'integrated schooling', *enhetsskole*, was to be achieved, and about some of the content of the curriculum, but when the standing committee on Church and Education reported to the Odelsting it was unanimous in supporting the aim of the reform.

Thus the Lagting's amendments to the Odelsting's resolution that the Secondary Education Bill be approved concerned matters of detail rather than principle. Only one delegate, Arne Kielland, a Labour member, opposed in principle the way the measure had been formulated — as he claimed, without adequate consultation with the teachers' and pupils' organisations — and wanted it returned to the government for redrafting;[34] however, he remained in a minority of one not only in the Lagting but in parliament as a whole. The Lagting's opposition centred on two main issues — the role of religious instruction in the curriculum and the position of private schools. As to the former, there was much discussion when the legislation was being formulated of the possibility of philosophy constituting an alternative option to religious education. However, this was rejected by a majority on the Schools Committee on the grounds that the objective of an advanced three-year course should be to broaden the student's knowledge and understanding of Christian values — in addition to a fundamental appreciation of the nation's cultural heritage, the ideals of a liberal democratic society, and scientific method. The majority in the Lagting did not dissent from the majority on the Schools Committee in seeing religious education as a necessary 'orientation subject', but held that a pupil should be exempted when not a member of the Established Lutheran Church of Norway. The Lagting also voted in favour of some redrafting of the section relating to the degree of central control over, and procedures for the local authorisation of, private secondary schools.[35] On 15 May 1973 the 'law' bill was returned to the Odelsting and on June 4 came before the United Storting following the adoption of unchanged positions at Second Reading in Odelsting and Lagting. As mentioned, the bill achieved a narrow majority of 70 votes to 68, but this did not constitute the two-thirds necessary for enactment under article 76 of the constitution.[36]

On the face of it, the episode suggests a victory for the Lagting, but the reality was in fact very different. In the first place, the governing coalition of Christian People's and Centre parties was vulnerable, for it commanded only forty-one seats in the Storting and while also containing a number of Liberal, *Venstre*, ministers, the majority of that party — which was divided over Norway's application for membership of the EC — refused to support the government. Secondly, all four successful Lagting amendments were tabled by the Labour Party and carried by the casting vote of the Labour Party Speaker following a tied ballot (18 votes to 18). Indeed, the rejection of the Secondary Education proposal was less a victory for the Lagting than a strategic triumph for the Social Democratic opponents of the bill in both divisions. Seen from another angle, opposition in the Lagting represented a tactical means of enforcing qualified majority acceptance for the measure in an assembly where overall the non-socialists had only a narrow plurality. Needing only one-third of the voting members to destroy the bill, the Labour Party had thus gained the whip hand. The Lagting debate showed a high level of partisanship — the sharp difference between the Labour and Conservative parties were particularly noticeable — something only marginally influenced by the fact that the next general election was only a few months away.

The final resolution of the issue in the United Storting was preceded by much moralising from the governing parties coupled with a generally resigned air over the likely outcome — the Conservative delegate, Lars Roar Langslet, compared the proceedings to those at a funeral. Yet it is difficult not to agree with the main points of his speech, namely that a majority of Storting members supported the aim of the government's proposal despite talk in the press about an imminent defeat for the coalition. Langslet identified two principal facilitating factors in the Labour Party's tactical victory: first that in the autumn of 1972 the votes of two anonymous non-socialist delegates had produced a Labour Party majority on the Speaker's Council, despite the absence of an absolute Labour majority in the Storting as a whole, and secondly that the continued existence of legislative procedures designed in the past to create stabilising 'checks and balances' now produced what Langslet described as 'completely unreasonable results' on the few occasions they were invoked.[37]

To sum up, there is little doubt that lacking a corporate identity, in the sense either of comprising a distinctive legal 'estate' or avoiding partisan conflict, the Lagting has lacked high status and in many ways a sufficiently meaningful role in the legislative process. Indeed, the significance of the historic 'three-*ting*' division of the Norwegian legislature for the development of modified unicameralism elsewhere in the Nordic region vastly exceeds that of the deliberative role of the modern Lagting in the policy adoption process, even within the context of 'law proposals'. In addition to its influence in Finland, the Norwegian constitution of 1814 served as a model for the division of the Althing into Chambers, which was proposed in 1867 and legalised by article 15 of the constitution of 1874.[38] The Upper Chamber of the Althing was to be elected by the United Althing in a way similar to that in which the Storting elects members of the Lagting. Furthermore, as in the event of deadlock between the two divisions in Norway, matters were ultimately to be referred back to the United Althing for resolution. For this to happen, a bill must have reached its ninth reading! In addition to the three plenary readings and one committee stage necessary in both divisions of the Althing for the enactment of ordinary legislation, as many as three more readings may be required if the two chambers cannot agree on a draft proposal. Precisely as in the United Storting, moreover, the matter to be adopted must then gain a two-thirds majority in the United Althing. The constitutional position of the Icelandic Upper Chamber emerged as stronger than that of the Lagting, for while the latter is not empowered to initiate or reject a bill altogether, these options are available to the Icelandic Upper Chamber. The influence of the Norwegian model in the structural development of the Icelandic parliamentary system is, however, unmistakable.

The Efri Deild

The development of the Icelandic Althing can claim a number of distinctive features. First, established in A.D. 930 and serving to unite the Norse settlements in Iceland, the 'ancient Althing' was, till its abolition in 1800, a unicameral assembly which was unique in the Nordic region in not being elected on the basis of 'estate'. Secondly, when sovereignty over Iceland was transferred from

Norway to Denmark as a by-product of the Napoleonic wars, the Althing was re-constituted — albeit only on a consultative basis — in 1843, but following the 'liberal risings' in Europe (and more particularly Denmark), the Danish King issued a decree summoning the Althing to express its view on the special position of Iceland within the Danish state. This led to the rise of a nationalist movement in Iceland led by Jón Sigurðsson which ultimately resulted in January 1874 in the Danish King presenting a constitution providing Iceland with self-government in domestic affairs and a two-divisional Althing along Norwegian lines. The Icelanders, incidentally, refused to acknowledge that they formed an inseparable part of the Danish kingdom.

In the ensuing sequence of events a number of points stand out. First, despite his leadership of a campaign for increased national freedom and constitutional rights, Jón Sigurðsson was not persecuted; indeed he was on surprisingly good terms with both Danish officials and ministers.[39] Secondly, in the countryside knowledge of and interest in the Althing was extremely limited: the official account, *Althingstidindi*, reached only a few hundred people, while the Althing itself met only every second year; Jón Sigurðsson's essays on major issues in *Ny felagsrit* had an even smaller readership; and newspapers generally published very meagre accounts. The hard core of nationalists among the Althing members was largely confined to farmers. All in all, as Olafur R. Grimsson has observed, 'the Althing did not create any deep or continuous public interest.'[40]

Initially, the division into two Chambers, incorporated into article 15 of the 1874 constitution, appeared to represent a victory for the nationalists: the Danish government had, after all, rejected an Upper Chamber and instead proposed *inter alia* a single assembly comprising twenty-one members and six high officials, the latter nominated by the Danish King and designed to prevent precipitate decisions against the Danish interest.[41] It had also proposed preserving for the Danes the discretionary right to hold a Third Reading stage at which a bill would either be rejected or approved *as a whole*, and it was the removal of this stipulation which prompted Iceland to push for a modified form of unicameralism or even a bicameral assembly. Yet if the two-divisional Althing represented an initial victory for the nationalists, Jón Sigurðsson was quick to observe that the King's prerogative of appointing personnel to the Upper Chamber ultimately gave him the power to block Icelandic measures. In reality, in other words, the nationalists wanted a fully unicameral assembly on their own terms. Their problem was highlighted between 1874 and 1903, when the Efri Deild contained six royal members with effective veto powers; it was not till 1915 that these members were abolished. Moreover, it was not until 1934 that the present system was instituted whereby one third of the members after a general election are chosen to sit in the Efri Deild for the statutory life of the Althing.

It is not intended at this point to discuss the modern role of the Efri Deild. Its standing committee system was examined in chapter 5, while the reasons for the evident dissatisfaction with it as an institution and the proposals to abolish it will be considered in chapter 7. Efri Deild is patently not an 'upper tier' committee in more than a notional sense — that is, the system of 'divisions' partakes somewhat of the character of modified unicameralism. In other respects, it would be no less apposite to describe the Icelandic legislative system as qualified bicameralism than as modified unicameralism. After all, unlike the Grand Committee and Lagting, any delegate in the 20-seat Efri Deild has the right to introduce a bill — government bills are also initiated in the upper chamber — and its powers and basic infrastructure (procedural arrangements, standing committees etc.) are identical to those in the 40-member lower chamber, Nethri Deild. It is true that recruitment to both chambers is controlled by the political parties, and the party balance in the United Althing is therefore reproduced in both chambers. But in contrast to the Grand Committee and Lagting, there is little evidence of a widespread predisposition on the part of delegates against membership of the Efri Deild. There is only one sentence on the subject in Gröndal, which states that the question of opting between the two chambers has not really been an issue. If anything, there would seem to be a preference among members for continuing in the Efri Deild, where the quality of debate tends to be higher than in the Nethri Deild.

Confirming the appearance of a legislative assembly in its own right, meetings of the Efri Deild — again unlike the 'upper tier' committees in Finland and Norway — are public, although the visitors' gallery in the lower chamber is often fuller simply because the greater number of delegates there, at least for important debates, creates more of the atmosphere of an assembly. Ultimately, however, the modern role of the Efri Deild must be open to question. Iceland is unambiguously a small society: there is no army, surnames were made illegal in 1925, although about 4% of the population are entitled to use them (they derive from the old commercial connection with Denmark), there are no dogs in the towns, no beer, no summer television and the population numbers less than a quarter of a million. Indeed, it is said that all Icelandic children could be provided with two bananas each grown in their own country[42] — an apt comment both on the diminutive population and the flourishing nature of the market garden industry. So why, in such a small society, should there be a need for two legislative chambers apparently lacking a clear-cut functional differentiation? Tradition, which is as rooted in the Althing as it is in the House of Commons, would explain much. Typically, for instance, the thirty or so foreigners who apply each year for Icelandic citizenship must adopt an Icelandic name and they are then listed together on a bill which goes through the Althing to effect their naturalisation. Tradition is doubtless a powerful factor militating against a move to a straight single-chamber assembly. However, the evolution of the peculiar type of modified unicameralism in Iceland reflects the devious course of the nation's history and in particular the influence of the legislative system elsewhere in the Nordic region.

This same process of institutional diffusion underpinned the incorporation of a Grand Committee, *stora utskottet*, into the parliamentary system on the Åland islands. The Landsting's Grand Committee, in short, bears a number of unmistakable resemblances to the Finnish Grand Committee model. First, like the parallel institution in the Eduskunta, it is twice as large as the four specialist standing committees — on Legal Affairs, Finance, Law and Economy, and Cultural Affairs respectively — and boasting ten of the thirty Landsting members is relatively larger than its mainland counterpart as a proportion of the total membership of the legislature. Secondly, the functions of the Landsting's Grand Committee are similar to the equivalent body in the Eduskunta: it deals in other words with almost all types of legislative initiative: the Presidential proposals issued from Helsinki (see chapter 1), the private member's bills, *lagmotioner*, and, in accordance with article 23 of the revised Landsting Orders of 1971, initiatives from the regional executive, *landskapsstyrelsen* — the most common of the three. Thus the Grand Committee reviews all legislative proposals — except financial matters and members' request proposals, *hemställningsmotioner*, which require only a single reading — after they have undergone preparation in the relevant standing committee and received a first plenary handling. The adoption process is identical to that in the Eduskunta and even involves a comparable system of qualified majorities (see chapter 7, which also discusses members' request proposals). Thirdly, in common with all the 'upper tier' committees in the region, the Åland Grand Committee has proved extremely durable. When on 8 March 1971 the committee set up to revise the Landsting Orders reported, there was no suggestion that the basic structure of the legislative process be changed — and there was little evidence of any influence derived from simultaneous discussions of reforming the Riksdag Orders in connection with Sweden's transition to unicameralism. Finally, however, the Åland Grand Committee appears to have differed significantly from the same body in Finland in one important respect. The absence until very recently of party-politicisation in the Landsting may well have facilitated the type of corporate identity and status as a Council of Elders which, despite original intentions, the Finnish Grand Committee has never achieved.

The Landsting is, of course, a small assembly marked by informality. Members, for example, normally vote simply by rising in their places — delegates voting 'yes' standing first — and a roll-call or the voting apparatus is used only when there is obvious uncertainty about the outcome, or when two delegates demand it. Only the winning proposal is minuted, not how every delegate voted. The Åland islands, as mentioned in chapter 1, are formally represented on the Finnish mainland through the single delegate they elect at Eduskunta elections.[43] He contributes only when matters relating to Åland — fishing, shipping and navigational questions — are being discussed, and in recent years he has preferred membership of the Eduskunta's Constitutional Committee. Significantly, the Åland Landsting also elects two members of the Finnish delegation to the Nordic Council and thus, like Greenland and the Faeroes, has separate representation at regional-level deliberations. The 'upper tier' discussions in the Nordic Council are the subject of the second part of this chapter.

An 'upper tier' assembly? The Nordic Council

The Nordic Council, as was noted in chapter 1, is not a parliament in the orthodox sense. Rather it is a consultative assembly, comprising 87 delegates elected on a *pro rata* basis by the five sovereign and three devolved assemblies in the region, and it may make recommendations but not enact laws. Via the phenomenon of overlapping membership, the Nordic Council and the other regional assemblies are interlinked, although their precise relationship is difficult to define. The Nordic Council is plainly not an 'upper tier' body in the way that the Norwegian Lagting and Finnish Grand Committee appear to be located at something of an angle to the national legislative process, but nonetheless function as an integral part of it. Yet it may not be altogether fanciful to depict the Nordic Council as an 'upper tier' assembly in so far as it deliberates on essentially supranational matters, i.e. issues over and 'above' the domestic concern of the individual states, while acting as a type of Consolidated Committee of the regional assemblies — nominated by them and ultimately subordinate to them. It is for this reason that we consider the Nordic Council at this point, focusing on three broad themes: the growing institutionalisation of regional co-operation and the feasibility of speaking of a Nordic political system; the development of the machinery of the Nordic Council and the changing nature of its role within the Nordic political system; and the impact of the Nordic system of co-operation on the individual parliaments in the region.

Unlike the EC parliament in Strasbourg, the Nordic Council was founded with a view to advancing practical forms of regional cooperation, not to binding the Nordic states into a single political entity, federal or otherwise. Federalist thinking has made little headway in the area, and a Swedish move soon after the Second World War, in January 1948, to co-ordinate the foreign and defence policies of Denmark, Norway and Sweden within the framework of a Scandinavian Defence Union — and thereby achieve a real measure of political integration — foundered on the rock of differing security needs. Prompted by a growing concern on the part of the three states in question at their exposed and vulnerable position with the advent of the Cold War, this would have committed them to remaining neutral in the event of world war, but would have required them to come to each other's aid in the event of one or more being attacked by an outside power. The plans for a Scandinavian Defence Union came to naught: Denmark and Norway proceeded to join NATO, while Sweden pursued a line of active neutrality. It was no coincidence that the Nordic Council was conceived in the aftermath of this attempt; however, it seems plain from both the timing and the Nordic Council's status as a purely consultative body that the venture constituted a cautious approach to co-operation taking account of the earlier failure to achieve a measure of integration, rather than representing a renewed attempt to achieve that goal. Moreover, the convention of excluding the discussion of security policy from the agenda of the Nordic Council is as an active reminder that, although in the words of the former Finnish President Urho Kekkonen, 'traditionally each Nordic country is accustomed to taking the others into account in its decisions,'[44] this has equally involved recognising that there exist real differences of interest between them.[45] Precisely because of this, there has been little concern on the governments' side to break with the conventional embargo on security policy discussions in the Nordic Council. At the thirtieth annual session of the Council in Helsinki in May 1982 the five Nordic Prime Ministers did meet specifically to discuss this matter, but they resolved not to deviate from established tradition, and at least the official government representatives were not to take up such questions in the Council.

As the Council's President (Speaker) Elsi Hetemäki-Olander put it, 'The Nordic Council is not a suitable forum for foreign and security policy debates.'[46]

Blueprints for economic union in the Nordic region, particularly two attempts to form a Nordic Customs Union in the 1950s and late 1960s, suffered a fate similar to that of the Defence Union and served further to underline the ultimate primacy of national interests. Denmark acceded to the EC in 1972 whereas Finland, Norway and Sweden, each for reasons of its own, signed only Free Trade Agreements with the Common Market. Finland also entered a commercial agreement with the Comecon countries. All this is not to imply that the early fruits of regional co-operation were sparse. In addition to a passport union and the synchronisation of much social policy legislation, perhaps the most notable early achievement was agreement on a Common Labour Market Treaty in 1954, revised in 1982 to include Iceland, which has so far enabled over 1 million inhabitants in the region freely to live and work outside their country of birth. For nearly twenty years, however, regional co-operation mainly involved regular meetings of Nordic parliamentarians: indeed, until the 1970s the Nordic Council was the only institutional expression of the undoubtedly strong sense of regional affinity felt among the Nordic peoples.

There are limited forms of inter-governmental co-operation which date back to 1914, when regular meetings of the Nordic Foreign Ministers were first organised. Between the wars, the Ministers of Social Affairs and then Ministers of Education did likewise. By the late 1950s the Nordic Council was itself seeking ways of developing an effective system of collaboration on the government side, and in 1960 a first step was taken when a Ministerial Committee on Economic Co-operation was created, attended by the Ministers of Trade, to be followed the next year by a similar committee coordinating aid to the Third World nations. The subsequent proposal of the so-called Fagerholm committee that a specific organ be founded to regularise co-operation between the governments was realised in 1971 with the foundation of the Nordic Council of Ministers, *Nordiska ministerrådet*. Its basic logic was well captured by Claes Wiklund who commented that 'in the absence of a permanent governmental organisation for the preparation of Nordic questions, it was far too often the case that the handling of Nordic Council recommendations dragged out for a long time.'[47] Since 1 July 1971 every government in the region has formally nominated a minister with special responsibilities, over and above his/her departmental duties, for co-ordinating Nordic co-operation — the so-called Minister for Nordic Co-operation, *Nordiska samarbetsminister* — and in Sweden the position of Under-Secretary for Nordic Affairs was created in 1982. The Council of Ministers is supported by two bodies of Nordic officials: the Secretariat for Nordic Cultural Co-operation, formed in 1972 and based in Copenhagen, serves the Council of Ministers in the fields of culture, science and education, and the Secretariat for General Co-operation, set up in 1973 and based in Oslo, covers no less than fifteen major sectors of policy co-operation.

Because of the heightened institutionalisation of regional co-operation in the early 1970s with the foundation of the Nordic Council of Ministers and the formation of international secretariats in the main policy areas, it is possible to refer to the existence of a fledgling Nordic political system. It would be tempting to liken the Council of Ministers to a regional cabinet, with the supporting secretariats playing an important role in the formulation of measures — significantly, pressure group lobbying has increasingly focused on the various Nordic agencies — and the Nordic Council coming to perform more of the control function classically associated with legislative assemblies. Corroboration of this scenario is perhaps to be found in the creation in 1975 of a ten-member Budget Committee. This comprises two delegates from each of the Nordic Council's standing committees and holds twice-yearly meetings with the Council of Ministers concerning the total amount of the two common Nordic budgets.

Three resemblances between the Council of Ministers and the national cabinets in the region stand out in particular. First, in accordance with the Helsinki Agreement of 1962, revised in 1971 and 1974, and in common with the five individual member-governments and the parliamentarians in the national delegations, the Council of Ministers has the right to make proposals to the Nordic Council. In short, it has an initiating role which, like the national governments in the region, it shares with the assembly.[48] For example, at the thirty-first ordinary session of the Nordic Council, held in Oslo in February 1983, the Council of Ministers put forward five proposals and like most cabinet initiatives at the national level, all five were approved in the assembly. They related to raising the ground capital on the Nordic Investment Bank; items for the two common Nordic budgets in General Affairs and Cultural Affairs respectively; a programme of co-operation in environmental matters; planning in the building and construction industries; and a development programme in the field of information science.

Secondly, like the national governments, the Council of Ministers must give regular account of itself to the assembly: it is required before every annual session to report on the state of co-operation in the foregoing year as well as to report on action taken on recommendations of the Nordic Council. A plenary debate ensues in much the same way as a full-sitting discussion takes place on the annual government report in the five sovereign parliaments in the region.

Finally like the domestic cabinets, the Council of Ministers is the centre of a nexus of official committees and committees of officials. There is a parallel committee of 'Nordocrats' concerned with the work of the Ministers for Nordic Co-operation and a complex of *ad hoc* working groups which the Council of Ministers is empowered to create. Their role in the formulation and preparation of measures should not be underestimated. Nor should the fact that the Nordic-level administrators tend to reflect the decision-making cultures of their separate states: in many ways, therefore, the initiation stage at the regional level embodies the norm in the individual countries in being slow-moving and highly deliberative. As Wiklund and Sundelius have observed, 'the Nordic policy process proceeds from detailed investigation to political decision'.[49] In the Common Market, the tendency has been the reverse of this.

On a number of counts, however, practice in the Council of Ministers differs from that in a typical national cabinet in the region. For example, the Council of Ministers has a membership which fluctuates according to the issue under consideration and, like the distinctive case of ordinary cabinet sessions in Finland, may involve the participation of officials and experts. Formal provision is even made in the work procedures of the Council of Ministers for Nordic Council delegates to be present at its meetings.[50] The Council of Ministers comprises the cabinet ministers of all the Nordic governments, except by convention the Prime Ministers and ministers in the area of Defence and Foreign Affairs, and so embraces both routine departmental ministers and the Ministers for Nordic Cooperation. In reality, its composition changes in relation to the question being discussed — a debate on labour market matters will require the presence of the various Labour Market ministers, and social policy the Ministers for Social Affairs. To be quorate, meetings of the Council of Ministers require a full attendance of member-governments: more than one minister from any Nordic state may be present, but each member-government has only one vote. In exceptional circumstances, a civil servant may represent his government, although if this happens at least three other countries must be represented by ministers.

The Council of Ministers also differs from national cabinets in the region as regards the formal rules on decision-taking. In the latter, votes are rarely taken and in practice the convention of collective responsibility prevails; in the Council of Ministers, not only are ballots taken, but collective authority is limited by the unanimity principle. The only exception concerns decisions on procedural matters, when a simple majority is sufficient (the chairman has a casting vote in the event of a tie). Abstentions do not prevent decisions being taken and once taken, decisions of the Council of Ministers are binding on member-nations — provided that the national constitution does not first require parliamentary acceptance of the measure, in which case the Council of Ministers is required to give advance notification of this fact. The chairman of the Council of Ministers is the minister representing the country in which the next ordinary session of the Nordic Council will take place. Meetings are convened if one minister so requires; there is a requirement that minutes of decisions are kept and provision too for a lengthier record to be made of meetings of the Council of Ministers.

Meetings of the Council of Ministers are held frequently, though less so than those of the national cabinets. When comprising solely the Ministers for Nordic Co-operation, the Council of Ministers held ten meetings in 1982 compared with nearly three times that number when the various departmental ministers made up the membership. As a college of Ministers for Nordic Co-operation, the Council of Ministers met the Nordic Council's Budget Committee three times, the Praesidium twice and the Communications Committee once in addition to arranging joint sessions with the Ministers of Cultural Affairs, the Ministers of Education and the Prime Ministers.[51] It seems that the post of Minister for Nordic Co-operation has typically gone to persons with relatively little experience in the national cabinet — a little over 2 years on average — although about one-third of the incumbents since the inception of the post in 1971 have had previous experience in the Nordic Council.[52]

The evolving role of the Nordic Council

In considering the evolution of the Nordic Council over the three decades and more of its existence, several developments warrant emphasis. Firstly, the work of the Nordic Council has been given an administrative underpinning, particularly in the form of the Secretariat of the Praesidium, which was set up in 1971. The Nordic Council, in short, now has a staff of its own. Secondly, there has been an institutionalisation of its standing committee system: the number of standing committees has risen, their substantive competence has been extended, and the frequency of meetings has increased. Finally, and contemporaneous with a similar phenomenon in the devolved assemblies, especially Åland's Landsting, there has been a marked party-politicisation of the basic proceedings of the Nordic Council. Private members' proposals have been affected, as have the appointments to positions of responsibility, while the 1970s and early 1980s have seen the appearance of four main party political blocs in the assembly. Before discussing these developments somewhat further and gauging their impact on the status and role of the Nordic Council within the Nordic political system, the structural machinery of the assembly should be briefly noted. The nature and working of the Nordic Council's Praesidium, standing committees and plenary sessions are not dissimilar to the comparable structures in the five national parliaments in the region.

The President and four vice-Presidents that make up the Council Praesidium are elected at the first plenary meeting of every ordinary session in accordance with a proposal from the Procedures Committee, *samlade arbetsutskott*. All five national delegations are represented in the Praesidium and so, if possible, are the different shades of partisan opinion[53] — a matter which acquired an extra pertinence during the 1972–3 session when the Praesidium contained no Social Democrats at all. The Praesidium handles the routine matters of the Nordic Council both at and between its annual sessions: one of its number or an elected deputy directs proceedings and may, as happened in 1975, call an extraordinary session (twenty-five delegates or two national governments have the same right). The Praesidium refers proposals, whether emanating from the national governments, Council of Ministers or individual delegates, to one of the standing committees, and in turn is required to produce an annual report on its activities which is placed before each ordinary session of the Nordic Council. Although members of the Praesidium are elected for a one-year term only, a much longer term of office has become commonplace: Sigurður Bjarnason of Iceland was elected no less than eleven times consecutively before 1970, and a number of others have been returned at least nine times. Very few women over the years have become members of the Praesidium; Ragnhildur Helgadóttir (at the time of writing Minister of Education in Steingrímur Hermannsson's centre-right coalition) became the first female President in 1975. Praesidium membership has tended to go to experienced male politicians, usually with considerable national standing in their own right. Typically they are senior figures with an average of 14 years' parliamentary service at the time of their election and exactly one-third of them in the period 1967–82 enjoyed cabinet status before or after their term in the Praesidium.[54]

The five standing committees of the Nordic Council are comparable in their essentials to those of the national parliaments. The committees are subject-specific, their deliberations secret — although government ministers and special experts can be invited to attend — and meetings are quorate when at least half the members are present. Decisions, in turn, are taken by a simple majority. The duties of the standing committees, as laid down in article 53 of the revised Helsinki agreement of 1971, involve the preparation of all private members', national government and Council of Ministers' proposals before a final division is taken at a plenary meeting. As in the various national parliaments, moreover, the standing committees of the Nordic Council issue written reports. They are also called upon to scrutinise reports from various Nordic-level organisations, and since 1972 have given particular priority to the annual reports of the Nordic Council of Ministers.

The five standing committees elect their own chairman and vice-chairmen and, as with the Praesidium, this has been for a term of one year at a time with the possibility of renewal. A number of committee chairmen have been returned for extended periods: the Norwegian Christian People's Party delegate, Asbjørn Haugstvedt, was elected continuously as chairman of the standing committee on Social Policy and the Environment from 1974 until 1983, when he became a member of Kåre Willoch's reconstituted centre-right coalition. The convention has been to distribute the positions of responsibility on standing committees between the five sovereign members of the Nordic Council so that each state nominates one chairman and one deputy-chairman. Since 1967, Denmark has elected the chairman of the Legal Affairs committee and Norway, Finland, Sweden and Iceland the chairmen of the standing committees on Social Policy and the Environment, Traffic, Economic Affairs and Cultural Affairs respectively. Claes Wiklund's research reveals the typical chairman of a Nordic Council standing committee, to be a man aged 58 at the time of his election who has been a Council member for $3\frac{1}{2}$ years. The youngest person who has assumed such office hitherto is the Finnish Liberal, Pekka Tarjanne, who was only 34 when he was given the head position in the Traffic Committee in 1971; in contrast, the Danish Conservative Knud Thestrup was 72 on becoming chairman of the Legal Affairs Committee in 1972. Again, women have unquestionably been under-represented: a female delegate has never been elected to the chairmanship of the standing committees on either Legal Affairs or Economic Affairs.[55]

In addition to the five standing committees, the Nordic Council possess two permanent committees — a Budget Committee, which handles budget and auditing matters and consists of the chairman plus one ordinary member from each of the standing committees, and a Communications Committee which has responsibilities *inter alia* for *Nordisk Kontakt* (liberally cited in this book) and comprises ten ordinary delegates, two from each member-nation.

The Orders governing the organisation of plenary meetings of the Nordic Council are unexceptional enough: sessions are quorate when at least half the total number of delegates are present, and for most purposes recommendations are approved when more than half of those present vote in favour. There are a variety of voting methods — delegates may be requested to hold a roll-call, to use the voting machinery or simply to rise in their seats — and, unlike the Storting, provision is made for members to abstain. Speeches are made in the order in which they are requested and there is the possibility of 'reply speeches' and, indeed, of delimiting the length of plenary contributions. At the request of 5 delegates (or the President), and with the backing of a two-thirds majority in the assembly, a clôture may be imposed, although no discussion is permitted on the clôture motion. Written questions to a minister in one of the national governments, or alternatively to a member of the Council of Ministers, must be submitted to the Praesidium at least three weeks in advance of the ordinary session at which an oral response is expected, and there are then restrictions on the time available for questioning the minister. It is a distinctive feature that, in order to emphasise the cross-national character of the assembly, ministers and delegates are seated in alphabetical order in the chamber.

Having thus briefly reviewed the basic infrastructure of the Nordic Council, we should now look at the three main lines of development which have marked the evolution of the Council over its 30-year history. The first two already mentioned — the provision of administrative back-up to delegates in the form of a purpose-specific assembly staff and the institutionalisation of the Council's standing committee system along with its growing centrality as a deliberative forum — need not be dealt with at length. The permeation of partisanship as the single most important determinant ofdelegate behaviour in the Nordic Council merits closer consideration.

The staff of the Nordic Council was significantly strengthened in 1971 by the creation of the Secretariat of the Praesidium. Based in Stockholm, it employs a staff of about thirty persons and prepares the meetings of the Praesidium and the Council's five standing committees. Moreover, in the last few years all the standing committees, with the exception of that on Legal Affairs, have acquired a full-time secretary. This is more than can be claimed for the standing committees in the Folketing and Eduskunta! The Secretariat of the Praesidium has played an important role in providing active, all-round support to Nordic Council members. Although still 'a young cuckoo in the Nordic nest', in the phrase of Ilkka-Christian Björklund, the chief secretary in the Praesidium Secretariat, it has acted as a prop to regional-level co-operation between the parliaments. Björklund has noted that at times when the impetus of Nordic co-operation has been thwarted by the twin menace of conflicting political ambition and divergent national interests, the administration has had simply to keep running, placing the application of formal rules ahead of the achievement of long-term goals. But, he argues, the urgency of the leading officials in the Secretariat of the Praesidium has been heightened by the fact that, in contrast to the staff of the various national secretariats, they enjoy only short-term contracts. The onus has thus been on achieving a tangible result quickly, which would partly explain why the Praesidium Secretariat has assumed a high work profile, acting as a counterpoise to the institutions on the government side which in the 1970s seem to have developed into the mainspring of Nordic co-operation.[56] Unlike the progression in the Common Market, the consolidation of Nordic co-operation has been achieved without a great degree of bureaucratisation — there remain, in short, relatively few 'Nordocrats'. The personnel of the three main Nordic secretariats, along with the staff of the national delegations to the Nordic Council, number less than 150 compared with over 10,000 officials employed in the service of the EC.

The recent attachment of a full-time secretary to most of the Nordic Council's standing committees might well be considered tacit recognition of the importance of their role in the work of the assembly. All measures are referred to a standing committee where they are either approved or rejected, and on occasions outside experts assist committees in the process of scrutiny. Their deliberations are invariably thorough: although in 1983 only 10% of private members' proposals were jettisoned by the standing committees, the figure for the previous year amounted to no less than 42%. Since the early years of the Nordic Council, moreover, the number of standing committees has grown, the scope of their policy responsibilities has widened, and the number of meetings they hold annually has increased.

Four standing committees were set up in the course of the first three annual sessions of the Nordic Council and a fifth, the Traffic Committee, was created in connection with Finland's accession in 1956. Before 1964, however, the standing committees convened only during annual sessions of the Council: *ad hoc* organs were nominated to deal with matters arising between sessions. In 1955, for example, a seven-man sub-committee of the standing committee on Legal Affairs was appointed to deal with the ramifications of

Finland's membership of the Council. The growth in the whole institutional structure of Nordic co-operation in the 1970s, and particularly the need to deal with the Council of Ministers' budgets, meant that standing committees were required to convene meetings throughout the year, and at present each committee deliberates between five and seven times annually and nominates internal working groups when the workload so dictates. The Nordic Council's standing committee system has also had to adapt to the increased membership of the Council, as well as when interest emerges in new areas of policy. In the latter context, the Social Policy committee broadened its remit in 1976 to become the standing committee on Social Policy and the Environment; in the former, successive increases in Council membership from 69 to 78 delegates in 1970 and again from 78 to 87 in 1983 (with the separate representation granted to the three devolved assemblies) has meant that the largest standing committee on Economic Affairs now comprises twenty-six members — larger than any standing committee in the five national parliaments. Table 6.5 shows the membership of the Nordic standing committees following the changes in the Council's representation in 1983.

Consonant with the importance of their work in the Nordic Council, the composition of standing committees and in particular their chairmanships have become the object of increased party-political attention. Indeed, although conventionally each nation controls the chairmanship of one of the standing committees — Sweden has held the top post on the Economic Affairs Committee since 1962 — appointments to these positions are nowadays made on a partisan basis. The same is true of nominations for the five national representatives in the Praesidium, while the organisation of the annual ordinary session also reflects the inroads made on proceedings of the Nordic Council by organised (cross-national) party activity. At the 31st session in Oslo in February 1983, the first day's

Table 6.5. MEMBERSHIP OF NORDIC COUNCIL'S STANDING COMMITTEES FOLLOWING GRANT OF SEPARATE REPRESENTATION TO THE DEVOLVED ASSEMBLIES, 1983

Standing committee	*No. of members*
Legal Affairs	13
Social Policy and Environment	13
Traffic	13
Cultural Affairs	22
Economic Affairs	26
Total	87

agenda set aside two separate times for party group meetings, the first starting the formal business of the week at 0830 on Monday morning.

At various points in this volume, the 'colonisation' of the infrastructure of the parliaments in the region by cohesive political parties has been referred to — in the context of the 'decline of parliaments' thesis and/or the erosion of the independent impact of standing committees and plenary meetings on the deliberative process. Contrary to sentiments expressed in earlier chapters, however, we shall not argue here that the growing significance of partisanship in determining delegate behaviour has necessarily been for the bad — it has not, anyway, advanced to anything like the same extent as at the national level. It has taken place at two reinforcing levels: within the national delegations and, more important, across national boundaries between parties with a common ideological background or outlook. Indeed, it may be considered an achievement of the Nordic Council that it has strengthened the cross-national linkages between the political parties and so helped to generate common policy programmes and to sharpen and improve the quality of debate both inside and outside Council sessions.

A watershed year in the party-politicisation of the Nordic Council was 1973, when the Social Democratic parties acted in concert on a private member's proposal on marriage rights, thus anticipating the subsequent practice of holding group meetings to agree a party line before meetings of the standing committees. Growing regional cooperation between the Nordic Social Democrats had produced a common programme by the autumn of 1976, and an economic policy manifesto followed in 1979. In the latter year, the Christian Democratic parties followed suit by founding their own Nordic group and proceeded to produce a joint policy programme. Nowadays there are four main party groups in the Nordic Council: the largest and best developed is the Social Democratic group which in 1983 had 29 seats; the heterogeneous group of Centre parties (14 in all) boasted 20 delegates; the Conservative group had 19 seats; and the Radical Left 8 members. Table 6.6 sets out the composition and relative strength of the party groups in the Nordic Council in February 1983. Another manifestation of the heightened party-politicisation of the Nordic Council has been an increase in the party group sponsorship of measures. The number of initiatives with the backing of delegates drawn exclusively from a party or related group of parties — the Social Democrat/Labour bloc, the centre-based groups etc. — has risen at the expense of the traditional cross-party initiatives supported by delegates irrespective of their ideological affinities. As Table 6.7 demonstrates, the proportion of

Table 6.6. COMPOSITION AND RELATIVE STRENGTH OF THE PARTY GROUPS IN THE NORDIC COUNCIL, FEBRUARY 1983

Left Socialists/ Communists	*Seats*	*Social Democrats*	*Seats*	*Centre parties*	*Seats*	*Conservatives*	*Seats*
Danish Socialist People's Party and Faeroese Republicans	3	Danish Social Democrats	6	*Denmark* Radicals, Liberals, Centre Democrats and Christian People's Party	4	Danish Conservatives and Faeroese People's Party	3
Finnish People's Democratic League	3	Finnish Social Democrats	5	*Finland* Centre Party, Swedish People's Party and Åland Union, Liberals and Christian League	6	Finnish Conservatives	4
Icelandic People's Alliance	1	Icelandic Social Democrats	1	*Iceland* Progressive Party	2	Icelandic Independence Party	2
Swedish Left-Communists	1	Norwegian Labour Party	8	*Norway* Centre Party and Christian People's Party	4	Norwegian Conservatives	6
		Swedish Social Democrats	9	*Sweden* Centre Party and Liberals	4	Swedish Conservatives	4
						Danish Progress Party*	2
Total	8	*Total*	29	*Total*	20	*Total*	21

Grand Total: 78

*The Danish Progress Party is not formally a member of the Conservatives' group but may be considered as such for the purposes of calculating the distribution of office-holders in the Nordic Council.

Table 6.7. PROPORTION OF MEMBERS' INITIATIVES IN THE NORDIC COUNCIL WITH PARTY GROUP SPONSORSHIP, 1953–83

	No. of members' initiatives	*% with Party Group Sponsorship*
1953–60	151	7
1975–9	125	18
1980	32	34
1982	24	29
1983	30	23

Sources: Claes Wiklund and Bengt Sundelius, 'Nordic Co-operation in the Seventies: Trends and Patterns', *Scandinavian Political Studies*, vol. 2 (New Series), no. 2, 1979, p. 106, 'Ärenden på dagordningen'. *Nordisk Kontakt* 3/83, pp. 158–84.

measures with party group sponsorship has risen from 7% in the period 1953–60 to 18% between 1975–9 and 34% in 1980. By 1983 it had fallen back somewhat to 23% — about a quarter of the total number of delegate initiatives.

Party group initiatives have ranged across the entire policy spectrum of the Nordic Council's standing committees. For example, at the Oslo session in 1983 the Traffic Committee dealt with a proposal from two Swedish Liberals urging the need for greater co-ordination in traffic policy in the region (1983 was officially 'Nordic Traffic Safety Year'), while the same committee also considered an initiative from two delegates, one in the Norwegian Labour Party and one in the Swedish Social Democratic Party, which pressed for the increased use of safety-belts in the back seats of cars. There was also an important Social Democratic/Labour group initiative in the Cultural Affairs Committee concerned to avoid cuts and to promote a programme of Nordic cultural development. More particularly, it argued for an increased concentration of resources on counteracting the commercialisation of cultural output by providing *inter alia* more adult education centres, sports clubs and youth clubs; extending co-operation in the telecommunications field within the framework set by *Nordvision*; establishing tourist exchanges and twin-town arrangements; and supporting literary and film projects. The proposal was given added weight by being underwritten by a number of senior politicians including Trygve Bratteli and Olof Palme. However, most party group initiatives in 1983, both relatively and absolutely, fell within the ambit of the Economic Affairs Committee.

Perhaps the most significant feature was that the Social Democratic-Labour group, the centre-based parties and the right-wing alliance all tabled proposals on the need for the regional economies to be managed in a way that would achieve growth and full employment. When these measures came up for plenary debate, differences in viewpoint between the party groups were much in evidence. On the Right the Swedish Conservative chairman Ulf Adelsohn, who also headed his country's delegation to the Council, was preoccupied with the reluctance of the West German government to give a lead in following up signs of a recovery in the world economy. On the moderate Left the Finnish Social Democrat, Ulf Sundqvist, wanted the appointment of a kind of Brandt Commission to analyse the role that might be played by the Nordic states in a future period of international growth. The former Danish Social Democratic Prime Minister, Anker Jørgensen, warned against what he considered a fixation with the battle against inflation at the expense of the battle against unemployment. Finally, for the Christian Democrats, the chairman of the Norwegian Christian People's Party, Kjell Magne Bondevik, without in any way making light of the economic maladies of the West, drew attention to the plight of Third World nations. Despite these differences, there was ultimately wide cross-party consensus behind the Economic Affairs Committee's report proposing a common Nordic campaign to achieve economic growth and full employment, albeit in a global rather than narrowly regional context: 55 delegates supported the report compared with 1 who voted against and 5 abstentions.[57]

One should not exaggerate the extent to which the Nordic Council has been party-politicised. The only other party group initiative in Oslo in February 1983 was a right-wing proposal on the need for concerted action in the Data Technology field. None of the delegate initiatives considered by the standing committee on Social Policy and the Environment had party group sponsorship, and one urging more active research co-operation in the energy and environmental areas was backed by no less than 28 delegates representing the major parties in all five sovereign states of the region, together with a delegate from the Faeroes. In short, cross-party initiatives are still the norm, and the party-politicisation of the Nordic Council has not proceeded to anything like the same extent as in the national assemblies.

How has the position of the Nordic Council been affected by the three main lines of development discussed above and what role does it perform in the evolving Nordic political system? Is it possible to argue that in providing a forum for bringing together parliamentarians from the national and Home Rule assemblies, the Nordic Council has provided an agency for the diffusion of ideas and thereby performed a valuable agenda-setting function? Or has power rather devolved to the Council of Ministers, with the Nordic Council assuming the type of control function classically associated with parliaments? The answer would seem to be, first, that parallel to developments in the national policy arena, where initiating powers have passed primarily to the cabinet and civil service (the executive arm of government), there has been a tendency in recent years for the onus in the instigation of broad co-operative measures to fall on the Council of Ministers and for delegates' proposals in the Nordic Council to lose their former importance. The Nordic political system, in short, appears *executive-dominant*. However, secondly and concurrently, through the institutionalisation of its standing committee system and the general process of party-politicisation, the *parliamentary character* of the Nordic Council has been accentuated, while the historic control function of legislatures has been emphasised in the case of the Nordic Council by the introduction of procedures for scrutinising the budget *in plenum*, along with the modernisation of techniques for interrogating the executive. We will elaborate these two points.

The appearance of executive dominance is sustained by the wide-ranging prerogatives exercised by the Council of Ministers in the initiation and implementation of policy. The Council of Ministers can set up Nordic-level commissions of inquiry and investigatory working groups — recruited mainly from the personnel of its two secretariats — as well as arranging conferences and seminars of experts, all of which enables it to approach the task of policy formulation in a slow-moving, deliberative and consensus-generating fashion. Next, it can create quasi-autonomous advisory councils: for example, there exist no less than thirty Nordic research institutes, and in March 1982 it was decided to found a Nordic Political Research Council to co-ordinate and further co-operation across the entire research field.[58] The Council of Ministers also produces consultative documents which, in consultation with the Praesidium, are placed before the Nordic Council and provide a framework for plenary discussion. In 1982 their two main themes were 'The Nordic Countries as a Home Market' and 'Technology and the Future'. Moreover, there are frequent cross-national ministerial meetings, and the ensuing statements, like those following on gatherings of the Nordic Prime Ministers, tend to carry considerable weight. Of major strategic importance is the fact that the five Nordic governments control the allocation of resources within the two regional-level budgets. Two final elements complete the picture of an executive-dominant Nordic political system: the growth in a regional administration and the high acceptance-rate of the Council of Ministers' proposals in the Council's annual session (all of them were approved in Oslo in February 1983). In sum, it appears that the major cooperative initiatives in the Nordic policy process stem from the

Council of Ministers, and increasingly from direct collaboration between two or three of the governments in the region.

In the last few years a far more incrementalist policy style has emerged. The broad-gauge approach which produced fruitless ventures such as the proposed Customs Union, *Nordek*, in the late 1960s has been abandoned in favour of a sectoral approach and what Gro Harlem Brundland, the Norwegian Prime Minister, described at the Nordic Council's ordinary session in Copenhagen in 1981 as the 'building-brick principle'. This has involved building from a relatively narrow base and by avoiding measures clearly likely to fail — such as wide-ranging plans to harmonise taxation and exchange rate laws — and acknowledging legitimate differences in national interest, maintaining the momentum of co-operation. The tendency to bilateralism and the agreement between Norway and Sweden on Energy and Industry in 1981, in particular, well illustrates the building-brick approach. Certain Nordic Council delegates have expressed reservations about developments: Ib Stetter, the Danish Conservative and retiring President, insisted at the Helsinki session in 1982 that bilateral arrangements should not be seen as a primary goal of co-operation, and the Swedish Conservative Allan Hernelius was in broad agreement with him. There has also been a certain amount of bilateral friction and tension — e.g. between Denmark and Sweden over atomic waste disposal and between Norway and Finland over unemployment and removal insurance for persons moving between the two countries. But if Denmark and Iceland have shown some scepticism towards bilateral and trilateral solutions, Norway and Sweden have been extremely enthusiastic and Finland too has taken a positive stance towards them.[59]

The building-brick approach is not of course the only *modus operandi* of Nordic co-operation which has emerged. A number of broadly conceived ventures like the so-called *Nordsat* project, a common TV satellite which would unite the Nordic-speaking areas, have also been high on the agenda. Although faring rather better than Nordek, the fate of Nordsat hangs in the balance at the time of writing.[60] Denmark, which has access to several European satellites, has withdrawn, and in Sweden the Social Democrats, who want a single Nordic programme, have been coolly disposed to it. Perhaps the most significant thing about Nordsat, however — and a measure of the increased resilience of regional co-operation — has been not so much the delay in its realisation as the fact that the other four Nordic nations have decided to proceed without Denmark. It appears that an early maxim of Nordic co-operation, 'proceed together or not at all' — or what Toivo Miljan has depicted as 'consensualism of the lowest common denominator'[61] — no longer has the validity it once had.

The role played by Nordic-level officials in tilting the balance of power towards the regional executive is difficult to estimate, although in the view of Helge Seip, a former general-secretary of the Nordic Council, it should not be underestimated. It has not been the growth in the size of the 'Nordocracy' *per se* — this, as we have seen, has been relatively small — but the extent of the cohesion between the two 'executive-side' secretariats and the Council of Ministers that has been the significant factor. According to Seip, the matter has been one of basic institutional relationships: the contacts between the governments (Council of Ministers) and the Nordic-level administration are better developed than those between the Nordic Council and the Praesidium Secretariat. Moreover, the Council of Ministers and its supporting organs have both resources and authority, whereas in Seip's view the Nordic Council officials serve in more of a consultative capacity.[62] The efficiency of the distinctive organisation of the Council of Ministers' bureaucracy along geographical lines — the division into twin secretariats, Cultural Affairs in Copenhagen and General Affairs in Oslo — was indeed reviewed by a commission appointed in 1981. Significantly, existing arrangements were confirmed.

As to the decline in significance of delegate initiatives in the Nordic Council — a corollary, though not an inevitable consequence of the domination of the regional executive — this has been in line with the rather uneven levels of parliamentary commitment to the question of Nordic co-operation. From the legislators' viewpoint, the challenge of the Nordic ideal has become more onerous. They have to cope with a mountain of documentation, to be read in addition to their heavy national workload; extensive preparation for an annual session which lasts only a week; and the reality that they are unlikely to gain any domestic advantage in terms of kudos, career advancement, or voter recognition unless they succeed in raising a topical national issue for discussion. Not surprisingly, therefore, the onus of initiation has passed increasingly from individual delegates to the party groups. It is also possible that the need for technical advice and assistance at the formulation stage has acted as something of a deterrent to individual legislators pursuing proposals. Certainly it seems that Nordic Council members are not infrequently mouthpieces for measures emanating from officials either in the Nordic or national secretariats. Precisely how many of the recommendations of the Nordic Council are in practice based on the initiative of officials it would perhaps be unwise to speculate, although Seip notes that it would scarcely surprise the more informed observer to learn that a majority come about in this way.[63] Finally, it is also conceivable that Nordic Council delegates increasingly see themselves fulfilling the traditional deliberating and scrutinising role of parliamentarians — the role they are accustomed to playing at the national level and doubtless feel best equipped to play.

It is significant in this last context that concurrent with, and in part a response to, the growing pre-eminence of the executive in the Nordic political system, the 1970s and 1980s have witnessed a marked strengthening in the parliamentary character of the Nordic Council. To members and officials alike, the Council has become less like a one-week 'international conference' and more like a parliamentary assembly. An institutionalisation of the standing committee system has played a manifest role in this development: as noted, standing committee meetings are now convened throughout the year rather than being confined to the annual weekly session. In November 1982, moreover, a full week was set aside experimentally for preparatory meetings of the five standing committees. The party-politicisation process has also contributed significantly by breaking down the barriers between the states and investing the Council with a Nordic quality, which in a real sense has exceeded the sum of its national parts. Like standing committee meetings, *ad hoc* gatherings of the party groups and group secretaries are staged throughout the calendar. More important, the year 1982 saw a decisive breakthrough in that for the first time all twenty-four positions of responsibility — the chairmanships and deputy-chairmanships in the Praesidium, standing committees and two permanent committees — were appointed on a partisan basis. In the autumn of 1981, the Swedish delegation had suggested the creation of a working group (formed from within the Praesidium) to work out a method of electing these leading positions, and in March the following year a distribution of 13:11 in favour of the non-socialist groups was unanimously concluded, based on a PR odd-numbers method. The party-politicisation of the national quotas — which have remained constant — is well illustrated in the case of the Praesidium. The Conservatives took the places allotted to Denmark and Finland, the Social Democrats got those reserved for Norway and Sweden, and the Icelandic position went to the Progressive Party. Recently, too, the introduction of new procedures for examining the common Nordic budgets, along with the introduction of 'short questions' to ministers, appear to have strengthened the Council's apparatus for controlling the executive — a classic function of legislatures throughout the world.

The present method of scrutinising the budgets grew out of an initiative from the Nordic Council's Budget Committee, which led in December 1981 to the creation of a working group to examine ways of consolidating the Council's influence in the allocation of common Nordic-level monies. Introduced provisionally in 1983, the revised procedure involves the engagement of the standing committees and Budget Committee at an earlier stage in the review process than heretofore and requires a proposal on the General Nordic Budget and the Nordic Cultural Budget to be placed before a plenary meeting as part of the Council of Ministers' report. Another innovation in 1983 was that following contributions from the floor — there were in fact ten speeches — delegates were permitted to vote on a proposal from the Council's Budget Committee. Indeed, the Cultural Budget was raised by 400,000 Danish kronor and the General Budget by the same amount in Norwegian kronor. It is, of course, quite possible that a comparable level of increase would have been effected under the former procedure, and it is certainly premature to assess the extent (if any) of the strengthening in the Council's financial control over the executive. A former secretary to one of the Council's standing committees has said that while 'one can have doubts about whether parliamentary influence over the [Budget] prioritisation exercise has really grown, it is not, of course, impossible.'[64]

Similar doubts concern the impact on 'legislative-executive' relations of the introduction in 1983 of a new mode of interrogating ministers — the short questions. In contrast to written questions, submitted three weeks in advance of an ordinary session, short questions can be tabled at only twenty-four hours' notice and thereby allow highly topical issues to be taken up. Slightly less than half of the thirty-nine questions answered in 1983 were short questions. Yet if these short questions constitute, potentially at least, a flexible vehicle for holding the executive to account, the reality has been rather different. Ministers responding to them cannot commit the Council of Ministers as a whole, and there has been a tendency for answers to be anodyne and devoid of practical significance. Nor are the plenary account debates (see chapter 8) an effective medium for taking the executive to task because they are restricted to a consideration of the annual reports of the Council of Ministers and Praesidium. Other general debate is very limited. Occasionally a statement from a Prime Minister early in the week's proceedings will lend muscle to the ensuing discussions — in 1969, the Danish Prime Minister made his ill-fated Nordek proposal at a Council session — but it is symptomatic that there is not the type of Report Stage or Final Reading debate (i.e., a decision-making plenary based on standing committee deliberations) that is endemic to the national parliaments.[65] Indeed, during the Nordic Council session in Copenhagen in 1981, the Speaker of the Folketing, K.B. Andersen, made the informal suggestion that general debate be scrapped and replaced by discussions focusing on the policy sectors covered by the five standing committees.[66]

Despite its accentuated parliamentary character in recent years, the Nordic Council falls short of being a legislative assembly both in its inability to pass binding laws and in the absence of a common Nordic taxation right which it can exercise. A proposal from the United Nordic Youth Organisation (FNUF) would remedy this situation by investing the Nordic Council with decision-making powers in certain policy areas — e.g. communications, culture and special education — as well as giving it the right to issue binding instructions in legislative questions (although every state would maintain a veto-right). The FNUF proposes a 200-member Nordic Parliament elected directly by the various peoples with seats distributed on a demographic basis and adjustments made to guarantee a fair representation for Iceland and the three Home Rule territories and to give a voice to the Lapps in the northern parts of the region.[67] Plainly the realisation of this blueprint is a long way off; equally, however, there has been an undoubted development in the Nordic Council, not only as an institution (in relation to its internal structures and practices) but legally and conceptually, since its foundation in 1952. Initially, the Council was grounded in five identical texts which were legally valid only in the individual countries and reflected the widespread apprehension that the new organ would encroach upon the sovereign position of the national parliaments. The so-called Helsinki agreement of 1962, revised in 1971 and 1974, gave the Council an international footing, and subsequent developments have consolidated its parliamentary character. In a strict sense, however, the Nordic Council remains a consultative body — an 'upper tier' assembly composed of, and ultimately subject to, the national parliaments in the region.

One question remains: what impact, if any, has the Nordic Council, and indeed the entire Nordic political system, had on the national legislative process? An immediate reaction might be: 'not much'. There is relatively little debate in the Nordic parliaments on issues related to regional-level co-operation, and outside the various national delegations parliamentarians are not at all sensitised to the workings of the Nordic political system. There is an annual debate in the Riksdag on the Swedish delegation's report, and another on the government's proposal concerning the two Nordic budgets. Otherwise, business growing out of Nordic co-operation finds little or no place on the national parliamentary agendas. The impact of the Nordic political system is felt almost exclusively at the initiation and formulation stages of the domestic policy-making process, either via proposals from the Ministers for Nordic Co-operation and routine departmental ministers, or on rare occasions through private members' bills. A delegate may table a private measure, alluding in the preamble to a recommendation of the Nordic Council and the way this has been implemented with favourable results elsewhere in the region.

At the adoption stage, however, the impact of the Nordic Council is not as great as 'upper tier' organs like the Finnish Grand Committee or the Norwegian Lagting, although ironically it clearly performs a more effective deliberative role in its own right than either the Grand Committee or the Lagting. The efficacy of these two organs as scrutinising bodies is limited, as we have seen, by the force of partisan allegiance: in both there is a duplication of the legislative-executive balance in the House as a whole. However, the Nordic Council has not been affected by party-politicisation to quite the same extent. The majority of private members' initiatives still enjoy multi-party sponsorship, and traditional norms of consensus continue to apply. It was not without significance that at a meeting of party secretaries organised by the Nordic Council's Communications Committee and held in the Faeroes in June 1983, a general commitment was made to greater co-operation between the four main party blocs in the Council. Anyway, there is evidence that developments have sharpened the quality of debate as well as heightening delegate interest. According to a Danish Social Democrat, the emergence of party group alignments was prompted by a concern to break down the widespread passivity which had existed among members, while on a related note a Swedish Centrist has pointed to a growing awareness among delegates that greater influence could be exerted through working as blocs or related parties.[68] Unity is strength and strength lies in numbers. Perhaps, in line with the thoughts of a senior Norwegian Conservative, the party-politicisation of the Nordic Council should be regarded as an expression of the advancing integration process in the region — integration by the backdoor, so to speak, and thus another strand in Nils Andrén's web of integration.[69] Whatever the truth of the matter, it has unquestionably enhanced the deliberative function of the Nordic Council.

Yet it is highly questionable whether the Nordic Council's impact on the deliberation and adoption of measures in the five national assemblies has been other than extremely marginal. It is true that experience as a Nordic Council delegate can, in principle, affect a parliamentarian's capacity to make a legislative contribution in the national forum. His views will doubtless profit from having a comparative perspective as well as from his access to Nordic-level documentation, statistical information etc. and he may even find that he can influence his parliamentary party group more easily as a result. However, the resulting impact of the Nordic Council on the domestic legislative process is likely to remain small. In fact, it is likely to be exceeded by the (admittedly) very rare amendments to 'law' proposals effected by the Lagting and the relatively infrequent amendments to bills occasioned by the Grand Committee.

REFERENCES

1. VJ 5:65–66.
2. FOF 3:8:9–10.
3. FOF 3:8:2.
4. RO 5:1.
5. FOF 3:12:4.
6. Nousiainen (1971), pp. 193–4.
7. O. Seitkari, 'Edustuslaitoksen uudistus 1906' in *Suomen kansanedustuslaitoksen historia*. Viides osa. Helsinki: Eduskunnan historiakomitea, 1958, pp. 44–5.
8. Nousiainen (1977), p. 398.
9. Ibid., p. 399.
10. VJ 4:42.
11. VJ 4:52.
12. Nousiainen (1977), p. 421.
13. *Suuren valiokunnan työjärjestys* (*SVT*). Hyväksytty 17 päivänä joulukuuta 1976. 17–18.
14. SVT 4.
15. SVT 5.
16. SVT 9.
17. SVT 12.
18. SVT 27.
19. Nousiainen (1977), pp. 403–4.
20. Voitto Helander, 'Kamari vai kirjaamo?' *Turun yliopiston valtio-opillisia tutkimuksia* 32, 1976, p. 71.
21. Helander (1976), pp. 61–6.
22. Ibid., p. 81.
23. Ibid., p. 84.
24. Ibid., p. 85.
25. 'Nimilain loppurutistus alkaa'. *Helsingin Sanomat* 26.1.1983.
26. 'Sukunimilain vahvistettava perheyhteyttä'. *Kristityn Vastuu* 20.1.1983.
27. Nousiainen (1977), p. 426.
28. Sverre Steen, 'Hvordan Norges Storting ble til' in *Det Norske Storting Gjennom 150 år*. Oslo: Gyldendal Norsk Forlag, 1964, pp. 171–2.
29. T.K. Derry, *A History of Scandinavia*. London: Geo. Allen & Unwin, 1979. p. 217.
30. SFO 5:30.
31. Information supplied by Erik Mo 27.9.1982.
32. Innst. 0 nr 43 (1972–3). *Tilråding frå kyrkje-og undervisningsnemnda om lov om gymnaset*.
33. *Forhandlinger i Lagtinget* 15 mai 1973 — Lov om gymnaset, p. 59.
34. *Forhandlinger i Lagtinget* 15 mai 1973, pp. 61–5.
35. Besl. L nr 53 (Jfr beslut 0 nr 44).
36. *Forhandlinger i Stortinget* nr 440, p. 3457.
37. *Forhandlinger i Stortinget* nr 439, p. 3447.

38. Bjarni Benediktsson, 'The Two Chambers of the Icelandic Althing', in *Legal Essays — A Tribute to Frede Castberg*. Oslo: Universitetsforlaget, 1963, pp. pp. 405–7.
39. Olafur R. Grimsson, 'Political Power in Iceland Prior to the Period of Class Politics'. Unpubl. Ph.D. dissertation, Manchester University, 1970, p. 97.
40. Ibid., p. 102.
41. Benediktsson (1963), p. 396.
42. 'God's Frozen People' *BBC 2 Television*, 29.12.1982.
43. Dag Anckar, 'Om öar och politik' in Åland i Utveckling (1982) pp. 150–66.
44. Speech made by President Urho Kekkonen at the Swedish Institute of International Affairs 8.5.1978.
45. Jacob Söderman, 'Utveckling eller stagnation?' *Nordisk Kontakt* 4/82, p. 249.
46. 'Fortsatt och utvecklat samarbete'. *Nordisk Kontakt* 4/82, p. 252.
47. Claes Wiklund, 'Det nordiska samarbetets ledning 11. De nordiska samarbetsministrarna 1971–82'. *Nordisk Kontakt* 15/82, p. 1134.
48. *Yhteistyösopimus Islannin, Norjan, Ruotsin, Suomen ja Tanskan välillä 23.3.1962* (Helsingin-sopimus). Helmikuun 13 päivänä 1971 ja maaliskuun 11 päivänä 1974 sopimukseen tehdyt muutokset on sijoitettu sopimustekstiin: 55 artikla. Pohjoismaisia yhteistyösopimuksia. Tukholma 1979.
49. Claes Wiklund & Bengt Sundelius, 'Nordic Co-operation in the Seventies: Trends and Patterns'. *Scandinavian Political Studies* 2 (New Series), 2, 1979, p. 114.
50. *Pohjoismaiden ministerineuvoston työjärjestys 17.2.1973*. Joulukuun 4 päivänä 1975 työjärjestykseen tehdyt muutokset on sijoitettu tekstiin. Artikla 12.
51. *Kertomus vuoden 1982 pohjoismaisesta yhteistyöstä*. Eripainos C1:stä. Pohjoismaiden ministerineuvosto, pp. 66–8.
52. Claes Wiklund, 'Det nordiska samarbetets ledning 11'. *Nordisk Kontakt* 15/82, pp. 1134–8.
53. *Stadga och arbetsordning för Nordiska Rådet*. Helsinfors 1958. Artikla 7.
54. Claes Wiklund, 'Det nordiska samarbetets ledning 1. Rådspresidiets sammansättning 1967–82'. *Nordisk Kontakt* 13/82, pp. 983–7.
55. 'Det nordiska samarbetets ledning 111. Förmännen i Nordiska rådets utskott 1953–83'. *Nordisk Kontakt* 11/83, pp. 751–6.
56. Ilkka-Christian Björklund, 'Om politiker och byråkrater.' *Nordisk Kontakt* 15/82, pp. 1132–3.
57. 'Full sysselsetting må gjenoprettes'. *Nordisk Kontakt* 5/83, pp. 337–8.
58. 'Forskningspolitiskt råd?' *Nordisk Kontakt* 7/82, pp. 502–4.
59. Claes Wiklund, 'Defaitism och partipolitisering?' *Nordisk Kontakt* 5/82, p. 354.
60. Allan Hernelius, 'Stora framgånger under Nordiska rådets 30 år'. *Nordisk Kontakt* 8/82, pp. 565–7.
61. Toivo Miljan, *The Reluctant Europeans*. London: Hurst, 1977, p. 101.
62. Helge Seip, 'Sekretariatenes roller, ansvar og samspill i det nordiska samarbeidet'. *Nordisk Kontakt* 13/82, pp. 977–82.
63. Ibid., p. 978.
64. Claes Wiklund, 'Samarbetsförhoppningar i krisens tecken. Intryck från Nordiska rådets 31: a session'. *Nordisk Kontakt* 4/83, p. 249.
65. Ralf Friberg, 'Nordiska rådet långsamt på veg att bli ett nordisk parlament?' *Nordisk Kontakt* 9/82, pp. 640–2.
66. Ibid., p. 642.
67. 'Nordiska rådet ett nordiskt parlament?' *Nordisk Kontakt* 14/82, p. 1069.
68. Claes Wiklund, 'Visionerna och verkligheten. Nordiska rådet och partipolitiseringen'. *Nordisk Kontakt* 3/83, pp. 146–8.
69. Nils Andrén, 'Nordic Integration — Aspects and Problems'. *Co-operation and Conflict* 2, 1967, pp. 1–25.

7

THE FINAL ADOPTION OF MEASURES: LEGISLATING OR DELIBERATING ASSEMBLIES?

> 'There is nearly always an element of uncertainty when the matter under discussion relates to the geographical placement of a public body, because then party lines are weak or, indeed, completely absent. — Speech by Kjell Magne Bondevik, Chairman of the Norwegian Christian People's Party, 1977

Having reached the stage at which legislative proposals are ready to be resolved on the floor of the assembly, we now have to consider two central questions. First, does the existence of a distinctive nexus of qualified majority and/or fixed minority provisions in respect of the approval of certain types of bills in Finland, Denmark and Sweden have a significant impact on legislative-executive relations in those countries? Secondly, and obviously not unconnected with the first question, how should the main patterns of legislative voting in the region be characterised? It is clear that where multiparty legislative coalitions — i.e. alliances between a party or parties in government and one or more parties in opposition — are commonplace, the deliberative influence of parliament is likely to be enhanced.

Later an inventory of the strengths and limitations of the Nordic assemblies in the adoption of public policy is compiled. A systematic reappraisal of their deliberative function is preceded by a detailed section on the independent legislative capability of the parliaments in the region — i.e. the proportion of initiatives that are accepted in the assembly from individual legislators, groups of delegates or, in Sweden and Iceland, parliamentary standing committees.

The final resolution of measures

All legislative proposals in the Nordic parliaments, after scrutiny in a standing committee, and whether in amended form or not, are ultimately resolved by a vote on the floor of the assembly in one of three ways: they may be accepted, rejected or deferred. Before considering the rules governing the final adoption of bills, however, we should note that attendance at parliamentary votes in the region has varied over time and in relation to the nature and importance of the issue being resolved.

In Sweden, for example, the average level of absenteeism at divisions of the unicameral Riksdag before the introduction of parliamentary deputies on 15 February 1974 was 60 delegates; shortly afterwards, it dropped to 20 but during the Spring session of 1981 had risen again to 40 delegates per vote.[1] In other words, an average of 309 out of 349 Riksdag members responded to the two-minute division bell. The crucial debate on reduced levels of state support to the hard-hit shipbuilding industry in June 1981, which Fälldin's Centre-Liberal minority won by 2 votes, saw 33 delegates absent from voting.[2] The position in Norway is less clear. Sven Groennings notes that between 1945 and 1957 the average absence rate of Storting members at votes was under 15% and that this later increased,[3] but it is not clear by how much; later statistics are not available. As in Denmark, at least half of all delegates must be present for valid decisions to be taken. In Finland, attendance at plenary votes deteriorated in the 1970s: a mean figure of no less than 60 of the 200 members in the Eduskunta were absent from votes in the autumn of 1979 compared with only 20 a decade earlier.[4] A Speaker's Council investigation revealed, however, that in many cases there were *bona fide* grounds for absence.[5] Even so, less than 10% of those missing were accounted for in terms of illness, while over 20% failed to explain their absence, despite the possibility of disciplinary action being taken against them. Since 1979 and the media exposure given to the matter, attendance at plenary votes has improved somewhat, as has the punctiliousness of members in making the necessary written request for official leave, *lomanpyyntö*.

Outside Finland, the proportion of delegates attending full-sitting divisions compares quite favourably with West European states although, with the exception of Finland, all the Nordic countries use a system of parliamentary deputies to cover when regular members are officially absent. Against this, absenteeism is inflated — it appears to be doubled — by the 'pairing' convention that operates throughout the region and which means that when a member on the government side cannot attend, a partner on the opposition benches is prevailed upon to stay away too. In Sweden a member of each of the parliamentary groups, the *kvittningsman*, is given special responsibility for 'pairing'. In Iceland pairing is organised through the chairmen of the parliamentary party groups, but is not common, but it does seem to hold up at the most tense divisions. When voting took place in the Lower Chamber of the Althing in April 1981 on a controversial opposition amendment to a government bill fixing the amount of public loans for the forthcoming fiscal year — an amendment which, contrary to government intention, provided for a loan to enable work to be started in co-operation with the United

States on a new terminal building at Keflavík airport — there was a tie and the opposition lost on the casting vote of the Speaker. However, at least one of the two opposition delegates absent from this critical division was known to be in Reyjavík at the time and could have swung the vote in favour of the amendment. Had he not respected the pairing convention, in other words, the government would undoubtedly have lost.[6]

In general, the greater the partisan importance of a vote, the greater is the pressure on delegates to attend — never more so, of course, than when the government has only a hairbreadth majority. In Iceland, participation at Althing divisions was markedly higher after the 1979 election and the ensuing split in the largest group, the Independence Party, than during the period 1974–8 when the centre-left coalition of the Progressive Party, People's Alliance and Social Democrats enjoyed a comfortable majority. The prelude to the Independence Party split was the long period of political crisis from December 1979 to February 1981, when repeated attempts to form a government foundered and the President was known to be considering nominating a civil-service administration along the lines of the one in 1942. Using this stalemate to good advantage, the deputy chairman of the Independence Party went behind the back of his chairman and, following approaches to the winning Progressive Party and the People's Alliance, succeeded in putting together a coalition which had an overall majority of only 4 seats. In the aftermath of these events, delegate attendance was at a premium. There was a similar situation in Sweden over the summer and early autumn of 1980. The debate on the nation's first-ever no confidence motion, tabled by the Social Democrats under the new constitutional arrangements against Fälldin's three-party non-socialist government in October that year, led to the only fully-attended division the Speaker Ingemund Bengtsson could remember.[7] The coalition won by a single vote. Two months earlier on August 26, during the only extraordinary session of the Riksdag to be held since the war, it was decided — again by a single vote, the size of the three-party non-socialist majority — to give Sweden the highest rate of Value Added Tax in Europe. By 173 votes to the 172 of the combined Left, the government raised VAT to exceed even Denmark's rate of 22%.

Attendance at parliamentary divisions has also been linked to the status of a proposal. For 'ordinary legislation' a simple majority at a quorate plenary meeting is sufficient for its enactment, although Norwegian 'laws' require a two-thirds majority in the event of repeated disagreement between the Lagting and Odelsting. Constitutional amendments, on the other hand, represent in their very nature 'exceptional legislation' and presume the backing of more than a simple plurality for final adoption. Article 112 of the Norwegian constitution states 'that if experience demonstrates the need for a modification to any part of the constitution, an amendment proposal shall be submitted to the first, second or third Storting after a general election . . . but it shall be left to the first, second or third Storting following the *next* general election to determine whether the amendment is to be adopted.' The amendment must then receive the support of two-thirds of the members of the Storting.

Distinctively in Finland, a broad category of bills 'at the constitutional level' need the approval of a qualified majority in the assembly. A bill introducing a new tax or increasing an existing one, when the provisions of the bill are intended to operate for longer than one year, is to be regarded as defeated unless two-thirds of the delegates present at Third Reading support it. If the proposal is defeated, it is returned to the Finance Committee, which reports on whether it should be enforced for one year only and, if this is the recommendation, supplies the necessary re-wording of the measure.[8] With tax amendments frequently incorporated into the annual Finance Bill, the Budget invariably needs a two-thirds majority for acceptance. So too do proposals involving reductions in the size of the national territory and those relating to the salaries of parliamentarians.[9] Proposals to enact a new constitutional law or modify existing constitutional legislation are anyway treated rather differently in Finland. If they receive simple majority support at Third Reading, they are postponed until the first parliamentary session after a general election and then they may be enacted in unchanged form if approved by at least two-thirds of the delegates present. If, however, a constitutional bill is declared 'urgent' — and this can be done by a five-sixths majority of the Eduskunta — it must be decided in the same legislative session; and then, to be accepted, it must gain the assent of a two-thirds majority.[10] This 'urgency' procedure has also become increasingly common in the case of Exceptional Laws — laws marking a departure from the prescriptions of the constitution but which do not in themselves involve any changes to the constitution's basic text. The Exceptional Law of 1974, which enabled parliament to extend President Kekkonen's term of office by a further 4 years rather than the 6-year term and indirect elections set out in the constitution, is a case in point.

The only other type of proposal in the region requiring a five-sixths majority — and then it is required for acceptance only rather than simply to be declared 'urgent' — is a law in Denmark involving the delegation of national powers to an international body. This needs either a five-sixths Folketing majority or a simple legislative plurality plus approval in a popular referendum.[12] Incidentally, it is not only Exceptional Laws that can create the need for decisions by a qualified majority: exceptional situations can do the same. According to the new constitution, if Sweden is occupied by a foreign power, no matter can be resolved except by a vote at which not less than three-quarters of the members of the Riksdag are present.[13] However, mindful no doubt of the experience of the Nygaardsvold administration in Norway during the German occupation from 1940 till 1945, and the possibility that an occupying power which convenes the Riksdag in order to take binding decisions might find its task facilitated by drafting in parliamentary deputies (the deputy system was introduced after the new constitution came into force), the Minister of Justice introduced a constitutional amendment in the autumn of 1981 requiring that the increased quorum of three-quarters be made up of full Riksdag delegates only. It is true that a qualified majority as such is not required, although a plurality of a minimum of three-quarters of all full delegates amounts in practice to much the same thing. Even an uncontroversial bill bearing on an extremely hypothetical situation was not without problems, however: when it was discussed informally by the secretaries of the Riksdag standing committees, the question was raised of whether the 'permanent deputies' — that is, persons substituting for cabinet ministers and the Speakers — would be included in the category of full members.[14]

Rather than being accepted or rejected outright, a bill may be deferred for renewed parliamentary consideration at a later date. In Finland, a bill which has gained a simple majority at Third Reading can be 'put to rest' *panna lepäämään*, if a proposal to that effect is moved before the formal announcement of the bill's acceptance. The matter is then put 'on the table' until the following plenary, and if at least one-third of Eduskunta members are in favour it is 'put to rest' in precisely its Third Reading form until the first parliamentary session after a general election, when it can be accepted by a simple majority. According to a constitutional amendment in 1979, however, bills cannot be postponed under this procedure if they relate to planned or existing strike action on the part of civil servants and public officials which is, or is likely to prove, injurious to society in general and to the welfare of individual citizens in particular.[15] Other matters that cannot be 'put to rest' include proposals for new or increased taxation, the approval of state loans, delegates' salaries and government bills not affecting the constitution which are discussed in an extraordinary session of the Eduskunta. A successful proposal to defer a bill does not prevent the government or an individual parliamentarian from introducing a new bill on essentially the same matter, and when this happens, the decision to put the original bill to rest is automatically revoked.[16]

Until after the Second World War, these constitutional provisions enabling a minority of parliamentarians to delay bills were unique to Finland: and there they remain the most integral part of any legislative process in the region. With one-third of the Eduskunta's delegates in a position to vote a bill over an election and as little as one-sixth able to prevent a measure from being treated as 'urgent', governments have traditionally been disinclined to introduce measures with little realistic prospect of achieving the overwhelming parliamentary consensus necessary for their enactment in a single parliamentary session. In many ways, moreover, the Finnish political system has been characterised by what Paavo Kastari has called an historic sense of 'legalism' — a legalism deriving from the last two decades of oppressive Russian rule at the beginning of this century, and which has expressed itself *inter alia* in a very strong respect for the letter of the constitution.[17] The elaborate system of qualified majorities and fixed minorities should be viewed as very much a legacy of this period of Russification — when parliament found itself in the vanguard of a movement to defend the provisions of the 1772 Swedish-Finnish constitution — and as a reflection too of the Eduskunta's subsequent concern when formulating a post-Independence form of government to protect citizens against any future violations of their basic individual rights and freedoms. That this latter objective was successfully achieved can be seen in the fact that alone of the new inter-war constitutions, the Finnish has survived, and has done so furthermore with a very minimum of amendments.

It was the practical impossibility, given Czarist attitudes, of amending the 1772 constitution which also gave rise to the highly distinctive system of Exceptional Laws: their enactment continued after Independence and around 600 such laws were passed in the five decades between 1917 and 1967. Whether a bill constitutes an Exceptional Law — they are normally in force for only a short period and can be amended or repealed by a simple parliamentary majority — or merely an ordinary law is not always clear. According to the Parliament Act of 1928, the Speaker[18] and if necessary the Constitutional Committee of the Eduskunta[19] determine whether a simple or qualified majority is necessary for the enactment of a bill, although the President on the advice of the Supreme Court, *korkein oikeus*, can withhold his consent from a bill not adopted according to the correct procedures.[20] In practice, as we shall discover later, challenges to the status of bills introduced as ordinary legislation and their consequent referral to the Constitutional Committee have afforded parliamentary opposition further tactical leverage.

In 1953 the new Danish constitution introduced regulations comparable to those in Finland (even if less comprehensive), permitting a minority of parliamentary delegates either to postpone the Third Reading of a proposal, vote a property expropriation bill over a general election or, uniquely in the region, make it obligatory for a bill successfully completing its passage through the Folketing to be submitted to a popular referendum. These three fixed minority provisions in Denmark, when stated in full, are as follows.

Two-fifths of the members of the Folketing can request that the Third Reading of a bill takes place, at the earliest, 12 (rather than the normal 2) weekdays after its acceptance at Second Reading; the request has to be made in writing to the Speaker and counter-signed by the members supporting it.[21] However, this type of Third Reading postponement is not possible in the case of Finance Bills, Supplementary Appropriation Bills, Provisional Appropriation Bills, Government Loan Bills, Naturalisation Bills, Expropriation Bills, Indirect Taxation Bills and various emergency measures. In the event of a proposal relating to the expropriation of property being passed, one-third of the Folketing's members can, within three days of its final approval, demand that the Royal Assent be withheld until after a general election has taken place and renewed acceptance has been gained in parliament.[22] Finally, when a proposal is adopted at Third Reading, one-third of the Folketing's members can, within three days of its final approval, petition the Speaker to submit it to a popular referendum. This request must be made in writing and be counter-signed by the members supporting it.[23] When a referendum is sought in this way, the Folketing can within five days of approving the relevant bill decide to withdraw it. This can be done through a motion for a resolution on withdrawal which is read once in the House in accordance with the rules governing the First Reading of bills, although the Speaker may decide to suspend the time limits on speeches to enable the Folketing to complete its consideration of the matter in time.[24] In the absence of such a resolution, the Prime Minister is notified as quickly as possible and he in turn makes a statement that a referendum will take place — this can happen at the earliest twelve and at the latest eighteen days after his announcement. For the bill in question to be rejected, a majority comprising at least 30% of *eligible* electors must have voted against it in the referendum, although exempt from this procedure are precisely the same category of measures that cannot be deferred at Third Reading. When a law is rejected in a referendum, a statement to this effect is made by the Prime Minister within fourteen days of the result being known, and at that point the proposal lapses.[25]

In Sweden, the case for incorporating qualified majority provisions into the new form of government came up in the early 1970s in connection with the only really fractious issue to surface during the constitutional reform debates — the protection of individual rights and freedoms. The main parliamentary battleground was the Riksdag's Constitutional Committee where the non-socialist parties came out strongly in favour of additional safeguards against the enactment of legislative proposals designed to curb fundamental freedoms, while the Social Democrats were equally vehemently opposed to any type of special protection. It took a compromise worked out in a special working group of the Constitutional Committee, and described by the veteran committee member, Hilding Johansson as the Stockholm Agreement, *Stockholmsöverenskommelsen*, to resolve matters: in classic Swedish style, a parliamentary-based commission of inquiry was set up to look again into the whole question of individual rights, and it was expected to report by the first half of 1975 to enable a proposal to be introduced into the Riksdag by the spring of 1976.[26] In the event the commission, which had all-party representation, was not created until January 1977 and did not report to the Minister of Justice before March the following year. It was 1 January 1980 before a constitutional amendment based on the commission's recommendations came into force. According to this amendment, a bill restricting fundamental rights and freedoms — such as freedom of expression and the right of assembly — can at the request of at least ten delegates be shelved for a minimum of twelve months from the date on which the first standing committee report on the matter was registered in the chamber. The Riksdag, however, can proceed to adopt the bill if at least five-sixths of its delegates so decide.[27] Rather like an 'urgent' constitutional proposal in Finland, in other words, one-sixth or 58 members of the Riksdag can contrive to delay the implementation of a measure seen as having a deleterious effect on the basic freedom and personal integrity of Swedish citizens. Although in the Swedish case only a small category of proposals affecting fundamental liberties may be challenged and delayed, it is plain that the requirement of qualified majorities for the resolution of a range of measures in the Nordic assemblies gives potential leverage to opposition groups at a very late juncture in the adoption process.

Before examining how far this leverage has been exercised through the qualified majority rules in Finland, Denmark and Sweden, a couple of points need emphasis. First, the influence of parliamentary oppositions plainly cannot be measured solely in terms of the exercise of formal voting sanctions — that is to say, the number of times a government proposal is successfully defeated or deferred on the floor of the assembly. Clearly the mere threat to delay a measure can be sufficient to prompt a government to withdraw it, while a failed attempt to postpone a bill does not necessarily leave the opposition empty-handed. Secondly, the existence of rules on qualified majorities, in so far as they dictate the need for a greater degree of parliamentary acquiescence in bills than is required under simple plurality arrangements, may tend to strengthen the consultative position of the opposition. Ultimately, the central question to be considered here is whether the formal rules governing decision-taking at the final reading plenary have a significant bearing on legislative-executive relations in the region?

In Finland the provisions for qualified majorities (and, of course, fixed minorities) were initially laid down in the Standing Orders of the new unicameral Eduskunta in 1907. As with the creation of the Grand Committee, they represented a lifeline for the established élites at a time when the introduction of universal suffrage threatened to sweep them into political oblivion. Not surprisingly, the Left has traditionally viewed the system of qualified majorities as 'the price the working-class movement had to pay the bourgeoisie for the present parliamentary system in Finland',[28] and hence has consistently argued for their abolition or modification. Space prevents detailed examination of the historic impact of the rules on qualified majorities, but we may merely note that a number of vital bills have been delayed or defeated by hard-core minorities in the House. In the autumn of 1918, for example, when 92 socialist delegates were absent following the Red defeat in the Civil War, a right-wing bill which attempted to foist constitutional monarchy on Finland failed to obtain the five-sixths majority necessary to declare it 'urgent', because it was supported by only 75 members of the rump parliament — two less than the number required. In more recent years, the existence of qualified majority rules has probably, more than any other single fact, served to ensure that the Eduskunta has not been a deliberating assembly in the minimal sense of merely authorising proposals formulated by the executive. Instead, the opposition has acquired real bargaining power in relation to the most important government measures. Put another way, despite the long period of predominantly majoritarian left-centre coalition since 1966 — the Koivisto 1 administration of 1968–70 enjoyed the support of no less than 165 of the 200 Eduskunta members — the opposition has always been able at the very least to prevent legislation being enacted in a single parliamentary session, and as such has exerted more real influence than (often numerically stronger) oppositions in systems where legislative decisions are taken exclusively on a simple majority basis. The government in turn has been obliged to anticipate the reaction of the opposition and, when adverse, to make the necessary concessions, albeit as unobtrusively as possible.

There is evidence, for example, of intended government bills being withdrawn in the face of an obvious determination by the opposition to defer them until after a general election. Two random examples from the 1979–80 Eduskunta session will illustrate the point. A government plan to postpone the payment of annual tax returns from the usual month of December to the following March, albeit paying the extra period of interest, was abandoned when it became clear that it would be opposed by all four non-socialist opposition parties, together with the minority wing of the Communists. Another proposal designed as a modest measure to deal with the problem of agricultural over-production, and which would have required farmers wishing to extend the cultivated area on their land by felling forest to obtain an official permit, was similarly withdrawn.[29] It is ironic, moreover, that while a left-right consensus on the desirability of qualified majorities has been conspicuously absent, the very existence of these rules has served to enforce a measure of practical agreement between the government and opposition regarding important legislation, particularly in the economic field. While the point should not be exaggerated, it appears that the central governmental task of economic management has been complicated in Finland by the fact that major initiatives — price freezes, tax amendments, incomes policy packages etc. — all represent legislation 'at the constitutional level' and in requiring a five-sixths majority to be enacted in a single parliamentary session have necessitated consultation with, and indeed the assent of, the main opposition party, the Conservatives. This is something which the government has acknowledged in practice. In 1968, when the first of a series of Economic Stabilisation Agreements was put before parliament, the Koivisto government had enough support to get the necessary constitutional amendment approved, but not enough to put it through in a single legislative session. The Conservatives accordingly occupied a strategic consultative position — they had to be (and were) consulted.[30] As a result, while they subsequently voted in principle against the Stabilisation Bill, they did not in practice prevent it from being declared 'urgent' legislation.

It could of course be argued that while the Finnish system of qualified majorities has contributed to consolidating the policy impact of opposition parties, it has not significantly strengthened the position of parliament itself. After all, the few government bills to be jettisoned have been withdrawn before reaching the Eduskunta and not afterwards, and although the bargaining position of the Conservatives has been enhanced by the need for co-operation in proceeding with 'urgent' legislation, deals with the main opposition party have been reached largely outside rather than inside parliament — i.e. in talks conducted in such places as suburban hotels, very much in the manner of the 'Haga agreements' in Sweden in the early 1970s (see chapter 5). In 1977 the 'Korpilampi spirit', *Korpilammen henki*, made its appearance in Finland, so-called because of the series of wide-ranging meetings convened initially at the Korpilampi hotel in the hinterland of Helsinki and involving the government and senior officials from the political parties, pressure groups and central administration. At the same time, however, the problem of interpreting the intent of a tightly-worded constitution — now almost 70 years old — coupled with the scope afforded by the unusually wide category of proposals considered 'at the constitutional level' have facilitated opposition challenges to measures both on the floor of the legislature and in standing committee. There is no doubt that in the right circumstances, opponents of controversial government measures have been able to give added demonstrative weight to their opposition by challenging the rightful status of a bill and, if successful in elevating it to 'the constitutional level', have then been far better placed to contest its passage through parliament. The Constitutional Committee in the Eduskunta is empowered to determine whether something is a constitutional proposal and significantly to do so by a simple majority. Hence with parliamentary standing committees reflecting the overall partisan balance in the legislature, ministers introducing a measure as an 'ordinary proposal' have normally enjoyed protection during periods of majoritarian government. But this does not prevent the opposition striving to 'promote a bill' — in such cases examination in the Constitutional Committee will usually cause a tactical delay in its progress through parliament — and if this proves unavailing, an attempt can be made to mobilise the necessary one-third of the Eduskunta's delegates to put it to rest over a general election. The highly controversial Gravel Excavation Law, *soranottolaki*, which was ratified by the President on 24 July 1981, is an illuminating illustration of the range of tactical ploys available to Finnish opposition groups as a result of the system of qualified majorities and which invariably produce at the very least residual gains in the form of amendments to the original bill.

The Gravel Excavation bill followed the broad lines of legislation in Sweden and Denmark in proposing that farmers wishing commercially to exploit the gravel deposits on their land be required to apply for a local council permit, and that in the event of official approval being withheld on environmental grounds they should be eligible for appropriate compensation. Divisions, however, became apparent even at the formulation stage of the bill. In Finland, where there was no Ministry of the Environment until one was created in September 1983, the Minister of the Interior, representing the farmer-based Centre Party, was in charge of the proposal. He precipitated a split in the centre-left government's ranks by deciding to deviate from the report of the committee of experts, *maankamaritoimikunta* — and indeed from the situation prevailing in Denmark and Sweden — by deleting the provisions for similar restrictions on the utilisation of peat. Subsequent differences both over the principle and the method of assessing compensation paid to farmers meant that the Interior Minister's draft bill spent no less than three years in various cabinet committees, and this in turn dictated that by the time it came before the Eduskunta in October 1980, a three-pronged opposition had developed in the legislature: there were those on the left who opposed the whole notion of compensation; those on the centre and right who argued that the bill was not compatible with the defence of property rights as defined in article 6 of the constitution; and environmentalists across the political spectrum who wanted the inclusion in the bill of restrictions on peat digging.[31]

In time, obvious internal divisions were to become apparent in this highly bill-specific opposition, but meanwhile two early and important victories were won. First, the opponents of the bill managed to enforce a rare parliamentary vote concerning the standing committee to which the bill should be sent, and then succeeded in overturning a recommendation of the Speaker's Council that it be handled in the Law and Economy Committee.[32] No secret was made of the fear that the matter would be delayed (to the tactical advantage of a divided government) in the heavily-worked Law and Economy Committee, and instead the bill was dispatched to the relatively underemployed Second Legal Affairs Committee. Secondly, although the government had discussed the Gravel Excavation bill with the Chancellor of Justice and a number of other constitutional experts, and was satisfied it could be treated as 'ordinary legislation', the Minister stated at the preliminary debate that in light of the widespread parliamentary opposition the matter would be sent to the Constitutional Committee for a statement on its constitutionality.[33] After a formal vote in the Constitutional Committee, however, a majority comprising the two left-wing parties, one Conservative delegate and the representative for the Åland islands ruled that the Gravel Excavation proposal could be handled as 'ordinary legislation', and the Second Legal Affairs Committee proceeded to consider the bill at great length, listening to many experts and even visiting Sweden and Denmark in the course of its deliberations. Most significantly, the committee saw fit to uphold a connected parliamentary bill (see later in this chapter) tabled by a Social Democrat and making commercial peat working subject to the same rules as gravel. This had the effect of reducing the number of delegates opposed to the bill, but intensifying the hostility of those on the centre and right concerned to protect the inviolability of fundamental property rights.

After its First Reading, bourgeois opponents of the bill on the Grand Committee managed by the narrowest of margins to force it back to the Constitutional Committee for another statement on its constitutionality. In a curious episode, a bourgeois plurality was obtained when the regular Christian League delegate on the Grand Committee, himself an opponent of further recourse to the Constitutional Committee, temporarily relinquished his place to his deputy out of respect for the predominant sentiments in his party's parliamentary group.[34] Unusually, too, the Grand Committee effected a number of lasting changes to the bill, in particular moderating the punishments suggested by the Second Legal Affairs Committee for those transgressing its provisions. When the Constitutional Committee repeated its previous judgement that the matter could be dealt with as 'ordinary legislation', there followed an all-night Second Reading during which the clause on peat was removed. In a final act of defiance, a number of Centre Party delegates attempted in vain to activate the third of the Eduskunta necessary to put the bill to rest over the period of an election.

Twice opponents had sought unsuccessfully to elevate the Gravel Excavation proposal to the status of a constitutional bill and so to jeopardise its progress through the House. They were at least instrumental in protracting the parliamentary consideration of the measure; though introduced in October 1980, the bill gained its Third Reading on Midsummer's Eve 1981, long after the traditional start of the Eduskunta's summer recess. Moreover, while the attempt on the part of a number of Centre Party delegates to invoke the fixed minority rule and vote the measure over a general election proved fruitless, it constituted the kind of demonstrative action not available to opposition groups in polities where decisions are taken solely on a simple majority basis. Significantly, the bill was in any event approved in a substantially modified form as a result of amendments tabled by bourgeois opponents in the Grand Committee. Two final points need to be made. First, the Gravel Excavation bill's experience was by no means typical: indeed, the minister intimated at the very start that, given the division in the government's ranks, parliament would be called upon effectively to decide the fate of the measure. Secondly, the matter was also not wholly atypical inasmuch as a controversial proposal at or around the constitutional level has allowed a determined opposition, using the weapon of the qualified majority rules, to introduce further complications into what is already perhaps the most complicated legislative process in the Nordic region. When this happens, the Eduskunta is a long way from merely authorising government proposals in the manner of an archetypal deliberating assembly.

In Denmark the fixed minority provisions prescribed by the constitution have apparently had a less decisive impact on the role of parliament in the policy adoption process than in Finland: although comparable in age to those in Finland and motivated by the same historic concern to protect existing élites, they have been used more sparingly and have had a generally marginal effect on the resolution of government initiatives. A fundamental difference of context needs to be noted. For a government really to be effective in Finland, in the basic sense of preventing its proposals from being voted over a general election (when, of course, a change in the balance of power could well see it ousted from office), it should enjoy the backing of two-thirds of the members of the Eduskunta. Hence a minimal winning or a bare majority coalition is not enough, with the result that the broad centre-left governments of the last twenty years have had a strictly numerical logic as well as a wider political one. The absence of a similar provision in Denmark enabling a minority of Folketing delegates to vote *all types* of bills over a general election has meant there has not been the same premium on welding broad-based administrations; minority governments backed by legislative coalitions have tended to be the typical Danish style. *Ad hoc* governmental consultation with opposition groups has accordingly become routinised, and the fixed minority rules are attractive to those parties excluded from the typical policy deals and packages, although they are not necessarily deployed by them. This of course represents a certain simplification of the picture. And, as for Finland, it should definitely not be presumed that the qualified majority rules have contributed *per se* to a moderation in government or that only those radical left and right-wing groups in the Folketing lacking clear links with the strategic labour-market organisations have had recourse to the qualified majority procedures. The central argument here, however, is that the potential sanction built into the fixed minority provisions in Denmark has not been realised because invariably a legislative consensus has been achieved before a measure reaches the point at which it can be delayed or deferred, i.e. Third Reading. The relatively infrequent use of special legislative procedures in Denmark warrants brief elaboration.

Although the rule exists (and it is a unique one in the region) that a substantial minority of two-fifths of all the Folketing's members can delay the Third Reading of certain proposals, it has been invoked only once. On 19 December 1975, a measure concerned with changes to the Tax Control Law, and in particular the obligations on financial institutions to divulge information, was postponed for the minimum period of 12 days laid down in article 41, paragraph 3 of the constitution at the written request of 76 Folketing delegates drawn from the opposition-based Liberal, Conservative and Progress parties.[35] As to the stipulation permitting one-third of the Folketing to vote measures relating to the expropriation of property over a general election, three such bills have been challenged, two successfully, since the re-incorporation of the provision into the 1953 constitution.

The second paragraph of article 73 on the deferral of property expropriation proposals was originally written into the constitution in 1915, partly as a counterweight to the growth of the socialist labour movement and its demand for the nationalisation of the means of production, and partly too as a consequence of the abolition of the privileged franchise to the upper chamber, the Landsting. It was retained in 1953 as one of the minority guarantees following the abolition of the Landsting and used unprofitably in 1960 in connection with a health insurance proposal (the relevant clause concerned sickness benefit funds) when the Prime Minister deemed the matter inappropriate under the terms of the constitution and allowed it to be ratified. In the case of the Icelandic manuscripts the following year, the government denied, as it had also done over the health insurance bill, that any expropriation was intended, but in August 1961 it decided to comply with the opposition's request that the measure be deferred. After the following general election in 1964, the bill was reintroduced and approved by the Folketing, only then to be declared invalid by the courts on the grounds that it had not been handled as an expropriation law. The Supreme Court, in its turn, reversed this latter judgement, although the various legal proceedings served to underline the highly specific as well as very limited terms of reference of the second paragraph of article 73 and hence the very narrow scope it affords opposition groups.

It was almost twenty years before this particular constitutional provision was again invoked. This occurred in June 1980 in connection with a government proposal on urban renewal and housing improvements which was blocked by precisely the same opposition alliance of Liberals, Conservatives and Progressives that had combined to delay the Third Reading of the Tax Control Amendment Bill. The measure itself was designed to stimulate public interest in a renewal programme for the older urban areas and the availability of improvement grants for modernising decaying individual properties. The responsibility for ensuring that the aims of the proposals were carried out fell to the lot of the local town councils which, because of the limited public resources available to support new housing development, were urged to give priority to urban renewal. The bill was handled in the Folketing in conjunction with several other related measures including a proposal modifying the legislation on housing subsidies, another dealing with slum clearance and the accommodation of displaced persons in private flats and a third on changes in the provisions relating to district and regional planning. It was twice referred back to the Folketing's standing committee on Housing and amended in the ministry before, having been accepted in substantially modified form at Third Reading, it was voted over a general election by 64 delegates from the Liberal, Conservative and Progress parties.[36]

Perhaps the most distinctive feature of the minority provisions in the Danish constitution is article 42, which allows 60 Folketing delegates to enforce a popular referendum with a view to killing off a bill on the absolute brink of its enactment, i.e. before the very last stage in the adoption process — its ratification by the monarch. Denmark is unique in the region in permitting a minority of parliamentarians to submit to a referendum a piece of ordinary legislation already approved by a majority in the Folketing. Of the other Nordic states, only in Sweden can parliament compel a referendum, and then solely in respect of constitutional laws. According to the *Regeringsformen*, a referendum on a constitutional question is to be held if requested by at least one-tenth of the Riksdag's members and if this initiative is subsequently backed by at least one-third of the assembly. The request must be tabled within fifteen days of the proposal being registered in the Riksdag, and the referendum is held at the same time as the next general election. The constitutional proposal will be regarded as rejected if there is a majority of votes against it, assuming that majority constitutes over half the valid votes cast at the simultaneous general election.[37] This relatively new Swedish procedure has not yet been invoked; in contrast, the Danish provision for referendums enforced by the legislature is much older, although it is little used.

With a logic similar to that underpinning the incorporation of qualified majority rules into the Parliamentary Standing Orders in

Finland in 1907, article 42 in Denmark was originally designed to protect the conservative forces against the consequences of a radical parliamentary majority at the time — in the early 1950s — when Denmark was making the transition to unicameralism. As early as the 1930s, when the reformist Social Democratic-Radical government gained a plurality in both houses of the Rigsdag, the Conservative Party leader viewed a referendum clause as a functional replacement for the Upper House, which both the coalition parties were committed to abolishing. In the event, a referendum under article 42 has been called only once since the new constitution came into force in 1953. This was on the last day of the 1962–3 Folketing session when the two main opposition parties, the Conservatives and Liberals, mustered 71 signatures and so forced four controversial land bills to a plebiscite, and less than three weeks later gained the majority of eligible voters necessary to defeat them. The high turn-out of non-socialist voters seems to have been the decisive factor in ditching the proposals which the opposition parties combined to present as embodying an attack on individual property rights and which certainly touched upon a number of sensitive matters. Persons buying agricultural property, for example, were required to live on the land within half a year of purchase, while both central government and local councils were given pre-emptive authority to purchase land for recreational and urban development purposes. If the referendum had an obvious side-effect, it was perhaps to sharpen the divisions between government and opposition in the 1960s although its effect on voting behaviour in the general election the following year, 1964, appears to have been small.[38]

Despite the highly-charged nature of the referendum campaign in the summer of 1963 and the subsequent defeat of almost half of a major package of government measures, there is no evidence to suggest that the constitutional rules permitting a substantial parliamentary minority to delay or instigate the overthrow of majority-backed proposals have had more than a marginal effect on policy adoption in Denmark. The fact that the 1963 referendum (held in accordance with article 42) has been the only one of its kind speaks for itself. There have been several unsuccessful attempts to use article 42. The 60 signatures necessary, however, constitute a sizeable number — which before 1973 would have entailed the cooperation of at least two, and possibly even three, of the 'old parties' and thereafter the (almost inconceivable) collaboration of most, if not all, of the small and highly disparate opposition groups that sprang up in the Folketing. Many types of proposal, including taxation bills, are any way excluded under article 42, while others may be of such a technical character as not to lend themselves to resolution by the voters. Above all, however, the government's search for *ad hoc* legislative coalitions in support of major proposals has meant that compromises have in reality been reached long before the Third Reading stage — not infrequently in inter-élite talks during the September 'cucumber season' — thus virtually nullifying any threat to delay or defeat bills. When broad — or indeed narrow — legislative coalitions on important issues have not been achieved, governments have invariably resigned — as Jørgensen's fifth minority administration did in September 1982. After talks with five other parties, it became apparent that support for further economic measures like the earlier 'March package', which was finally backed by the two other left-wing parties, was not forthcoming and the Social Democratic Prime Minister decided not to continue in office.

If this is to put matters a little strongly, the thrust of the argument is implicitly substantiated in Kenneth E. Miller's work on Danish policy-making by referendum, where it is shown that of 2,537 laws accepted in the Folketing between the 1963–4 and 1978–9 sessions — and excluding the 704 measures not falling within the provisions of article 42 — a mere 2.5% had 60 or more votes cast against them at Third Reading.[39] It seems arguable moreover that it was as much a reaction to the breakdown of talks on the Social Democratic government's package of economic measures, which were simultaneously on the political agenda, as hostility to the land laws by itself which prompted the opposition Liberal and Conservative parties to turn the property measures into a referendum issue. In a rare situation of majority government, negotiation with the opposition had not been strictly necessary but had been conducted in what was seen as a rather summary manner and not surprisingly had failed to produce the desired effect. In the longer term, it may be surmised that recourse to, or the threatened use of, referendums under article 42 would have a damaging effect on legislative-executive relations and endanger the consultative position of opposition groups in the Folketing, even during periods of minority government. Far from strengthening the hand of opposition groups, repeated referendums could ultimately serve to erode the sovereignty of parliament in the decision-making process. After all, referendums constitute a form of extra-parliamentary machinery which is mandatory in a number of questions — e.g. the lowering of the voting age[40] — and as a result they have been held more frequently in Denmark than any other West European nation except Switzerland. Faced with the reality of a high level of voter passivity at these referendums, opposition groups doubtless hesitate to deploy the provisions of article

42 and would scarcely demur at Sten Sparre Nilson's observation, based on his examination of government-initiated consultative referendums in the entire Nordic region, that 'as a result of their recent experience of referendums, many Scandinavian politicians have grown wary of using the institution.'[41]

Article 2, paragraph 12 of the Swedish *Regeringsformen*, allowing ten Riksdag delegates to instigate a minimum twelve-month postponement of measures threatening to restrict fundamental personal freedoms, has been operational only since 1 January 1980, thus ruling out generalisations concerning its impact on the legislative process. Like article 42 of the Danish constitution, it has been successfully used once, in connection with a government bill in March 1981 on the circulation of video material depicting scenes of violence. As with the Gravel Excavation bill in Finland, the case illuminates the dynamics of policy adoption at the parliamentary stage.

Designed to come into force on 1 July 1981, the bill imposed a dual ban: first, on the sale or hire to persons under the age of fifteen of video material depicting violence or the threat of violence against people or animals; and secondly, on the organisation of profit-making screenings of such material when children under 15 were present.[42] When the Cultural Affairs Committee reported on the bill, the Social Democratic and Centre delegates making up the majority held that it was necessary to implement wider-ranging proscriptions than those the government envisaged, which they felt did not adequately protect young persons *over* 15. In their opinion, only a complete embargo on the commercial showing of video violence would suffice. The Cultural Affairs Committee entrusted the task of formulating a revised legal text to the Constitutional Committee,[43] which unanimously decided — without compromising its ultimate position on the government bill — to request a statement from the Law Council. This in turn left open the question of whether the government's proposed ban was compatible with the constitutional requirement that any delimitation of individual liberties should absolutely not exceed that necessary to achieve the desired goal — in this instance, protecting the mental health of children. It did, however, venture to advocate that all showings of violent video material should be made illegal irrespective of whether they were intended for commercial gain or not. The Constitutional Committee's response was to disagree — at least to the extent of stating that such a step would infringe parental rights as well as enacting something which would be impossible to implement, given the finite nature of police resources. The committee nevertheless went further than the government proposal in contemplating a total ban on the commercial distribution of all video tapes containing the most extreme and sadistic forms of violence. It was this addition to the original bill which prompted ten Conservatives, in a letter to the Speaker on 3 June 1981, to invoke the procedure set out in article 12, paragraph 2 of the constitution. Ironically, this put the Constitutional Committee in the position of having in effect to adjudicate on the fate of its own proposal by ruling on whether section 1 of the revised bill, namely the stipulation on sadistic content which the committee itself had included, posed a possible threat to fundamental freedoms and could therefore be held over for twelve months in accordance with 2:12.[44] Voting on section 1 then took place on the floor of the Riksdag and although it was favoured by 237 votes against only 68, this did not comprise the five-sixths majority necessary for immediate enactment, and accordingly the matter was returned to the Constitutional Committee until at least 3 June 1982.

A number of points stand out in connection with the video violence issue when seen in relation to our earlier discussion of the tactical deployment of qualified majority and fixed minority rules in Finland and Denmark. First, the legislative opposition was directed towards what was in reality a parliamentary proposal, i.e. a government bill significantly modified in Riksdag standing committee. The government bill, the Minister of Justice emphasised, had quite deliberately refrained from imposing a total ban on extreme video violence, preferring to wait for the recommendations of a commission which was examining the whole question of individual rights. Secondly, like the Gravel Excavation bill in Finland but not the Land Law proposals in Denmark, opposition emanated from within the ranks of the governing alliance. True, the Minister of Justice was latterly a non-partisan government member, Carl Axel Petri, although the rebellious Conservatives did not oppose the original government bill — which, incidentally, the Riksdag adopted — but rather the amendments to it prompted in the first instance by the Social Democratic and Centre Party delegates on the Cultural Affairs Committee. Finally, although article 2, paragraph 12 has been invoked only once, its capacity to sabotage bills should not be underestimated. In the case of the Constitutional Committee's proposal on video violence, the Riksdag was prevented from adopting a recommendation which more than two-thirds of parliamentarians, both socialist and non-socialist, clearly supported. It should be remembered that any party with 59 Riksdag delegates can enforce a twelve-month postponement of measures seen as jeopardising individual freedoms and, in the process, compel parliament to review the matter again.

If this seems *prima facie* to reinforce the scrutinising function of the assembly, one might question whether it does so at the expense of investing relatively small legislative minorities with disproportionate influence. To this an immediate rejoinder might be that disproportionate influence is not necessarily synonymous with undue influence: checks and balances and minority safeguards are widely regarded as fundamental to the healthy working of parliamentary democracy, while the price of abusing the qualified majority and fixed minority rules would ultimately be the discrediting of the parliamentary system itself — an objective attractive only to anti-system parties in the strictest sense of the term. There is, however, no evidence in the region of these rules being exploited in an attempt to cause significant dislocation to the legislative process.

Denmark and Finland have in recent years each had more than eight parliamentary groups, including anti-system parties with obvious blackmail potential, approximating to the extreme multi-party system of post-war Italy. But the protest parties have been too small, and the parliamentary opposition generally too divided, to profit from the qualified majority provisions, and the result has been that the irresponsible opposition of Sartori-style polarised pluralism has not been evident, at least in terms of legislative behaviour. For the larger opposition parties, moreover, particularly the 'outcast' Finnish Conservatives, any such irresponsibility could jeopardise its strategic bargaining position and thus quickly prove counterproductive. The tabling of a few interpellations annually (see chapter 8) rather than the threat to block bills using the qualified majority regulations, has been the characteristic style of the Finnish Conservatives who, in being able consistently to prevent measures being declared 'urgent' (and so enacted in a single parliamentary session), have enjoyed an established consultative role, especially over economic policy. All in all, disruptive activity in the Nordic assemblies has been extremely rare and what little there has been, namely occasional American-style filibustering in Finland, has tended to exploit the absence of prescribed time limits on plenary speeches rather than the qualified majority provisions.

Before commenting briefly on filibustering in the Eduskunta, it is necessary to note that the strength of the Finnish Conservatives' bargaining position should not be exaggerated. True, the influence of the opposition groups in the Norwegian parliament has appeared weaker than theirs (though not in 1981–83), especially with regard to economic policy decisions. In practice, government negotiations with interest groups have seemed to present Storting members with little more than a *fait accompli*. The Centre Party leader, Johan J. Jakobsen, for example, stated in an interpellation debate in October

1980 that 'in reality the Storting is obliged to approve, down to the very last letter, the draft incomes policy legislation formulated by the government and labour-market leaders.' However, even the extra negotiating clout created by the qualified majority rules would scarcely enhance the position of the Norwegian opposition if, as Jakobsen observed, parliamentary amendments to an incomes policy bill 'produce chaos and the torpedoing of the agreement on the labour market'.[46]

It could similarly be argued that the Finnish Conservative Party's influence stems less from its direct consultations with the government (compelled by the qualified majorities needed to pass most economic legislation) than from its ensconced position in the employers' organisation SAK. Incidentally, responding to Jakobsen's interpellation, the Finance Minister Ulf Sand offered sympathy but few solutions. 'I consider it in practice necessary and in principle correct that the government should have direct contact with interest organisations,' he maintained. 'If it is held desirable to preserve the government's freedom of action as well as a clear separation of responsibility between the government and Storting, I can envisage no solution which would bring parliament more directly into the incomes policy system.'[47] There were, however, two proposals that Sand did make: first, the need to develop contacts between the Minister of Finance and the Storting's Finance Committee and, secondly, the strengthening of contacts between the parliamentary group leaders. However, the opposition Conservative Party leader Kåre Willoch replied that neither the Finance Committee nor the group chairmen could reasonably act on the Storting's behalf, and the deputy chairman of the Finance Committee echoed Willoch's assertion that the Storting must accept a diminished role arising from the fact that the Finance Committee received incomes policy packages which in practice had merely to be accepted or rejected.

We shall conclude this section on the final resolution of measures with a brief note on parliamentary filibustering. Finland is the only Nordic state to have witnessed occasional filibustering: the tactical prolongation of debate has been facilitated there by the fact that — along with Iceland and Liechtenstein — it is one of the few European democracies not to restrict the number and length of parliamentary speeches. Although the old Swedish constitution also gave delegates extremely wide speaking rights, filibustering did not occur in the bicameral Riksdag. It has also been relatively rare in Finland, and cannot be regarded as a central part of the nation's legislative culture. Yet the 59-hour filibuster organised against proposed reforms in the internal administration of higher education institutions on the eve of the 1970 general elections, together with the recent Conservative propensity for protracting the discussion of important issues beyond the normal 11 o'clock full-sitting closure so as to capitalise on the diminished numbers in the chamber and send matters back to standing committee, shows that filibustering is a recognised phenomenon in Finnish parliamentary life. Uniquely in the region, the Eduskunta Standing Orders do not specify a quorum for decision-taking at plenary sessions.

Filibustering can occur in a standing committee as well as on the floor of the House: the Exceptional Law introduced into the Eduskunta in January 1973 to enable parliament to extend President Kekkonen's term of office by four years in what were described as 'exceptional circumstances' is a case in point. The filibuster this prompted was very much a last resort because the 30 or so opponents of the bill were insufficient to prevent the measure being declared 'urgent' under the qualified majority procedure. Their action was nonetheless facilitated by the decision of the Speaker's Council to complete consideration of the matter in only two days: the preliminary debate was to take place on Tuesday, 9 January, beginning at six o'clock; the Constitutional Committee stage was planned for Wednesday morning; and the First Reading, Grand Committee and Second Reading stages for later the same day, with the close of the parliamentary session scheduled for the following Tuesday. However, when opponents in the Constitutional Committee made the tactical proposal that a statement be sought from the Foreign Affairs Committee and combined this with an insistence not only on hearing experts but on getting their normal written statements, the committee had still not completed its report by Thursday afternoon. Its deliberations had then to be interrupted to accommodate the opening of a plenary debate on a finance bill which was itself curtailed at 2100 hours to allow the Constitutional Committee to reconvene and, if necessary to continue in unbroken session until Friday noon. So it proved to be. No fewer than three regular and two deputy committee members managed, by citing constitutional literature and the welter of letters in the press on the subject, to filibuster for an unbroken 15 hours, and at mid-day on Friday the Constitutional Committee meeting had to be adjourned to allow for a pre-arranged full-sitting of the Eduskunta. At this point, a number of delegates outside the Constitutional Committee engineered a compromise: in return for an end to the filibustering, the written reports from all the experts heard by the committee, except the Foreign Secretary, would be procured and opponents of the bill would also be given two hours in which to prepare their reservation. This would be considered at the Third Reading stage the following Wednesday — one day after the projected end of the parliamentary session.[48]

At one level, the filibuster against the Exceptional Law was simply a protest gesture undertaken by delegates who possessed a common mistrust of the incumbent Head of State. At another, it showed that even when seven main parties favour a measure and the opponents are numerically too weak to prevent its enactment in a single Eduskunta session, parliamentary minorities are able to use filibustering as a *bona fide* legislative device with which to make their hostility known to the electorate at large.

Patterns of legislative voting

The ultimate adoption of policy proposals, whether emanating from a government or private member's initiative, involves in most cases (i.e. with the exception of *unanimous decisions*) a formal vote at a Final Reading plenary; this, as often as not, is preceded by ballots in one or more of the parliamentary standing committees. The emergent patterns of legislative voting generally reflect the impact of parliament in the adoption process: clearly its autonomy is greatest when the assembly is characterised by what Loewenberg and Patterson describe as *individualistic* voting,[49] i.e. where each legislator contributes to the decision of parliament by casting a vote arrived at individually and determined by a wide variety of influences. The measure then passes or fails but — as in the most distinctive case of individualistic voting, the United States Congress — there are no further consequences. It is important that legislators take their cue from their constituencies and from individual Congressmen rather than their party. The independent impact of the legislature is plainly least when patterns of *government and opposition voting* predominate — as at Westminster, where there is a division of votes between a government which (usually) has a majority in the House and an Opposition which is sufficiently united to constitute a potential alternative government. In these circumstances, the outcome of parliamentary votes is invariably a foregone conclusion. Finally, in assemblies where *multiparty legislative coalitions* are commonplace, the influence of parliament is enhanced by the fact that measures are passed by fluctuating party majorities. In the Netherlands, for example, Arend Lijphart notes that 'major pieces of legislation are often passed with the help of some "opposition" parties and with a "governmental" party voting against.'[50] Applying Loewenberg and Patterson's typology of legislative voting patterns[51] to the Nordic region, three initial observations are in order.

First, the level of party cohesion in the Nordic parliaments has been consistently too high to permit significant or recurrent patterns of individualistic voting on major policy issues. In Sweden and Finland, the evidence indeed suggests that partisan solidarity has been higher on issues that present clear-cut ideological divisions, and in the case of parties on the extreme right and extreme left of the political spectrum. However, throughout the region the entrenched party loyalties of parliamentarians have militated against individualistic voting along Congressional lines.

Secondly, the predominant Nordic pattern of legislative voting has been government and opposition voting: i.e. voting which can be depicted on a left-right or, more precisely, socialist/non-socialist continuum. Damgaard's analysis of parliamentary divisions in the Folketing in 1953–70 demonstrated that of those votes on which the parties disagreed, almost 90% aligned the parties in order from the radical left to the radical right.[52] Party loyalties and bloc allegiances, in short, have been paramount. In this light it was hardly surprising that on 26 May 1982 the bourgeois parties in Sweden achieved a majority of one — 169 votes to 168 — favouring the introduction of controversial cutbacks in health insurance benefits, *karensdagarna*, although the Conservatives, the largest non-socialist party, were in opposition and the Social Democrats resisted the proposals to the last. True, the Centre Party delegate Arne Andersson made it clear that he was voting against his conscience on the matter and accordingly would not stand for re-election in September 1982. Nevertheless the bourgeois ranks held firm.[53]

Finally, even allowing for the primacy of government and opposition voting, shifting multi-party legislative coalitions have been commonplace in the Nordic parliaments and not only during periods of minoritarian government, as typically occur in Denmark. Stjernquist and Bjurulf's analysis of Riksdag voting in the mid-1960s concluded that 'cases when a strict division between the socialist and non-socialist parties occurred constituted a minority of the total number of divisions'[54] and that during an extended period of single party Social Democratic majority government, variable legislative coalitions characterised balloting on both government and non-governmental measures.

A number of important caveats are necessary, however. Individualistic voting is not unknown when the character of the decision to be taken is essentially non-partisan: moral questions in Sweden, significantly the only mainland Nordic parliament without a religious-specific party, are a case in point. A small but determined group of parliamentarians has worked to defend traditional standards over issues like the liberalisation of the abortion laws, the spread of sex shops, and the circulation of grossly pornographic video material. A religious-secular dimension has consequently been evident in patterns of legislative voting, and recruitment to the 'moral lobby' has drawn heavily on delegates belonging to 'low church' Inner Mission groups within the Established Lutheran Church and denominations like the Free Church and Pentecostalists outside it. It is probably fair to say that patterns of individualistic voting have been the norm rather than the exception on questions with a moral dimension. Indeed, although the Social Democratic government's bill relaxing the abortion law so as to permit women to obtain an abortion up to the eighteenth week of pregnancy was ultimately approved by the comfortable margin of 214 votes to 103 (with 6 abstentions) following a marathon debate in the Riksdag in May 1974, the only party that showed internal unity on the matter was the Left-Communists. A government and opposition pattern of voting collapsed in the face of low-church Brethren, *broderskapare*, in both Social Democratic and Centre parties uniting to oppose the bill.[55] Incidentally, there is a cross-party Christian group in the Riksdag at present numbering over 100 members, linked informally to the various extra-parliamentary religious organisations, including the small Christian Democratic Party[56] which polled 1.9% in September 1982.

Individualistic voting has also occurred, in defiance of the party line, over regional economic questions. There is widespread evidence of a Congressional-style constituency orientation or 'localism' — as it is referred to in chapter 8 — on the part of delegates in the Nordic parliaments, which has created strong cross-pressures on party loyalties when relevant regional questions have come up for resolution. In these circumstances, renegade voting has been no rarity. In Pekka Nyholm's study of party cohesion in the Finnish Eduskunta in the late 1940s and 1950s, it was shown that the solidarity of parliamentarians in the Agrarian (nowadays Centre) Party — the 'hinge group' of post-war governments — was strained by the strong regional allegiances of the delegates representing northern and eastern Finland. This was partly because of tough electoral competition from the newly-legalised Communist Party, but also because the Agrarian delegates from the southern constituencies represented a larger and wealthier type of landholding than those in the north and east.[57] Similarly in Norway, the chairman of the Christian People's Party, Kjell Magne Bondevik, has noted that 'there is nearly always an element of uncertainty when the matter under discussion relates to the geographical placement of a public body for then party lines are weak or, indeed, completely absent.' Bondevik cited as an example the decision in the early

1970s on whether to locate the state oil directorate in Trondheim or Stavanger.[58] It should be remembered that while American Congressmen 'vote their constituencies' because it is the natural thing for them to do, given the manner in which they are recruited to office,[59] parties in Norway and elsewhere in the Nordic region are by no means so decentralised. Nonetheless, delegates are elected on regional rather than (as in the Netherlands) national lists, and to a degree the regional seating of delegates in the Storting and Riksdag serves as a reminder that traditionally they are constituency before party representatives. In any event, in prompting delegates to take their cue from their constituency or from legislators elected for the same district, regional economic issues have fostered limited patterns of individualistic voting — expressions of maverick behaviour on the part of individual delegates contributing substantially to reducing group solidarity at key votes.

A controversial case in point was the Swedish bourgeois government's defeat over the Öresund shipyard in June 1980, when in the teeth of cabinet intentions a parliamentary majority comprising Social Democrats, Left-Communists and two dissident Liberals voted to make money available to save the publicly-owned Öresund shipyard in the depressed Landskrona region. The previous January the State Shipbuilding Corporation, *Svenska Varv*, had submitted its long-term structural plan to the Department of Industry proposing, in the face of economic recession, a rundown and closure of the Öresund yard by 1983. However, the government, mindful of the consequences of this action for the economy of the whole Landskrona region, made its policy contingent upon what it claimed to be the ready supply of redeployment opportunities in the area and did not specify a timetable for the closure of the yard.[60] Instead it decided on a line of continued temporary subsidies and a review of the position during the autumn. Although the Riksdag's Industry Committee associated itself with the government's proposal in all essentials,[61] the House ultimately backed connected parliamentary bills from the Social Democrats and two Liberal Party rebels from the Landskrona region providing for continued activity at the yard and setting aside money both to offset losses and to stimulate new production. In his otherwise moderate contribution at the plenary reading stage, the Social Democratic spokesman on Economic Affairs, Thage Peterson, was extremely critical of the Minister of Industry: 'Never before to my knowledge has a cabinet minister in Sweden set region against region and worker against worker in this way.'[62]

The government's defeat over the Öresund yard was by no means unique: on a number of other occasions, issues connected with regional policy and planning led to defeats for Fälldin's three-party bourgeois coalition between 1979 and 1981. In December 1980, its policy of maintaining commercial flights at the main domestic airport at Bromma, situated relatively near the city centre of Stockholm, was overturned in the assembly. Despite its pledge to impose stricter noise controls, division in the government's ranks was apparent from the start, for while the Minister of Communications insisted in the Riksdag that 'Bromma is the hub of the national air traffic system and Sweden's interests must come before those of Stockholm,'[63] all but one of the Liberal and Centre Party delegates representing greater Stockholm initially opposed the continued use of Bromma on environmental grounds. Even after Fälldin personally applied pressure on the dissidents[64] (see chapter 3), Stockholm Liberals still voted against the government's proposal. A Social Democratic move[65] to transfer domestic traffic from Bromma to the international airport at Arlanda, situated well outside the capital, ultimately carried the day, but not before a number of provincial Social Democratic delegates from Gotland, Skåne and Värmland had opposed the party line, believing that the concentration of traffic at Arlanda would involve increased domestic costs particularly on freight.[66] The end-result was that after a seven-hour parliamentary debate just before Christmas 1980, the Riksdag voted by 168 votes to 167 with 3 abstentions to shift domestic traffic to Arlanda during the second half of 1982, a date later postponed to the autumn of 1983.[67] The winning legislative coalition comprised the entire Left-Communists' parliamentary group, a majority of Social Democrats, together with the renegade Stockholm Liberals.

All in all, individualistic voting at times caused the Swedish non-socialist governments of 1979–82 acute embarrassment. Obviously, with a majority of only one in the assembly, a single turncoat was able to cause a major upset, and this is precisely what happened in November 1980 when the Fälldin administration was defeated over a plan for building a hydro-electric plant on Sölvbacka streams in the area of norra Härjedalen. The rebel in the case, Tore Nilsson, was not a member of the Civil Affairs Committee that had earlier considered the matter,[68] but stated in a plenary speech that the scheme was economically unsound and ecologically indefensible. Supporting a 10-year local campaign against the development, Nilsson put a passionate case for individualistic voting: 'A man who denies his conviction, rejects the test, goes under like Peer Gynt, kills his conscience — that man is lost.'[69]

Far more common overall than individualistic voting, and prevalent enough to justify referring to *mixed patterns of legislative voting* in the Nordic states, has been the regular incidence of multi-party legislative coalitions, i.e. collaboration between parliamentary groups across the line dividing government and opposition, socialists and non-socialists. Perhaps the most common form of multi-party winning coalition has occurred with one or more parties in opposition co-operating to support a government bill. This is what happened in Norway in 1981 following the introduction of the Social Democratic minority government's bill banning professional boxing. This proposal emanated from the Sports Section of the Church and Education Department and followed the Nordic Council's recommendation of 1969 and Sweden's example in imposing a fine or up to three months' imprisonment on those promoting and participating in professional bouts, along with persons engaged in the coaching and training of professional fighters. Criticism was particularly strong against the commercial exploitation of an activity which could lead to serious injuries, particularly brain damage. While the opposition-based Centre and Christian People's parties supported the ban — the Christians in fact wanted it extended to include amateur boxing, as in Iceland — the Conservatives were against the measure, arguing *inter alia* that interest in professional boxing in Norway was very limited, that there were few fights, and that the evidence of permanent brain damage was not based on Norwegian statistics. Moreover, even if such injuries could be proved, the Conservatives argued, the risk was no greater than in other sports. When the matter came to a vote in the Odelsting in June 1981, however, the Conservatives remained alone in their opposition to the bill and the ban was favoured by a majority of 54 votes to 22 with the Christians and Centre backing the government.[70]

Although multi-party coalition voting takes place most often during periods of minority government, and in Denmark especially has become the characteristic *modus operandi* of the post-war period with governments 'log-rolling' for support in the assembly on an issue-by-issue basis, it is by no means confined to periods of minority administration. True, in Erik Damgaard's seminal analysis of Danish legislative coalition-building, it is shown that the Agrarian Liberals, *Venstre*, participated in 87% of agricultural bill coalitions and tended to be included irrespective of whether they were strongly opposed to the government or not. However, there have been occasions, during periods of majority government, when winning multi-party coalitions have been formed, although it has been difficult to differentiate multi-party coalitions from individualistic voting. At the end of September 1980, the Finnish parliament accepted a government bill, *kapinalaki*, concerning the use of the army as police auxiliaries in such situations as traffic control, searches over wide areas, and the temporary protection of property. Much of the ensuing controversy was focused on a clause in the bill stating that the army could be deployed in putting down riots and revolts at the request of the Ministry of the Interior and with the approval of the cabinet. The bill was supported by the hardline Stalinist minority wing of the Communist Party and a majority of Conservatives from the opposition benches, a fact which infuriated the other small opposition parties, particularly the Christian League, which held that the request for military auxiliaries should not be dependent upon the initiative of a single person in the Ministry of the Interior. What would happen, the party inquired, if the Minister of the Interior represented the hardline Communists and his comrades decided to instigate violent revolution?[71]

To sum up, government and opposition — or, in practice, socialist/non-socialist bloc voting — has been the dominant form in the Nordic assemblies. Broadly, the smaller the size of the governing majority, the higher the level of bloc cohesion. High levels of bloc cohesion, in turn, have implied high levels of conformity within the individual parties. The goal of vote maximisation has generally ensured that parties are united, while the increased workload of delegates and their resultant tendency to specialise in one area of policy has worked in the same direction in so far as it has led to an increased reliance in the parliamentary groups on the guidance of the various standing committee spokesmen and internal policy committees.

It is significant that there was little apparent decline in the levels of partisan cohesion in Denmark during the 1970s, despite the fragmentation that occurred in the party system. In Palle Svensson's analysis of Folketing voting, it was shown that breaks in the party line had taken place in less than 14% of all Third Reading votes in the 1970s, compared with 11% for the late 1960s and 12% for the period 1953–65.[72] Much of the slight increase in the 1970s was explained by the Radical Liberal, *Radikale Venstre*, split over the EC issue *before* the rise of Glistrup *et al.* When other breaks occurred, they involved a relatively small number of dissidents — two or three rebels at most — suggesting that disunity was expressed in terms of individualistic voting. When the government's majority is a hair's-breadth one, as in Sweden in 1979–82, individualistic voting — which has been most common in the Nordic assemblies on moral and regional questions — has caused acute embarrassment. In such circumstances, parliament is a potent forum for the registration of intra-party dissent.

If individualistic voting has been intermittently important, multiparty coalition voting in the Nordic countries has been commonplace. Legislative voting coalitions have their greatest functional logic during periods of minority government, but occur too when broad-ranging agreements reached in standing committee are ratified on the floor of the House. The incidence of multi-party legislative coalitions in the Nordic states has not been unrelated to the generally pragmatic style of politics in the region. Also, a high percentage of the legislative resolutions in the regional assemblies are taken by unanimous decision without a formal vote. In sum, it seems reasonable to speak of the existence of mixed patterns of legislative voting in the Nordic parliaments; although a division of ballots along government and opposition lines has been paramount, parliament has afforded an arena for the expression of both individualistic and more organised dissent within the parliamentary party groups, as well as for cross-party co-operation 'across the blocs', *över blockgränsen*, as it is known in Sweden, i.e. between socialists and non-socialists.

We will look briefly at two final facets of the adoption process. One concerns the final ratification of bills by the Head of State, but first a few remarks on the method of voting at the Final Reading plenary and, in particular, the possibility the ordering of proposals gives for tactical voting. In practice, a resolution by formal ballot is often unnecessary. In Sweden a majority of decisions are taken by acclamation without the need for a vote.[73] When a formal 'division' (in Westminster parlance) is required, however, the Speaker puts a proposal on voting, *omröstningsproposition*, which must then be approved by the whole House.[74] In Norway, the Storting's Standing Orders state that motions shall be put to the vote 'in a logical sequence'[75] and it may be regarded as the index of a Speaker's effectiveness that he is able to contrive agreement among delegates on the way of doing things. As to the method of voting, three procedures are used in the region.

A universal procedure in the Nordic parliaments is the roll-call of members. In the Riksdag the Speaker requests two delegates to take up places at the podium to keep a record of the vote, and balloting proceeds with the deputy Speakers announcing their preference first — either 'yes', 'no' or 'abstain' — followed by the rest of the delegates in order of their seat numbers in the chamber.[76] In the Folketing, delegates are called in alphabetical order, whereas in the Storting and Odelsting it is on the basis of a previously-held lottery.[77] Distinctively in Finland, different coloured cards are used in the roll-call: they are printed with the delegate's name only, along with the words 'yes' or 'no' and the delegate calls his decision and places his ballot on the relevant pile.[78] In Iceland roll-calls are used only for the resolution of controversial issues, and elsewhere in the region — in Norway for instance — it is specified that they should be used in 'the more important matters'.[79] In Denmark, 17 Folketing delegates may submit a prior request in writing for a roll-call on a particular question, although on an initiative from the Speaker an ordinary majority of members can overrule this request.[80]

A common procedure for voting in the region is to request delegates simply to stand up. The Speaker requests those voting 'yes' to the bill to rise first and then those intending to vote 'no' to stand. In Iceland when the Speaker puts a question to the vote, he merely requests all those in favour to raise their right hands first and then those against to do the same. If the Speaker of any of the Nordic parliaments is at all doubtful about the outcome of a division conducted by requesting members to stand or raise their right hands, a formal 'machine vote' is likely to take place.

Voting with the aid of the special voting apparatus — the third type of voting procedure — is possible everywhere except in Iceland, although it was the summer of 1982 before it was introduced into the Folketing. Typically, in Sweden, each member has on the front panel of his desk a 'Yes', 'No', 'Abstain' and 'Correction' button, which light up in contrasting colours when pressed. The result of the vote, showing how every member has voted, is photographed and distributed to members about half an hour later. In Norway the system is even more efficient and delegates receive a photocopy of the result within one minute of the voting — a fact which persuaded the Swedes to install the same voting apparatus in the Riksdag when delegates moved back to the old parliamentary building at Helgeandsholmen in October 1983. Incidentally, there is no provision at divisions in the Storting (which uses mechanical voting equipment) for delegates to abstain, an anomaly which has led to some resentment and compelled those members wishing not to take sides to absent themselves from votes altogether.

It is the job of the Speaker to determine the order in which voting on legislative proposals will take place and to present the proposals in such a way that they can be responded to in simple 'Yes/No' terms. Strong convention, however, governs his task. Standing committee proposals, for example, are invariably placed last when three or more alternatives are to be decided and, in so far as the committee proposal tends closely to resemble the original government bill, that affords the incumbent administration a tactical advantage. The vast majority of roll-calls in Finland and Sweden involve only two alternatives, and tactical voting is ruled out. However, when three or more motions are at issue, the so-called 'amendment procedure' is invoked, whereby two alternatives are voted on and the winner goes forward to face the remaining proposal(s). When this 'knock-out' style of balloting occurs, and it is particularly common during periods of minority government, strategic voting is commonplace. Bjurulf and Niemi note that in the Finnish Eduskunta in 1957–9, there were several occasions when the Social Democrats used Conservative Party proposals to eliminate what appeared to be majority-backed measures from the centre-based Agrarian and Finnish People's (Liberal) parties. In short, in Finland, and also in Sweden, strategic voting in roll-calls is widespread, albeit not always successful, and not undertaken on every occasion when the parliamentary conditions appear conducive.[81] In Denmark and Norway, however, it is extremely rare that more than two alternatives are voted on; instead, motions are taken one at a time until one receives a majority — the so-called 'successive procedure'. This prompts any inter-party deals to be concluded at an earlier stage in the legislative process than under the 'amendment procedure'.

The ratification of bills by the Head of State

Once bills are approved at the Final Reading, they are submitted to the Head of State for formal ratification. This is the case in all the Nordic countries except Sweden, where the King is no longer part of the legislative process. In Iceland, a bill must be referred to the President for countersignature not later than two weeks after it has been passed in the assembly, while in Denmark a proposal completing its passage in the Folketing becomes law if it receives the Royal Assent within 30 days.[82] Since parliament decides on a bill on the basis of a standing committee report, the Swedish government is informed of the outcome through an official parliamentary letter, *riksdagsskrivelse*, and implements the measure by issuing the necessary legal orders incorporating it onto the Swedish statute-book, *Svensk författningssamling*.

Constitutionally, a majority of the Nordic Heads of State have delaying powers, though not an ultimate veto over legislation. In Norway, a bill which the King has refused to ratify is returned to the assembly and cannot then be re-submitted for his approval in the same Storting. However, a bill which has been passed unamended in two ordinary sessions of the Storting separated by a general election and at least two intervening Storting sessions — without a divergent bill having been passed in the mean time — is submitted to the King with the request that he does not withhold his assent to something which 'after the most mature deliberation the Storting considers to be for the benefit of the country'.[83] In such cases, the matter becomes law even if the Royal Assent is not forthcoming. Article 26 of the Icelandic constitution states that if the

President refuses to undersign a bill it nevertheless becomes law, although it is then submitted to a referendum and if rejected by the people forfeits its legal status. In neither Norway nor Iceland has the Head of State's power to delay legislation had any practical significance; in the latter, for example, Presidential assent has not been refused on a single occasion since the inception of the Republic in 1944.

The same has not been true in Finland. According to the 1919 constitution, a bill passed by the Eduskunta is sent to the President for ratification and he, in turn, is entitled to request a statement on it from either the Supreme Court or Supreme Administrative Court. The bill is then to be ratified in precisely the form approved by parliament. If the President declines to give his assent — and this normally involves his failure to countersign it within three months of receiving the bill — the measure shall still become law if following a general election it is re-adopted in unchanged form by a majority vote in the Eduskunta. Otherwise, it is considered to have lapsed.[84] In the first half-century of Finnish Independence, the President exercised his suspensive veto on approximately 50 occasions, albeit after extensive consultation with the cabinet and for reasons of technical deficiencies in the bill following amendments in the assembly. Invariably, the government comes up with a refurbished measure which quickly gains the approval of both Eduskunta and Head of State. The suspensive veto, in short, has not been deployed to frustrate the will of parliament, and consequently it was not necessary for the Eduskunta to invoke the constitutional provisions relating to the re-adoption of measures following a general election on more than four occasions in the aforementioned period.

In the 1970s, the suspensive veto (or more exactly its threat) was perceived by the long-serving Head of State as an overtly political weapon: in November 1976, President Kekkonen broke an illegal strike of railway traffic controllers by stating, quite unprecedentedly, that he would refuse to approve any parliamentary bill meeting the strikers' claims for a reduction in the retirement age.[85] The sanction of non-ratification, however, was directed against a strategically-placed labour market organisation rather than against the elected representatives of the people in parliament.

LEGISLATING OR DELIBERATING ASSEMBLIES? AN INVENTORY

An analytical framework for the comparative evaluation of the strengths and weaknesses of the Nordic assemblies in the adoption and resolution of public policy is presented in Table 7.1. Later in

Table 7.1. FRAMEWORK FOR COMPARATIVE EVALUATION OF POLICY ADOPTION IN THE NORDIC PARLIAMENTS

Structural variables	*Denmark*	*Finland*	*Iceland*	*Norway*	*Sweden*
Number of compulsory plenary readings of bills	3	3	6	1	1
Nature of parliamentary standing committees viz subject-specific (SS) or bill-specific (BS)	SS	SS	SS	SS	SS
Existence of 'upper tier' committees	—	Grand Committee	Efri Deild	Lagting	—
Existence of qualified majority rules	Yes	Yes	No	No	Yes
Rate of Parliamentary Adoption of Private Initiatives. High-Medium-Low	Low	Low	High	Low	Low

this concluding section, the deliberative function of the regional assemblies will be reappraised. However it is vital first to examine the importance of the legislative function of the five parliaments — i.e. to consider the proportion of initiatives from individual legislators, groups of delegates and in Iceland and Sweden parliamentary standing committees, that are adopted in the House.

The parliamentary adoption of private initiatives

There are three main types of legislative initiative available to parliamentarians in the Nordic region. First, there are *private members' bills* proposing the enactment of a new measure or the modification of existing legislation. The one legal restriction on this form of initiative is to be found in Norway, where only members of the government and the Odelsting are empowered to introduce 'law bills', *lovsforslag*.[86] Private members' bills must be submitted in writing, usually during prescribed periods in the parliamentary calendar: in Sweden, for example, this is during the fifteen-day period after the introduction of the annual budget proposal in January.[87] It is nonetheless possible to introduce a private member's bill at any time in the Swedish parliamentary year, except the period before the summer recess, provided the bill is sponsored by at least 10 Riksdag members and relates to a matter of sufficient importance.[88] Such bills have been few. In March 1976 a number of 'extraordinary' private members' bills on alcohol policy were taken up when an earlier government proposal was cancelled, while in October 1978 and again in 1979 similar private measures on the economic situation were allowed. In Finland, an amendment to the work procedures of the Eduskunta in March 1983 enabled delegates there to table private members' bills, *lakialoite*, at any time during the parliamentary calendar, although at the time of writing it is too early to gauge the impact of this change. In addition to private members' bills, parliamentary standing committees have the right to initiate proposals in Sweden and Iceland.

In practice, 'free-standing' private bills can emanate from groups of delegates — even an entire parliamentary group — as well as individual delegates and standing committees. In Sweden, especially, so-called party bills, *partimotioner*, signed by a senior figure on behalf of his party group, have become common practice, although they have no constitutional status and no greater chance of success than any other private initiative. During the Riksdag's General Initiatives Period, *allmänna motionstid*, in 1983, just over 5% of all private proposals comprised party bills as Table 7.2 demonstrates. The growing extent to which private members' bills have in practice been party-politicised, with the distinction between 'private' and 'party' accordingly being blurred, can be seen from the Swedish case.

As Isberg's interviews with the party staff directors have shown, the Riksdag parties in opposition use an informal ranking system with regard to free-standing private initiatives. First in importance are the party bills which are underwritten by the Executive Committee after broad-ranging discussion in the parliamentary group, and which present the main lines of opposition policy. Next come the group policy committee bills — not to be confused with the

Table 7.2. NATURE OF PRIVATE MEMBERS' BILLS SUBMITTED IN THE RIKSDAG DURING THE GENERAL INITIATIVES PERIOD, 10–25 JANUARY 1983

Party	*Individual & standing committee initiatives*	*Party bills*
Conservatives	530	8
Liberals	170	22
Social Democrats	450	—
Centre	480	20
Left Communists	170	55
	1,800	105

Source: Från Riksdag & Departement, 4:1983

initiatives of the parliamentary standing committees — which are proposed by the group policy committees within the parliamentary group (see chapter 5) and deal with somewhat more narrowly focussed matters than the party bills. Finally, there is the numerous category of individual initiatives (in which several delegates may in fact be involved), many of them generated outside the policy framework of the parliamentary group, often with the aid of the non-partisan Riksdag Information Service.[89] Significantly, while a party's delegation on a parliamentary standing committee is granted a good deal of latitude when the Riksdag considers individual initiatives, it is expected to toe the party line in the case of party bills and group policy committee bills. Incidentally, while party bills as such are peculiar to Sweden, initiatives signed by the entire membership of smaller party groups in Finland amount in practice to much the same thing.

Unlike their counterparts in Westminster, Nordic parliamentarians have the right to endeavour to amend proposals under consideration in the assembly by tabling *connected parliamentary bills* — the second form of legislative initiative in the region. These are connected with and/or arise out of cabinet proposals, particularly the budget, either at the point of their introduction into the legislature *or* in connection with their consideration in one of the parliamentary standing committees. In Sweden, the majority of connected parliamentary bills have been tabled during the General Initiatives Period in January and have invariably proposed the spending of larger sums of money, *finansmotioner*. They have derived from both individuals and collective partisan action. In connection with the 1981–2 Budget, for example, Svante Lundkvist and a number of other Social Democrats proposed the expenditure of an additional 5 million kronor on sport, while the entire parliamentary group of the Left Communists, the other party in opposition, produced a bill demanding that an extra 500 million kronor be set aside for the Swedish railways! Incidentally, during the second phase of constitutional reforms in 1973–4, no less than 70 connected bills were tabled in the Riksdag.

In Finland, an enormous post-war increase in their number meant that until recently connected parliamentary bills, *rinnakkais/raha-asia-aloite*, were accepted only when they could be considered without clarification or modification alongside the government proposal. The preference of delegates for connected parliamentary bills is evident from the fact that out of 147 private initiatives tabled by the small opposition party, the Finnish Christian League, during the General Initiatives Period in January 1982, no less than 103 were connected bills, compared with only 6 private members' bills.[90] One reason for this is doubtless that in contrast to private members' bills — many of which, as we saw in chapter 5, lapse through lack of time — bills connected with government measures are invariably handled by parliament and hence produce an outcome one way or the other. However, the importance of connected parliamentary bills in the Nordic states lies in the way they facilitate 'second-stage' members' initiatives — i.e. individual measures which may be tabled, at a later stage in the legislative process than is possible in, say, the British House of Commons or the French National Assembly.

In all the Nordic legislatures, a third type of private initiative is possible: delegates can apply pressure on the government by petitioning for some form of executive action. This can range from a request for the creation of a commission of inquiry, or the preparation of a particular bill, to the amendment of existing legislation and even the repeal of an unworkable law. The widespread increase in the number of these *members' request proposals* has been due not least to the fact that the technical expertise and assistance essential to drafting private members' bills has not been so necessary. Members' request proposals are short, and couched in direct terms with the minimum of elaboration. They are also a genuinely universal form of private initiative in the region.

In Norway, request proposals, *søknader*, which must be countersigned by more than ten members of either the Odelsting or the Lagting and submitted in writing to the appropriate division of the Storting, have provided a useful channel for the mediation of citizens' complaints to the executive authority.[91] In Finland, request proposals constitute the sole vehicle of parliamentary initiation in certain policy areas: in accordance with article 33 of the constitution, assembly initiatives on matters relating to, e.g., foreign treaties and Finland's international relations can be introduced only through the machinery of a member's request proposal, *toivomusaloite*.[92] In Sweden, delegates frequently use members' requests, *hemställningsmotioner*, to seek the formation of a commission of inquiry to examine a specific legislative question, rather than proceeding directly to venture a private member's bill on the matter. The thinking here is that there is a greater probability of the individual delegate gaining the necessary amount of cross-party support for an objective (or at least neutral) investigation into a particular topic than in attempting to canvass an already formulated bill.

Although members' request proposals may ultimately result in a legislative response from the government, they do not involve the same handling in the assembly as private members' bills. In Iceland, for example, request proposals require only a single parliamentary reading: after the request has been debated in a plenary meeting, it is sent to one of the standing committees of the United Althing whose report provides the basis for a continued First Reading on the floor of the assembly before the matter is submitted to the cabinet or to a resolution of the Althing. Despite similarly truncated scrutiny procedures elsewhere in the region, the vast majority of the greatly increased number of members' request proposals are simply not dealt with by parliament through lack of time. In Finland in the 1979–80 session of the Eduskunta about 96% of all members' request proposals were not treated as Table 7.3 illustrates.

Shortage of time has been only one of the factors contributing to the niggardly approach of the Nordic parliaments to adopting initiatives from their own members. The increased workload of the assemblies, particularly since the war, has meant that in practice priority has been given to public over private bills in standing committee. Also, shortcomings in the legal drafting of members' bills have occasionally forced their withdrawal, and above all the high levels of partisanship have doomed the main opposition initiatives — the party bills etc. — at least during periods of majority government. The result has been that the proportion of private initiatives reaching the statute book has been extremely small.

In Denmark a mere 1% of all successful bills in the period 1953–70 derived from private initiatives;[93] in Finland, only two private members' bills became law in 1980 and that was the highest figure in over a decade; in Sweden, and in Norway to only a slightly smaller extent, the private member's bill has become almost obsolete as a form of legislative initiative. The success in November 1981 of a private bill from the Swedish Liberal delegate Daniel Tarschys, which required the government when submitting measures to the Riksdag to include provisional estimates of their costs, was conspicuous by its very rarity. Supporting Tarschys' bill and following the lead of the Constitutional Committee, parliament also decided that 'framework proposals' from the government (see chapter 3) should be included in the cost-accounting brief.[94] The amendment to the Riksdag Standing Orders was then achieved at a stroke

Table 7.3. THE PARLIAMENTARY HANDLING OF MEMBERS' REQUEST PROPOSALS IN FINLAND, 1970–1980

	No. tabled	*Accepted*	*Lapsed*	*Rejected*	*Not considered*
1970	2,233	10	69	64	2,090
1972	2,749	17	62	101	2,569
1980	2,881	3	—	102	2,776

Source: Eduskunnan kansliasta saatua neuvoa.

because more than three-quarters of the voting members favoured the change and they in turn constituted a plurality of all Riksdag delegates.

Some variation over the years in the rate of successful private bills must be allowed for, of course, influenced not least by the numerical strength of governments and changes to the party system in the legislature. It was no coincidence that in 1973–1981 successful private bills in Denmark made up almost 4% of the total volume of enacted legislation, and in the 1974–5 Folketing session it reached 9% (over 13% of all the private members' bills laid down) as Table 7.4 shows.

Of the small percentage of private initiatives that reach the statute book, cross-party bills, or those with a significant degree of backing across a spectrum of backbench delegates, clearly stand the best chance of success. Significantly, four out of the five private members' bills adopted in the 1977–8 Folketing session were of this kind.[95] A random example of more recent date was the proposal sponsored by delegates drawn from no less than seven parliamentary parties in Denmark which passed into law in February 1982. The bill focussed on the question of the compensation due to housing associations whose properties were affected by clearance schemes, and the measure represented an amendment to existing legislation.[96] The reaction of the Social Democratic minority government proved favorable, and at the First Reading debate the Minister of Housing affirmed that the bill touched on a real problem, and one which his department was committed to act on.

Table 7.4. THE RATE OF SUCCESSFUL PRIVATE MEMBERS' AND GOVERNMENT BILLS IN THE DANISH FOLKETING, 1973–81

Parliamentary session		*No. of government bills passed*	*Private bills accepted*	*Total*
1973–4		119	5	124
1974–5		174	17	191
1975–6		161	11	172
1976–7		186	4	190
1977–8		146	5	151
1978–9		146	1	147
1979–80		160	1	161
1980–1		152	7	159
	Total	1,244	51	1,295

Source: Antal fremsatte og vedtagne lovforslag fordelt efter oprindelse 1953/54 — 1980/81. *Folketingetsåret 1980–81*, p. 3.

Despite a number of specific reservations, moreover, he was positively disposed towards its progress in standing committee.[97] As may be inferred from this Danish example, government support for a private member's bill is a telling factor if not exactly a *sine qua non* in its acceptance in the legislature. Certainly when a majority government opposes a private member's bill, its chances of becoming law are remote. Frequently, of course, government support has to be won through sheer persistence. During the General Initiatives Period in January 1982, a private member's bill proposing to amend the Riksdag Standing Orders so that, with the consent of committee members, standing committee meetings would be open to the public along the lines of the American Congressional 'hearings', was introduced for the fifteenth consecutive time! On the non-socialist side, it is at present supported by the Liberals and Conservatives, but opposed by the Centre Party.[98] The Social Democrats who were previously against the idea are now more evenly divided. Plainly, then, the policy influence of private members' bills is not necessarily direct; it is more likely to be incremental because in a changed climate of opinion, a government may find it judicious to accommodate some of the main points of private measures with growing support in the assembly.

There are, of course, occasions when a private member's bill may be adopted complete by a government, and when this happens the original source of the measure will be obscured in the annual statistics. An example from Norway illustrates the point. In June 1980, two individual parliamentarians, Kjell Magne Bondevik of the Christian People's Party and a Centre delegate Ambjørg Sælthun, tabled a private 'law' bill requesting that parliament modify the criminal law in such a way that persons purveying printed and visual matter of a violent and/or grossly offensive nature aimed at the commercial exploitation of children and young persons should be liable to a fine or up to six months' imprisonment.[99] When the Justice Committee reported on the private bill in February 1981, it recommended that the government take up the measure, and the Labour Party Minister of Justice acceded to this request during the Odelsting report debate the same month. Private members' bills on matters of 'law' are only very rarely successful and have almost fallen into disuse. That this one engendered a positive government response owed not a little to the perseverence of Bondevik, who was widely recognised as a pioneering campaigner in the field of violent pornography. Throughout the 1960s he had worked to eradicate flagrant sex and violence from radio and television programmes,[100] and in 1974 he tabled a request proposal during an interpellation debate urging the government to stamp out 'decadent influences' in schools.[101] The timing of the bill was crucial, because it caught a mood of growing public concern over the content of video material. Moreover, in such a sensitive matter, bearing on the social development of young people and consequently mobilising opinion across partisan boundaries, the cost to the government in adopting Bondevik's bill was acceptably low. The change of Norwegian administration in September 1981 did nothing to jeopardise the bill's chances — on the contrary, with a Conservative minority dependent on the support of the Centre and Christian People's Party, it probably enhanced them.

The practice of a government taking up a private member's bill at the recommendation of the appropriate parliamentary standing committee, as in the case of the Bondevik-Sælthun proposal on violent child pornography, should be regarded as the exception rather than the rule: indeed, it is probably fair to surmise that a majority of successful private initiatives suggest largely technical amendments and modifications to ongoing government measures and are tabled as connected parliamentary bills. In Finland, the two private initiatives to be enacted in the 1980–1 session of the Eduskunta were both of this kind. One, sponsored by a Social Democrat, contained *inter alia* the important principle that the state-subsidised special retirement benefit should be paid to all war veterans, regardless of income, as an explicit acknowledgement of services to their country;[102] and the other concerned the statutory creation by local government authorities of committees to promote cultural and artistic activity in their districts.[103] Both of these private bills extended the scope of parallel government proposals.

During this same parliamentary session of 1980–1, there was a significant Constitutional Committee ruling broadening the remit of connected parliamentary bills and in the process reversing a previous judgement of this same committee in 1957. It was in that year that the Eduskunta had challenged the Speaker's decision not to allow a connected parliamentary bill seeking to widen a government proposal on the provision of tax relief for firms in northern Finland, although when the issue was referred to the Constitutional Committee, it found in the Speaker's favour.[104] There the matter rested for more than twenty years, until in the autumn of 1979 the Speaker refused to sanction a connected parliamentary bill which proposed to increase expenditure on study support grants — funding for which the government had incorporated into the 1980–1 budget.[105] On this occasion the Constitutional Committee, while associating itself with the opinion of the legal experts that the Speaker had acted correctly in respect of established practice, nonetheless held that the introduction of the connected bill would not be in violation of the Constitution.[106] The decision of the Constitutional Committee was scarcely welcomed in government quarters: the Prime Minister, Mauno Koivisto, voiced his concern at the likely consequences for minority cabinets if the new interpretation of connected parliamentary bills were to gain currency,[107] and the fear was expressed elsewhere that it could be cynically exploited by the smaller protest parties. For his part, Juuso Häikiö, the author of the bill (himself a deputy speaker, albeit acting here in his private capacity) believed such fears to be exaggerated, arguing that the 1957 interpretation was better suited to the Czarist days when government proposals were merely read out and automatically rubber-stamped in the Eduskunta.[108]

To sum up so far, the number of legislative proposals tabled by backbench Nordic parliamentarians has risen sharply since the last war. Of the three main types of private member's initiative, connected parliamentary bills, invariably of a non-partisan or cross-partisan character and proposing technical amendments to ongoing government legislation, stand the greatest chance of success. The enactment rate of free-standing private members' bills, notwithstanding some fluctuation caused by the changing dynamics of the legislative-executive balance, is very low and in Sweden and Norway particularly they have become a largely outmoded form of delegate initiative. However, the impact of private members' bills is probably greater than at first appears. Occasionally, one is adopted directly by the government, or alternatively the main substance may be incorporated into a subsequent government proposal. Members' request proposals are easier to formulate than private members' bills, very numerous and by no means an inconsequential parliamentary input into the policy process. In Sweden it has been estimated that 5–10% of private initiatives, most of them members' request proposals, produce a positive outcome, usually in the shape of a new commission of inquiry.[109] In sum, the influence of private members' initiatives should not be underestimated; yet neither should it be exaggerated, for the Nordic assemblies are certainly not legislating assemblies in the sense that major public policies are initiated there.

Exceptionally, the two most important constitutional laws in Finland, including the 1919 constitution itself, were enacted as connected parliamentary bills and as such provided the basis for much-needed inter-party compromise. But in contrast to the U.S. Congress, important measures of social and economic policy do not derive from private proposals, and the Nordic legislatures cannot therefore be said to legislate in the significant sense of generating major public policy, the latter being the sole responsibility of the governments in the region. It is imperative to establish that for many parliamentarians private initiatives are not tabled in any serious anticipation of their becoming law, but rather to vent constituency grievances and put pressure on the government to remedy them. For parliamentary groups in opposition, too, private bills are less designed to initiate legislation than to criticise and scrutinise the executive. In Sweden, for example, partisan deployment of connected bills has afforded the opposition an opportunity for a detailed review and critique of executive proposals. During the early phase of the interlude of non-socialist government in Sweden between 1976–82, connected party bills from the Social Democrats tabled in the form of 'alternative budgets' had the important function of challenging government policy.[110] Private bills, in short, are frequently part of the ammunition used by the opposition in opposing the government. Indeed it may be hypothesised that, despite the enormous number of parliamentary initiatives tabled annually, the Nordic assemblies do not strive to be legislative assemblies; rather, they rely on private proposals to challenge government policies, so enhancing the legislature's scrutinisation function. One important exception is the Icelandic Althing, which is close to being a legislative assembly. It warrants discussion as a special case.

The legislative role of the Althing

Quite uniquely in the Nordic region and indeed in Western Europe as a whole, the bulk of legislation entering the statute book in Iceland before the Second World War emanated from private members' bills. Even in 1940, as Table 7.5 shows, successful private proposals outnumbered government bills enacted by a ratio of three to one. True, the rules relating to the submission of private bills have been particularly liberal: a private member's initiative can be tabled in either chamber of the Althing and the days on which it can be debated are in no way restricted. But as Benedikt Gröndal has observed, perhaps the most important factor in the pre-war primacy of private legislation was that until the 1930s Iceland was essentially an uncomplicated society, and hence individual parliamentarians were mostly competent to draft their own bills.[111] In the two decades following the Second World War, however, coincident with the emergence of an increasingly interventionist state, the situation changed and there was a marked drop in the proportion of successful private members' bills. However, in 1950–70 approximately one-fifth of the annual number of enacted bills were still the result of private members' initiatives, and during the sec-

Table 7.5. RATIO OF SUCCESSFUL PRIVATE AND PUBLIC BILLS IN THE ICELANDIC ALTHING, 1920–80

	Government bills		*Private members' bills*	
Session	*Introduced*	*Passed*	*Introduced*	*Passed*
1920–1	15	8	27	11
1930–1	31	18	87	33
1940–1	14	14	77	47
1950–1	61	53	74	24
1960–1	65	55	72	14
1970–1	79	61	105	16
1976–7	71	50	51	13
1977–8	115	88	76	20
1978–9	92	60	80	22
1979–80	87	52	36	11
1980–1	98	84	84	13

Source: Data provided by Thorsteinn Magnusson 22.11.1981.

ond half of the 1970s this figure rose to nearly 25% — a powerful reminder that the legislative role of the Althing remains without parallel in Western Europe.

In order to probe further the scope and nature of these private bills, the thirteen enacted in the 1980–1 Althing session — all but two introduced into thè Lower House — are analysed in Table 7.6. The most numerous category of successful members' initiatives were all-party private bills, i.e. proposals signed by delegates from all four parliamentary parties. Broad delegate consensus was thus achieved on a number of issues ranging from the development of a cultural exchange programme between Iceland and Greenland[112] and the exemption from sales tax of certain specialist instruments used in the key fishing industry,[113] to the structure of the nation's health authorities in respect of the employment of another (part-time) doctor at a medical centre on the east coast.[114] There was also broad parliamentary support for the creation of an independent board to assess the salaries of Althing members.[115] Only

Table 7.6. TYPES OF SUCCESSFUL PRIVATE MEMBERS' BILLS IN THE ICELANDIC ALTHING, 1980–81

Type	*Number*
All-Party Private Bills	5
Single/Double-Member Bills	4
Committee Initiatives	3
Private Initiatives from Government Ministers	1
Total	13

slightly fewer in number than the all-party backbench initiatives were single-member and double-member private bills — i.e. proposals signed by one or at most two delegates. Even in the more complex structure of post-war Iceland, individual delegates have been routinely successful in getting their proposals on to the statute book. Typical of its kind was the bill from Albert Guðmundsson abolishing import duties on children's foods.[116] Neither can measures enacted as single- and double-member bills be regarded as politically marginal: for example, the successful request from the government backbencher and People's Alliance delegate Guðrún Helgadóttir that the Minister of Education define the rules relating to day-nurseries was both significant and controversial.[117]

In the 1980–1 Althing, there were also an unusually high number of initiatives from parliamentary standing committees. The right of permanent assembly committees to move policy initiatives — found in only two countries in the region, Iceland and Sweden — is potentially, of the utmost importance in any appraisal of the legislative role of the Nordic assemblies. In practice, Swedish committee initiatives have generally been infrequent and relatively minor. According to the Riksdag Standing Orders, all standing committees are entitled to introduce measures in their particular area of competence: a majority is needed to proceed with them, and reservations to committee initiatives are permitted.[118] As a random instance of one of the more significant initiatives, the Foreign Affairs Committee took the lead in December 1974 in proposing an increase in the level of aid to those Third World countries affected by desperate conditions of starvation and famine.[119] More typical, perhaps, was the successful initiative of the Constitutional Committee in the spring of 1981 bringing about a number of small changes to the rules governing questions and interpellations. Indeed, although the Constitutional Committee has produced most of the committee initiatives[120] since the facility was incorporated into the Standing Orders of the unicameral Riksdag, it is doubtful how far the intention of consolidating the assembly's legislative role really has been affected by the provision.

In Iceland too, committee initiatives have been of limited importance, although in general bearing on matters of rather more than a purely technical character. Of the three successful initiatives in 1980–1 one, introduced by the Health and Social Insurance Committee, related to the question of increased taxation to support a building fund for elderly people and was part of a government bill that had proved too unwieldy;[121] another from the Agricultural Committee concerning fur-farming was straightforward enough;[122] but the third represented an unusual occurrence in so far as the

Minister of Education delegated the task of formulating legislation on the rules governing the election of bishops in the State Lutheran Church to the Committee on Education.[123] In such cases strong convention dictates that the committee's proposal be given broad cross-party backing. To complete the analysis of private bills enacted in the 1980–1 Althing, we must take note of a measure urging the re-establishment of the right to fish for plaice in Faxaflóa bay, tabled by the Progressive Party Minister of Fisheries in his capacity as a private member. The bill reflected dissension in the cabinet and, in particular, strong opposition from the Minister of Justice who represented the governmental wing of the Independence Party.[124]

Looking at the whole range of members' initiatives enacted in the 1980–1 Althing, three things stand out. First, as elsewhere in the region, successful private bills are not uncommonly founded on cross-party sponsorship. Secondly, far more than in the other Nordic states, individual Althing delegates can achieve significant policy reforms through the medium of private members' bills. And finally, the parliamentary standing committee's right to initiate legislation has been exercised more often, and to effect more wide-ranging legislative outcomes, than in Sweden. In general, the issues covered by the thirteen cases analysed indicate that successful private bills amount to more than technical amendments of existing legislation; rather, important facets of cultural and regional policy are touched upon, although at the same time members' initiatives clearly fall short of matters of 'high politics'. In sum, while the significance of the legislative role of the Althing is distinctive in Western Europe, it would clearly be erroneous to regard it as a legislating assembly in the sense of generating the major lines of public policy.

The deliberative function of the Nordic parliaments: a reappraisal

The comparative evaluation of the deliberative function of the Nordic parliaments involves at least four main structural variables: the extent of the plenary scrutiny of bills (and by extension, delegate involvement in full-reading sessions); the nature (i.e. the subject-specific or bill-specific character) of the parliamentary standing committees; the existence (or not) of 'upper tier' committees and the existence (or not) of qualified majority voting rules. A brief recapitulatory note on each is in order.

It is evident from Table 7.1 that there exist significant variations in the formal length and complexity of the enactment process in the region. In Iceland there are six plenary readings and two committee stages before a bill completes its progress through the two divisions of the Althing; in Finland and Denmark there are three plenary readings, and in the former two committee stages, whereas in Norway and Sweden a single committee stage is followed by one compulsory plenary. There is of course no necessary connection between the length of the parliamentary adoption process and the efficiency with which the deliberative function is performed in the Nordic assemblies. Irrespective of the number and indeed the timing of plenary sessions, i.e. whether it is a broad First Reading of the principles of a bill or a detailed scrutiny of a standing committee report involving the tabling of amendments from the floor of the House, full sittings are largely a formality. They serve either as a vehicle for individual members to place their views on record — as well as advertising them to their electors through the parliamentary reports in the press — or for parties, mainly through their parliamentary group leaders or committee spokesmen, to register their standpoint on an issue.

Nordic plenaries are dull and poorly attended, and the influence of individual contributions must be regarded as very small. Debates lack 'cut and thrust' or any theatrical element; pre-written speeches often fail to pick up points from earlier speakers and in consequence statistics are duplicated and errors compounded. Legislative plenaries tend to be better attended than routine plenary account debates which often do not lead to a vote. In Sweden, for example, even such a highly-charged interpellation as the one tabled by the Social Democratic leader Olof Palme in November 1981, criticising the Defence Minister over the exact interpretation of a remark he had apparently made on Swedish neutrality around the time of the Russian submarine incident (see chapter eight), failed to produce an attendance of many more than 200 delegates.[125] In Finland a roll-call of attendance does not take place at plenary account debates, at which only oral questions are considered.[126] Even in Iceland, however, where uniquely in the region parliamentarians generally use a minimum of notes and there is much impromptu speaking accompanied by a lively exchange of views, attendance at plenary debates is often poor.[127]

Some speeches are, of course, better attended than others. Inge Krogh, the Danish Christian People's Party delegate, recorded amusingly how in Spring 1982 her three weekly plenary contributions were generally well-patronised because, as a member of the smallest Folketing party, she spoke last in the debate, just before the minister, and as the majority of delegates were returning to the chamber for the imminent division![128] However, the policy increment of her contributions — as with the great majority of plenary speeches — was not likely to be very great. Erik Ninn-Hansen, as Conservative First Speaker of the Folketing (1981–2), could remember only about ten occasions during his three decades in parliament when statements on the floor of the Folketing had influenced the outcome of policy — every case, moreover, had occurred during a period of minority government, and the impact had been indirect.[129] One final point on plenaries. Although plenaries in the Nordic parliaments tend to be grey, élitist affairs — it is significant that in Norway the Speaker rings a bell when a minister is about to speak — proceedings can occasionally spring to life. The Third Reading of a Finnish government proposal to amend article 23 of the 1919 constitution so as to increase the number on the Presidential electoral college from 300 to 301 (and so avoid a deadheat when electing the Head of State) in the autumn of 1981 is a case in point. Though a very minor amendment, the debate was punctuated by interjections from the floor, and ranged from the merits of Swiss democracy, and a suggestion that Presidential candidates should be at least forty years of age, to allegations of male chauvinism against the Finnish Rural Party's parliamentary group for appearing to criticise the female Presidential candidate of the Liberal Party.[130] Yet even when the occasional debate is lively and produces touches of humour, delegates feel the pressure to conform and toe the party line, making the outcome a largely foregone conclusion.

Not that British-style whipping is practised in the Nordic region. Typically, every main Finnish party, with the exception of the People's Democratic League, has two whips, *piiskurit* — usually young and/or first-time members — whose duty it is to ensure the attendance of their 'people' at full-sitting divisions. Lacking the necessary authority with their senior colleagues, however, the system has not worked well. In the Centre Party, for example, it has only really functioned in connection with the vital annual budget voting in December, when a careful record of a delegate's whereabouts is kept and a telephone number is requested if he or she is likely to be outside the Eduskunta building at all. Groups do, of course, possess sanctions in the form of a reprimand or even the temporary suspension of members. In the 1979–83 Eduskunta, one Social Democrat was reprimanded in connection with the controversial Gravel Excavation bill. But measures of this kind are seldom deployed. In general, delegates feel the pressure to conform more informally — in terms of the possible damage to their future careers etc. Obviously the permission of the group is needed if a member wishes to deviate from the party line, and in the case of 'conscience questions' this is usually granted.

Throughout the region there exist subject-specific standing committee systems of varying degrees of institutionalisation, and this is undoubtedly where much of the detailed parliamentary deliberation of bills takes place. Longevity of committeeship tenure and, besides, the substantive knowledge delegates bring to their work make the parliamentary standing committees potential arenas for the development of a corporate identity — an identity which might be expected to act as a brake on executive intentions. Up to a point this may happen as the Swedish case illustrates. The Riksdag standing committee on Housing, and indeed the Taxation Committee, are good examples of legislative organs which, by dint of the expertise of their members and the highly specific nature of their policy remit, have contrived something approaching the unitary character of corporate committees.[131] The Legal Affairs Committee, albeit at a still more technical level — witness its redrafting in the spring of 1982 of the so-called Name Bill in a less liberal direction than that proposed by the government — has also generated an intermittent cross-party identity. The power of common interests has occasionally fostered cross-party alliances on other standing committees. So it was in 1974 when members of both socialist and non-socialist parties on the Riksdag Industry Committee joined forces to defend the interests of small firms in the context of a State loan fund.[132]

From a broad West European viewpoint, the policy perspective of the Nordic standing committee members, as distinct from the narrowly partisan perspective, is noteworthy. The regional norm has been for delegates to remain on the same standing committee and to work their way up. Some standing committees have enjoyed a particularly stable personnel: the composition of the Riksdag's Legal Affairs Committee changed little in the decade before the 1982 general election. Distinctively in Sweden, moreover, the policy competence of delegates has been enhanced by overlapping membership of a parliamentary standing committee and one or more parliamentary commissions of inquiry in the corresponding legislative area. The Riksdag Labour Market Committee's united recommendation that an investigation be set up to examine the working of the Labour-Market Board, *ams-utredning*, resulted in a commission in May 1982 on which a quarter of the total membership were full or deputy members of the Labour Market standing committee.

Yet while this is clearly conducive to the development of a common interest orientation, when differences do emerge between a party and its standing committee members on a commission of inquiry, it is invariably the party line that prevails. Partisanship is also the major obstacle to the development of a corporate identity in standing committee. As a general rule of thumb, the bigger the issue, the more fixed the partisan position and the lower the temperature of committee deliberations.

Whereas during the long era of Swedish Social Democratic supremacy (1932–76) budgets were approved unamended in the standing committees, marginal changes to the Finance Bill were effected during the period of bourgeois coalitions 1976–82. In the spring of 1982, for example, 20 million Swedish kronor — a modest enough sum — was effectively added to the budget when leading members of the governing Centre and Liberal parties on the Industry Committee joined the Social Democrats in opposing proposed cuts in employment subsidies. But paradoxically the action of these bourgeois opponents was motivated by essentially partisan considerations and did not involve party loyalties being subsumed in a greater corporate identity. Neither of the two dissident members of the Industry Committee was standing for re-election at the 1982 general election, and both perceived the widespread unpopularity of the proposed cuts and doubtless hoped to salvage some of the anticipated vote losses for their parties by opposing the measure.[133] The personal cost of their rebellion was low, whereas the possible electoral advantage to their parties from their nonconformity seemed to justify embarrassing their senior party colleagues in government. In fact it was precisely these senior colleagues who had failed to observe the conventional practice of consulting with high-ranking standing committee members before proceeding to introduce a controversial measure into the legislature. A vital item of policy etiquette had been flouted.

In short, there is only very limited evidence that the subject-specific character of the parliamentary standing committees has been conducive to cross-partisan alignments on important policy issues. A corporate impact is most likely when a standing committee has a narrow and highly specific policy focus, i.e. Housing, Taxation, Legal Affairs and/or where the issue in question has a regional or moral dimension. For example the case, mentioned above, of the proposed cuts in the Swedish employment subsidies had important regional implications. However, conflicts on standing committees almost invariably follow partisan lines — just as in the bill-specific standing committees at Westminster — with the result that the Nordic standing committees must be viewed as essentially of the permeable type. They do, however, act as a signalling system pointing to disagreements which are resolved either in the various parliamentary groups or, in some cases, by informal negotiation between the party leaders. Standing committee members, moreover, do possess considerable influence over their policy sector within the parliamentary group: in this sense there is a reciprocal flow of influence between the standing committee and the parliamentary party group. The increased workload of parliamentarians has created a feeling of extremely limited competence in matters outside the concern of a delegate's own standing committee, and as a result group members have become reliant on the information and opinions of colleagues on other standing committees. Gudmund Hernes' interviews with Storting delegates in 1977 revealed that no less than nine out of ten parliamentarians admitted an enormous dependence upon their party colleagues on other standing committees.[134]

Contrary to what was originally intended, the existence of 'upper tier' committees in the region, in the form of the Norwegian Lagting and Finnish Grand Committee, has been of only ephemeral importance in strengthening the deliberative function of the Nordic legislatures. Like the specialist standing committees, the 'upper tier' committees have proved highly permeable organs. In February 1981, the Labour Party Speaker of the Odelsting, Per Karstensen, proposed a commission of inquiry into the whole procedure of dividing the Storting for the handling of 'law' proposals.[135] According to Karstensen, the Lagting duplicated rather than complemented the work of the Odelsting since the partisan balance was similar in both chambers, and there was therefore little interest in the Lagting's handling of matters.[136] As Morten Malmø commented in *Aftenposten*, 'Today the Lagting lives an existence completely hidden away from the glare of media publicity and except on a few occasions is largely forgotten.'[137] One defence of the Lagting might be that it does ensure that laws are given at least two readings, and that this is desirable both to remove any technical deficiencies in the wording of proposals and to allow parliament a thoroughgoing engagement in the policy adoption process. At the same time, it is evident from a study by Asbjørn Kjønstad that the average period for the enactment of each of ten central 'laws' in the 1960s and 1970s was nine years and eleven months (from the creation of the commission of inquiry to the final ratification of the 'law') and that the Lagting was responsible for some of this delay.[138]

As for the Grand Committee in Finland, it is one of the least popular committees among delegates, even if it provides a useful training in legislative practice for newer parliamentarians. A member of the Centre Party's parliamentary group staff recalled how a newly-elected delegate for south-west Finland announced excitedly on her first arrival at the Eduskunta that she wanted to be a member of the Grand Committee. She was later to be bitterly disappointed with her choice.[139] A Communist delegate also confirmed how in the parliamentary group of the People's Democratic League the name 'Grand Committee' had proved tantalisingly misleading to new delegates.[140]

Although the position of the Grand Committee in Finland is clearly not under threat, there has been extensive talk in recent years of abolishing the upper division of the Althing. It is argued that the system of divisions is meaningless, given that the Althing has been elected as a single legislative body since 1934 and that the Danish and Swedish experience of making the transition to unicameralism has been favourable. More prosaically, it has also been pointed out that the existing arrangements require the government to have a working majority of 32 rather than 31 delegates, i.e. 21 against 19 in the Lower Chamber and 11 against 9 in the Upper.

It should also be emphasised that rules on qualified majority voting in Sweden, Finland and Denmark (in Norway a two-thirds majority is required for constitutional amendments), while theoretically allowing legislative minorities to delay or even to defeat government proposals, have had little more than a marginal effect on executive proposals. Obviously, the majority of Nordic oppositions possess formal sanctions greater than in systems like the British where only simple plurality voting arrangements prevail. On paper, moreover, this would appear to strengthen their bargaining position, insofar as the threat of exploiting the qualified majority provisions could have a feedback effect on the government's approach to parliamentary management, and more particularly on the degree of consultation with the opposition before the presentation of bills to the legislature. Only in the case of the Finnish Conservatives, however, has the opposition's negotiating stance been consolidated by the power to prevent a measure being declared 'urgent' (and thus enacted in a single parliamentary session) or to vote a bill over a general election.

In conclusion, it is clear that generically the Nordic parliaments belong to the family of deliberating assemblies and spend most of their time scrutinising executive proposals. They are not, however, deliberating assemblies in the minimal sense of mechanically authorising and approving government bills. Government and opposition voting is the dominant pattern of balloting on the floor of the regional assemblies, although marathon debates also occur regularly enough, amendments are frequently made to legislation in standing committee, and multi-party coalitions at final plenary reading are commonplace. Furthermore, the Nordic parliaments are able to exert considerable *informal* influence in the adoption of policy. In the Riksdag, this happens in at least three distinct ways. First, there is a tradition of holding discussions between the cabinet and leaders of the opposition over controversial issues such as proposed cuts in marginal taxation, changes in the level of VAT, or the question of foreign submarines in Swedish territorial waters. Next, it has become conventional for senior-ranking members of the governing party or parties in standing committee to be consulted before a bill is submitted to the Riksdag. And thirdly, there are important 'non-political' contacts between the secretariats of the standing parliamentary committees and the staff of the government ministries. It is precisely because informal channels work so effectively that the right of Riksdag standing committees to initiate legislation — usually this involves tidying up and slightly adjusting government bills — has not been used more than infrequently; it has been viewed, in short, as a last resort rather than a first option, undertaken when parliamentary and ministry officials fail to produce the required measures, usually through lack of time, and when no other means are available.

The substantial informal influence exercised by the Riksdag in the deliberation and adoption of government legislation is integrally tied to the attitude of ministers. Ministers still tend to regard themselves as members of parliament, albeit temporarily estranged, and o perceive the legislature as the rightful forum for policy discussion. The 'parliament-directedness' of cabinet ministers is common to the region as a whole, although the consultative character of legislative-executive relations is probably more accentuated in Sweden than elsewhere.

The heavy workload placed on delegates has made it increasingly difficult for them to maintain a broad overview of legislative matters, and so, as the result, the deliberative function of the Nordic parliaments has been weakened. According to the Conservative member, Gunnar Biörck, Riksdag delegates often have as little as two days in which to read a standing committee report before a plenary decision is taken on it, and frequently they only have a single day to register their intention to speak on the matter at the relevant full-sitting debate. In a private member's bill tabled during the General Initiatives Period in January 1983, Biörck insisted that an outline of committee reports would be helpful to enable hard-pressed delegates to gain a broad idea of the subject-matter in time. In particular, he requested that a summary of the main content, together with an indication of the number of motions considered in connection with the bill, be set out on the first page of the standing committee report.[141]

Significantly, too, an overwhelming majority of the Storting delegates interviewed in 1977 admitted they felt competent only on questions dealt with in their own standing committee, as Table 7.7 documents. Indeed, when in August 1982 news broke of the effective

Table 7.7. THE PERCEIVED LEGISLATIVE COMPETENCE OF STORTING DELEGATES, 1977

Competence in	*Questions handled in a member's own standing committee* %	*Outside own standing committee* %
Virtually all	41.3	0.0
A large proportion	51.6	5.2
About half	5.2	14.2
Less than half	1.3	65.2
Very few	0.6	15.5

Source: Dagbladet 3.9.1982, p. 2.

collapse of Nye Tofte — a company set up to direct the operation of a new pulp mill which in turn was designed to rationalise the Norwegian paper industry — it became clear that only just over 20 Storting delegates had attempted to discover what the Tofte question was all about before voting extra subsidies to the firm earlier the same year,[142] and of these 14 were members of the Industry Committee which was the parliamentary standing committee specifically handling the matter. Even a number of the Industry Committee members conceded that they had been hard pressed to keep up with developments and they included none other than the Centre Party chairman of the committee, Reidar Due, who was also chairman of the Board of Norske Skogindustrier, the major private shareholder in the bankrupt firm! 'We are confronted with such a pile of documentation that it is not possible to read it all,' Due commented in the context of a letter which Nye Tofte had sent to the Industry Department in January 1982 informing the government that the firm's deficit was likely to be greater than anticipated.[143] The heavy burden of some Riksdag standing committees actually became the subject of an investigation which in the spring of 1982 recommended hiving off some areas of responsibility from the two most overworked committees — Industry and Labour Market Affairs. Energy questions, the commission proposed, should be shifted from the Industry Committee to the Housing Committee, while Consumer Affairs should be transferred from the Labour Market to the Legal Affairs Committee. The dilemma, of course, is that despite being overworked, delegates still tend to resist any reduction in the policy competence of their own standing committee: there was strong opposition to the proposed reforms from members of the Industry Committee interested in energy questions.[144]

Thus a significant challenge to the effective performance of the deliberative function of the Nordic legislatures has come from the increased workload of delegates. In order to cope, parliamentarians have not been able to make time stand still; rather, the old axiom *ars longa vita brevis* has been apposite to their dilemma; faced with a daunting quantity of proposed legislation to scrutinise, individual delegates have had time to master little more than the essentials of bills in a relatively narrow policy sector. The result, it cannot be doubted, is that the *collective capacity* of all the Nordic assemblies to examine executive programmes has been reduced.

REFERENCES

1. Conversation with John H. Hagard 10.11.1981.
2. 'Uppgivenhet präglar Åslings varvspolitik'. *Dagens Nyheter* 3.6.1981.
3. Groennings (1960), p. 5.
4. 'Eduskunnan poissaolot ovat kasvaneet räjähdysmäisesti'. *Helsingin Sanomat* 21.9.1980.
5. 'Tilinpäätös'. *Suomen Kuvalehti* 19.12.1980.
6. Information provided by Thorsteinn Magnusson 19.1.1982.
7. Interview with Ingemund Bengtsson 10.9.1981.
8. VJ 5:68.
9. VJ 5:69–70.
10. VJ 5:67.
11. VJ 4:23.
12. DRG 3:20:2.
13. RF 13:10.
14. Interview with John H. Hagard 18.12.1981.
15. VJ 5:66, 68.
16. VJ 5:70, 72, 73, 74.
17. Paavo Kastari, 'The Finnish Constitutional System and its Development', in *Constitution Act and Parliament Act of Finland*. Helsinki: Valtion painatuskeskus, 1967, pp. 27–33.
18. VJ 5:55.
19. VJ 5:80.
20. HM 3:19.
21. DRG 5:41:3.
22. DRG 8:73.
23. DRG 5:41:3.
24. FOF 4:15:3.
25. DRG 5:42.
26. Johansson (1976), pp. 27–8.
27. RF 2:12.
28. Esko Riepula, 'Eduskunnan asema Suomen poliittisessa järjestelmässä'. *Aika* 4–5, 1972, pp. 232–7.
29. Interview with Esko Almgren 9.7.1980.
30. Oksanen (1972), pp. 40–1.
31. Olavi Jouslehto, 'Kuka tuntee soralain?' *Uusi Suomi* 9.10.1980.
32. 'Soralain valiokunnasta äänestetään'. *Uusi Suomi* 10.10.1980. *Vuoden 1980 valtiopäivät*. Pöytäkirjat 10, p. 2323.
33. Ehdotukset soranottolaiksi ja eräiksi siihen liittyviksi laeiksi sisältävä hallituksen esitys no. 88. *Vuoden 1980 valtiopäivät*. Pöytäkirjat 9, p. 2221.
34. 'Soralain käsittely otti lujille'. *Kristityn Vastuu* 25.6.1981.

35. *Folketingstidende* 1975–76, 19 December 1975. pp. 3613–14.
36. 'Forslag til lov om byfornyelse og boligforbedring'. *Folketingsårbog* 1980–81, pp. 120–4.
37. RF 8:4:15. RO 1:4, 2:7:1, 3:17, 5:2:8.
38. Kenneth E. Miller, 'Policy-Making by Referendum: the Danish Experience'. *West European Politics* 5, 1, 1982, pp. 54–67.
39. Ibid., p. 63.
40. DRG 4:29.
41. Sten Sparre Nilson, 'Scandinavia', in David Butler and Austin Ranney (eds) *Referendums: A Comparative Study of Practice and Theory*. Washington, DC: American Enterprise Institute for Public Policy Research, 1978, p. 190.
42. *Regerings proposition 1980/81*: 176 med förslag till lagstifning mot viss spridning av videogram med våldsinslag m.m.
43. *Kulturutskottets yttrande 1980/81*: 8y över proposition 1980/81: 176.
44. *Konstitutionsutskottets betänkande 1980/81*: 29 med prövning av fråga om tillämpligheten av 2 kap 12§ tredje stycket RF i visst fall (KU 1980/81: 28).
45. *Riksdagens protokoll 1980/81*: 163–65, pp. 3–5.
46. 'Stortingets innflytelse svekkes?' *Aftenposten* 30.10.1980.
47. 'Stortingets innflytelse redusert'. *Aftenposten* 13.6.1977.
48. Ilpo Toivonen, *Jarrutuskeskustelut Suomen eduskunnassa itsenäisyyden aikana*. (Pardem 2). Tampereen yliopisto: politiikan tutkimuksen laitoksen tutkimuksia 51, 1979, pp. 67–72.
49. Loewenberg & Patterson (1979), pp. 212–26.
50. Cited in Loewenberg & Patterson (1976), pp. 224–5.
51. Ibid., pp. 212–26.
52. Damgaard (1973), pp. 35–66.
53. 'Besviken centerpartist hoppar av'. *Dagens Nyheter* 27.5.1982.
54. Cited in Lowenberg & Patterson (1979), p. 225.
55. Stefan Swärd, *Ett förklaringsförsök av en inrikespolitisk förändring — om fri abort i Sverige*. Stockholms universitet: Statsvetenskapliga institutionen, 24.8.1981.
56. Interview with Swedish Christian Democratic Party Research Secretary, Mats Odell 28.9.1981.
57. Pekka Nyholm, *Suomen eduskuntaryhmien koheesio vuosien 1948–51 vaalikaudella ja vuoden 1954 valtiopäivillä*. Helsinki: Keskuskirjapaino, 1961, pp. 96–7.
58. 'Det viktigste skjer i grupper og komitéer'. *Aftenposten* 14.1.1977.
59. Loewenberg & Patterson (1979), p. 219.
60. *Regerings proposition 1979/80*: 165.
61. *Näringsutskottets betänkande 1979/80*: 69.
62. *Rikdagens protokoll 1979/80*: 164–172, p. 20.
63. 'En röst avgjorde Brommas öde'. *Nordisk Kontakt* 1/81, pp. 53–4.
64. 'Fälldin låter partipiskan vina'. *Expressen* 5.10.1980.
65. *Trafikutskottets betänkande 1980/81*: 8 om Bromma och Arlanda flygplatser m.m. (prop. 1980/81: 30), p. 2.
66. Interview with Bo Fagerberg, a research secretary in the Swedish Social Democratic Party 16.9.1981.
67. 'Brommatrafik till Arlanda hösten 1983'. *Från Riksdag & Departement* 19.6.1981.
68. *Civilutskottets betänkande 1980/81*: 3 om en överenskommelse angående Sölvbacka strömmarna.
69. *Riksdagens protokoll 1980/81*: 25–28, pp. 83–7.
70. *Innst O nr 89 (1980/81)*. Innstilling fra kirke og undervisningskomitéen om lov om forbud mot profesjonell boksing (Ot. prp. nr 52).
71. 'Kapinalaki'. *Kristityn Vastuu* 2.10.1980.

72. Palle Svensson, 'Party Cohesion in the Danish Parliament during the 1970s'. *Scandinavian Political Studies* 5 (New Series), 1, 1982, p. 29.
73. RO 5:4.
74. RO 5:5:1.
75. SFO 7:43.
76. RO 5:5:2.
77. FOF 12:35. SFO 7:43.
78. Eduskunnan työjärjestyksen muutokset 45a. Lisätty Edusk. päätöksellä 4.12.1980.
79. SFO 7:44.
80. FOF 12:35.
81. Bo H. Bjurulf and Richard G. Niemi, 'Strategic Voting in Scandinavian Parliaments'. *Scandinavian Political Studies* 1 (New Series), 1, 1978, pp. 5–22.
82. DRG 3:22.
83. NG 79.
84. HM 3:19.
85. 'Avainryhmä aiheuttaa suhteettomat tappiot'. *Uusi Suomi* 11.10.1976.
86. SFO 5:30.
87. RO 3:11.
88. RO 3:15.
89. Isberg (1982), pp. 19–21, 30–4, 55–7.
90. 'Kristillisen Liiton kansanedustajat jättivät 147 eduskunta-aloitetta'. *Kristityn Vastuu* 18.2.1982.
91. SFO 5:31.
92. Kauko Sipponen, 'Lainsäädäntövalta', in *Suomen kansanedustuslaitoksen historia* 11. Helsinki: Eduskunnan historiakomitea, 1977, p. 47.
93. Damgaard (1973), p. 39.
94. Riksdagsordningen ändrad. Bättre beslutsunderlag krävs. *Från Riksdag & Departement* 27.11.1981.
95. Fitzmaurice (1981), p. 66.
96. *Folketinget 1981/82* (2 samling). Lovforslag nr L 75. Forslag til Lov om ændring af lov om sanering.
97. Fortryk af folketingets forhandlinger (39), 26.1.1982.
98. Interview with Daniel Tarschys, the author of the bill in 1982, 21.9.1981.
99. *Innst O nr 28 (1980/81)*. Innstilling frå justiskomitéen om privat lovframlegg frå stortingsrepresentantane Ambjørg Sælthun og Kjell Magne Bondevik om endring i straffelova §211.
100. Interview with Johannes Østtveit, Research Secretary (*utredningsleder*) of the Norwegian Christian People's Party 1.10.1981.
101. Information supplied by Lars Nerheim 2.10.1981.
102. *Vuoden 1980 valtiopäivät*. Ahde ym. Ehdotus laiksi rintamasotilaseläkelain muuttamisesta: Lakialoite no 188.
103. *Vuoden 1980 valtiopäivät*. Kortesalmi ym. Ehdotus laiksi kuntien kulttuuritoiminnasta: Lakialoite no. 166.
104. Antero Jyränki, 'Aloiteoikeuden tulkinnalla tärkeä periaatteellinen merkitys'. *Helsingin Sanomat* 21.9.1980.
105. *Vuoden 1979 valtiopäivät*. Lakialoite no. 450. Asiakirjat E1, pp. 895–6.
106. *Vuoden 1980 valtiopäivät*. Perustuslakivaliokunnan mietintö no 17 eduskunnan puhemiehen kieltäytymisen johdosta esittelemästä ed Häikiön lakialoitetta.
107. 'Eduskunta pohtii aloiteoikeuttaan'. *Uusi Suomi* 26.9.1980.
108. 'Tekikö eduskunta vallankaappauksen?' *Uusi Suomi* 12.10.1981.
109. Interview with Daniel Tarschys 21.9.1981.
110. Interview with Bo Fagerberg 16.9.1981.
111. Gröndal (1981), p. 21.

112. *1980 (103 löggjafarthing)* — 29. mál. um Grænlandssjóð.
113. *1980 (103 löggjafarthing)* — 139. mál. um breyting á lögum nr. 1022 mars 1960, um söluskatt með áorðnum breytingum.
114. *1980 (103 löggjafarthing)* — 133. mál. um breyting á lögum um heilbrigðispjónustu, nr. 57/1978.
115. *1980 (103 löggjafarthing)* — 85. mál. um pingfararkaup alpingismanna.
116. *1980 (103 löggjafarthing)* — 138. mál. um breytingu á lögum nr. 120/1976, um tollskrá, með síðari breytingum.
117. *1980/81 (103 löggjafarthing)* — 270. mál. um breyting á lögum nr. 112 frá 1976, um byggingu og rekstur dagvistunarheimila fyrir börn.
118. RO 3:7.
119. Staffan Edmar & Göran Hagbergh, *Arbetet i riksdagens utskott*. Stockholm: Norstedts tryckeri, 1976, p. 5.
120. Interview with Magnus Isberg 7.9.1981.
121. *1980/81 (103 löggjafarthing)* — 335. mál. um framkvændasjóð aldraðra.
122. *1980/81 (103 löggjafarthing)* — 325. mál. um loðdýrarækt.
123. *1980 (103 löggjafarthing)* — 152. mál. um biskupskosningu.
124. *1980 (103 löggjafarthing)* — 173. mál. um breyting á lögum nr 81 31. maí 1976, um veiðar í fiskveiðilandhelgi Íslands, sbr. lög nr. 42 13. maí 1977 og lög nr. 67 30 maí 1979.
125. Försvarsministerns uttalanden förvanskade. *Från Riksdag & Departement* 13.11.1981.
126. Eduskuntamuistio 1979, p. 27.
127. Interview with Thorsteinn Magnusson 21.11.1981.
128. Interview with Inge Krogh 22.4.1982.
129. Interview with Erik Ninn-Hansen 21.4.1982.
130. Copy of the then unpublished manuscript kindly made available by the staff of the Eduskunta library 22.12.1981.
131. Interview with the Chief Secretary to the Riksdag Industry Committee, Lars Foyer 17.9.1982.
132. *Näringsutskottets betänkande 1974*:33. Statens hantverks- och industrilånefond.
133. Interview with the Deputy Secretary to the Riksdag Industry Committee, Gösta Fischer 17.9.1982.
134. 'Et mindretall på Stortinget setter seg inn i sakene'. *Dagbladet* 3.9.1982.
135. 'Nye regler for lovbehandling'. *Aftenposten* 23.2.1981.
136. Dag Hofoss, *Det politiske Norge. En innføring i politisk analyse og norsk samfunnsliv*. Oslo: Universitetsforlaget, 1975, p. 103.
137. 'Lagtingets fremtid avgjøres av neste Storting'. *Aftenposten* 24.6.1981.
138. 'Utredning av lovgivnings praksis'. *Aftenposten* 13.2.1979.
139. Interview with Tapani Katila 23.3.1983.
140. Interview with Inger Hirvelä 23.3.1983.
141. Sammanfattning behövs av utskottsbetänkanden. *Från Riksdag & Departement* 4.2.1983.
142. '112 på Stortinget forstod ikke Tofte'. *Dagbladet* 3.9.1982.
143. 'Jeg burde ha lest Toftebrevet!' *Aftenposten* 23.8.1982. Skytøen beklager. *Norges handels og sjøfartstidende* 2.9.1982.
144. Interview with Gösta Fischer 17.9.1982.

Part III
THE POLICY IMPLEMENTATION STAGE: PARLIAMENTARY INSPECTION AND CONTROL OF THE EXECUTIVE OUTSIDE THE ENACTMENT PROCESS

8
CONTROLLING THE EXECUTIVE ON THE FLOOR OF THE LEGISLATURE

'So far, the opposition has not used the question period in the Storting to challenge the Prime Minister. He is seldom questioned and very rarely by other party leaders.' — Johan P. Olsen, *Governing Norway: Segmentation, Anticipation and Consensus Formation* (1980), p. 212

Not all plenary debates in the Nordic assemblies form an immediate part of the enactment process in that they constitute a First, Second, Third or, in Norway and Sweden, only Reading of a government bill. At fixed intervals throughout the parliamentary calendar, time has traditionally been set aside for *plenary account debates* — the Speech from the Throne in Norway, the so-called 'Kitchen Debate' in Iceland, the bi-annual Foreign Policy Reports in Sweden and so on — at which, on the basis of information provided by the government, parliament is able to inspect the work of the executive and assess the overall state of the nation. The present chapter is concerned to examine the means available to the Nordic parliaments to control the executive on the floor of the assembly. It is divided into four sections: the government bulletins which lead to full-sitting debates; the regular plenary account debates; motions of no confidence; and parliamentary questions and interpellations.

If not all plenary debates relate to the consideration of legislative proposals, so equally parliamentary standing committees in the Nordic states can and do function outside the immediate orbit of the policy-making process. It will be recalled from Part II that standing committees operate as *policy initiators*, exercising formal or conventional powers to instigate measures of their own — usually, though not always, connected with government bills — and as *policy deliberators* concerned to assess, scrutinise and, where necessary, amend proposals falling within their remit. Chapter 9 focuses *inter alia* on parliamentary standing committees exercising their authority to investigate and review the activities of governments — standing committees in their third main role in the region as *inspectors of the political executive*.

At this stage an important caveat needs to be made. The weight in the last part of this book is on procedures for the control of the executive outside the enactment process. A plenary account debate may indeed bear on a government's future legislative programme, while an interpellation or even no confidence vote can spring from a perceived shortcoming in a measure currently under scrutiny in the assembly; but although these procedures may be connected with the process of enacting laws, they do not themselves form part of it. At the same time, of course, the line dividing matters inside from those outside the lawmaking process is in practice difficult to draw. Ministers are questioned in standing committee on government proposals under examination by the committee at the time, as well as on their use of delegated powers and matters related to the implementation of previously enacted measures. No attempt is made to fix an arbitrary and rather artificial distinction between these activities, although, as has been mentioned, the emphasis is on the control of the executive outside bill-related matters.

Government bulletins to parliament

Outside the immediate ambit of the enactment process but in line with a fundamental prerequisite of parliamentarism — that the government formally accounts for its actions to parliament — the Nordic governments supply the regional assemblies with a flow of information which in many cases leads to a plenary account debate.

Much of this information is contained in government bulletins to parliament, which are common to all the Nordic assemblies. In Norway, the *Stortingsmelding*[1] is a device used by the government when matters do not require a concrete decision and resolution: the future guidelines of policy are delineated in general terms — cf. the so-called 'framework proposals', *riktlinjepropositioner*, in Sweden — and after a debate in the Storting the government often introduces a related bill if a grant of money is required. Typical subject-matter for *meldinger* are agricultural policy, the handicapped in society, the condition of adolescent children etc. In addition, this mechanism is used for the annual reports of public corporations and other forms of state activity — e.g. Norwegian participation in all types of international organisations. In Finland, there are two basic types of government statement to parliament. The government communiqué, *hallituksen tiedonanto*, has become relatively infrequent since 1969 when a similar procedure, a government progress report, *selontekomenettely*, was incorporated into the constitution. The latter has the advantage of not involving the risk of subsequently leading to a no-confidence vote in the assembly.[2] In Iceland, members of both divisions of the Althing can request a minister to produce a report about a particular policy matter, *Beldni um skýrslu:* some eight ministerial reports are submitted to the Althing annually, the majority on the initiative of the appropriate minister. In the Folketing Standing Orders, provision is made for a special statement to the House by the Prime Minister, *en udtalelse af særlig karakter*, and for ministers to address the House on a matter of public interest, *en redegørelse for et offentligt anliggende*. In the latter case, a written account or an oral statement not exceeding half an hour is permitted. At the discretion of the Speaker, a subsequent plenary debate may then be held not later than the first sitting after the ministerial account, or at the written request of 17 Folketing delegates not later than five days after the Speaker has received the request or communicated his decision on it.[3] Finally, in Sweden the Riksdag Standing Orders accommodate both written and oral statements to the assembly at short notice, *skrivelse från regeringen*.[4]

Three points concerning these government bulletins to parliament need to be emphasised. First, they afford a *prima facie* case for a marginal strengthening of the legislative function of the Nordic parliaments by delegating decisions — frequently in the event of government divisions — to the legislature. However, as the following instance illustrates, there is no ultimate guarantee that the cabinet will act upon assembly resolutions. Thus the less common government communiqué machinery was used in the mid-1970s on energy policy, as it was again in May 1982 when Kalevi Sorsa's broad centre-left coalition in Finland presented parliament with three alternatives relating to the structure and substantive competence of the proposed Ministry of the Environment. All this was consonant with the rejuvenation of the legislature advocated by President Koivisto, although the decision to issue the communiqué owed much to deep-seated divisions in the cabinet,[5] and the particular alternative on the new Ministry favoured by the Eduskunta, was shelved anyway.

Secondly, the sheer quantity of government bulletins, particularly in Norway, has contributed further to undermining the deliberative capacity of individual delegates. According to information from the Prime Minister's Office in Norway, Kåre Willoch's Conservative minority administration proposed issuing no less than 104 *Stortingsmeldinger* during the spring of 1982.[6] One, for example, concerned petroleum activity in the central and northern parts of the country and suggested a co-ordinating committee to enhance contacts between the various authorities and the oil companies with a view to the future expansion of oil and gas finds.[7] The increase in the number of bulky reports has given the backbench delegate something of a satiated feeling. It is simply not possible for him to study the thousands of documents (100- or 200-page *meldinger*) received from the executive thoroughly enough, with the result that the Storting's role in controlling the policy implementation function of governments has deteriorated — a tendency accentuated by the individual delegate's propensity to specialise in order to survive. All in all, the advice to newly-elected delegates from Tor Oftedal, an experienced member of the Storting's Administration Committee, remains pertinent: 'If you are not absolutely sure that you need a document, throw it out.'[8] Thirdly, government bulletins *per se* afford the assemblies only a limited opportunity for the inspection and review of the executive; much more can be achieved in standing committee. Even then, the initiative in reporting to the assembly rests very firmly with the government of the day.

The regular plenary account debates in the Nordic parliamentary calendar

Over and above bulletins to parliament, the governments of the Nordic states are obliged to give a periodic account of their activities to a plenary meeting of the assembly. These plenary account debates are non-legislative and public — not infrequently they are televised — at which the administration outlines plans, answers for its past actions, and subjects itself to examination on the floor of the House. Most commonly this happens at the beginning of a new parliamentary session. Only in Finland does an initial statement of government intent not lead to a plenary account debate; instead the President merely outlines the main government proposals — usually rather briefly and selectively, and concentrating on those measures which he believes to be important and/or likely to prove contentious. Much later in the Eduskunta calendar, however, there is a general debate on the statements on the government's annual report, *hallituksen kertomus*, prepared by the parliamentary standing committees on the Constitution and on Foreign Affairs (see chapter 9). Elsewhere in the region, the new session of the legislature is traditionally launched with a plenary account debate based on a report and policy declaration from the government.

In Norway this takes the form of the Speech from the Throne, *trontaledebatten*, composed by the government but read by the King at the official state opening of parliament in a manner reminiscent of the Queen's Speech in the British House of Lords. No debate takes place in the United Storting until the monarch has left, and a discussion (often protracted) is then initiated by the leader of the largest opposition party. Norway is the only Nordic state where the Speech from the Throne has retained its original form. In Sweden, since the introduction of the new constitution, a government declaration, *regeringsförklaringen*, has been read by the Prime Minister in the presence of the King who, although seated prominently, is required to make only the shortest of contributions when formally opening the new session of the Riksdag. Later the same week there is a so-called 'general political debate,' *allmänpolitisk debatt*, on the government's declaration and this is one of a number of such account debates in the Riksdag. In Denmark since 1953, the parliamentary nature of the political executive has been given even more visible and symbolic expression in that despite the official opening of parliament being the only time the monarch attends the Folketing, he/she has been relegated, following a radical leftist lobby, to the safe distance of a box in the visitors' gallery! The government declaration in Denmark is usually extremely long: part of it is given verbally by the Prime Minister and part in the form of a handout to delegates. The 'opening debate' itself follows two days later.

Notwithstanding a republican constitution, the procedure is very much the same in Iceland. The President officially opens parliament[9] and a government declaration is made not later than two weeks after the beginning of the new session. The Prime Minister is allocated half an hour in the declaration debate and representatives of the other parties twenty minutes each in the first instance; the second time round, all speeches, including the Prime Minister's, are restricted to a maximum of ten minutes. Interestingly, the institution of an opening plenary account debate has recently been introduced at the Nordic regional level. At the initiative of the Nordic Council, the chairman of the Council of Ministers, Arne Skauge, opened the week's proceedings for the first time in Oslo in 1983 by presenting a Council of Ministers' declaration, *ministerrådsdeklaration*.

In addition to these opening debates, all the Nordic parliaments have provision for deliberations of a general review nature: in Norway, for example, the Foreign Secretary's bi-annual report to the Storting leads directly to a plenary debate which is usually a lively affair; it is not vetted by the standing committee on Foreign Affairs and the Constitution. The same is true in Sweden. However, the degree of executive control achieved through plenary account debates is limited on three counts. First, they tend to be formal and routinised in character and are invariably dominated by a few senior party figures, themselves operating within strictly-prescribed time limits. Iceland provides a case in point. In accordance with article 54 of the 1976 Althing Standing Orders, a general account debate — affectionately known as the 'Kitchen Debate' due to the Icelandic penchant for culinary chit-chat — is held about two weeks before the end of the parliamentary session in late April or early May.[10] Each party, however, is allowed only half an hour in which to state its views, and with three spokesmen per party customarily sharing the half hour this has meant in recent years that as much as four-fifths of the total Althing membership has been denied the right to take part. The 'Kitchen Debate' is poorly attended: partly because it is broadcast nationally (and delegates can hear it without being in the chamber), partly because it does not conclude in a vote, but most of all because the limited right of participation has undermined the incentive of members to attend.

Secondly, in a majority of the Nordic states, there is no provision whatsoever for shifting the parliamentary Orders of the Day so as to hold a topical account debate. In Iceland 'urgency questions', *umræða utan dagskrá*, tabled by individual delegates usually from the opposition ranks, can lead — at the discretion of the Speaker and if deemed to be of sufficient general importance — to the Orders of the Day being suspended to allow a wide-ranging general debate. But this is the exception in the region. Even in Iceland the 'urgency questions' (literally, 'deliberations outside the agenda of the day') have no formal status; there is no reference to them in the Althing's Standing Orders and their extensive use is based on convention alone. The Speaker, however, only very exceptionally refuses to accommodate them by deferring the business of the day (which may, of course, be returned to if the debate on the 'urgency question' only lasts a short time); they always attract media attention and as such are popular both with the political parties and new delegates wishing to establish a name for themselves. In the 1978–9 Althing, 'urgency questions' were even put by the many newcomers on the government side. The flexibility which these afford to Althing proceedings is remarkable in the Nordic perspective — they are so commonplace that there is even a feeling in some circles that there is a need for some regulation!

Finally, account debates often lack immediacy — a corollary of the second point — and hence delegate interest is slight. In Finland, for instance, the government's annual report is introduced into parliament in May and then, in accordance with article 29 of its Standing Orders, it is sent for scrutiny to the Constitutional Committee and the Foreign Affairs Committee.[11] The Constitutional Committee requests answers to the government document from the other Eduskunta standing committees before it compiles its own report, usually around Christmas. A general debate subsequently takes place at which the sections dealing with the government's foreign and domestic policy are dealt with in turn. It is not unusual for there to be considerable delays in this sequence of events: the Finnish government's annual report for 1980 was not discussed in the Eduskunta until well into the spring of 1982. Moreover, while this debate allows delegates their only real opportunity to debate issues like foreign policy, there has been growing disenchantment among rank-and-file members with the way they are called upon to consider matters which now belong to the past and about which little in reality can be done.

All this is not, of course, to suggest that plenary account debates do not play a useful parliamentary role: indeed, like Supply Days at Westminster, they give opposition parties an opportunity to project their policies to the voters. During the long periods of post-war Social Democratic rule in Norway, for example, account debates enabled the non-socialist parties to demonstrate their credibility as an alternative government. The first-ever co-operation between the centre-based groups in the Storting involved their taking a common line during the debate on the Speech from the Throne in 1960, and delegates from the Liberal, Christian People's and Centre parties met subsequently to try further to formalise collaboration in advance of the 1961 general election.[12] Against the background of the Swedish Social Democrats' energy programme of February 1975, envisaging the continued expansion of nuclear power, the Centre Party leader Thorbjörn Fälldin used the forum of the general political debate in the Riksdag in April that year tactically to underline his conviction that an embargo on the development of nuclear power was necessary at least until a number of safety issues had been satisfactorily resolved.[13] The issue was thus placed high on the agenda of the 1976 election campaign, although the result did not indicate that the Centre Party profited much from it at the polls. Also, the small opposition parties not well represented on parliamentary standing committees and commissions of inquiry tend to use account debates to deploy their generally adversarial style in the legislature: they denounce the government, demand information from it, and above all heighten their profile with voters. In the debate on the Speech from the Throne in Norway in 1979, the leader of the miniscule Left-Socialist Party, Hanna Kvanmo, spoke on no less than ten occasions and this, coupled with her 150 speeches during the previous parliamentary session, made her an undoubted thorn in the government's side.[14]

Plenary account debates are a *sine qua non* of responsible government. The executive accounts for its past actions, elaborates its future plans, and is called upon to debate the niceties of both on the floor of the assembly. Account debates receive plenty of publicity, afford contenders for office an opportunity to ventilate and publicise their policies, and provide a useful barometer of the intensity of opposition sentiment. However, they do not lead to a vote and therefore lack immediate sanctions. Points can be scored and psychological gains made, but cabinets cannot be ousted. If it is obvious that a government does not enjoy the confidence of the legislature, the parliamentary principle clearly requires its resignation. This can be enforced through the successful passage of a motion of no confidence, which represents the ultimate parliamentary weapon for exercising political control over the executive.

Motions of no confidence

In the multi-party Nordic assemblies, the operation of the parliamentary principle has tended to protect governments with a numerically weak following in the legislature — whether they are minority ones in the formal sense or exclusively comprise experts and officials, as sometimes happens in Finland — in so far as cabinets are assumed to enjoy the confidence of the legislature unless an actual vote of no confidence is carried against them. In the classic Swedish formulation, governments are required merely to enjoy 'the tolerance of the Riksdag'; in Finland reference is made in the constitution to the principle of 'negative parliamentarism'.[15]

Irrespective of the balance of power in the assembly, this last-mentioned principle can be used to sustain an ailing government. In the spring of 1981, Koivisto's broad but badly-divided centre-left coalition in Finland soldiered on — there were suspicions of collusion involving the Centre Party and the ageing President Kekkonen with a view to unseating Koivisto and so discrediting the popular Prime Minister before the 1982 Presidential election — because, as the Prime Minister tersely remarked, 'the cabinet has not received a vote of no confidence in the Eduskunta.'[16] The whole episode was heavily tinged with irony, for Koivisto invoked the ground rules of parliamentarism to remain in office — and in defying the Presidential plot further enhanced his standing in the public opinion polls; yet many in the country had felt that the spirit of these rules were violated in the initial building of the very coalition which was now threatened by internal division. Before the crisis, the government did indeed have the backing of a large majority in the assembly, but still excluded the very party, the Conservatives, who made the greatest gains at the polls in 1979! With the parliamentary opposition numerically too weak to be a serious threat to the government's position through the no confidence procedure, it was hardly surprisingly that when Koivisto's successor as Prime Minister, Kalevi Sorsa, finally dismissed the Communists from his cabinet in December 1982 — they had received official sanction to disavow the tradition of collective ministerial responsibility in connection with the devaluation crisis two months earlier — it was hailed in the ranks of the smaller parties as an 'object-lesson in parliamentarism'![17] After all the Communists seemed to want, not for the first time, to offer open opposition from within the cabinet and to be loath to resign despite repeated criticism from the parliamentary opposition that condoning such practice was incompatible with established notions of accountable government. In any event, and notwithstanding the changing legislative-executive balance in the Nordic assemblies, cabinets do not need actively to seek a vote of no confidence from the legislature, either at their inception or later, and rarely do so.

In Sweden, of course, the parliamentary vote on the Speaker's candidate for the Premiership amounts in effect to a vote of confidence in a new administration, or rather 'not no confidence', *non sfiducia*, in the distinctive Italian term. When the Fälldin I bourgeois coalition collapsed following disagreements over whether a referendum should be held on the nuclear power question, its successor, a single-party Liberal minority under Ola Ullsten, obtained the support of only 39 Liberal delegates when it submitted itself to the Riksdag in October 1978. The Social Democrats and Centre Party abstained, which meant that the Conservatives and Left-Communists voting against failed to obtain the absolute majority necessary under the new constitution to defeat the Speaker's nominee.

A Prime Minister, moreover, may decide for tactical reasons to make an issue one of confidence in the government, which is what Olof Palme did in December 1982, threatening to resign and call new elections if his three-month-old cabinet (with 166 seats in the 349-seat Riksdag) were defeated over a proposal for a 2% increase in VAT. The government scraped home by two votes following a deal with the Left-Communists, who abstained and thereby won an increase in the subsidies on milk, cheese and fish.

In Denmark two months earlier, on 14 October 1982, the bourgeois coalition's Employment Bill was turned into an issue of confidence in the government using the machinery of the Special Prime Ministerial Statement to the Folketing, *udtalelse af særlig karakter af statsministeren.*[18] Poul Schlüter requested the opportunity of making a parliamentary statement to clarify the situation following the success of a number of opposition-party amendments to the government's Employment Bill — amendments which, he claimed, had rendered the bill out of line with the content of the government's 'opening declaration', *åbningstale*, as well as its goal of reviving the Danish economy. Schlüter expressed his concern at developments on two main counts. First, he noted that the amendments had cut many millions of kronor from the total amount the government believed necessary to affect the colossal deficit in the state's finances; secondly, he stressed that a majority of Folketing delegates had consistently torpedoed the government's plans for an incomes policy which, he was convinced, would significantly improve the nation's employment capacity. All this, the Prime Minister observed, would mean *inter alia* a continuation of the fully-automatic cost-of-living adjustment machinery. Schlüter noted that the Third Reading of the government bill was scheduled to take place two days later, and would indeed take place. However, he said he felt obliged to tell the Folketing that if the opposition amendments were ultimately incorporated into the government bill, the coalition could no longer remain in office; rather, it would be forced to construe the parliamentary majority against the Employment Bill as expressing a desire for a general election. Schlüter pointed out in conclusion that the government did not want an election, which he claimed would undoubtedly lead to economic chaos. Before the Third Reading, the government would explore all reasonable channels with a view to finding an accommodation. Schlüter remarked: 'I hope we succeed, but in the event of failure, the Folketing now knows the consequences.'[19] In the event, the coalition survived.

However, if Nordic governments do not need actively to seek a vote of confidence at any stage in their tenure of office — precisely as in the United Kingdom — neither are they protected by the device of the 'constructive vote of no confidence' as in West Germany, which protects an incumbent administration in the event of the opposition — following a successful no confidence vote — failing to agree on an alternative head of government. This was, admittedly, used against Helmut Schmidt in the autumn of 1982 when the Social Democratic Chancellor was replaced by the Christian Democrat Helmut Kohl, although general elections soon followed against a background of some dissatisfaction with the constitutional mechanism. In short, for a government to be unseated in the Nordic region, a motion of no confidence must be passed against it and even then an absolute majority of delegates in opposition is required for the move to be successful. No confidence motions can be tabled against whole governments, or alternatively against individual cabinet ministers either directly or, as in the Finnish case, in connection with ongoing parliamentary business. In no confidence motions in the Nordic parliaments, all votes cast are counted in contrast to the practice in France where, according to article 49 of the Fifth Republic constitution, only the ballots in favour of a motion of censure are calculated.

As noted earlier, the constitutional powers vested in the Presidency — *inter alia* the appointment of governments, the right to take decisions against the majority view of the cabinet and the right to dismiss governments and dissolve parliament — have conspired significantly to weaken parliamentarism in Finland. For example, a government can be dismissed by the Head of State — as was done in practice to the Karjalainen II centre-moderate left administration in the autumn of 1971 — even if it has not received a vote of no confidence and appears still to possess the tacit support of a majority in the legislature. In the latter instance, Kekkonen simply informed the Prime Minister that unless the deadlock between the farmer-oriented Centre and consumer-based Social Democratic parties were resolved by October, the government would be removed and new elections held. The same Karjalainen administration also received a note from the President — an unprecedented action on Kekkonen's part and in the strict sense scarcely constitutional — warning it of the importance of getting its forthcoming budget right in view of what he believed to be an impending international currency crisis.[20] When the coalition failed to settle its differences, it duly resigned.

There have been numerous occasions, moreover, when individual ministers have been obliged to accept parliamentary responsibility for decisions which the President has made in opposition to a majority of ministers or sometimes even a unanimous cabinet. So much is perfectly constitutional. That said, there is no question that if a President tried consistently to assert his will and enforce policy without the backing of the government, he would ultimately be forced out of office. This at least was the view of Urho Kekkonen who noted in a seminal speech on the powers of the Presidency at Helsinki University in 1967 that 'disagreement between the President and cabinet can easily be transformed into a confrontation between parliament and President, and this eventually to a situation where the Head of State is unable to form a government enjoying the support of parliament as required by article 36 of the constitution.' Such a situation where the government is 'on strike', *hallituslakko*, i.e. where prospective ministers refuse to serve in anticipation of conflict with the President and a lack of legislative backing, 'is bound to lead to the resignation of the President.'[21] However, it has not yet arisen; indeed, when the usual consultations with parliamentary party groups have been circumvented or particular ministers have fallen foul of the Eduskunta, the no confidence vote has worked unerringly. When, for example, a government of experts under von Fieandt was nominated in the autumn of 1957 by Kekkonen without the conventional inter-party preliminaries and the following April 1958 received a vote of no confidence, it promptly resigned. When Leino, the Communist Minister of the Interior, failed to resign following a no confidence vote in May 1948, President Paasikivi intervened, the minister was removed and a new one appointed to replace him. In sum, an attempt to conjoin the American-inspired principle of a separation of powers with a Westminster type of parliamentary government may have produced a constitutional hybrid tending, in the complex multi-party situation of Finland, to bolster the powers of the President at the expense of a cabinet directly responsible to parliament; yet potentially at least, the no confidence vote constitutes an important check on the unbridled use of Presidential power. Certainly, as Paavo Kastari has indicated, there has never been an attempt to form Weimar-style 'combat cabinets', *Kampfregierung*, in Finland, defying the assembly and serving as a pawn of the President.[22]

As we have mentioned, motions of no confidence in the region can be tabled against individual ministers as well as entire cabinets, as the following brief examples will illustrate. In Norway the Storting's discussion of the 1983–4 Defence Budget occasioned two motions of no confidence against the Minister of Defence in Willoch's Conservative minority, Anders C. Sjaastad — one by the Labour Party, the other by the Left-Socialists — both alleging that in a vital matter of security policy, information had been withheld from parliament. More precisely, the Labour Party claimed that the Defence Minister had misled the Storting standing committee on Defence, which was clearly under a misapprehension when it declared in May 1982 that 'thus far, Norway has not been charged with any part of the 49 million kronor representing the national share of the collective costs towards developing NATO's new middle-distance atomic rocket programme.'[23] In this situation, the Labour Party claimed, the Defence Minister was under an absolute obligation to set the record straight in the Storting. Sjaastad denied the charge and said that in June 1982 he had told the assembly that a smaller sum had already been allocated for the planning and building of atomic rockets. After many hours of debate, the Labour motion of no confidence was defeated by 88 votes to 65. Subsequently, by only the narrowest of margins (77 to 76), the Storting agreed to pay its share of the costs towards the rockets although with the main opposition group, the Labour Party, voting against the programme, this constituted the first serious breach in the national consensus on defence since Norway's accession to NATO in 1949. However, the Labour Party's no confidence motion was motivated not least by a concern to distract attention from grass-roots divisions in the party over the rocket question.

In Finland, in connection with the 1981–2 Budget, two small-party delegates, Samuli Hautala of the Finnish Christian League and Pekka Vennamo of the Rural Party, argued that as the level of unemployment had remained unacceptably high, the Communist Party's Minister of Labour Arvo Aalto had failed in his task and therefore no longer enjoyed the confidence of the Eduskunta. Of these two separate motions of no confidence, only Hautala's was voted on and predictably it was defeated by 118 votes to 18, although significantly there were 42 abstentions — many, doubtless, from the leading opposition party, the Conservatives.[24] Incidentally, in Finland and Denmark interpellations leading to a plenary vote can be tantamount to motions of no confidence; we will return to this below.

Perhaps the most celebrated example of a no confidence motion tabled against an entire government was the Social Democratic challenge to the three-party non-socialist coalition in Sweden in October 1980, the first of its kind since the provision for no confidence votes was incorporated into the new constitution. The backing of 175 delegates in the 349-seat Riksdag was needed for success — more than the combined membership of the two left-wing groups — and even a result of 174 votes to 1 against the government would not have sufficed. Needless to say, both politicians and journalists had a herculean task in explaining the logistics of this situation (namely that for all the excitement the outcome was a foregone conclusion) to a Swedish public that was politically highly sensitised, but largely ignorant of the constitutional niceties of the matter. In the event, the Fälldin government had a majority of one. The three-party Icelandic coalition led by the dissident Independence Party Prime Minister, Gunnar Thoroddsen, held on in a vote of no confidence in November 1982 by the only slightly greater margin of two votes — his vital support coming from 17 Progressive Party delegates and

11 from the radical leftist People's Alliance. The debate on this no confidence motion marked the first occasion when proceedings of the Althing had been televised live.[25]

It is almost a truism to say that the function of no confidence motions in the region is to bring sitting governments down, either directly or indirectly. However, we will be suggesting that this is only a part of the story, albeit an important one. True, after the departure of a majority of a group known as the Liberals and Leftists from the Icelandic coalition in May 1974, the opposition parties, principally the Independence and Social Democratic parties, tabled a vote of no confidence to press the point that the rump administration no longer had majority support in the Althing. As it turned out, the Prime Minister decided to dissolve parliament rather than face the inevitable outcome of the no confidence vote. Also, the centre-based executive on the Åland islands was defeated by 16 votes to 12 (one delegate abstained and one was absent) in March 1983 when the Right, Social Democrats and Liberals backed a no confidence motion tabled against the executive's handling of traffic questions — although dissatisfaction in the opposition camp ran much deeper than that.[26] In general, however, the success rate of opposition measures of no confidence against incumbent Nordic governments has been low and even the threat of such action has had only limited effect. When, following the withdrawal from the Swedish government of the Conservatives in May 1981 over the question of promised cuts in marginal taxation, Fälldin offered to form a centre minority government — it became the first of its kind — Palme, the Social Democratic Opposition leader, advised that he would immediately move a vote of no confidence in such a minority. However, Bohman for the Conservatives responded that his party would never vote out a non-socialist government when it meant allowing the Social Democrats to take office.

Yet if it appears self-evident that no confidence motions in the Nordic region have been tabled with the serious intent of dismissing the political executive, it is still arguable that a majority of them have not been put down with any realistic such hope. Instead they have tended — as with Palme's gesture mentioned above — to have an essentially demonstrative character, indicating the depth of opposition feeling and affording it an outlet for frustration and, on occasions, sagging morale. Obviously the greater the parliamentary majority behind a government, the greater will be the likelihood of tactical no confidence motions. But even when the parliamentary arithmetic makes the outcome largely academic, no confidence motions can be telling enough — witness the one tabled by a united opposition of People's Alliance, Social Democrats and Liberals and

Leftists in Iceland in February 1976. It inveighed against what it claimed to be the manifest inability of the coalition to manage the nation's economic problems as evidenced by the general strike taking place at the time. The mathematics of the situation in the Althing ensured that the result was a foregone conclusion — the no confidence division registered only 18 votes against the government, 41 for and a solitary abstention — but the desired effect of pointing to an alternative plan of campaign was largely achieved. In situations where the idea of overturning the government is largely theoretical, no confidence motions acquire a strategic importance. To be effective they need to be used sparingly and on matters of real importance. In Sweden there has only been one since they were incorporated into the new constitution and not a single one has been moved against an individual cabinet minister. Similarly in Iceland, only two no confidence motions were laid before the Althing in the period 1971–81.

On occasions, the deployment of no confidence motions reveals as much about the state of the parliamentary opposition as the vulnerability and/or unpopularity of the government. This certainly appeared so in Norway in the early 1960s when, after abortive attempts by the Liberals, Centre and Christian People's parties to cement a three-party 'centre alternative', the entire opposition concerted its efforts against the Social Democratic government. Between February 1963, when de Gaulle's 'no' to British (and thereby Norwegian) membership of the Common Market reunited the non-socialist camp, and August the same year the entire bourgeois bloc — the three already mentioned plus the Conservatives — put down three motions of no confidence. The first concerned the appointment of a new Principal at the Police School; the second the construction budget for the coke network, *koksverket*; and the last and decisive one a mining accident at Kings Bay on Svalbard. The radical left-wing Socialist People's Party joined the rising chorus of criticism over the Svalbard incident and on 22 August 1963 the Storting debate on the no confidence motion culminated in the fall of Gerhardsen's government.[27]

Precisely because the motivation underlying no confidence motions is variable, extending beyond their ostensible aim of toppling the government, any attempt to estimate their utility as vehicles for controlling the executive is best restricted to particular cases. It might rather paradoxically be argued, for example, that the introduction of no confidence motions into the new Swedish constitution has led to restraints on the government being weakened and not strengthened. Defeats for the government on central matters of economic policy have been condoned — the issue of subsidies to the

Öresund shipyard in June 1980 to cite a case in point (see chapter 7) — and do not lead to the government's resignation unless the matter is specifically made one of no confidence. As one commentator has observed, 'under the present arrangements, a government can be defeated regularly and still not resign unless the matter is pushed to a no confidence vote'.[28] In reality, this amounts to a growing protection for the political executive.

Parliamentary questions

Parliamentary questions constitute an easily accessible channel for the routine inspection of the executive. They afford an opportunity for delegates, especially from the opposition parties, to acquire information, articulate a wide variety of interests, and above all to criticise the government. We now deal with the two main modes of querying ministers — interpellations and ordinary questions. A brief description of both types is followed by a consideration of who uses parliamentary questions — for what purposes and with what results. Are there, in other words, any patterns to be discerned from the submission of questions? The main conclusion is that the main plenary machinery for interrogating the executive has been much less party-politicised than the other basic structures of the legislature, although ironically the degree of parliamentary control over the executive has not been measurably increased.

Interpellations are the oldest form of parliamentary question in the region, dating back in Denmark to the 1849 constitution and in Sweden to the transition to bicameralism in 1867. They are addressed in writing (and with a suitable explanatory preamble) to a minister in relation to an action of his department or to the Prime Minister on a matter of general policy. Interpellations bear on matters of broad political concern — 'great general interest' in the phrase of the Swedish Constitutional Reform Committee in 1972. They require the appropriate cabinet minister to respond within a prescribed period — ranging from fifteen days in Finland to four weeks in Sweden — or to explain why he/she is unable to do so. Unlike ordinary questions, interpellations lead to a plenary debate in the legislature. Ministers very rarely refuse to reply: every interpellation in Sweden since 1975 has been answered, and in Finland an answer has not been forthcoming only when a change of minister has taken place before the expiration of the response period.

In general, parliamentarians themselves control the destiny of interpellations. In Denmark, the Folketing decides without debate whether an interpellation is to be placed on the agenda, whereas in

Sweden, following an initiative in the spring of 1981 from the Riksdag's Constitutional Committee, an interpellation which the Speaker refuses to put can be referred for decision to the whole House. Norwegian interpellations can be rejected by the Speaker only when the matter is under scrutiny in a standing committee, relates to a committee report that has not been debated in the assembly, or is the topic of an earlier interpellation which has not yet been answered. As noted earlier, the Althing Speaker seldom rejects an 'urgency question' which we will consider in the present context in so far as it leads to a general debate. Uniquely in the Nordic states, though in common with Austria and West Germany, interpellations in Finland require collective sponsorship: the backing of at least one-tenth of the Eduskunta, i.e. a minimum of twenty delegates, is necessary before an interpellation can be put. Before 1917 a parliamentary majority was needed!

The most important difference in the formal rules relating to interpellations in the Nordic region is whether or not they conclude in a vote. In Denmark and Finland, where they do, interpellations can cause the fall of a government. In Denmark in November 1981, a motion from the Radical Party to proceed to the next item of business, the so-called resolution on the order of business, *forslag om motiveret dagsorden*, tabled during an interpellation debate — in accordance with the Folketing Standing Orders (24:3) — brought about the fall of Anker Jørgensen's (fifth) Social Democratic minority government. In Finland there have been four occasions since 1917 when an interpellation, *välikysymys*, has led to the resignation of a cabinet, the last in 1957 when von Fieandt's civil service administration fell.

The more recent Danish case is of particular interest. The Radicals' motion tabled by Niels Helveg Petersen read thus: 'The Folketing requests the government to abandon its plans for compulsory measures on the sale of pension funds and insists too that before 1 December 1982 a bill should be introduced to improve the financing of agriculture and building.'[29] Ironically, the Liberal delegate Ellemann-Jensen who had earlier tabled a similar motion — though without any reference to agriculture and building — tactically withdrew his proposal when the Speaker placed it after Petersen's in the order of voting,[30] leaving the Social Democrats to fall foul of their traditional allies, the Radicals, in their attempt to use the pension funds to bolster the Danish economy. Jørgensen could simply have resigned on receiving the adverse vote without calling fresh elections,[31] but in the event he chose to go to the country. Although it is customary for a government to resign if a resolution on the order of business is successfully moved against its wishes, much seems to depend on the nature of the issue. When the Left-Socialist delegate Steen Folke and Socialist People's Party member Gert Petersen tabled an interpellation leading to a resolution on the order of business which inquired what light the government could shed on NATO's plans to place 572 new atomic missiles in Western Europe during 1983, Schlüter, the Conservative Prime Minister, made it clear he would not resign even if it was successful.[32] In fact, a rather anodyne countermanding resolution on the order of business, *prevens dagsorden*, from the Social Democrats, who were rather equivocal on the missiles issue, was carried by 49 votes against 13, though with no less than 90 abstentions.

Outside Denmark and Finland, interpellations lack a real sanction. In Sweden they never culminate in a vote and may therefore be likened to the 'debated oral question', *la question orale avec débat*, in the constitution of the Fifth French Republic. Even the amount of debate tends to be limited although there are no time limits on speeches in interpellation discussions. In recent years, only about one-third of interpellation debates have involved contributions from delegates besides the interpellator, and as a result they have lasted on average no more than half an hour. In Norway, interpellation debates are restricted to a maximum of two hours and can indirectly lead to a vote: a bill proposed during an interpellation debate is referred by a decision of the Storting either to a standing committee or the government or, alternatively, is simply placed on the table for later handling.

Ordinary questions differ from interpellations in three obvious respects. The prefatory explanation is minimal or not required at all; the debate is generally confined to the questioner and the appropriate cabinet minister; and questions do not lead to a vote. Not surprisingly, perhaps, the rules on supplementary questions vary across the region, as does the period of time within which governments are required to respond. However, the practice of interrogating ministers has been institutionalised in the Nordic states in the post-war period by the introduction of a regular weekly question time. This does not, as Johan P. Olsen has noted of Norway, entail the grilling which British ministers face at Westminster. Opposition party leaders very seldom use question time in the Storting to challenge the Prime Minister;[33] and the type of 'rowdyism' which a Speaker's inquiry in February 1983 reported was inescapable in the House of Commons[34] is precluded by the Standing Orders of the Nordic parliaments. Yet, consonant with the enormous post-war expansion in government, particularly in the direction of welfarism, the number of questions has grown, and so has their utility as a means of probing a highly technocratic state. In this latter context, a majority of the answers to written questions in the Eduskunta between 1980–1, almost 18% of the total, emanated from the Ministry of Health and Social Affairs.[35] This is not a comment on the efficacy of parliamentary questions: indeed, the pre-requisites of effective questioning may be thought to have developed in response to the increased specialisation and bureaucratisation of government.

The post-war growth in the rate of parliamentary questions has been particularly marked in Iceland. Since 1945 there has been no less than a thirteenfold increase in the number of questions tabled annually in the Althing, the vast majority of them receiving a ministerial response. The institution of Question Time itself is the oldest in the Nordic region dating back to the creation of a two-division Althing in 1874, although until the Second World War the number of questions submitted each year amounted to single figures only. Questions, *syrirspurnir*, are tabled for oral or written response: the Speaker of the United Althing calls on a member to introduce his question, after which the appropriate minister reads out a prepared reply. The questioner is allowed to speak twice, including a supplementary, though not for more than five minutes at a time; the minister in responding usually makes two speeches which must not last longer than ten minutes each. In a format later introduced into Denmark, other ministers and parliamentarians can speak in question debates for a maximum of two minutes each. Question Time in the United Althing lasts on average about two hours.

The interrogation of the administration was regularised in Denmark in 1947 when it became possible for the first time for Folketing delegates to put questions to cabinet ministers. This must be done in writing and accompanied by a request for either a written response, *skriftlige spørgsmål til ministre* — which is not discussed in plenary, but should be answered within six days — or alternatively an oral reply from the minister, *mundlige spørgsmål*, at the Folketing's weekly Question Time. Oral questions, which have become the more popular of the two forms, are submitted only two days in advance — theoretically the swiftest rate of ministerial response in the region — the minister being limited to a reply of three minutes. With a view to a more thoroughgoing and lively elaboration of the matter at hand, the opportunity for members other than the questioner to speak after the minister's reply was introduced into the 1972–3 session of the Folketing. Conventionally, two other delegates at most can make short contributions, with the result that question debates last on average about fourteen minutes.[36]

A concern to enhance delegate participation and enliven proceedings on the floor of the Storting underpinned the institution of Question Time in Norway in 1950. This meant there are now two sub-types of question. 'Long questions', *grunngitt spørsmål*, must be answered within two months of their submission: when taken up in the assembly, a delegate can elaborate on his question for not more than five minutes, and the cabinet minister has the same length of time to reply — although with the Storting's permission this can be extended to ten minutes. Thereafter both questioner and minister have the right to one further, albeit brief, contribution and, in the former's case, this can take the form of a supplementary question. 'Short questions', *spørretimespørsmål*, are answered at the regular Wednesday question time and should be submitted by the previous Friday morning. They are printed and distributed to members of the Storting at the beginning of Question Time. A delegate puts his question without any exposition to the appropriate minister and, assuming he consents to answer, both he and the questioner have the right to a further short contribution.[37]

In Sweden the possibility of putting questions to ministers was introduced into both chambers of the Riksdag in 1938; then in 1949 it was ruled that only the questioner and responding minister could participate in question debates. Questions were used sparingly in the 1940s but, inspired by Norwegian practice, interest grew in introducing a regular Question Time. A Constitutional Committee initiative in 1955 recommended that individual questions should be answered at regular intervals a few days after their submission and that, to increase general interest in Question Time, both questioners and responding ministers should voluntarily impose a time limit on their statements. Nothing came of the matter then, although following a subsequent government proposal, the first Question Time was held in Sweden on 21 April 1964. The result was a significant increase in the number of questions tabled: from about a dozen a year in 1964 to 70–90 in the First Chamber in the late 1960s and nearly 300 in the Second Chamber in the last years of its existence. Even in the year when Question Time was introduced, questions became more numerous than interpellations in both houses of the Riksdag.[38]

The transition to unicameralism in Sweden brought a restatement of the rules on questions. Today the Riksdag's Standing Orders recommend that a question be answered at a question time held at the earliest six days after its submission, while by a parliamentary decision of autumn 1972 the first speech of both questioner and minister is limited to 3 minutes, the second 2 minutes and subsequent contributions to no more than one minute.[39] In consequence, question debates in Sweden last about seven or eight minutes. Question Time itself is held twice weekly on a Tuesday afternoon and on Thursday at noon.

Finland adopted Question Time in 1966, two years after Sweden. Previously, there had only been the so-called 'written question', *kirjallinen kysymys*, introduced by legislation in December 1917 and confirmed by the Parliament Act of 1928 where it was referred to as an 'ordinary question' — in contrast to the interpellation. A cabinet minister is required to respond to a written question within 30 days, and following legislation in 1948 this has invariably been in writing. At question time, however, 'oral questions', *suulliset kysymykset*, are put — in precisely the same form as in the text submitted earlier and ministers are not obliged to respond until the third day after receipt of the question. Question Time lasts a maximum of one hour (unless the Speaker decides otherwise), no more than two supplementaries are allowed and delegates may not table more than two 'oral questions' in one week.[40]

Hardly surprisingly in view of the post-war growth in the scale and scope of government, there has been a general increase in the rate of parliamentary questions in the Nordic region. Evidence of this in Iceland and Sweden has already been presented *en passant*. Equally, however, the increase has been uneven. Denmark illustrates the point. The average yearly rate of questions from their inception as a parliamentary institution in 1947 to the introduction of a single chamber system in 1953 was only 66 for the Folketing and less than one for the Landsting. It remained under 100 per year in the 1950s, but rose markedly from the end of the 1960s. From an annual mean of over 300 parliamentary questions in the late 1960s, the rate rose to an all-time record of 476 in 1973–4.[41] How is this fitful progression to be explained? Why has the enormous post-war increase in the number of parliamentary questions tabled annually in the Nordic states tended to take place in short 'surges', often followed by a period of retrenchment and decline? What do the oscillations on the graph, so to speak, indicate about the deployment of questions in the region?

The unsteady growth curve can perhaps be understood in the light of three factors. The first, can be described under the heading 'technical factors'. Clearly, changes in the formal rules relating to parliamentary questions can affect the frequency with which they are tabled. At least part of the recent increase in the rate of questions submitted in Sweden, for instance, has been tied to a liberalisation of the regulations relating to the questioning of ministers. Thus in the autumn of 1972, the Riksdag abolished the restriction that a delegate be limited to two contributions per question. This has meant that Sweden, alone of the Nordic countries, although restricting both the extent of participation at question debates and the length of speeches, imposes no limit on the *number* of exchanges that are permitted.

A more substantial second variable in the analysis has been the changing dynamics of the legislative-executive balance. To emphasise this point, we must ask: Who uses parliamentary questions? In this connection, have there been any discernible trends in the distribution of questions in the assembly? And finally, in what circumstances are they likely to prove most effective? When, in short, do groups inclined to use questions perceive that they will be most effective? The distribution of questions in the Nordic parliaments reveals — perhaps not unexpectedly — that opposition parties have a far greater propensity for using questions than groups in government. Typically, over the twenty-year period following the transition to unicameralism in Denmark in 1953, an average of no less than 80% of questions in the Folketing were tabled by opposition parties. In Finland, a breakdown of 'oral questions' in the Eduskunta during the spring session of 1981 showed that the largest governing party, the Social Democrats, with over 25% of the parliamentary seats were responsible for only 12% of the 'oral questions' and their main non-socialist coalition allies, the Centre Party, for only 8% (see Table 8.1). Moreover, in the 1979–80 session of the Althing, ten times as many 'urgency questions' were submitted by the opposition as by the government side, and although the ratio between the two has varied somewhat in recent years, it has rarely been less than 2:1 in the opposition's favour.

In so far, therefore, as questions plainly constitute a weapon in the opposition's armoury, it would seem reasonable to suggest that there is likely to be a higher incidence of parliamentary questions

Table 8.1. DISTRIBUTION OF ORAL QUESTIONS BY PARTY IN THE SPRING 1981 SESSION OF THE FINNISH EDUSKUNTA

Party	*No. of delegates*	*No. of oral questions*	*% of Total no. of oral questions*
Social Democrats*	52	34	12
Conservatives	46	30	11
Centre*	37	23	8
People's Democratic League*†	35	53	19
Christian League	10	33	12
Swedish People's Party*	10	19	7
Rural Party	6	72	26
Liberal People's Party	4	11	4
	200	275	100

*Governing party.

†The hardline Sinisalo Communists within the People's Democratic League remained in opposition.

Source: Suullisia kysymyksiä. Eduskunnan kevätistunto 1981.

during periods of unstable and/or minority administration — when the opposition will naturally tend to intensify its activities — than in conditions of stable majority government. There is evidence in support of such reasoning. Damgaard notes that in Denmark the mean variation in the rate of parliamentary questions is largely explained in terms of the parliamentary base of the administration in power. The proportion of opposition questions to ministers dropped to 69% of all questions during the two periods of strongest post-war government — 1957–60 when the Social Democrats, Radicals and Justice Party were in office, and 1968–71 when a three-party bourgeois coalition was in power — but increased to 96% during the very weak Liberal minority of 1973–4.[42] In sum, the rate of parliamentary questions is likely to rise during periods of numerically weak and/or unstable government.

A third and final element in the uneven post-war rise in parliamentary questions in the Nordic region appears to be the structure of the legislative opposition. It is a fair surmise that when the parliamentary opposition is fragmented by the existence of small and/or radical parties — tangential to the formal power structure in being denied significant access to committees and commissions — the rate of parliamentary questions will be greater than when there is a cohesive and unilateral opposition. In this context, the impact of the general polarisation of the Nordic party systems in the last decade and more has been unmistakable. In Finland, although over one-third of the governing Social Democratic Party's backbenchers did not table a single 'oral question' during the spring 1981 Eduskunta session, the populist-style Rural Party, the second smallest group with only 3% of all parliamentary delegates, accounted for 26% of the total number of these questions (see Table 8.1). Its former chairman and founder Veikko Vennamo, the Rural Party's Presidential candidate in 1968, 1978 and 1982, tabled himself a mere six questions less than all the Social Democrats put together. In Sweden, the Left Communists, successfully negotiating the 4% electoral threshold, put down more interpellations per delegate than any other party in the unicameral Riksdag in the 1970s as Table 8.2 illustrates. Finally, the heightened incidence of interpellations in Denmark in recent years appears directly attributable to the activity of the small, radical parties, especially those of the Left. Ten interpellations, *føresporgsler*, were tabled in the Folketing between October 1982 and January 1983: one from the Social Democrats, the main opposition party, asking what initiatives the government had taken to alleviate the serious state of unemployment was routine enough (earlier the same year the Social Democrats in power had pushed through their so-called 'March package' of measures — see

Table 8.2. NUMBER OF INTERPELLATIONS PER DELEGATE PER PARTY IN THE UNICAMERAL RIKSDAG, 1971–80

Parliamentary Session	*Conservatives*	*Liberals*	*Centre*	*Social Democrats*	*Left Communists*
1971–3	0.9	1.1	0.8	0.2	1.7
1974, 1975/6	0.8	0.6	0.7	0.1	1.3
1976/7, 1977/8	0.2	0.5	0.4	0.4	1.6
1978–1979	0.4	0.2	0.5	0.3	1.6
1979–1980	0.4	0.6	0.5	0.4	2.6

Source: Konstitutionsutskottets betänkande 1980/81:25. *Granskningsbetänkande*, p. 161.

chapter 3 — precisely to deal with unemployment, particularly among the young); a second, signed by a number of governing parties as well as the anti-tax Progress Party and the Radical Left, concerned the question of humane adoption and was not of a partisan character. All the rest were instigated by the tiny Socialist People's Party either alone or in league with other groups. The extraordinarily large number of interpellations tabled during the first three months of Schlüter's bourgeois minority coalition should be seen in perspective: over much of the post-war period, the rate of interpellations was low at about 5 or 6 annually and Damgaard was able to note in the late 1970s that it had not exceeded ten per annum for 100 years![43]

We have, therefore, the fragmentation and radicalisation of opposition in the Nordic parliaments in the 1970s; periods of minority or weak majority government; a liberalisation and development of the rules relating to the interrogation of ministers; and of course the government's record of handling controversial issues, together with the number and nature of these issues. These together provide a framework within which we can analyse the uneven character of the growth in the rate of questions tabled in the region after the war.

Particularly for the larger opposition parties, putting down parliamentary questions has been a useful method of being seen to oppose the government. Questions have also represented a means of forcing the government to be accountable for its actions, and a way of contriving a general debate at which alternative policy options can be paraded. The highly visible nature of the opposition generated through parliamentary questions is remarkable in a group of democracies which have traditionally tended towards inter-élite consultation on important issues and the role of what Giovanni Sartori calls 'hidden politics' — backstage negotiation, bargaining and consensus-building away from the spotlight of day-to-day parliamentary affairs. A controversial or topical issue raised through an opposition party question or interpellation has invariably involved a degree of posturing for public consumption. For the smaller opposition parties, often with nothing more than the slenderest toehold on the parliamentary standing committees, questions provide the means of heightening their profiles with voters and defying both government and larger opposition party(ies). This is somewhat obvious; however, in the absence of days specifically set aside for the opposition in the manner of Supply Days at Westminster, the strategic importance of questions is considerable.

As a procedure for launching a partisan offensive against the government, interpellations have been more effective than questions, simply because they permit a plenary account debate. During the crisis caused by the discovery of a Soviet submarine in Swedish territorial waters in October 1981, the Social Democratic leader Olof Palme used the vehicle of an interpellation strenuously to criticise remarks reputedly made by the Minister of Defence in a press interview the previous August. According to Palme, the Minister's comments implied that Swedish neutrality was in reality a fiction and would not prevent military co-operation with those nations which Sweden regarded as her 'natural friends' if the need arose.[44] It cannot be doubted that Palme's interpellation was, in large part, a signal directed to a highly-charged public opinion; for it is equally certain that consultations between government and opposition must have taken place behind the scenes on a matter of such delicacy. Nevertheless, the Social Democratic leader was clearly putting a question of genuinely widespread concern and in turn making legitimate political capital out of it.

In Finland, even interpellations which fail to secure the necessary sponsorship by 20 delegates can attract a measure of publicity. An interpellation tabled by a Liberal delegate in February 1981 on the need to return taxation powers to the legislature gained the backing of only the 4-strong Liberal group in parliament and was lost.[45] The same fate, moreover, befell an attempted interpellation in September 1981 from Pekka Vennamo and the 5 other Rural Party delegates on the condition of war veterans, despite its bold assertion that Finland's war veterans had waited over 40 years for the recognition and support they deserve from society.[46] Both, however, were widely covered in the organs of the two parties and indeed beyond. Equally fruitless, though tactically more adroit, was the attempt in November 1982 by the Christian League (with 10 parliamentarians) to mobilise support — that is at least 10 delegates from the ranks of the Rural and Conservative parties — for an interpellation criticising the increase in fuel costs in the middle of a government price freeze. The Conservatives' backing, a *sine qua non* of the interpellation being adequately supported, was not forthcoming and the proposed interpellation was submitted in the form of an ordinary 'written question'.[47] The Conservatives in fact waited until just before the 1983 general election to table an interpellation — on the economy, unemployment, taxation and state debts — and in this way secured themselves some added election propaganda. Even if interpellations succeed in getting the necessary backing from delegates, they invariably fail in a second sense, namely in not bringing about a defeat for the government in the ensuing vote. Nonetheless, as soon as the data of the Prime Minister's reply to the interpellation is announced, media interest grows; and although, in the nature of the legislative-executive balance, the outcome is usually a foregone conclusion, this does not prevent a hard-hitting debate in which the opposition can score a few tactical points. The opposition, in short, is seen to be opposing.

Given the foregoing analysis, it is somewhat surprising that interpellations are not the exclusive preserve of opposition parties: even in Finland, where they imply the possibility of a no confidence vote in the government, they are tabled by members on the governing side. This has usually happened during periods of majority coalition, although interpellations and questions have also been submitted by members of parties involved in a minority government, especially a non-socialist one. As Kari Joutsamo has observed, there has been a tendency for centre-based groups in particular to table interpellations when in government.[48] Why should this be? Why do rank-and-file delegates in the Nordic states publicly interrogate their 'own' cabinet ministers when not only could this be construed as evidence of division in the party, but the dialogue could also take place in the privacy of a meeting of the parliamentary party group? Two explanations suggest themselves.

First, it is quite conceivable that one source of interpellations and questions on the governing side is the minister himself in that suitably primed questions can provide him with an excellent opportunity to explain himself to parliament, announce future legislative plans, and point to other developments such as the creation of a commission of inquiry, the completion of a commission report, an intended visit and so on. This is a common practice at Westminster where government MPs are fed questions by the minister, and it can surely not be discounted in the Nordic states. Equally, however, Magnus Isberg's interviews with the staff directors of the various Riksdag party groups indicate that the vast majority of routine questions and interpellations constitute independent action on the part of parliamentarians — not only in the formal sense, but in the real political sense that the party organisations (the executive committees, policy committees and party staff) only rarely initiate parliamentary questions, even when a party is in opposition.[49] This being the case, an alternative explanation appears in order: namely, that delegates on the governing side (as well as those in opposition) use parliamentary questions to seek out information and/or promote a debate on a matter relating to the interests of their region or constituency. They act in short in one of the basic roles of the Nordic parliamentarian — the role of localist. But before considering the validity of this view, we should briefly note the primary roles of delegates in the region.

It was argued in chapter 1 that the increasing body of survey evidence pointing to a decline in the popular standing of the Nordic parliaments does not *ipso facto* confirm what Coombes and Walkland refer to as a fundamental decline of parliaments relative to the classical ideas of parliamentary democracy.[50] On three counts, however, the Nordic legislators scarcely appear representative in the traditional sense set out by Edmund Burke. First and foremost, they are *partisans* — party members before members of parliament — and this is reinforced by the stranglehold parties exercise over candidate recruitment. In the present context, evidence of the all-pervasive party-politicisation process — in relation to the plenary machinery for interrogating ministers — was observed in the distribution patterns of questions in the assembly, the use of interpellations to launch partisan offensives against the government etc. Secondly, delegates soon become (if they are not already) *specialists* — long periods of service on a subject-specific standing committee and the personnel overlap between the standing committees and the internal policy committees of the parliamentary groups are responsible for this. The questions and interpellations tabled by members clearly reflect the nature of their expertise: indeed, a significant number of parliamentary questions fall within the policy sector of the standing committee to which the questioner belongs. Finally, Nordic legislators are *localists* — spokesmen for the main interests in their own localities rather than proponents of the national interest. In short, they are members for Norrköping, Buskerud or Vestmannaeyjar rather than members of the Riksdag, Storting or Althing. Sten Sparre Nilson notes that 'in many matters the men and women of the Storting feel they represent the particular interests of a specific region.'[51] The role of localist is encouraged by the regional seating of delegates in the Storting and Riksdag and it can come into conflict with the partisan loyalties of members. In practice, of course, it is difficult to separate the roles of specialist and localist: a delegate for example, might develop an expertise on a standing committee to which he was elected initially on the basis of its relevance to the predominant interest of his region — e.g. Traffic, Agriculture, Shipping and Fisheries, Communal Affairs, or Housing. The two roles overlap and reinforce each other. Indeed, while it is true that many questions are located in the area covered by the questioner's standing committee — an apparent case of him acting as a specialist — this is not to say the delegate was not mainly preoccupied with regional matters when tabling the question. Hence the Nordic parliamentarian's role of localist is analytically distinct and important, and is reflected in the content and type of question tabled in the assembly, as a few examples will illustrate.

The subject-matter of a question or interpellation tabled by a delegate on the government side will often deal with a matter of essentially local character. There was a question from a Centre Party delegate in late 1981 which was concerned with whether a textile firm managed along co-operative lines in the small Swedish town of Enköping would receive financial support from the government in order to expand production.[52] It elicited the useful information from the Centre Party's Minister of Industry, Nils G. Åsling, that a related bill was planned for the spring of 1982. Much less encouraging was the response given by the Social Democratic Minister for Labour Market Affairs, Anna-Greta Leijon, in March 1983 to an interpellation from a delegate for the pro-government Left-Communist Party which requested a package of measures to deal with unemployment in Värmland along the lines of the government's proposal for the outlying province of Norrbotten in northern Sweden. His demand for a working group to produce a long-term plan on industrial development and redeployment in Värmland was rejected.[53] The previous autumn, the Social Democratic Defence Minister was called upon to answer a question from a backbench member of his party which expressed concern that the facilities for the emergency transportation of the sick by military helicopters — particularly relating to round-the-clock manning of these helicopters — were inferior in his area of Söderhamn in northern Sweden than those in central and southern Sweden. The minister responded that he agreed with the point of the question, but that in practice limited resources had compelled a prioritisation exercise.[54] Examples from the other four Nordic states would confirm that delegates on the government side regularly function as localists when putting questions to their 'own' ministers.

Secondly, there is further evidence of localism in the concentration of parliamentary questions on those government ministries involved in the management of regional policy. Again Swedish data are appropriate. During the 1979–80 Riksdag session, just over 23% of all interpellations were directed to the Ministry of Industry. This was well over twice the amount going to the Ministry of Agriculture (which received the second highest number) and almost three times as many as the Foreign Ministry with the third highest number. The Industry Minister, in fact, answered almost one-fifth of all interpellations and questions in that session, which undoubtedly reflected the importance to delegates of promoting the regional economic interests of their constituencies. In 1977 the Ministry of Industry, already charged with responsibility for the industry and energy fields, took on regional questions too. In Finland, the three main departments dealing with regional matters, Trade and Industry, Agriculture and Forestry and Transportation accounted between them for almost one-third of the total of written questions answered in the 1980–1 Eduskunta session. Throughout the region, moreover, the parliamentary standing committees on Industry have been among the most sought-after in recent years.

The heightened propensity of Finnish delegates to table 'written questions' provides yet further evidence of the way Nordic parliamentarians act as localists. The number of written questions tabled annually in Finland grew almost threefold between 1970 and 1980, whereas the number of 'oral questions' fell slightly. Replies to 'oral questions' have in practice been delayed and their consideration in the Eduskunta postponed sometimes as many as 3–4 times before a ministerial response has been forthcoming. Despite the formal rules, in other words, 'oral questions' have not afforded a significantly quicker response than 'written questions'. The latter, however, tend to focus on local issues and permit the delegate a useful means of obtaining a detailed and official statement on a matter of particular interest to his constituents.[55] Put another way, answers to written questions invariably sent to, and reported in, the press provide an important link with constituents and one consolidating the localist perspective and role of parliamentarians, not only in Finland but in the rest of the region.

Hence the institution of parliamentary questions in the Nordic states performs a number of valuable functions. In the hands of individual delegates, questions serve as a channel of communication between legislature and executive, and one relatively little dominated by the political parties. Parliamentarians have generally had greater licence in tabling questions than in promoting legislative initiatives, for in the latter case they frequently act as the mouthpiece of their party. Parliamentary questions have often served as the vehicle with which delegates, whether in government or opposition, have been able to pursue local issues, pressurise the government into action, and of course justify themselves to their electors. However localism, although important, is not the only motivation behind parliamentary questions. Recent questions in Sweden have ranged across a wide variety of issues — the possible transportation of Norwegian war materials across Swedish territory, the inclusion of the Baltic Sea in a non-nuclear zone, inter-Nordic consultations on the question of so-called internationally adopted children, the co-ordination of Cable TV projects, a new system of state support for child care, the operation of a reduced rate travel system for pensioners on the railways, stiffer penalties on illicit fishing within Sweden fishing zones and a change in the procedures for admitting pupils to the sixth form of schools, to cite but a few. Moreover, precisely because questions — unlike private initiatives which (outside Finland) are effectively confined to a brief General Initiatives Period — may be tabled throughout the legislative calendar, they may be used to originate new ideas and place fresh issues on the political agenda. In the hands of the party spokesmen and party leaders, interpellations give greater visibility to the opposition by enforcing discussion on politically sensitive and topical issues: this is equally true of those Nordic countries where interpellations lead to a vote — and therefore possess an implicit sanction — and those where they do not. In the former countries media interest is of course likely to be greater, particularly in Finland where, since the advent of broad centre-left coalitions in 1966, the one or two interpellations moved annually by the leading opposition party, the Conservatives, invariably dealing with major economic issues, have amounted to motions of no confidence in the government. Finally, parliamentary questions are used across the region by the small radical parties not well represented on the important commissions and parliamentary standing committees to criticise those in power, extract information on government plans and above all identify and project themselves to voters. They deploy, in short, a more adversarial style in the chamber than the larger groups.

It might be contended that the task of controlling the executive on the floor of the assembly cannot be seen in isolation from other control mechanisms (dealt with in chapter 9) and that, in any case, checks operate through the whole institutional apparatus of the legislature: the parliamentary appointment of governments, their corresponding accountability to the assembly, the detailed examination and inspection of the executive by the standing committees, and the involvement of legislators on commissions of inquiry. When seen thus, questions, although the most overt means of controlling the government, are perhaps the least important one. It might be argued, too, that attempts to modernise the traditional system of interrogating ministers with the introduction of Westminster-style question times have proved largely cosmetic and that the primary function of questions is to allow delegates a heightened sense of personal competence.

Obviously parliamentary questions cannot be divorced from trends occurring throughout the policy process. More particularly, questions are plainly a reflection of the growing specialisation of parliamentary proceedings which has in turn resulted from the growth in the scope and complexity of central government. This is amply demonstrated in Erik Damgaard's detailed analysis of two Folketing sessions in the early 1970s, in which a clear majority of questions fell within the policy area of the questioner's parliamentary standing committee.[56] In many ways, of course, this is the product of the need for legislators to concentrate their attentions on one area of policy. A detailed survey among Finnish parliamentarians by Matti Oksanen showed that 56% of delegates believed specialisation to be more important to the work of the Eduskunta than retaining a generalist's perspective, whereas only 14% held the opposite view. Significantly, only 9% of delegates admitted to not having specialised in a single policy field.[57] Obviously such expertise is likely to enhance the capacity of individual delegates to cross-examine the executive: it is even conceivable that a delegate will be more familiar with a topic than an incoming minister. Equally, the level of delegate expertise required to probe the activities of the governmental machine has, potentially at least, important implications for the ability of the Nordic parliaments *as a whole* to check the executive. As the studies by Gudmund Hernes in Norway and Erik Damgaard in Denmark have demonstrated, the Storting and Folketing comprise a number of specialist sub-systems that are mutually interconnected to a far smaller extent than each is integrated with the parallel structures in the central administration.

In view of the sectoral specialisation evident both in parliamentary questions and contributions to plenary account debates (the inspection work of standing parliamentary committees will be discussed in the next chapter), it seems probable that the assemblies in the region do not exercise sufficient overall control over decisions made within the various sectors. Yet if the collective *policy control* of the Nordic parliaments is limited by the demands of interrogating ministers who are responsible for a highly technocratic state machine, the classical machinery for the *political control* of the executive from the floor of the assembly — via interpellations and no confidence votes — has continued to function impeccably.

REFERENCES

1. SFO 5:29.
2. VJ 3:36.
3. FOF 8:19:3–5.
4. RO 3:6.
5. 'Ympäristöhallinto eduskuntaan'. *Kristityn Vastuu* 6.5.1982.
6. 'Mange saker i vårsesjonen'. *Nordisk Kontakt* 4/82, p. 324.
7. 'Stortingsmelding om oljevirksomheten i Nord'. *Nordisk Kontakt* 4/82, p. 324.
8. 'Stortinget "drukner" i omfangsrike meldinger'. *Aftenposten* 21.1.1978.
9. 'Glatt á hjalla aður en alvaran tekur við.' *Dagblaðið* 12.10.1981.
10. Thingsköp Althingis, pp. 33–4.
11. *Ulkoasiainvaliokunnan mietintö no 26* hallituksen toimeenpiteistään vuonna 1980 antaman kertomuksen johdosta siltä osin kuin koskee suhteista ulkovaltoihin 8.12.1981.
12. Rommetvedt (1981), p. 9.
13. Birgersson *et al.* (1981), p. 287.
14. Skard (1980), p. 181.
15. Kastari (1977), p. 164.
16. 'Uutisankka, Vaihtoehdot'. *Nykypäivä* 14, 1981.
17. 'Parlamentarismin oppitunti'. *Kristityn Vastuu* 6.1.1983.
18. FOF 8:19:3.
19. Fortryk af folketingets forhandlinger (42), 14.10.1982, pp. 663–4.
20. Kekkonen (1976), 30.8.1971.
21. Urho Kekkonen, *Vallankäyttö ja vastuu*. Eduskunta, valtioneuvosto, tasavallan presidentti. Juhlajulkaisu Urho Kaleva Kekkonen 1900.3/9.1975, p. 5.
22. Paavo Kastari, 'The Position of the President in the Finnish Political System'. *Scandinavian Political Studies*, 4, 1969, p. 158.
23. 'Strid om sikkerhetspolitikken'. *Nordisk Kontakt* 16/82, pp. 1258–60.
24. *Vuoden 1980 valtiopäivät*. Pöytäkirjat 4, pp. 4190–4.
25. 'Mistillit til regjeringen avvist med 31 mot 29 stemmer'. *Nordisk Kontakt* 16/82, pp. 1248–9.
26. 'Hallitus kaatui Ahvenanmaalla'. *Uusi Suomi* 19.3.1983.
27. Rommetvedt (1981), p. 10.
28. Interview with Magnus Isberg 5.10.1981.
29. *Folketinget 1981/82*. Til forespørgsel nr F2. Blad nr 210. Forslag om motiveret dagsorden (Den 12 november 1981) af Niels Helveg Petersen.
30. *Folketinget 1981/82*. Til forespørgsel nr F2. Blad nr 208.
31. Discussion with the Deputy Information Secretary in the Folketing, *Kurt Andersen* 19.1.1983. The press highlighted the alternatives open to Jørgensen.
32. *Folketinget 1982/83*. Forespørgsel nr F4. Blad nr 148.
33. Olsen (1980), p. 212.
34. Discussion on 'Newsnight'. BBC 2 Television 3.2.1983.
35. Information provided by Jouni Vainio 1.10.1982.
36. Erik Damgaard, *Folketinget under forandring. Aspekter af Folketingets udvickling, virkemåde og stilling i det politiske system*. København: Samfundsvidenskabeligt forlag, 1977.
37. SFO 9:51–3.
38. *Konstitutionsutskottets betänkande 1980/81:25*. Granskningsbetänkande. Bilaga 8. PM angående interpellationer och frågor, p. 149.
39. RO 6:1:2–6:2:2.
40. VJ 3:37a. ET 52a.
41. Damgaard (1977), p. 44.

42. Ibid., p. 45.
43. Ibid., p. 44.
44. 'Försvarsministerns uttalanden förvanskade'. *Från Riksdag & Departement* 13.11.1981.
45. *Ed. Kivitie. Verotusvallan palauttamisesta eduskunnalle* 24.2.1981 Esitelty 27.2. 1981. Rauennut.
46. P. Vennamo ym. Välikysymys, joka koskee sotaveteraanien ja invalidien aseman parantamista. *Valtiopäivät 1980/81*. Pöytäkirjat, pp. 1848–9.
47. 'SKL yrittää välikysymystä'. *Kristityn Vastuu* 2.12.1982.
48. Kari Joutsamo, *Välikysymys parlamentarismin ilmentäjä Suomessa*. Turun yliopisto 1972, pp. 147, 159, 161.
49. Isberg (1982), p. 73.
50. Coombes & Walkland (1980), p. 3.
51. Nilson (1977), p. 2.
52. 'Framtidsutsikter för Eisers textilföretag'. *Från Riksdag & Departement* 4.12.1981.
53. '"Norrbottens-satsning" inte möjlig i alla län'. *Från Riksdag & Departement* 25.3.1983.
54. 'Sjuktranporter med helikopter'. *Från Riksdag & Departement* 3.12.1982.
55. Interview with Jouni Vainio 22.12.1981.
56. Damgaard (1977), p. 194.
57. Oksanen (1972), pp. 127, 145–6, 310.

9

INSPECTING THE GOVERNMENT IN PARLIAMENTARY COMMISSIONS, COUNCILS AND STANDING COMMITTEES

> 'The Riksdag Constitutional Committee's review is nearly as much politicised as its consideration of legislative matters. It could hardly be otherwise when one political body, the Committee, is judging the actions of another, the Government.' — Magnus Isberg, *The First Decade of the Unicameral Riksdag* (1982), p. 68

In this chapter we examine the inspection and control of the executive in parliamentary commissions, councils and standing committees, and attempt to gauge the influence of the Nordic parliaments over policy implementation. The opening section focuses on the use of *ad hoc* parliamentary commissions appointed by the assembly to investigate a range of administrative matters including suspected ministeriai malpractice and incompetence. In exceptional circumstances these can lead to impeachment proceedings. The next section deals with the distinctive category of special Parliamentary Advisory Councils on Foreign Affairs, located in the three constitutional monarchies in the region, which afford parliament a role in what was a traditional preserve of the King. All Nordic standing committees have inquiry powers: they can cross-examine ministers, under-secretaries and civil servants in connection with both the deliberation of legislative proposals before the committee and, more widely, the application of previously enacted legislation. The third section considers the inspection of the executive in standing committee and concentrates on the handful of standing committees with statutory inquiry functions — the Government Review Committees of Parliament. Outside Iceland, all the Nordic parliaments elect Parliamentary Ombudsmen (one or more) to act as agents of the legislature in overseeing the detailed application of laws by officials. The fourth section discusses the work of the Ombudsmen and their relations with parliament. Finally, after a recapitulation of the main themes of Part III of this book, the role of the Nordic parliaments in policy implementation is evaluated in a wider comparative perspective.

Ad hoc parliamentary commissions of investigation and the impeachment of ministers

On the basis of article 19 of the Danish constitution, the Folketing is empowered to set up commissions of its members, *parlamentariske kommissioner* — elected to reflect the partisan balance in the assembly — to investigate matters of general importance, these commissions being entitled to demand written and oral evidence from private citizens as well as from public officials.[1] Exactly the same right exists under article 39 of the Icelandic constitution. These parliamentary commissions of investigation should not be confused with commissions of inquiry, which are primarily engaged in the policy formulation process and, although they occasionally result from parliamentary pressure, only rarely involve parliamentarians. Rather, in Denmark and Iceland the constitution allows elected representatives of the people to create *ad hoc* commissions to investigate a range of matters, including suspected ministerial incompetence. However, parliamentary commissions have been rare in recent years: the last was nominated in Iceland in 1955 and the last in Denmark in 1945. Elsewhere in the region, the procedures for investigating matters of public significance — *inter alia* the legality of ministerial actions — are rather different.

The right to form parliamentary commissions of investigation in Denmark, which was initially incorporated into the 1849 constitution, should be seen as a further step in the development of the Folketing's machinery for controlling the executive, while the extensive deployment of these commissions in the second half of the nineteenth century was very much a response to the inadequacy of the rules on interpellations which were also built into the 1849 constitution. Before the breakthrough of parliamentarism, commissions of investigation were used partly to examine general legislative matters and partly too as a way of analysing the case for the possible impeachment of a cabinet minister or ministers. Since 1901, however, there have been only two of these commissions — one in 1918 and another set up on 15 June 1945 to look into the German invasion in 1940, the concessions after the occupation, and more particularly whether action was necessary against the government or any of its members. The commission's mandate was renewed after each of the first three post-war general elections in 1945, 1947 and 1950, and by 1953 it had produced no less than fourteen comprehensive reports. However, in 1955 the Folketing resolved by 153 votes to the 8 of the Communist delegates not to go ahead with an impeachment.[2] Since then, the practice has been to reject proposals to set up parliamentary commissions of investigation. Folketing pressure may of course result in the creation of an independent commission to examine the conduct of a cabinet minister. Following a scandal in the Post and Telecommunications Service which surfaced in October 1981 and broad cross-party agitation for an inquiry, the Minister of Justice Ole Espersen took the relatively unusual step in January 1982 of setting up a three-person legal commission, *kommissionsdomstol* (members of legal commissions must all possess formal training as judges) to appraise the whole affair.[3]

If, following the report of a parliamentary commission of investigation (or similar inquiry), the Folketing decides to proceed with an impeachment case against a minister, this is conducted, according to article 16 of the constitution, in the High Court of the Realm — half of whose members are elected by the Folketing. Ministers sentenced in the High Court may, however, be granted a royal pardon subject to the Folketing's consent. Unlike Norway, a strict separation of legislature and judiciary is maintained by the rule that no Folketing member can be elected to serve on the High Court of the Realm.[4]

In Sweden and Finland, where there are no provisions for the creation of *ad hoc* parliamentary commissions of investigation, any evidence of illegality, or maladministration relating to a cabinet minister or ministers is examined by the Constitutional Committee of Parliament. Distinctively in Sweden, the decision to proceed with a trial is also the prerogative of the Constitutional Committee. In the words of the new constitution, a person who is or has been a minister can be prosecuted only when he has gravely neglected his duties or abused his office. The decision to go ahead with a prosecution is taken by the Constitutional Committee and heard in the High Court of the Realm, *högsta domstolen.*[5] Evidence of such palpable dereliction of duty is invariably collected as part of the Constitutional Committee's annual review of government (see pp. 381 ff.) in the course of which the offending minister(s) will be cross-examined by committee members. The Constitutional Committee is free to initiate any investigation it sees fit into the work of the government and its departments. If the Riksdag is not satisfied with the conclusions contained in the Constitutional Committee's annual report regarding a question of ministerial misdemeanour, a motion of no confidence can, of course, be tabled when the report is debated on the floor of the assembly. An individual minister was last forced to resign following action in the Riksdag in 1929. As in Denmark, it is commonplace for ministers under pressure from the Riksdag to set up independent commissions of inquiry, *utredningar*, to examine other matters of general public significance.

In Finland the preparatory work in the event of the possible impeachment of one or more members of the government is undertaken by the Eduskunta's Constitutional Committee acting as in Sweden as a type of permanent parliamentary commission of inquiry. In accordance with the Parliamentary Standing Orders of July 1906, confirmed by separate statute in 1922, the Constitutional Committee has authority to inspect the legality of the actions of cabinet ministers and the Chancellor of Justice. This can happen in three ways: at the instigation of the Constitutional Committee in connection with a matter it is examining; as a result of another parliamentary standing committee referring a question to the Constitutional Committee; or when a request for a reprimand to a government minister is tabled by at least five delegates in the assembly (this is sent to the Constitutional Committee for scrutiny without a plenary debate).[6] The provision facilitating a members' request for a minister to receive an official reproach was last invoked in 1978 when a special sub-committee was created within the Constitutional Committee to investigate a petition from the Rural Party against the entire cabinet concerning the financial problems of the state-owned enterprise Valco. This was highly unusual. That impeachment proceedings were not ultimately resorted to — despite the exhaustive and protracted investigations undertaken by the Constitutional Committee — was due in no small measure to the high ceiling placed on culpability by article 7 of the 1922 statute. In line with this, the accused person(s) must have been guilty of plainly illegal activity or have deliberately abused his office to the detriment of the nation at large. Even so, the Constitutional Committee was unanimous in reprimanding two ministers who had distorted facts about the parlous state of the Valco company.

If the Eduskunta decides to impeach a minister, a special Court of Impeachment is set up with half its members elected by parliament and the other half comprising the Presidents of the Supreme Court, Supreme Administrative Court and all four Courts of Appeal together with one member of the Law Faculty in the University of Helsinki. On two occasions, in 1952 and 1961, this procedure has resulted in ministers being fined for corruption and carelessness.

In Norway complaints about the legality of a ministerial action, along with evidence for possible impeachment proceedings, are investigated by a Protocol Committee, elected in accordance with article 14a of the Storting's Standing Orders from among the members of the Odelsting. The Protocol Committee may be regarded for all practical purposes as an ad hoc parliamentary commission of investigation. It was abolished as a permanent institution in 1972, but following subsequent doubts as to whether this had been a wise action, its more general functions were assumed in 1981 by the Scrutiny Committee, *kontrollkomitéen*, which, uniquely in the region, is a permanent committee of parliament exclusively with inquiry powers.

Article 16 of the Norwegian constitution states that the Constitutional Court of the Realm shall pronounce judgement on actions brought by the Odelsting against members of the Council of State, Supreme Court of Justice or Storting for criminal offences committed in their official capacity. The ordinary members of the Lagting and permanent members of the Supreme Court of Justice are judges of the Constitutional Court, and proceedings take place in the Lagting chamber under the direction of the Lagting Speaker. All the eight cases of impeachment since 1814 have involved ministers, severally or collectively; five have resulted in acquittals. There was serious talk in 1977 of impeaching two Left-Socialist delegates for violating article 60 of the Storting's Standing Orders — the delegates' obligation to remain silent on all matters discussed behind closed doors in the assembly — over the question of releasing information from the confidential parts of the Schei committee's report on the navigation systems Loran C and Omega.

Initially impeachments in Norway involved technical charges of maladministration against individual ministers — the Minister for the Army over the question of military supplies and the abandonment of the summer war with Sweden in 1814, and Minister of Finance in 1822 for selling copper to Amsterdam at a loss and reputedly using his department as an 'exchange office'.[7] By the last quarter of the nineteenth century, however, impeachment had assumed a completely different character: it was used by the Storting as a political weapon in its struggle for power with the Swedish King and Norwegian cabinet in Stockholm. This contest ended with the dramatic impeachment of Christian August Selmer in 1883 which led to the fall of his government and the establishment of parliamentarism in Norway. Selmer's government had repeatedly refused to sanction a constitutional amendment requiring the Prime Minister and cabinet to participate in Storting proceedings, although after the 1882 general election — and the considerable advances made by the ('old' non-socialist) Left — there was a solid parliamentary majority in favour of the amendment. There has been only one impeachment case this century, against Abraham Berge's government in 1926–7 and concerning sums paid without authorisation in the Storting to the Commercial Bank of Norway in an attempt to avert a serious banking crisis.

In addition to the eight impeachment cases that have come to trial in the Lagting, the Protocol Committee proposed on four occasions in the nineteenth century that action be taken against the

Cabinet Office, *statsrådsavdelingen*, in Stockholm — as well as several individual cabinet ministers — but all were rejected by the Odelsting. There was also discussion of the possible impeachment of Johan Nygaardsvold and members of his government after the Second World War, although in the end nothing was done. The Protocol Committee was abolished as a permanent committee of the Storting in 1972, not least because it was unpopular with delegates who, if they were members of it, were precluded from belonging to any other committee of the Storting. It was, however, retained on an *ad hoc* basis; indeed a specially enlarged Protocol Committee (containing 11 rather than the usual 9 members) under the chairmanship of the Odelsting Speaker Per Karstensen was appointed in 1977 to examine the cases of Berge Furres and Finn Gustavsen, the two Left-Socialist delegates at the centre of the Loran C and Omega affair. When it reported in January 1979, a clear majority (Labour, Conservatives, Christians and Centre) held the Furres and Gustavsen had violated the secrecy oath, but the parties, and Labour in particular, did not believe it was a sufficiently grave matter to warrant impeachment proceedings.

Significantly, in its report on the controversial 'Document 7' — relating to the question of the Storting's control over the central administration and dating back to the King's Bay Crisis in 1963 — the Storting's standing committee on Foreign Affairs and the Constitution cast doubt on the wisdom of abolishing the Protocol Committee before real consideration had been given to providing an alternative channel for examining such matters as citizens' complaints, government resolutions and issues affecting the Parliamentary Commissioner for Administration, *Stortingets ombudsmann for forvaltningen*. The possibiliy of creating a new organ with responsibility for these matters was suggested and the Speaker's Council was asked to investigate.[8] As a result, a new committee, the 9-strong Scrutiny Committee, heralded by a unanimous vote of the Storting, came into being in October 1981 and was given the broad remit of inspecting the executive. Matters are referred to the Scrutiny Committee by the Storting, although the Standing Orders do permit the formal decisions of the Council of State together with the individual ministerial proposals and their premises (the government protocols) to be sent directly to the Scrutiny Committee. Much of the Committee's work arises out of citizens' complaints and one of its important functions is therefore to redress grievances. One of the first cases it dealt with involved two officials in the Naval Defence Supply Command who, having had their case examined by the Ombudsman for Military Affairs, *Ombudsmannen for forsvaret*, decided to complain to the Storting that they had been unfairly overlooked in the matter of an internal promotion.[9] In the first three months of its existence, the Scrutiny Committee also examined the constitutional comments from the Auditor-General's Department on Norway's public accounts for 1980,[10] a report from the Auditor-General's Department in respect of the latter's control over certain public corporations,[11] and a Storting report on the appointment of higher officials.[12] In short, the Scrutiny Committee deals with essentially the same matters as its predecessor, the Protocol Committee, although unlike the latter its members are not excluded from membership of other Storting committees. Like the legislative committees, moreover, its composition reflects the balance of power in the assembly: in 1981–5 there were four Labour, three Conservatives, one Christian and one Centre Party members.

In all the Nordic states, the assembly, either by means of *ad hoc* parliamentary commissions (Denmark and Iceland) and committees of investigation (the Protocol Committee in Norway), or the regular standing committee machinery (the Constitutional Committees in Sweden and Finland), can instigate an inquiry into possible ministerial incompetence, maladministration or illegality, which may result in the impeachment of a minister or ministers. In most cases, the legislature is also involved in nominating the personnel of the Impeachment Court, and in the Norwegian case Lagting members actually participate on it. The unique judicial function vested in the Lagting underlies the original conception of the 'upper division' as an 'estate' of lawyers. In practice, the initiative in probing matters of general public significance has largely passed to the government, albeit frequently responding to pressure from the assembly — the Swedish government commission into the activities of foreign submarines in its territorial waters, which reported in the spring of 1983, is a case in point. The *ad hoc* and exceptional machinery discussed so far has operated outside the routine enactment process: this type of inspection and control of the executive in other words has focused on the implementation of laws and their interpretation by officials, authorisations of the cabinet which do not require parliamentary approval, or simply unforeseen events and their handling by ministers and/or their advisers. The second category of 'control committees' examined in this chapter are also engaged in an area of decisions which often do not need to undergo the normal adoption process in the assembly and over which parliament has traditionally had least hold — foreign policy decisions.

The special parliamentary advisory councils on foreign affairs

In accordance with article 19 of the Danish constitution, the monarch is empowered to conduct international relations — albeit with the consent of the Folketing when any increase or diminution in the size of the national territory is being proposed, or when an international treaty is to be undertaken or rescinded.[13] Even in Sweden, where the King was precluded from meetings of the Council of State in 1973, the monarch's historic role in the direction of foreign policy is implicitly acknowledged in the new constitution.[14] Nowadays, of course, it is not the King (except in his ceremonial duties) but the King's 'officials' — the cabinet and not least the Prime Minister and Foreign Secretary — who conduct the nation's foreign policy. However, inasmuch as foreign policy was long the personal preserve of the Head of State and his *confidants*, parliament's participation in the management of foreign policy has traditionally been weak. In Sweden, for example, it is still not necessary for the government to seek parliamentary approval on matters such as the making of treaties and international agreements if the 'national interest' dictates otherwise.[15] However, against the background of the First World War, the completion of mass democracy, and the general strengthening of the parliamentary principle in the region, attempts were made to 'democratise' the running of foreign policy. Thus the assemblies in Denmark, Norway and Sweden — or more exactly a select parliamentary delegation — acquired the right via the creation of foreign affairs' councils to be consulted and informed and even to exercise some control over the executive before significant decisions were taken. Moreover, despite the subsequent formation of 'orthodox' parliamentary standing committees on foreign affairs, all three constitutional monarchies still have the special parliamentary advisory bodies on foreign policy set up in the early 1920s and comprising the King (in Sweden), leading ministers (in Sweden) and senior-ranking legislators. The advisory councils on foreign affairs are not standing committees of the legislature, and have neither a legislative function nor decision-making powers. Rather, they are consultative organs, with the onus in initiating consultations resting mainly (though not exclusively) on the government. In states renowned for their open style of government, the secrecy surrounding proceedings of the parliamentary advisory councils on foreign affairs seems rather anachronistic — no minutes or related documents are available for inspection and, on occasions, members are bound by an oath of secrecy. But what role do they play? Are they regularly consulted and in consequence able to inspect and even influence government policy?

Formed in 1921, the Swedish Foreign Affairs Council, *utrikesnämnden*, preceded the Riksdag standing committee on Foreign Affairs by sixteen years: prior to the so-called 'partial constitutional reforms' of 1968–9, however, its composition was identical to the latter. Thereafter it was reduced in size and given a membership of its own.[16] The Foreign Affairs Council (FAC) currently comprises a chairman who is the Head of State and nine other members elected by the Riksdag. Should the chairman be absent — King Karl Gustav has in fact proved an enthusiastic participant at meetings — the vice-chairman (the Prime Minister) deputises; when other members are prevented from attending, nine reserve members elected by parliament are available to take their place.[17] The Foreign Minister always attends meetings of the FAC but the Prime Minister can authorise the presence of other cabinet ministers or officials where this is judged necessary or desirable.[18] Membership of the FAC is proportionate to the strength of the parties in the Riksdag, which has meant that the Left-Communists have not yet served on it; at the same time its members are eminent public figures, i.e. senior personnel from all the main political parties.

The FAC is a permanent organ which continues to function between sessions of the Riksdag. Meetings are convened by the government and held in private. Because its powers are purely consultative, no decisions can be taken, and accordingly there are also no votes. Nonetheless, a member of the FAC is obliged to be prudent in divulging any information that relates to meetings, and where appropriate the chairman is empowered to insist on unconditional secrecy.[19] Unlike parliamentary standing committees, the FAC is neither responsible to, nor an integral part of, the Riksdag as a whole. The presence of the monarch as chairman is of course a distinctive feature (cf. Denmark and Norway) and a timely reminder of an era when the separation of powers was both legal fact and political reality. As Neil Elder has written, the FAC continues to provide the King 'with an opportunity to enjoy the classical rights of a constitutional monarch to bc consulted, to encourage and to warn'.[20] Yet if to insist that it has served significantly to control the executive is to overstate the facts, if not the original intentions of the FAC's activities, two provisions in the form of government have ensured that on the whole regular consultations with it have taken place. First, although the government normally takes the initiative in calling meetings of the FAC, they must also be called if at least 4 members request discussions on a particular issue. Secondly, while the government is obliged to gain Riksdag approval for international treaties etc. involving amendments to existing legislation or the generation of new laws (indeed generally to consult parliament if the matter is of real foreign policy importance), the cabinet is not required to obtain the Riksdag's consent when, as mentioned, the national interest dictates otherwise. It is, however, obliged to liaise with the FAC in such an eventuality before the matter is finally decided.[21]

The government's freedom of manoeuvre, it should be noted, has scarcely been restricted by these stipulations. On three notable occasions since the early 1960s, Swedish governments of both socialist and non-socialist colours have taken important foreign policy decisions either before or without consulting the FAC. The first occasion concerned the Undén plan, so called after the long-serving Social Democratic Foreign Minister who in 1962 proposed an alliance involving all those states who did not possess nuclear weapons.[22] The second related to the Swedish cabinet's decision in the spring of 1971 not to seek full membership of the European Common Market: the dramatic antecedent events are well illuminated in a biography of the Centre Party leader, Gunnar Hedlund, published soon afterwards.[23]

It transpired that at a lunch given on 13 March 1971 by Tage Erlander, the former Social Democratic Prime Minister, which was attended by the Finnish President, Urho Kekkonen (coming straight from Moscow), the Swedish Minister of Trade emphasised the political as well as economic character of the EC.[24] The next day the Foreign Secretary made a statement in cabinet ruling out an application for full membership, mindful no doubt of the need to preserve the notion of the 'Nordic balance' (see chapter 1). More significantly, the government's decision on the EC was not communicated to the FAC until March 18. Indeed the television announced that the Prime Minister Olof Palme would announce the government's position on the EC at a workers' meeting in Stockholm, which evoked a protest from the Liberal leader, Gunnar Helen. Although the latter was rather ambivalent towards full membership,[25] compared for instance to the unequivocal support of Gösta Bohman and the Conservatives,[26] he was indignant at the lapse in protocol and requested that the FAC be convened before the matter was finally decided.[27] A meeting was held at mid-day on March 18, but the outcome was a foregone conclusion.[28]

A further instance of the FAC being by-passed by the government on a controversial foreign policy question occurred over the Sundvik case in February 1981, when the three-party non-socialist coalition led by Thorbjörn Fälldin granted three firms exemptions to the investment ban contained in the South Africa Act of 1979. In the deliberations on the Sundvik company's application to allow a South African subsidiary to replace two outdated drilling machines — a step which, it was argued, would not involve any increase in the firm's overall capacity — the cabinet was divided and the Liberals registered the view that permission ought not to have been granted. Despite these divisions in the cabinet and protests from the Social Democrats, a meeting of the FAC was not called.[29] In sum the available evidence compels us to conclude that the government's hands are not in practice tied and that, contrary to its original purpose, the FAC does not afford the Riksdag much influence or control over the executive in the foreign policy sphere.[30]

The history of the Danish Foreign Affairs Council, *Det Udenrikspolitiske nævn*, is similar to the parallel organisation in Sweden. It became a permanent organ by law in 1923, and its role was reaffirmed in the revised constitution of 1953. It comprises delegates elected by the Folketing from among its number, and the government is required to consult it before every important foreign policy decision is taken. True, the monarch is not present at meeting's of the Danish FAC but, as in Sweden, it is a body on which the party chairmen or senior party figures are well represented. However, the Danish FAC, like its Swedish counterpart, has no decision-making powers: it may disagree with a government line, but cannot enforce its viewpoint. In its general character, it has features in common with the Market Relations Committee — both receive confidential information from the government without producing written reports or recommendations to parliament — but unlike the Market Relations Committee, it possesses no formal sanctions. Any general evaluation of the Danish FAC's role is bound to be speculative. At times of international crisis, it is unquestionably important in allowing governments, through consultations with FAC members, to gauge the reactions of parliament while at the same time maintaining the confidentiality of its own position.[31] Clearly, too, the FAC provides a vehicle for limited government accountability on foreign policy questions. If the Danish FAC is really to function as a sounding-board for parliamentary opinion on international questions, the importance of informal contacts between FAC members and rank-and-file Folketing delegates cannot be exaggerated. The evidence suggests that regular discussions between the government and FAC do indeed take place, although the FAC may be slightly less important in its 'routine' role of influencing the government than the corresponding body in Norway. Ministerial cross-examination also, of course, takes place in the standing committee on Foreign Affairs although, as in Sweden, this is mainly concerned with budgetary questions and matters related to Denmark's Development Aid programme.[32]

The Enlarged Foreign Affairs and Constitutional Committee, *utvidet utenriks-og konstitusjonskomité* — EFACC — is substantially larger and more integrated with the legislature than its Swedish equivalent, although with a mandate to discuss important foreign, commercial and security policy questions before government decisions are taken, its objective is fundamentally the same.

According to the Storting's Standing Orders, the EFACC consists of regular members of the parliamentary standing committee on Foreign Affairs and the Constitution (or their deputies where necessary), the Speaker and deputy Speaker of the Storting (if they are not already members), the chairman of the standing committee on Defence, and up to 11 other members nominated by the Election Committee of the Storting on the basis of the proportional representation of parties. In the 1981–5 Storting, the EFACC comprised 26 persons: 11 from the Labour Party, 8 Conservatives, 3 Christian, and 2 Centre Party representatives together with one delegate each from the Liberals and Left-Socialists. Like the FACs in Denmark and Sweden, the EFACC includes party leaders and senior parliamentarians and therefore shares their prestigious nature. Meetings are called by the chairman, or alternatively when the Prime Minister, Foreign Minister or one-third of the committee's members request them, and this can be between sessions of parliament. Deliberations are secret (unless otherwise decided), as are the occasional joint consultations between the EFACC and various standing committees of the Storting. If at least 4 members so demand, the EFACC can report to the Storting: in reality, this never happens and, as with the FAC in Sweden, proceedings have remained strictly secret.

Founded after the First World War as an expression of the Storting's concern for more information and consultation with the executive in the wide area of foreign and commercial affairs, the considerable size of the EFACC has allowed for representation of the smaller parties which have lacked seats on the standing committee on Foreign Affairs and the Constitution. The radical left has had a voice on the EFACC, unlike the Swedish FAC. This has not always been so, and there have on occasions been disguised attempts to exclude it. Certainly the election of 11 Communist delegates to the Storting in 1945 engendered a feeling of unease which in 1948 prompted the Speaker's Council to propose on the one hand the formation of a special committee on foreign and security policy matters, and on the other the broadening of the EFACC's terms of reference to cover the nation's civil and military preparedness. In the face of strong Communist opposition, because the size of the special committee and the EFACC were now small enough to preclude their having a say, a proposal to reduce the size of the EFACC to 15 members was carried in the Storting. However, it was reversed by the Storting on 10 January 1950 when the special committee was abolished and the EFACC restored to its original composition.[33] Although the secrecy surrounding EFACC business has necessarily obliterated its traces as far as the analysis of documentary evidence is concerned, interview data suggest that the Enlarged Foreign

Affairs and Constitutional Committee in Norway plays an active and important role in the foreign policy process.[34] In short, consultations with the EFACC initiated by the Foreign Minister are regular and meaningful, with the result that it is those matters raised in the parliamentary standing committee on Foreign Affairs and the Constitution that tend to be of a procedural nature.

Although the three special parliamentary councils on foreign affairs were formed soon after the First World War, the debate which culminated in the reduction in size of the Swedish FAC about half a century later had an effect on the creation of a fourth advisory organ in the same genre as the others in the region — the Self-Government Council of the Åland islands, *självstyrelsepolitiska nämnden*. There is evidence, in other words, that the general discussion touched off by the revision of the Riksdag Standing Orders in the context of the transition to unicameralism, and in particular, the restatement of the work procedures of the Swedish FAC, influenced the way the powers and functions of the new Self-Government Council were formulated in the amended Standing Orders of the Åland Landsting in 1972.[35] The foundation of the Self-Government Council meant the provision of a central advisory body overseeing the legal rights of the Åland islands in respect of international agreements under consideration by the Åland executive, *landskapet*. However, matters that have completed the process of consideration by the Self-Government Council are submitted to the Landsting for scrutiny — unlike the practice in the Swedish FAC.

On the subject of the devolved assemblies, it has been noted earlier in this volume that their internal structure and organisation closely mirrors that of the 'mother parliament': there are, for example, Grand Committees in both the Finnish Eduskunta and the Åland Landsting, specialist standing committees in both the Folketing and Faeroese Lagting, and so on. The standing committees, as elsewhere in the region, may call witnesses — including ministers and officials — in relation to matters under consideration in the committee. It is to this inquiry function of standing committees and above all, the special inquiry powers vested in small groups of them — the government review committees of parliament — that we must now turn.

Standing committees with an accentuated inquiry function — the government review committees of parliament

In common with the United States Congress and West German Bundestag, the standing committees of the Nordic legislatures possess long-standing inquiry powers. They are entitled to interrogate the executive — that is, the ministers, under-secretaries, departmental officials, experts and indeed the representatives of affected interests that man the multitude of 'policy communities' within the modern governmental machine. Such cross-examination of witnesses is entirely commonplace. In fact, closely corresponding to the structure of the government ministries, the standing committees in the region are plainly themselves part of the policy community covered by their subject area. In the absence of a clearly-defined separation between the deliberative and inquiry functions of Nordic parliamentary committees, like that institutionised in the standing and select committee systems of the British House of Commons, it is of course extremely difficult to differentiate questioning related to the deliberation of bills presently before the committee from the wider probing of matters connected with the implementation of policy. In the case of the government review committees of parliament, however, their inquiries are essentially directed at matters outside the enactment process.

Concerning the cross-examination of the executive by 'ordinary' parliamentary standing committees, there are two points to be made. First, it is far more likely that an under-secretary and/or his departmental officials will attend the formal proceedings of a standing committee than the responsible government minister. Ministers may answer, in writing, a large number of written questions from committee members, as in Denmark, but personal appearances are the exception. In Sweden, where before 1974 it was not possible to bring a minister before a Riksdag committee, the custom has been for the under-secretary accompanied by one or more civil servants to attend three times a year: only once since 1974 has a minister been cross-examined on the important Riksdag Industry Committee.[36] In Finland, lacking a special advisory council on foreign affairs (exclusively a Presidential preserve), standing committee cross-examination of cabinet members has in reality been confined to questioning the Ministers of Foreign Affairs and Overseas Trade on the basis of the quarterly reports on foreign and commercial developments provided by the Foreign Ministry. Even in Norway, where of all the states in the region, ministers are most frequently present to answer questions in standing committee, under-secretaries nonetheless bear their share of the task.

Secondly, the relatively rare oral questioning of ministers on parliamentary standing committees has focused on issues of a topical and/or politically sensitive nature not infrequently with broadly national or international implications. Thus in April 1979 the Riksdag Industry Committee called on Carl Tham, the Minister of Industry in Ullsten's Liberal minority government, to appear before the committee to clarify the measures being taken by the Swedish government in the aftermath of the nuclear reactor failure at Harrisburg in the United States.[37] The committee considered tabling an initiative, *utskottsinitiativ*, asking the Riksdag to request a government inquiry into the causes of the fault on Three Mile Island, as well as the implications for Sweden of a total embargo on her nuclear energy programme. In the event the Industry Committee was satisfied, on the strength of Tham's evidence, that the government had done everything that could be reasonably expected of it and the matter rested there.[38] In Denmark a minister in Jørgensen's Social Democratic minority administration was questioned at a special session of the Folketing Energy Committee in 1982 over the controversial issue of constructing twin gas and oil pipelines across Jutland. The minister's claim that the pipelines could run in parallel was disputed on technical grounds, a member of the Energy Committee took this up, and amid much media publicity, the minister attended the committee to answer questions on the matter.[39] The standing committee questioning of the Finnish Foreign Minister can also touch on matters of real public concern and speculation. In the context of the foreign policy report for March 1980, for instance, and a question from a committee member, the minister, Paavo Väyrynen, proceeded to scotch rumours that in connection with the Afghanistan crisis there had been unusual military activity on Finland's border or indeed on the border of Russia and Norway.[40]

The specialist standing committees in the region appear well equipped to perform their inquiry function. The experience of focusing on one legislative area for a minimum of three to four years (often much longer) enables delegates to develop a substantive grasp which can be turned to good use in interrogating the executive. This was implicitly recognised by the Social Democratic government when introducing its proposal on a new constitution in 1973, for it was argued that the reformed subject-specific standing committees would be better equipped than their bill-specific predecessors to undertake inspection work. In fact, however, Riksdag committees seldom undertake reviews of their own. When necessary, it has been customary for the assembly to request the government to set up a commission of inquiry. Since 1979 it has also been possible for the standing committees to propose that the Riksdag Auditors undertake such an investigation.[41] To be sure, the inquiry powers of the Nordic standing committees facilitate a more exhaustive and comprehensive examination of the executive than is possible at Question Time. Yet unlike the United States, and despite a Nordic tradition of 'open government', committee hearings are not open to the public. Indeed there is evidence of a growing awareness in the region of the need to develop the inquiry function of parliamentary standing committees.

In Sweden there has been a succession of members' request proposals in recent years urging that standing committee meetings be opened to the public with the unanimous consent of the committee. Former Liberal Party delegate Daniel Tarschys, the author of a number of these proposals, has expressed the belief that allowing the public to observe the inquiries of parliamentary standing committees would inspire a deeper probing and inspection of the government. While accepting that the public could not be admitted to every meeting, Tarschys nonetheless argued that in addition to witnesses drawn from among ordinary citizens, more civil servants would be encouraged to attend than presently do so.[42] Similar views have been canvassed elsewhere in the region, notably by the veteran Social Democrat Benedikt Gröndal in Iceland and the Progress Party leader in Norway Carl I. Hagen. In November 1973, the Norwegian Labour Party requested information on how the practice of committee hearings operated in other countries, but the office of the Storting took four years to produce it — a matter which Hagen took up in connection with the question of individual amendments to the Storting's Standing Orders in 1977. He was subsequently informed that the time was not yet ripe for investigating further the issue of committee hearings.[43] In Denmark there was much talk of introducing Congressional-style committee hearings in the mid-1960s as part of a debate on the need for more open government — a debate which spawned several amendments to the Folketing's Standing Orders and, *inter alia*, permitted the author of a private member's bill to participate in the meetings of the appropriate standing committee when his/her bill was being discussed. Discussion of public hearings has continued ephemerally since then though hitherto without any result.[44]

In the absence of public committee hearings, practice in the Nordic states must be regarded as less well-developed than in Britain where a 'watchdog' select committee system — a network of committees with exclusively inquiry powers — was set up by the Thatcher I administration in 1979. Meetings of these select committees are open, their reports published and proceedings invariably recorded for later radio broadcasting. The working of the select committees, moreover, may well provide evidence to confirm Tarschys' thesis about a more penetrating inspection of the executive. True, there were MPs who, as a matter of principle, would not initially participate: Dennis Skinner, for example, referred dismissively to the 'kind of sloppy consensus which is the basis of the activities of the select committees'.[45] But there is nowadays widespread enthusiasm among MPs for the new committees. On the Conservative side, in particular, membership of select committees is seen as part of a career structure and to solidifying an appropriate expertise, which today is essential for the building up of a desirable *curriculum vitae*.[46] The type of delegate expertise generated through the select committee system may be seen as vital to enhancing parliamentary control over the executive. The Liberal leader David Steel argued, at the time the Franks Commission report on the South Atlantic war was published in January 1983, that had the select committees been better established, parliamentarians might well have provided the new thinking necessary for fresh ministerial initiatives on the Falklands question and have made the Argentinian invasion of the islands avoidable.[47]

What is certain is that had the South Atlantic war involved Denmark, Finland or Sweden, the government's conduct of proceedings would have been monitored or subsequently investigated by one of the distinctive government review committees of parliament. Indeed, if the inquiry function of standing committees in the Nordic states is less developed than in the United States and less publicly performed than in Britain, there are nonetheless standing committees in the region with an accentuated inspection role. In these cases there is a clear separation of the deliberative and inquiry functions of the committee, and the latter is often emphasised through the production of an annual report reviewing the activities of the entire government. Special hearings take place on issues selected by the committee, any area of policy-making may be covered and ministers present themselves for cross-examination more frequently than on 'ordinary' standing committees.

In the case of the Folketing's Market Relations Committee, *Folketingets markedsudvalg*, the committee's task is to inspect Common Market matters of essential political importance to Denmark and to scrutinise those decisions of the Council of Ministers whose implementation requires action by the Folketing. The Market Relations Committee, in short, keeps a check on the negotiating stance of government ministers in Brussels and may ultimately refuse to mandate the official line. This considerable sanction is offset by the fact that consultation with the Market Relations Committee (technically at least) depends on the discretion of the government.

The Eduskunta's Constitution and Foreign Affairs committees inspect the activities of the government on the basis of the latter's annual report to parliament. Although the choice of topics for investigation by the committees is not in itself circumscribed, they are of course reporting on a report. As with the Market Relations Committee, in other words, inquiry follows an initiative from the government (a cabinet decision on a particular position in Brussels, the production of an annual report etc.) However, a sanction exists in the plenary debate on the statements of the two committees, when a minister may be censured.

The Riksdag's Constitutional Committee is required annually to inspect the cabinet and government departments and to produce a report on its findings. The committee's review function is the oldest in the region, considerably pre-dating the breakthrough of parliamentarism. Unlike the review committees in Denmark and Finland, the Swedish Constitutional Committee has a free hand to instigate inquiries, and is not tied to a presentation by the government.

There are other obvious differences in the working of these three bodies: it is not the norm in Finland and Sweden for cabinet ministers to appear before the review committees — although it is common enough — whereas in the case of the Danish Market Relations Committee, civil servants are precluded from attending and only ministers are cross-examined. In Finland and Sweden, moreover, the committees direct their attention towards the past, examining the government's record over the previous year; in Denmark, the review committee 'looks forward', monitoring decisions before they are finally resolved. All the review committees, however, are standing committees of the assembly and are required to consider ongoing legislative proposals (though to sharply varying extents): all are elected by parliament from among its members; and all have a broad remit and are not confined to inspecting one department or one policy-making sector. In every case, the central analytical question is also the same: how effective is the inspection and control of the executive achieved by the government review committees of parliament?

The Folketing Market Relations Committee has a unique place among the national legislatures of the EC countries in that it is a permanent standing committee exclusively comprising parliamentarians, which the government is required to consult over the more important facets of Denmark's Community policy. The purpose-specific character of the Market Relations Committee (MRC) needs emphasis. In West Germany, for example, where the system of specialist standing committees approximates to the Danish system, Community matters are dealt with primarily by a sub-committee of the Bundestag's External Affairs Committee and not infrequently thereafter in the standing committees on Finance and Economic Affairs too. There has in fact been little discussion of emulating Danish practice and creating a single parliamentary organ for dealing with EC questions; rather, the Bundestag groups content themselves with holding informal workshops on Market matters.

The modern role of the MRC is enshrined in article 6 of Denmark's accession treaty of 1972, which says that 'the Government shall report to the Folketing on developments in the European Communities and shall notify a committee of parliament of proposals for Council decisions that will become directly applicable in Denmark and whose implementation requires action by the Folketing.'[48] The MRC had in fact existed from the time of Denmark's first application to join the Common Market in 1961, and had long functioned as essentially a deliberative forum in which to review the various options in Community policy and discuss the possible terms of Denmark's future admission. Following the parliamentary decision to adhere to the EC in September 1972 and the affirmative popular referendum two months later, the status of the MRC underwent a marked change. This was particularly the case after the political crisis of February 1973 when the Minister of Agriculture in the Social Democratic minority administration concluded a highly unfavourable provisional price agreement for Danish export bacon without getting the backing of the Folketing, and so prompted the Liberals and Conservatives to table a motion of no confidence in the government. A compromise hammered out between the Social Democrats, Radicals and anti-EC Socialist People's Party did indeed save the government, but a by-product of the crisis was an agreement significantly strengthening the position of the MRC as a parliamentary control mechanism.[49]

The revamped MRC contains 17 full members (and 14 deputies) who, like the other parliamentary standing committees, mirror the relative strength of the political parties in the assembly. As one of the regular Folketing committees, the MRC can and very occasionally does function routinely as part of the legislative process — e.g. when the rules governing elections to the European Parliament are being considered. Its members are senior politicians, former ministers, party leaders and the like, who have relatively little time to devote to MRC business. Consistent with the practice throughout the Nordic region, however, there is preliminary discussion of forthcoming committee business in the parliamentary party groups and their internal policy committees, and MRC members can also receive expert advice from the standing committee spokesmen in the parliamentary groups.[50] Despite the highly purpose-specific character of the committee and the obvious potential for corporate behaviour 'in the national interest', the MRC thus represents very much the permeable type of standing committee on which partisan factors are paramount.

In consultations with the MRC the onus, it must be emphasised, rests firmly with the government. Indeed a consensus has developed that consultations with the MRC should be discretionary and not obligatory for a government, although discussions would be expected to take place relating to all important political questions — in such a way as to respect both the will of parliament and the government's freedom of action. It follows therefore that it is the cabinet's prerogative to estimate whether a Community matter is of 'essential political importance' (in the phrase of the MRC annual reviews of 1973 and 1974), and the right of the Minister (or the MRC chairman) to require members where necessary to maintain secrecy on matters discussed within the committee. The confidentiality rule has in practice been applied in only a very few cases and may really be said to apply only when the position of other countries is being debated or when Danish ministers are receiving their (oral) mandate for a particular stance in Brussels. In so far as it has been felt desirable to avoid a majority forming in the MRC which is opposed to the Danish government's negotiating position on an important Community question, the formal quorum rules applying to the other Folketing standing committees, i.e. that at least half the members be present, have been waived. The issue of the need to bring the attendance regulations in the MRC into line with the other standing committees was pressed by the Justice Party delegate, Ib Christensen, in 1974 for he was not present at an MRC decision which he disliked and in consequence demanded the standard 50% quorum. In fact, a 50% turn-out of members is required only on the very rare occasions when the MRC is functioning as part of the domestic legislative process, although, if the committee is granting authority to a minister, it is normally expected that representatives of half the opinion in the Folketing — at the time of writing this could be one delegate each from the Social Democrats, Christian Democrats and Conservatives — should be present and support the step. Furthermore, in recent years the chairman of the MRC has not been a member of a governing party, so absolving the administration from any charge of not being prepared to subject the main lines of its Community policy to adequate examination.

Thus far the cards seem to have been stacked very much in the government's favour; after all, it is the government that is empowered to assess whether discussions with the MRC are necessary, whether confidentiality is required etc., and moreover to do so without the quorum constraints of the other standing committees. However, consultations between the two have worked well enough, and the MRC is not without a number of trumps of its own. Foremost among these is the sanction of refusing to mandate the negotiating position of a Danish minister in the Council of Ministers, a matter to which we will return shortly. Suffice it for the moment to emphasise the mutually satisfactory nature of most of the contacts between the MRC and government. In many respects, their relations might be likened to those between the government and Foreign Affairs Council (FAC). The FAC, as we noted earlier in this chapter, must be consulted by the government on major foreign policy issues and, in the manner of the MRC, it may also receive confidential information from the government. Unlike other parliamentary standing committees, the MRC and FAC do not produce written reports, nor do they make recommendations to the Folketing. In so far as there is some overlapping between EC policy and, say, the international role of the Community which falls within the orbit of foreign policy, occasional joint meetings between the MRC and FAC are not unknown. Unlike the MRC, the FAC does not mandate ministers: it may on occasions indicate a contrary view to that of the government, but the government is not in any way bound by this. We should add that a high level of co-ordination between the Danish government, the MRC and the FAC is achieved informally through the responsible minister. During the South Atlantic crisis in the spring of 1982, for example, the Foreign Minister wanted talks with the MRC to be able to inform the FAC of the MRC view before a meeting between himself, the Minister of Overseas Trade and the MRC. The MRC for its part had already approached the Minister of Overseas Trade for an audience.

The real inspection powers of the MRC, in respect of the Minister of Trade or indeed any other minister, should not be underestimated. The committee's working methods are extremely thorough. MRC agendas are very detailed, setting out those items on which consultations with the appropriate minister will take place. Before every meeting of the Council of Ministers, moreover, the MRC holds a joint session with the minister on the basis of the Council of Ministers' provisional agenda which all committee members receive. During this dialogue members may request additional oral and/or written information. The MRC cross-examines ministers with great regularity, and the minister must maintain close contact with the MRC throughout crucial discussions. Before all negotiations in Brussels on important political matters, the Danish government presents its initial stance to the MRC in verbal form. If the chairman reports a majority in favour, or if the MRC is undecided — formal voting never takes place — the government will go ahead as planned. However, fresh developments in negotiations invariably require the minister to obtain renewed authorisation from the MRC — as a result, meetings often take place at short notice and at inconvenient times — and the outcome of continued talks is again presented to the MRC. Before the Danish government's discussions in Brussels with Britain and subsequently the entire Commission over the controversial fisheries question in the autumn of 1982, the MRC was thoroughly briefed about the line the government intended to take (which it opposed) and was also kept extremely well versed about the implications for the Danish fishing industry of the deadlock that had affected the dispute by the beginning of 1983.

It might be contended, therefore, that the Danish government's position in Brussels is in unnecessary jeopardy and that the national interest is adversely affected by the way in which the minister's hands are tied at each move to those of the MRC. The minister needs constantly to consult the MRC or at least the 'contact men' in it before modifying an agreed stance, whereas he might well have achieved a better deal had he been free to act on his own initiative at the conference table. Equally it could be countered that Danish ministers can use their relationship with the MRC as leverage, achieving a favourable deal with the argument that 'my committee will certainly not stand for anything less.' In the inevitable absence of systematic evidence, a balanced view is difficult to achieve, although recent events suggest that the Danish government's position has indeed been hamstrung by the need to carry along the MRC with it. (If the MRC were to be ignored in circumstances which seemed to call for consultations, the Folketing could deploy the usual parliamentary procedures for expressing no confidence.)

To aid the task of scrutinising a mass of Community material and in particular assessing the implications for Danish industry of a wide range of EC directives, the MRC may enlist the resources of other Folketing standing committees. In other words, a special statement from another parliamentary committee can be requested, although as critics of the MRC outside Denmark have been quick to point out, this is a relatively rare occurrence. Indeed, the only Folketing standing committee from which statements are always required is the Committee on the Environment and Regional Planning, a requirement as old as the MRC itself and one based on the special expertise vested in that committee.[51] On 19 November 1982, for example, the MRC made a written approach to the Committee on the Environment and Regional Planning concerning *inter alia* the limits on the discharging of cadmium into waterways; a proposed EC ban on the importation of certain sealskins; and a Commission statement on the dangerous substances listed in a Council of Minister's document on the marine environment. Incidentally, on a number of these issues, the Committee on the Environment and Regional Planning was not able to produce a unanimous response because the Socialist People's Party members and the single Progress Party delegate deviated from the majority view.[52]

Recently, too, the practice has developed of the MRC receiving deputations like other standing committees of the Folketing. In December 1982, a lawyer representing three Danish shrimp vessel owners wrote to the MRC with a description of the problems of the shrimp fishing industry off the Greenland coast. He had previously approached the Ministry of Fisheries, the Foreign Ministry, the Ministry of Greenland and the Prime Minister's Office on his clients' behalf and indeed twice earlier contacted the MRC over the same matter. The lawyer's letter contended that, exactly as during Jørgensen's Social Democratic governments, Schlüter's new four-party bourgeois coalition had failed to give a declaration of intent either concerning shrimp quotas for 1983 or on the wider issue of the historic rights of the Danish shrimp industry. The vessel owners, he noted, were distressed by two recent developments in particular. The first was the announcement by Norway (not, of course, a full Community member) that she would co-operate in the implementation of a common EC fisheries policy in respect of shrimp fishing rights off the Greenland coast; this, it was feared, could entail Danish shrimp boats being sacrificed on the altar of a Common Market fisheries policy. Secondly, there were the press statements from the chairman of the Greenland executive, *hjemmestyre*, Jonathan Motzfeldt, insisting that by the end of 1982 fishing opportunities for the three shrimp vessels off the Greenland coast be terminated. Invoking a Commission ruling that vessels with historic rights in an area be allowed to maintain a quota there, the lawyer closed his communication by requesting a general clarification of the position on whether the Danish right to fish and earn a living around the Greenland coast would be upheld and licences granted, or whether for political reasons no statements would be forthcoming.[53] The MRC was urged to take the matter up with the government.

Although we have been focusing exclusively on the activities and procedures of the MRC, the committee is obviously far from operating in a policy vacuum. It forms part of a distinct and largely self-contained sub-system within the Danish political process, having the Ministry of Foreign Affairs as its apex. This organisational nexus includes a special EC cabinet committee chaired by the Minister for Overseas Trade (often with the Prime Minister in attendance), a parallel committee of senior civil servants, and an infrastructure of 23 supporting civil service committees ranging from Customs, Agriculture and Fisheries to Euratom, the EC Budget, and Faeroes and Greenland. The detailed inspection and consideration of EC questions originates in one of these special civil service committees. The government ministry corresponding to the particular competence of the committee provides the committee chairman and undertakes the secretarial functions; members are drawn from both the 'anchor' ministry and other relevant departments. The civil service committees' primary charge is to scrutinise a mass of Commission documentation, and above all to ascertain the implications for Danish interests. Pressure groups are frequently consulted at this stage. The task of the EC committee of senior officials which meets every Tuesday is then to prepare recommendations for the government. As the Permanent Secretary at the Foreign Ministry has observed, 'In reality, the EC committee of civil servants has responsibility for briefing the government on all those important questions that are likely to affect relations between the EC countries.'[54] Thus the committee directly serves the government of the day. To ensure the necessary continuity between the two, the chairman of the EC committee of officials acts as secretary to the EC cabinet committee. Civil servants, however, never attend meetings of the MRC. A diagram of the Market sub-system within the Danish policy process is presented in Table 9.1.

In summing up the role of the MRC, we should emphasise three points. First, in a situation of minority government, the MRC can exercise significant *political* control over the Danish executive in relation to important Community questions. A majority can easily form against the government's view, as happened in January 1981, when the Fisheries Minister was due to sign an agreement on fishery quotas. In the event, another minister had to act *pro tempore* as the Fisheries Minister and present a new governmental stance. As there was not a majority of the MRC against this, negotiations were able to proceed.[55] It was more serious when the MRC opposed the bourgeois minority coalition government of Poul Schlüter in December 1982 on the question of a common EC fisheries policy, and this led to open conflict with Britain, losses to the native fishing industry, and ultimately a compromise solution which was widely seen as a defeat for the Danish government. There are, at the time of writing four anti-Market parties represented on the MRC, and by dint of very thorough preparation they have contrived substantially to protract meetings and, more important still, sustain the essentially political character of the organ. There is in fact co-operation between the anti-Marketeers on the MRC and Denmark's anti-Market delegates in the European Parliament at Strasbourg. Euro-delegates receive the same information as MRC members, except for material stamped 'confidential' which is distributed to the latter

Table 9.1. THE EC DECISION-MAKING PROCESS IN DENMARK

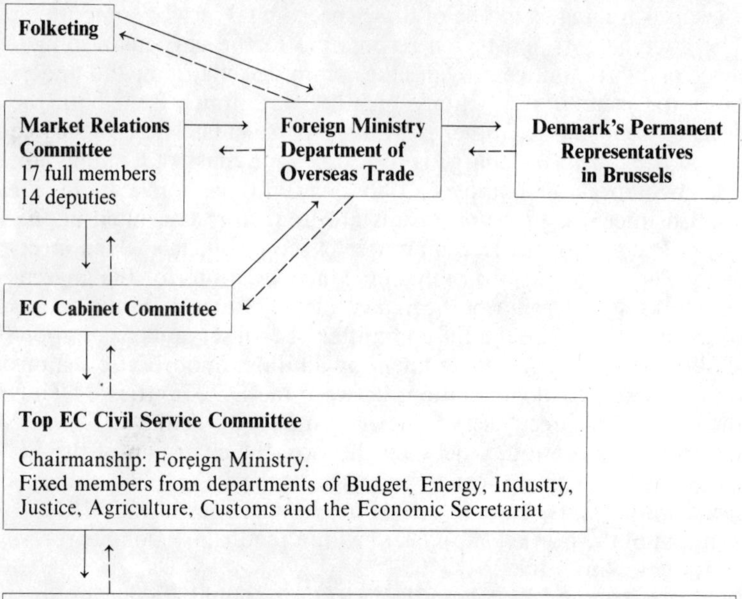

Folketing

Market Relations Committee
17 full members
14 deputies

Foreign Ministry Department of Overseas Trade

Denmark's Permanent Representatives in Brussels

EC Cabinet Committee

Top EC Civil Service Committee

Chairmanship: Foreign Ministry.
Fixed members from departments of Budget, Energy, Industry, Justice, Agriculture, Customs and the Economic Secretariat

Special Civil Service Committees

Customs	Indirect Taxation	Investment Bank
Agriculture	Direct Taxation	EC Personnel questions
Fisheries	Trade & Commerce	Faeroes & Greenland
Social & Labour-Market questions	Industrial & Regional Policy	Legal questions
Establishment & official costing	Energy	Science & Research
Political Economy	Environment	
Transport	Aid Policy	
Education	Euratom	
Competition Regulations	EC Budget	

Source: Otto Møller, 'Koordinerer danske interesser'. *Europæisk Samling*, 3, 1981, p. 5.

only. As one senior Folketing official wryly observed, there has been an increasing tendency for material to be marked 'confidential' in order to minimise the risk of leagues, made up of anti-Market Euro-delegates and anti-Market members of the MRC, forming against the government. Any documentation which is not so marked is also available to newspapers. In recent years the MRC has paid more attention to the popular perception of its work and to heightening the visibility of its activity by releasing as much information as possible to the press.

Secondly, the degree of control exercised by the MRC in the *technical* inspection of EC policy is significantly less. The committee staff is very small, and delegates receive agendas only three days before meetings and in consequence find it difficult to assess the implications for Denmark of marginal adjustments to, say, the Community's agricultural budget. Members of the MRC, it should be remembered, are senior politicians — party spokesmen, former ministers of agriculture etc — who have relatively little time to vet topics that range over so wide an area from fisheries to pollution, and from education to taxation.

Thirdly, and distinctively, the MRC speaks with the full political (if not legal) authority of the Folketing;[56] ministers are obliged to follow the MRC line. Moreover, although MRC delegates normally consult their parliamentary groups, they can as party leaders commit their parties unilaterally where necessary. There are precedents among the standing parliamentary committees for the type of decision-taking power delegated to the MRC: for example, the Finance Committee is authorised to approve supplementary estimates etc. on behalf of the Folketing as a whole. But the central role of the MRC reflects the strong Danish tradition of parliamentary involvement in shaping public policy, and the prevalence of minority government has perhaps been the vital factor. Thus it will be recalled how in the winter of 1973 the Social Democratic minority government was forced to accept a compromise deal including the strengthened control function of the MRC as a *sine qua non* of its continuing in office. There is not a great risk that a continued period of majority government might significantly depoliticise the MRC.

In an entirely different way from that in which the MRC controls EC policy in Denmark, the Eduskunta inspects the activities of the Finnish executive on the basis of the statements which the Constitutional Committee and Foreign Affairs Committee make on the Government's annual report to parliament. The Government Report, a substantial document often containing more than 500 pages and prepared by the separate ministries, is ready for presentation to the legislature by May, and is examined privately by members of the two mentioned standing committees over the summer recess. When the new Eduskunta session opens in October, members of the Constitutional Committee request that particular matters be taken up, and generally between two and five issues yearly are chosen for special hearings. The actual decision on the subjects for investigation is normally taken without a vote, although in practice the larger committee groups, the Social Democrats and their long-standing coalition partners the Centre Party, effectively dominate the process of selecting topics. Before Christmas short written requests are ready to be sent out to the persons concerned, and hearings are held in January. When information and/or opinion is asked from ministers they invariably produce written responses, although during the 1980–1 parliamentary session, two ministers did appear in person at Constitutional Committee meetings in connection with the Government Report. Ministers can refuse to attend; however, according to the secretary of the Constitutional Committee Martti Manninen, this would be to risk infringing article 53 of the Eduskunta Standing Orders relating to a standing committee's right to receive information.[57] In pursuance of its duties, the Constitutional Committee, like the MRC, may request statements from other parliamentary standing committees — nine of them altogether were requested to give special statements apropos facets of the 1981 Government Report — and a wide range of persons attend committee hearings (24 in the winter 1982).

As to the topics raised for further investigation by the Constitutional Committee, these are often narrowly technical and do not have a particularly partisan flavour. Often they arise out of perceived shortcomings and inequities in recently-enacted legislation — lacunae in the implementation of programmes that can be plugged quite easily once the deficiency has been made apparent. The two cases taken up for further analysis in the 1981 Government Report will illustrate the point. In the first, the Constitutional Committee recommended the need for uniformity in the wage conditions applying to senior public sector officials. The Constitutional Committee accordingly urged the amendment of a government act which had come into operation in October 1982 so as to make a particular category of high-ranking public sector officials (including the Chancellor of Justice and his staff, the staff of parliament and the parliamentary library, and persons employed in the Bank of Finland, the Post Office Savings Bank, the Pensions Board and the Office of the Finnish Delegation to the Nordic Council) eligible for the same long-service increment, *määrävuosikorotukset*, as other classes of civil servant. In other words, the Ministry of Finance regulations on the matter were to be modified.[58]

The second issue was the need to ensure that the appropriate car tax rebate should be available to all disabled drivers. In connection with the government's Invalid Care Amendment Bill, parliament had urged the government to investigate how the costs of vehicles for the badly disabled might be reduced. According to the Government Report, however, the cabinet had decided on 22 December

1981 that the investigation it had authorised on the matter required no further action. The Constitutional Committee expressed disquiet at this outcome, and produced several recommendations on the broad question of tax relief to the owners of these vehicles. A definition of the concept of invalidity was urged so that common norms could be applied by doctors and others in assessing invalidity status; those persons certified as disabled but not driving their own vehicles, i.e. those in need of a driver, were not to be excluded from the tax relief provisions; preferential treatment for disabled persons with a high professional background was to be avoided; and a miscellany of technical loopholes in the law plugged. The Constitutional Committee noted, for example, that under existing arrangements applications for car tax rebate from the disabled could be forwarded to two offices and get contradictory responses. These and other irregularities in the implementation of the law were to be stopped.[59]

Matters in the government's annual report bearing on foreign affairs and Finland's external commercial relations are dealt with separately by the standing committee on Foreign Affairs. However, because of the overwhelming cross-party consensus on national foreign policy management — for the first time in the post-war era, foreign policy was not a campaign issue at the polls in March 1983[60] — the ensuing committee statement is both uncontroversial and uncritical. Progress is monitored, achievements are recorded and assertions of continuing commitment are given. In the Foreign Affairs Committee's statement on the 1981 Government Report, for instance, the increasingly favourable development of commercial relations with the Soviet Union was noted, as was Finland's contribution to the overriding goal of international detente. The Foreign Affairs Committee observed with satisfaction that there had been growing regional interest in the notion of a nuclear-free Nordic zone; it expressed the hope that there would be a favourable conclusion to the European Conference on Security and Co-operation in Madrid, and also emphasised the need to explore new markets so as to facilitate the expansion of Finland's export trade. Finally, the enormous significance for Finns of the new language agreement between the Nordic states was acknowledged, and the point made that its vigorous and consistent implementation was vital for Finnish citizens living in the other Nordic countries, particularly Sweden.[61]

As effective pieces of machinery for the inspection and control of the executive, the Constitutional and Foreign Affairs Committee statements on the government's annual report are limited in two important ways. First, there is a significant time-lag between the initial action of the government (a legislative measure or whatever), the subsequent annual report on it, the related standing committee statements and finally the full Eduskunta debate. The standing committee responses to the Government Report for 1981 were not ready before February 1983, and it was not surprising that they lacked immediacy for most delegates. For the relatively high number of new Eduskunta members elected the following month in particular, the annual report debates in the spring were without real interest. The debate on the Foreign Affairs Committee statement, one of the rare occasions for a full-sitting airing of foreign policy issues, has been especially criticised for lack of topicality. (In theory, the Preliminary Debate on the Budget affords delegates a further opportunity of raising foreign policy matters, like the size of Finland's development aid contribution, in so far as these are related to allocations in the Finance Bill.) In February 1980, parliament gave a single reading to the Foreign Affairs Committee statement on the Government Report for 1978.[62] Yet although the debate took place shortly after the Afghanistan crisis broke, there was no provision for considering the implications of the Soviet action and delegates were confined to pondering the issues of 1978. Not surprisingly, there were expressions of disquiet, not least from the Rural Party, and the proceedings were poorly attended.

A second aspect of the annual report machinery as a vehicle for inspecting the political executive in Finland is that when matters arising out of the standing committee responses to the government's annual report come to the vote in the assembly, delegates on the government side tend to protect their ministers on all important matters. In other words, the annual report affords the parliamentary opposition an opportunity to gain some tactical capital without really disturbing the government or threatening it with a serious reverse in the assembly. This is not to say that the Constitutional Committee's report has never unearthed matters that are politically embarrassing or that the ensuing debate has not led to action being taken against a minister. The Constitutional Committee's annual report for 1945 contained evidence of irregularities in the Ministry of the Interior which by 1948 had caused the (very unwilling) resignation of the responsible minister, the radical leftist, Eino Leino.[63] In general, however, the main government review committee in Finland, the Constitutional Committee, has been engaged in the work of technical inspection rather than the political control of the executive. In the case of the Swedish Constitutional Committee, both elements — technical inspection and political control — have been attempted in its annual review of the cabinet and government departments.

According to the new Swedish constitution, the Riksdag, in addition to 'enacting laws, determining state taxation and deciding how public resources are to be deployed', is required 'to inspect the government and central administration'[64] — this last duty being performed by means of an annual report, *granskningsbetänkande*, from the Constitutional Committee. The Finance Committee is also invested with special inspection functions: it is obliged to make a yearly review of the administration of the Bank of Sweden, and although fairly routine this has become a sizeable task, frequently involving the appointment of auxiliary members of the committee staff on short-term contracts.[65] But the vital point about the Constitutional Committee's review is its overtly political nature — the investigators are parliamentarians and those under investigation are cabinet ministers and their departments. In short, the committee monitors the organisation of government in the ministries along with the commissions of inquiry that are formally *ad hoc* extensions of government departments. The rest of the public administration — the central boards, *verk*, and provincial agencies, *länsstyrelser* — does not come within its remit.

The Constitutional Committee's task of inspecting the government was written into the constitution of 1809. Between the committee's inception in that year and the constitutional reforms of 1971, the Constitutional Committee supervised the Council of State through its examination of Council minutes and related documents. Immediately the Riksdag convened, the Constitutional Committee would receive the set of minutes for the previous year (the government had the right to withhold certain foreign policy documents[66]) and if, on the evidence of the minutes, a majority of the committee held that a minister had acted negligently or imprudently, a formal complaint could be lodged against him in its consolidated report on the minutes. Technically (this in fact never happened) the Riksdag was then able to petition for the removal of the minister or ministers in question, though the monarch was not bound to acquiesce in this request. As a result, parliament occasionally decided to stress that a complaint was justified by minuting it 'with approval'. If the procedure of vetting the minutes of the Council of State was largely overtaken by events — the more expeditious interpellation machinery, which was incorporated into the constitution in 1867, and the subsequent rise of cohesive political parties in the legislature — it cannot be dismissed as simply a fruitless exercise. As Elis Håstad has commented, the fact that governments could not avoid Riksdag supervision of their minutes was of 'great, though indirect, preventive significance'.[67]

The new constitution does not prescribe limits on the nature of the Constitutional Committee's annual review; in practice, however, the committee has tended to restrict itself to examining government activities from a constitutional viewpoint. Two random examples from its Annual Report for 1980–1 will serve to illustrate the type of routine inspection work it undertakes. The first issue concerned the implications of the new rules on Law Council statements, incorporated into the constitution in 1979 and taking effect from 1 January 1980. The new regulations stipulated that legal proposals in a number of specified areas — e.g. freedom of the press, individual rights, local government taxes, Swedish citizenship, and restrictions on an individual's economic situation — should in principle be examined by the Law Council. This could be obviated only if the bill was judged to be of minor importance or if the Law Council's examination would so delay deliberation of the matter as to cause harm. In chapter 3 we saw that if the government presents the Riksdag with a proposal in any of the mentioned areas without first consulting the Law Council, it is required to explain its reasons for not doing so in a preamble or appendix to the bill. Reviewing the situation at the end of its first year of operation, the Constitutional Committee observed that the new rules had led to a significant increase in the number of government proposals sent to the Law Council — 37 in 1980, compared with 23 in 1979. However, it noted that it had not been possible to maintain the same division of manpower resources within the Council to deal with the increased workload. Between January and May 1980, the Law Council had functioned with three sections (a maximum of four is permitted by law), whereas for the remainder of the year it had been reduced to only two. The Constitutional Committee also identified a number of cases of government proposals in which the advice of the Law Council had not been sought, without any explanation being given in the introduction to the bill. These included a Budget Department proposal concerning tax relief on certain types of shares, a Foreign Ministry initiative on Swedish membership of an African Development Bank, and a bill submitted by the Trade Department to change the law on customs duties. The committee accordingly underlined the importance of adhering to the new rules as laid down in the constitution.[68]

A second case of the routine inspection of the government by the Constitutional Committee in 1980–1 concerned the presentation of government proposals to the Riksdag.[69] Two questions in particular were to the forefront of its deliberations: the distribution of bills during the parliamentary year and the connection between government plans for introducing bills and their actual presentation to parliament. On the question of the distribution of bills, the Constitutional Committee pointed to the detrimental effects to the Riksdag of concentrating the load of government initiatives — e.g. within the week immediately before the expiration (on March 31 each year) of the period for introducing government proposals, *propositionstid*, or even on the very last day of this period. Between 1971 and 1979 it discovered that an average of 39% of government bills in the spring session of the Riksdag had been introduced during the final week of 'proposals time' and as many as 14% on the final day itself. In 1980, the proportions were 42% and 24% respectively. This type of overloading, it was argued, was likely to reduce the chances of delegates having sufficient time to study government bills and to generate related parliamentary motions. The work of standing committees was also likely to be complicated by bottlenecks, and there would be problems of organising sufficient plenary meetings. Even the capacity of the mass media to give an adequate account of parliamentary proceedings would be jeopardised.

As to the relationship between the outline plan for introducing government bills and their actual submission to parliament, the Constitutional Committee held that a close correspondence between the two was essential in order that parliament could work effectively. If more bills were presented than set out in the plan, or if bills were introduced that did not form part of the plan, the result would be the dislocation of standing committee work and, beyond that, the work of parliament as a whole. The Constitutional Committee concluded by stating that only a very approximate date for the introduction of a measure — e.g. a particular month — was at present indicated in the outline of forthcoming government proposals, and that during 1980 delays of about two weeks had been experienced. It expressed the hope that departments would in future specify a more precise schedule of bills and that the appropriate standing committee would be informed in advance if a delay was likely.

In addition to these two examples, the Constitutional Committee regularly urges the need for swifter ministerial responses to parliamentary questions and interpellations, and criticises the shortness of the time-span between the government's publication of laws and the date on which they are designed to be implemented. Topics like these, which are taken up for scrutiny every year, are exclusively the responsibility of the staff of the Constitutional Committee — the largest of any Riksdag standing committee — whose task it is to identify the problems and produce the necessary supportive evidence. In addition, almost every year a specific sector of government decision-making is held up for inspection at the instigation of the committee staff who work on it intermittently during the summer and autumn months. In recent years, the government's handling of appeal cases in the field of zoning and immigration legislation has come in for close attention primarily with a view to determining whether a consistent line is being pursued and whether delays in hearing such cases are being avoided. Within the Constitutional Committee, the examination of routine matters like those cited is known as the *administrative review*.[70]

The Constitutional Committee does not review its own administrative review. Judging by the recurrence of problems and the absence of sanctions at its disposal, however, it would probably be fair to say that the tangible return on the committee's administrative review has on the whole been small. Typical perhaps was the response to action prompted by an amendment to the Riksdag's Standing Orders in the 1981–2 session which required the government to cost so-called 'framework proposals' in addition to the detailed government bills. In its annual report for 1981–2, the Constitutional Committee pointed to the need to observe both rules. The government's response was an inter-departmental circular sent out by Claes Eklundh, the Chief Legal Officer in the Prime Minister's Office, which reminded ministries both of the established constitutional prescription on pricing orthodox government bills, and of the import of Daniel Tarschy's successful private measure requiring the same exercise for 'framework proposals'.[71] However, as Eklundh commented, the matter was already on the inter-departmental agenda in that during an economic recession the ministries are inevitably under pressure from the Budget Department to undertake the costing of proposals. As to the government adhering to the rules on consulting the Law Council, the importance of which the Constitutional Committee had stressed in its previous annual report, Eklundh's response was to notify his fellow Chief Legal Officers at their regular monthly meeting. The matter, in short, was treated informally and probably not taken any further.

The majority of matters reviewed by the Constitutional Committee, it should be emphasised, are not of the routine administrative type. Rather, they are political in nature and are identified by the parliamentary members of the committee acting as individuals or frequently as partisans. In these cases, a member of the committee staff does the initial detective work in examining the background to the problem and then produces a paper — usually without any conclusions — which is considered by the full committee. Unlike the Law Council, the internal work procedures for the annual review — which occupies the Constitutional Committee at intervals over February, March and April every year — do not involve the creation of sections within the committee, although inside the party groups represented on the committee only one person will normally specialise in a particular matter under review. As for this *political review*, there has been no more controversial issue in recent years than the Telub case, which well illustrates the inherent weakness of the control function of the Constitutional Committee during periods of majority government.

Telub is a medium-sized, state-owned telecommunications company specialising in radar and radio technology along with advanced electronic equipment and based at Växjö in southern Sweden. Most of its work has always come from Swedish defence service orders. In 1977, it was rather surprisingly contracted by the Libyan government to provide advanced technological education to a group of 100 trainee Libyans who had been sent to Sweden. The trouble arose when claims were made that the fourth year of the special course involved giving military as well as technological instruction. It transpired that the Director of the Telub Institute had concealed the real nature of the agreement and when, following his resignation, the main safe was opened, the clause in the contract about military education was discovered! The government subsequently managed to renegotiate what was a very valuable deal for Sweden: indeed, the deal itself, worth an estimated Sw. Kr. 200–300 billion was obviously of decisive importance for Telub's fortunes. By then, however, adverse publicity and revelations in the newspaper *Expressen* had dictated the need for a thorough investigation of the whole affair.[72]

There were two distinct, albeit overlapping, approaches to the Telub case. For many, the central question was whether it was right and proper for a state-owned concern to educate Libyans in techniques which could be used for military purposes: the issue, in short, was viewed as essentially one of political morality, i.e. that Sweden was assisting a military and moreover a militant dictatorship. For others the real question was whether a number of accountable officials and persons in positions of public confidence had taken sufficient pains to grasp the nature of the proposed instruction: whether they were simply ingenuous about it, or whether they had subsequently kept silent or even lied about their knowledge of the facts. For this group, the matter was essentially a technical and administrative one of ministerial competence and it was mainly this angle on which the Constitutional Committee focused when it began its review. By now one thing was clear: while the agreement with the Libyans did not contravene Swedish law, the Telub affair had grown slowly but surely into a political scandal and one ready-made for exploitation by the opposition parties.

The Social Democratic leader Olof Palme in particular scented blood, and while not making specific allegations of lying, he singled out the former Foreign Secretary Karin Söder of the Centre Party as the main object of his wrath. Speaking on radio and television, Palme claimed that she had shown naivety and incompetence, and expressed incredulity that the Foreign Minister had no inkling of the real nature of Telub's deal with the Libyans. For her part, Söder maintained throughout that she had never been exactly informed that the Libyans would receive a military education in Sweden. Here, obviously, was the vital point in the whole affair: did Söder, along with the Minister of Trade Staffan Burenstam-Linder and the Defence Minister Eric Krönmark — all members of Fälldin's first bourgeois coalition — actually know about the contents of the Telub deal in 1978? They all maintained, at least until early in 1981, that they had simply been misled by the Telub director at the time. However, in a dramatic turn of events, it came to light on 11 March 1981 that there had been a highly confidential letter from the Swedish ambassador in Libya, dated 11 January 1978, which made it clear (while expressing misgivings) that the Telub deal did indeed involve the giving of military training.

On same evening of 11 March, the Defence Minister conceded that he for one had been party to the contents of the letter and shared the ambassador's anxieties, but he claimed to have had no authority to prevent the agreement. If anything could have been done, he argued, it would have had to be through the Industry Department to which Telub is subordinate. It also seemed that at no point had the Trade Minister been able to find legal grounds for preventing co-operation between Telub and the Libyans. Even so, the Fälldin II government was able to cancel the military part of the education when the occasion demanded it.[73] At this stage two things were very clear. First, the ministers in question apparently knew more than they had been prepared to admit, and secondly, although in addition to the Constitutional Committee's review of the case, a one-man commission of inquiry, *enmansutredning*, had been set up to look into the nature of the education given at the Telub Institute, both inquiries were being undertaken when several of the facts had already come publicly to light. In view of what they regarded as the gravity of the matter, the Social Democrats also wanted the parallel commission of inquiry broadened to include members of the Riksdag.

The Constitutional Committee proceeded to interrogate no less than sixteen persons, including several ministers and former ministers, in the course of its protracted inquiries. The time expended on the case is indicative of the magnitude of the investigation:

according to committee statistics, the annual review had consumed 21 hours over the winter of 1980 whereas the following year this had risen to no less than 38½ hours of which as much as 25 were devoted to the Telub case. No single review issue has engaged the Constitutional Committee for longer since the transition to unicameralism in 1971. When the committee published its annual report in May 1981, however, it did not recommend any criticism of the government, although the Social Democratic members tabled a reservation to the report. An individual minister, the Conservative Party Minister of Trade Staffan Linder, was ultimately rebuked for having misled the Riksdag and not told the whole truth on the matter of military education. Yet despite the pressure from the Social Democrats, the former Foreign and Defence Ministers emerged unscathed.

There can be no question that the partisan composition of the Constitutional Committee worked to protect the government of the day: the majority decision not to criticise the Fälldin administration derived from the non-socialist committee members. Indeed, it may be that a weakening of its inquiry function has been an inevitable corollary of the party-politicisation of the Constitutional Committee. As Magnus Isberg has observed, 'the Constitutional Committee's review is nearly as much politicised as its consideration of legislative matters. It could hardly be otherwise when one political body, the Constitutional Committee, is judging the actions of another, the Government.'[74]

There are some final points to be noted on the Telub affair. First, the former Minister of Trade, Linder, gained a measure of official exoneration when the special one-man commission of inquiry reported that the minister had done a good deal to ascertain the truth. Secondly, on the orders of their government, the 100 Libyan soldiers being educated at the Telub Institute discontinued their studies at the beginning of 1982 and returned home. This happened almost a year after the Swedish government's decision of February 1981 to terminate the provision of education in all those areas with a military connection. Although Telub's parent-company subsequently offered an alternative programme with a more general character, this proved unacceptable and in the event the Ministry of Industry accepted on the Swedish government's behalf the ultimate liability to pay damages to the Libyans.[75] Finally, although the meetings of Riksdag standing committees are closed, a record of proceedings in the Telub case was published in conjunction with the Constitutional Committee's annual report. The apparent illogicality of this situation further reinforced the case for experimenting with a system of American-style 'open hearings'.

Taking the government review committees of parliament together, what can be said by way of summary? All are prestigious bodies which include senior delegates, even group chairmen, among their number and represent in their varying ways a distinctive consolidation of the classical parliamentary function of limiting the executive. The work of the review committees divides conveniently into two parts: technical inspection and political control. The former is constrained by the human factor — the finite amount of time and energy that committee members can devote to the review coupled with the modest staff resources at their disposal — and the vastness and complexity of the task at hand. For example, the evaluation of the ramifications for Danish industry of a particular EC decision plainly demands both delegate commitment and technical assistance. Moreover, in Finland and Sweden the Constitutional Committee reviews are confined to investigating the cabinet and government departments. The primary institutional structures of policy implementation — the central boards and agencies — are outside their terms of reference. In Sweden the public boards are scrutinised by a body of 12 Riksdag Auditors who are elected by the Riksdag from among its members and who can examine any subject or organisation within the purview of the national budget. In practice, however, the Riksdag Auditors are a weak organ of control. In all the review committees, matters of a politically sensitive and controversial character are raised from time to time. However, the fact that the committees reflect the partisan balance in the assembly has meant that the extent of their political control is inevitably tied to the changing dynamics of the legislative-executive balance. When a minority government is in power, the review committees can exercise political influence, as was evident during the Danish fisheries dispute with Britain at the beginning of 1983; when a majority government is in power, committee members ultimately tend to protect their own ministers, as in the Telub case. The party-politicisation of the government review committees of parliament has meant that they are no more 'corporate' bodies than the other parliamentary standing committees.

Control of the executive through Parliamentary Ombudsmen

The institution of the Parliamentary Ombudsman is indigenous to the Nordic region. The office originated in Sweden in the eighteenth century where it was formally incorporated into the 1809 Constitution. A second Swedish Ombudsman, dealing with Military Affairs, had been created in 1915 before Finland (formerly, of course, part of the Swedish realm) followed suit, adopting an Ombudsman in her post-Independence form of government in 1919. Constitutional reform led to the inception of a Danish Ombudsman in 1955, and seven years later a Norwegian Ombudsman for Administration, on the Danish model, was instituted. The latter complemented Norway's Ombudsman for Military Affairs, set up a decade earlier. Meanwhile, reorganisation in 1968 had seen the demise of Sweden's Military Ombudsman and led ultimately to the appointment in 1976 of four Ombudsmen, all with equal powers. Thus at present, there is a Parliamentary Ombudsman in Denmark, Norway and Finland (where since 1971 there has also been an Assistant Ombudsman), four hold office in Sweden, and only Iceland lacks a comparable office.

All the Ombudsmen are appointed by parliament, usually after a general election, and their term of office is in the first instance four years. All the Ombudsmen must have received a legal training — according to the Finnish constitution they are required to be 'eminently versed in the law'[76] — and, unlike the British Parliamentary Commissioner for Administration, they have wide-ranging powers of supervision which include the investigation of unreasonable as well as illegal decisions by public authorities. All have powers to initiate investigations, often following reports in the press, and outside Norway the Nordic Ombudsmen conduct tours of inspection of bodies such as prisons, local administrative districts, police headquarters and military garrisons. By comparison with Britain, the Ombudsman is highly visible: the investigation of complaints can generate considerable publicity, journalists frequently visit his office to peruse the files, and as a result the general public is far more aware of his existence than is the case in Britain. Not surprisingly, therefore, the workload of the Ombudsman is great: most of his cases stem from the large volume of citizens' complaints he receives and inevitably the personal interviewing of officials in the course of scrutinising these grievances (which is the norm in Britain) is relatively limited. In such circumstances, how effective is the control of the executive achieved through the network of Parliamentary Ombudsmen in the region?

We will first consider the formal variation in the powers vested in the office of the Ombudsman and the still greater discrepancies in the scope of the post which exist in practice. Primary attention is given to the 'old model' Ombudsmen in Finland, and in Sweden. Somewhat more summary consideration is given to Denmark and Norway, where the post was instituted after the Second World War and where the right of investigation is more circumscribed. Over and above his powers of inspection, it is obviously important to consider the accountability of the Ombudsman to parliament. How does this operate and how assiduous are parliamentarians in overseeing the Ombudsman's activities? Has parliament any operational control over his work and has the office been party-politicised to the same extent as the 'control committees' we discussed earlier in this chapter?

The powers of the Nordic Ombudsmen are greatest in Finland and Sweden, where there is the right to instigate a prosecution against an official or, more commonly, to authorise the public prosecutor to do so; in Denmark the Ombudsman has analogous legal powers but never deploys them in practice.[77] According to the Finnish constitution, the Ombudsman has the same authority as the Chancellor of Justice to attend sittings of the cabinet, the courts and official bodies, to obtain information from the records of the proceedings of the cabinet, ministries, courts and other official bodies, and, with the official responsibility prescribed in law for public prosecutors, to press charges or have charges pressed for official error or neglect of duty in office.[78] His terms of reference, moreover, include scrutinising not only the legality of the actions of officials and authorities, but also the procedures by which decisions are made. Uniquely in the region, the Finnish Ombudsman can propose legal proceedings against a member of the cabinet for an illegal act committed in the exercise of his duties; if this is upheld by the Eduskunta, he acts as the prosecutor at the special Court of Impeachment. This has happened twice, although in all cases where it is legally permissible, the Ombudsman exercises his power to order the public prosecutor to bring the action.

Prosecutions have been unusual, though by no means rare. In 1975, there were eight cases of prosecution: those against whom action was taken included two policemen accused of causing bodily harm through an official error, and a military doctor and a company commander and training officer accused in quite separate cases of continually violating their official responsibilities. However, it is far more common for the Finnish Ombudsman to issue a reproach or reminder, *huomautus*, which does not lead to disciplinary measures but sets out his view as to how and why a ministry or central board, for example, has been acting illegally. In recent years, reproaches have been sent to the Ministry of Education and National Board of Education, *kouluhallitus*, for delaying the payment of state subsidies to private schools; to the National Health Board for undue delay in the handling of a complaint before it; and to the National Forestry Board which had incorrectly, and without granting a personal hearing, required a landowner to repay to the state compensation that he had received for forest-planting work.[79] Although reproaches lack a formal sanction, they invariably lead to corrective action. Indeed, the Ombudsman is empowered to submit to any public authority proposals based on his observations in supervising the action of these authorities. These are not legally binding, but the Orders of the Ombudsman (1920) specifically require him to make such representations.

Thus each year the Ombudsman presents the cabinet, individual ministries and central boards with proposals for the development of legislation. Taking 1976 as a typical year, the Ombudsman put a wide-ranging proposal to the cabinet on the need to re-draft the laws relating to guardianship, particularly the provisions concerning the supervision of guardianship, and also drew its attention to the logjam in the handling of applications from associations seeking official registration. Another proposal was made regarding the improvement of the legislation dealing with the implementation of confinement orders by the military courts, while another urged the cabinet to remedy deficiencies in the law regarding the rights of foreigners taken into custody. A suggestion was made to the Ministry of Justice that in preparing for the next national and local elections more detailed instructions should be given to the election officials regarding the application of the election laws — the ballot paper used in the October 1976 local election was so thin as to be transparent and thus endangered the secrecy of voting — and another was directed at the Ministry of the Interior recommending consideration of whether the training of policemen should include a familiarity with certain diseases, such as diabetes, which could be crucial when detaining persons on charges of intoxication etc. Representation was made to the Social Welfare Board on the importance of giving local boards guidelines for the production of court statements concerning the care of children, divorce, separation etc., and the National Health Board was approached with a view to achieving uniform instructions regarding medical statements for presentation to the courts in guardianship cases. All in all, the Ombudsman made 25 proposals in 1976 regarding the development of legislation, the courts and central administration.

Finally, the Finnish Ombudsman is also involved in a number of general rulings which adequately reflect the status of the office. Most notable, given the closed nature of committee proceedings in the region, was the statement which the Ombudsman was called to give to the Finnish delegation of the Nordic Council on whether there were juridical obstacles to amending their procedure so as to allow committee meetings to be open to the public. No such legal barriers were discovered.

In accordance with the provisions of the 1974 constitution, the four Swedish Ombudsmen exercise a watching brief over the application of laws and other regulations in the public sector: they are allowed to prosecute in line with an authorisation of the Riksdag and may also be present at the deliberation of courts and administrative bodies as well as having the right of access to their protocols and minutes.[80] Unlike their Finnish counterpart, the Swedish Ombudsmen cannot move a prosecution against a cabinet minister, but on the other hand the public boards and agencies that implement the law do fall within their charge. This limitation in the scope of their inquiries — even the Danish and Norwegian Ombudsmen investigate complaints against ministers — should be seen in the context of the historic separation of government and public administration in Sweden and in particular the distinctive autonomy of the Swedish civil service.

Thus the 1809 constitution envisaged a body of central officials acting as a neutral connecting link between the policy-makers and parliament: the King nominated a government accountable to the Riksdag through the Constitutional Committee's inspection of its minutes, but the civil servants were to be answerable for their decisions only before a court of law. Neither government nor parliament was allowed to interfere in the activity of public officials, and conversely the government's political responsibility to the Riksdag — as set out in articles 49 and 90 of the 1809 constitution — did not include decisions taken by civil servants. The King's ministers were to formulate proposals; the Riksdag ratified them; and the central officials carried out the laws. In the process of executing the law, the officials were liable in a legal sense only: they could not be dismissed by cabinet or parliament. It is in this light that the incorporation of an Ombudsman into the 1809 constitution and the powers vested in him to supervise the legality of the action of those implementing the laws assumed such obvious importance.

The former Swedish constitution was undoubtedly influenced by the principle of the separation of powers written into the American constitution somewhat earlier, although it also reflected the social structure of Sweden at the beginning of the nineteenth century. As Hans Esping has noted, 'it is not necessary to be a committed Marxist to recognise that the 1809 constitution gave the upper class — the high nobility and above all officials — a position from which to dominate the conduct of public affairs. The only centres of power strong enough to direct the administration — the King and his ministers on the one hand and the Riksdag on the other — were forbidden by the constitution from influencing them'.[81] The salience of the Ombudsman's classical role was even maintained when the 1974 form of government perpetuated the tradition of a highly independent public administration: officials, in short, are still exempted from political responsibility for their actions.

Since it was defined in the 1809 constitution, the role of the Swedish public administration has changed markedly. An autonomous and impartial body of central officials was possibly a tenable notion as long as the position of the state remained essentially that of a nightwatchman. However, the development of a welfare state from the 1930s onwards has meant an increase in the number of civil servants, and in the volume and complexity of the business they handle. Inevitably, the scope for administrative discretion in the interpretation and application of legislative programmes has increased as well. The number of central boards has grown from about 50 in the early 1970s to rather more than 100 a decade later. Because the size of government departments (the formulating bodies) has remained small, a majority of civil servants are today located in public boards and agencies. Yet ministers still neither bear responsibility for, nor exercise any control over, the operation of these boards. It remains, as one commentator has observed, a distinctive feature of the Swedish system of public administration 'that once a decision has been reached through executive-legislative channels, the ministers and the departments exercise no direct authority over the actual implementation of policy.'[82] Nor are the actions of central boards subject to parliamentary control since, as noted earlier, the Constitutional Committee's review is restricted to the cabinet and government departments.

Certainly there is an overlapping membership between parliament and the central boards: as Isberg has indicated, Riksdag representation on the executive boards of the major public agencies increased from 13% in 1971 to 21% in 1979,[83] and moreover, the representation of Riksdag delegates on agency boards in recent years has reflected fairly accurately the partisan balance in the assembly. But such informal personnel links plainly do not constitute a vehicle for scrutinising and controlling the process of implementing laws in Sweden. A Director-General appointed, like the Riksdag delegates, by the government acts as chairman of the board and exercises a good deal of discretion in deciding whether to resolve a matter himself or bring it before the monthly board meeting, while the growing body of parliamentarians on the boards in the 1970s appears to have been designed to provide a counterweight to the pressure groups and civil servants also represented. Delegates, in short tend to serve as experts and spokesmen of a particular interest, precisely as they do on many of the policy-formulating commissions of inquiry (see chapter 2). Riksdag members, of course, have nothing to do with the day-to-day operation of the agency, nor is there yet any systematic reporting of their activities in their parliamentary party groups.[84] At most Riksdag representation on the executive boards of public agencies could be said to provide a potentially important channel through which parliament can influence broad decisions relating to the implementation of policy — resource allocation between the various administrative bodies, the size of their annual budget requests etc. However, it is only through the Ombudsman's powers to probe actions of the staff of the public agencies — and if necessary to bring a prosecution against one or more of the officials therein — that a degree of control over the non-political arm of the executive, impossible through parliamentary machinery, has been obtained.

In reality, resort to a prosecution instigated by, or brought on the instruction of, the Ombudsman has been even less common than in Finland, running at no more than one or two cases annually. True, it has been commonplace for the Swedish Ombudsman, like his Finnish counterpart, to initiate an investigation leading to an agency being reprimanded, sometimes following a report of suspected corruption or malpractice in the press or alternatively if the evidence has been uncovered by one of the Ombudsman's periodic tours of inspection. In Sweden the Ombudsman's terms of reference are wide: he supervises not only the legality of the application of laws, viz. procedural questions, but also whether they are reasonable.[85] But the need to order a formal prosecution has seldom arisen since there have hardly been any occasions when an official or public authority has failed to react to a recommendation from the Ombudsman. Like the Finnish Ombudsman, his Swedish counterparts can, and do, suggest the development of legislative proposals to the cabinet and parliament, although their heavy workload has acted as a powerful constraint on this important task.

The office of Ombudsman is less deeply-rooted in Denmark and Norway than in Finland and Sweden, and his powers of criticising the executive are more limited. Indeed, lacking an institutional separation of the formulation and implementation functions of the executive as in Finland and Sweden, the activities of the Danish and Norwegian Ombudsmen in investigating complaints against a 'department-dominant' administration may be readily compared to those of the British Parliamentary Commissioner for Administration (PCA). The Danish Ombudsman has a much wider remit than the PCA, since included in the scope of his investigations are the nationalised industries, the armed forces and local authorities' planning powers, though (unlike in Sweden) they exclude the courts. But in practice criticism against unreasonable decisions has been extremely cautious — there are similarities here with the 'injustice in consequence of maladministration' that are the PCA's terms of reference — and, as in Britain, many complaints cannot be taken up because of the rule that the complainant must have exhausted the remedies available through appeal to the higher courts before approaching the Ombudsman. As much as one-third of the complaints he receives annually cannot be investigated as a result of this stipulation, which however does not apply to grievances against the conduct of officials. Unlike in Sweden, moreover, the Danish Ombudsman cannot require all the documents — e.g. the internal memoranda — in a particular matter to be made available.

According to article 55 of the Danish constitution, statutory provision shall be made for the appointment by the Folketing of one or two persons (the same wording as in the 1971 Swedish constitution) to supervise the civil and military administration of the state. In Norway the overseeing of the military administration is the responsibility of a special Military Ombudsman set up in 1952, leaving the Ombudsman for Administration — unlike his counterparts elsewhere in the region — to concentrate solely on civil matters. On the Danish model, the Norwegian Ombudsman possesses similar restrictions over access to documentation, complaints not having had prior recourse to higher bodies, and criticism of discretionary decisions. In both Denmark and Norway, however, the work of the Ombudsman is far more publicised than that of the PCA in Britain.

On the question of their accountability to the legislature, it should be emphasised that all the Nordic Ombudsmen are appointed by parliament, and parliament can as a last resort refuse to re-elect them. On the matter of appointing the Ombudsmen, the Standing Orders of the Riksdag state that within 20 days of it being named after a general election, the Riksdag Constitutional Committee shall elect a 6-person working group, *JO-delegationen*, to prepare the election of the Parliamentary Ombudsmen, and this shall work in consultation with the nominated representatives of the party groups in the Speaker's Council.[86] The regulations in Finland are less precise — the Ombudsman is elected by a secret ballot of the Eduskunta, though without the formal nomination of candidates. Throughout the region, appointments are initially for a four-year term which by convention may be renewed at least once in Sweden and for longer periods elsewhere. In Denmark, Stephan Hurwitz held the post from its creation in 1955 to his retirement in 1971.

The main line of accountability to parliament is scarcely through the possible sanction of not being re-appointed, which in practice is never invoked, but through the presentation of the Ombudsman's annual report to one of the standing committees of the assembly — the Constitutional Committee in Sweden and Finland and the Justice Committee in Denmark and Norway. The annual reports, however, are subject to only the most cursory inspection in standing committee. In Denmark, delegates on the Justice Committee do show interest in the ten or so special reports which the Ombudsman submits yearly (in addition to his annual report), while in Finland the Constitutional Committee usually calls the Ombudsman to a personal 'hearing' at which questions on the annual report may be put and further information sought on cases in which committee members may be particularly interested. The Constitutional Committee then reports on the Ombudsman's report, and this is subsequently considered in a plenary sitting. In Sweden, however, the Ombudsman's report receives a largely mechanical consideration in the Constitutional Committee, although it might be noted here that the Riksdag Standing Orders do permit private initiatives to be tabled on the basis of the Ombudsman's annual report.[87]

Despite his formal accountability to the legislature, a number of factors have emphasised the functional separation between parliament and the parliamentary Ombudsman in the region. His office is no longer located in the parliament building. He has his own staff: it is relatively small — in Sweden a little over thirty persons serve the four Ombudsmen — but it is independent nonetheless. Complaints to the Ombudsman do not need to be directed via parliamentarians, as in the case of the British PCA and French *Médiateur*, and very few are. Nowhere in the region, moreover, can a member of parliament hold the post of Ombudsman, although in Finland this was possible before 1928. Indeed, the role of party considerations in the election of the Ombudsman has been more prominent in Finland than in the other Nordic countries — partly because there is no formal nomination of candidates — and this was particularly so in the 1920s when Eduskunta members were on occasion elected to the position of Ombudsman. In none of the Nordic states, however, can the post of Ombudsman remotely be considered a party-political appointment. Distinctively, the Finnish Ombudsman has the right to attend a plenary sitting of parliament and to take part in debates — although not of course to vote.[88] If the Ombudsman requests to speak he is given precedence over ordinary delegates and on more than twenty occasions since 1919 the incumbent Ombudsman has exercised this right, though seldom in connection with the plenary reading of his annual report.

Thus only in the strictest sense are the Ombudsmen part of the parliamentary control system. Their investigations are technical rather than political — to employ the dichotomy used in relation to the work of the government review committees of parliament; their appointment is non-partisan and parliament exerts no influence over either the selection of cases for investigation, the action taken or the remedies proposed. In the words of Frank Stacey, the role of the Ombudsman in the Nordic states is very much that of 'an independent critic of the executive'.[89]

Parliamentary inspection and control outside the enactment process: Conclusions

The inspection and control of the executive are classical functions of the Nordic legislatures, entrenched as early as 1814 in article 75 of the Norwegian constitution. The latter includes among the rights and duties of the Storting: to control the finances of the Kingdom; to decide how much shall be paid annually to the King for the royal household; to have laid before it the records of the Council of State and all public reports and documents; to have communicated to it the treaties and agreements which the King has concluded with foreign powers; to have power to summon anyone before it on matters of state except the King and the royal family; and to appoint five auditors who shall examine the accounts of the state. Well over 150 years later, paragraph 1, sub-section 4 of the new Swedish constitution encapsulated these same historic rights and obligations in the terse statement that the Riksdag shall review the activities of government and public administration. We have been concerned in Part III of this volume to examine the varying means which the Nordic parliaments have at their disposal for inspecting and controlling the executive outside the process of enacting laws — in short, the inquiry function of the Nordic parliaments.

What is initially most striking is the way traditional structures for overseeing the executive have proved so resilient. Indeed the Nordic assemblies have witnessed the survival into the modern era of control machinery born of a period of constitutional and parliamentary reform considerably pre-dating the completion of mass democracy and designed to keep a check on the King and royal officials. The Constitutional Committee's review of government in Sweden thus dates back to 1809, interpellations and parliamentary commissions of investigation in Denmark to 1849, and questions to ministers in Iceland to 1874. All these devices arose at a time when there was a clear-cut separation between the legislature and executive. The primary function of the Riksdag Constitutional Committee's inspection of cabinet minutes was to ensure some measure of government accountability before the breakthrough of the parliamentary principle. The rise of cohesive parliamentary parties, however, has meant that the degree of real accountability is largely dependent on the balance of parties in the committee: as the Telub case illustrated, the majority can protect its own ministers. The party-politicisation of the Nordic assemblies has also affected the way the classical instruments of parliamentary control are used. Interpellations, for example, with the opportunity they afford for a plenary debate, were originally a means of questioning ministers and so calling the executive to account. In the hands of opposition party leaders, however, interpellations are today vehicles for opposing the legislative intentions of the government and for promoting opposition counter-programmes. Nowadays the ultimate weapon of parliamentary control is the motion of no confidence — only quite recently introduced in Sweden — though here again this is not infrequently seen by the opposition as a tactical ploy with which to bluff the government.

The party-politicisation of the Nordic assemblies, together with the growing bureaucratisation of government after the Second World War—a corollary of the development of state welfarism — have highlighted the need to distinguish two contrasting objectives in the deployment of the parliamentary procedures for interrogating the executive. First, they can be used to produce some form of *political control* over the executive — the criticism of government policy, the dismissal or even impeachment of a minister, the resignation of an entire cabinet, and so on. In such cases, delegates invariably divide into a government and opposition camp. Secondly and more routinely, the inquiry powers of the assembly are used to achieve a measure of *technical inspection* of administrative practices. They are designed in other words to bring out discrepancies in the way that certain policies are implemented, delays in acting on parliamentary directives, improvements in the technical details of a law after scrutinising its application over a particular period etc. In the government review committees of parliament particularly, the political control and technical inspection functions are intertwined. The technical inspection of the executive should be viewed in the context of the growing scale and complexity of state activity. Indeed to keep pace with developments, there has been a modernisation of the parliamentary control and inspection procedures in the region since the Second World War.

The plenary machinery for interrogating the executive has thus been extended with the introduction of a Westminster-style Question Time. Members' questions have not been abrogated by the party machines to any significant extent. However, 'supplementaries' are limited both in number (outside Sweden) and in length, and cannot be compared with the lengthy (often 20 minute) preamble which accompanies their British counterpart and which can give ministers an extremely harrowing time. Question Time is plainly not the ordeal for the Prime Ministers of the Nordic states that it can be for the British Premier in the House of Commons. In cross-examining ministers, delegates tend to trade off their expertise in a particular policy area and to table questions which come within the legislative scope of the standing committee to which they belong. The collective capacity of the Nordic parliaments to inspect administrative practices is accordingly limited. It is symptomatic of the increased workload of government departments and of the concentration of questions on relatively few ministries — often those with responsibilities for regional economic policy — that delegates experience delays in gaining a ministerial response to their questions.

Next, the parliamentary standing committee systems were reformed to create (in Denmark and Sweden) or institutionalise (in Finland) a network of subject-specific, department-oriented committees with inquiry powers. Standing committees in the region conjoin scrutiny of ongoing government proposals with the wider inspection of the implementation of policy. There is not a distinct system of departmental review committees like the select committees at Westminster; nor is there an 'open hearings' procedure like the one so well established in the United States Congress. On the subject of Congress, the schema used by Jewell and Patterson in their analysis of the American legislature provides a sensitive tool for evaluating the extent of parliamentary influence over policy implementation in the Nordic states. Three levels of influence are identified: first, *oversight* or parliamentary observation of the administration; secondly, *supervision* or parliamentary involvement in the formulation of administrative policy; and finally, *control* or parliamentary determination of administrative policy.[90] How then should we sum up?

First, only a few standing committees in the Nordic parliaments possess statutory review duties. This is unlike the United States where since 1946 every Congressional standing committee has been required by law to undertake a continuous review of the work of the agencies under its jurisdiction, or Britain where since 1979 a comprehensive network of select committees has been empowered to inquire into administrative practices and obliged to report regularly to the House of Commons (their reports being debated and sometimes compelling a response from the executive). All the specialist standing committees have powers to oversee the administration, and ministers, under-secretaries and departmental officials are indeed cross-examined, but the weight of oversight activity is concentrated on one or two committees with accentuated inquiry powers — the Constitutional Committees in Sweden and Finland, the Scrutiny Committee in Norway — which are required to report back to parliament on their investigations.

Secondly, the influence of the Nordic parliaments over policy implementation is almost entirely limited to administrative oversight — that is, inspection and surveillance involving the standing committees, interpellations and questions from the floor of the assembly, and, outside Iceland, the election of a Parliamentary Ombudsman to act as agent of the legislature in overseeing the application of laws by officials. In Sweden, where the Riksdag is precluded from monitoring the central boards and agencies which form the basic structures of policy implementation, the increased representation of legislators on the executive boards of these public agencies in the 1970s has provided a potential channel through which parliament might subsequently be involved in the formulation of administrative policy viz the size of the allocation to a public agency within an existing legislative programme, the annual budget request of the agency, and so on. For the time being, however, the Nordic parliaments are effectively restricted to overseeing executive practices.

In a category of its own is clearly the Market Relations Committee in Denmark, which not only supervises, but on occasions controls administrative policy. However, although it is a 'control committee', the MRC exerts its influence not over the implementation of policy at the national level, but rather over the policies of the implementing or administrative agency — the Danish government — which bears responsibility for the domestic application of EC regulations.

Finally, if in comparative perspective the influence of the Nordic parliaments is seen to be relatively weak, particularly compared with the US Congress — where the separation of powers principle has created an entirely different set of circumstances — the extent of delegate participation in oversight activity should certainly not be minimised. All the standing committees exercise inquiry powers; the volume of parliamentary questions (oral and written) has grown continuously if unevenly; and attendance at Question Times, although by no means impressive, exceeds that for a typical legislative plenary. Indeed a credible defence could be made out in the region for Loewenberg and Patterson's assertion that 'legislatures play a larger role in the implementation of policy than in the formulation of policy which they are commonly expected to influence strongly.'[91] Equally, of course, delegate participation cannot be equated with parliamentary influence over the application of legislative programmes.

REFERENCES

1. DRG 5:51, 52.
2. Lo Folkman & Hans Peter Hilden, *Lovgivningsprocessen og mulighederne for indflydelse på folketingets arbejde*. København: Schultz Forlag, 1979, pp. 145–6.
3. Forslag til lov om en undersøgelse af visse forhold vedrørande post- og telegrafvæsenet. Lovforslag nr L 64. *Folketinget 1981/82* (2 samling). Blad nr 77, pp. 226, 242.
4. DRG 3:16, 24. 6:59.
5. RF 12:3.
6. Laki eduskunnan oikeudesta tarkastaa valtioneuvoston jäsenten ja oikeuskanslerin virkatointen lainmukaisuutta (*ministerien vastuunalaisuus*) 25.11.1922. 2§.
7. 'Riksretten — en "politisk domstol" '. *Aftenposten* 11.11.1977.
8. 'Politkere utelukkes fra offenlige verv?' *Aftenposten* 27.4.1977.
9. *Innstilling* (*S. nr 101, 1981/82*) fra kontrollkomitéen om klager fra avdelingsingeniør Hans J. Rogde og kommandørkaptein Finn Holtar.
10. Information provided by Erik Mo 24.2.1982.
11. *Innstilling* (*S. nr 121, 1981/82*) frå kontrollkomitéen om Riksrevisjonen sin konstitusjonelle kontroll av statsbedrifter og statsbanker under kommunal- og arbeidsdepartementet.
12. *Innstilling* (*S. nr 112, 1981/82*) fra kontrollkomitéen om embetsutnevnelser m.v. 1 juli 1980 — 30 juni 1981 (St. meld. nr 6)
13. DRG 3:19:3.
14. RF 10:7.
15. RF 10:2.
16. *Ny utskottsorganisation. Statens offentliga utredningar 1969:62*. Stockholm 1969, pp. 92–5.
17. RO 8:7.
18. RO 8:8.
19. RF 10:7.
20. Neil Elder, *Government in Sweden. The Executive at Work*. Oxford: Pergamon Press, 1970, p. 33.
21. RF 10:2.
22. Birgersson *et al.* (1981), pp. 273–4.
23. Jorma Enochsson & Roland Petersson, *Gunnar Hedlund*. Stockholm: Norstedt & Söners Förlag, 1973.
24. Ibid., pp. 179–80.
25. Ulf Svensson, 'Folkpartiet och EEC'. *Tiden* 63, 6, 1971, pp. 342–9.
26. 'Avvaktande i EEC- frågan'. *Nordisk Kontakt* 3/71, pp. 173–4.
27. 'Nej till EEC-medlemskap'. *Nordisk Kontakt* 5/71, pp. 307–8.
28. Jan-Olof Sundell, 'Sverige och EEC'. *Svensk tidskrift* 58, 4, 1971.
29. 'Regeringens Sydafrikabeslut attackerat av Carl Lidblom'. *Från Riksdag & Departement* 13.2.1981.
30. Karl E. Birnbaum, 'Hur den Svenska utrikespolitiken tillkommer', in Gunnar Jervas (ed.), *Utrikespolitik i Norr*. Lund: Studentlitteratur, 1973, pp. 88–123; Nils Andrén, *Svenska Statskunskap*. Stockholm: Liber, 1968, pp. 473–82.
31. Interview with Arne Marquard 20.4.1982. DRG 3:19:3.
32. As Nils Stjernqvist has put it in the Swedish case: 'Only such foreign policy matters as do not belong to another committee shall be considered by the Foreign Affairs Committee'. Nils Stjernqvist, 'Riksdagens arbete och arbetsformer', in *Samhälle och riksdag* IV. Uppsala: Almqvist & Wiksell, 1966, p. 232.
33. Reidar Omang, *Stortinget og de utenrikske saker etter unionsoppløsningen 1905*. Oslo: Gydendal Norsk Forlag, 1964, p. 160. Finn Moe, 'Stortinget og den utenrikspolitiske avgjørelsesprosessen'. *Internasjonal Politikk* 6, 1969, p. 691–713.

34. Interview with Erik Mo 1.10.1981. On the role of the Storting standing committee on Foreign Affairs and the Constitution, see *St. meld. nr 35* (*1980/81*) om Noregs samarbeid med utviklingslandene i 1979. *Innst S nr 255* (*1980/81*). Tilråding frå utanriks- og konstitusjonsnemnda om Noregs samarbeid med utviklingslanda i 1979.
35. Gustafsson & Johansson (1982), p. 62.
36. Interview with Lars Foyer 17.9.1982.
37. *Näringsutskottets betänkande 1978/79*:60, pp. 2, 26.
38. Information provided by Gösta Fischer 17.1.1983.
39. Interview with Jens Adser Sørensen 26.4.1982.
40. On the standing committee interrogation of the Overseas Trade Minister, see Arvo Rytkönen, *Kauppapolitiikkamme 1980-luvun kynnyksellä*. Alustus Paasikivi-Seura ry:n kokouksessa 29.1.1979. Paasikivi-Seuran monistesarja 18, 1979. In general, however, Eduskunta control over foreign policy is very weak. Parliament receives the occasional government bulletin on a foreign or commercial policy issue — e.g. one annually between 1970 and 1975 — but, significantly, the Constitutional Reform Committee in its interim report in 1974 was unanimous that the Eduskunta should be able more actively to participate in foreign policy management through strengthening the powers of the Foreign Affairs Committee. See Olavi Borg, *Suomalaisen parlamentarismin muutospaineet*. Tampereen yliopiston politiikan tutkimuksen laitoksen tutkielmia. 20, 1980. Hannu Soikkanen, *Eduskunnan toiminnasta sota-aikana* (*valtiopäivät 1939–44*). Helsinki: Tammi 1980.
41. Isberg (1982), p. 69.
42. Interview with Daniel Tarschys 21.9.1981.
43. 'Komite-høringer er ikke aktuelt'. *Aftenposten* 28.5.1977. 'Nei til "høring"?' *Aftenposten* 11.6.1977.
44. Interview with Arne Marquard 20.4.1982.
45. Anne Davies, *Reformed Select Committees: The First Year*. London: Outer Circle Policy Unit, p. 65.
46. Interview with Keith Hampson, Conservative Parliamentary Private Secretary at the Ministry of the Environment 12.2.1983.
47. Interview with David Steel, leader of the Liberal Party, 'Newsnight', BBC 2 Television 18.1.1982.
48. John Fitzmaurice, 'The Danish system of parliamentary control over European Community policy', in Valentine Herman & Rinus van Schendelen (eds), *The European Parliament and the National Parliaments*. Farnborough, Hants: Saxon House, 1979, p. 217.
49. Ibid., p. 210.
50. Interview with Lo Folkmann, Secretary of the Market Relations Committee of the Folketing 21.4.1982.
51. Information from Lo Folkmann 20.1.1983.
52. Miljø- og planlægningsudvalget (alm. del/EF — bilag 7). Markedsudvalget (alm. del/EF — bilag 37) *Til folketingets markedsudvalg* 25.11.1982.
53. Niels Gangsted-Rasmussen. Vedr: 3 danske rejefartøjers rejelicenser 1983. 15 december 1982. *Markedsudvalg bil. 62*.
54. Otto Møller, 'EF- udvalgets opgaver og funktion'. *Europæisk Samling* 3, 1981.
55. Lo Folkmann, 'Sådan fungerer folketingets markedsudvalg'. *Europæisk Samling* 3, 1981.
56. Ibid., p. 8.
57. Interview with Martti Manninen, secretary to both the Eduskunta Constitutional Committee and the Foreign Affairs Committee 21.3.1983.
58. *Perustuslakivaliokunnan mietintö no 56* hallituksen toimenpiteistään vuonna 1981 antaman kertomuksen johdosta, pp. 1–3.

59. Ibid., pp. 3–8.
60. David Arter, 'Rural sway in Finnish vote'. *Yorkshire Post* 26.3.1983.
61. *Ulkoasiainvaliokunnan mietintö* no 28 hallituksen toimenpiteistään vuonna 1981 antaman kertomuksen johdosta siltä osin kuin se koskee suhteita ulkovaltoihin.
62. *Valtiopäivät 1980*. Pöytäkirjat 1, pp. 139–171.
63. Hallituksen kertomus 1945 sisäasiainministeriön toimiala. *Perustuslakivaliokunnan mietintö* 17 ja 17a, 1948. Eduskunnan pöytäkirjat A IV, 1948.
64. RF 1:3.
65. Interview with Bengt Johansson 18.9.1981.
66. Håstad (1957), pp. 131–4.
67. Ibid., p. 133.
68. Konstitutionsutskottets betänkande 1980/81:25. Granskningsbetänkande, pp. 6–7, 96–105.
69. Ibid., pp. 7—8.
70. Information provided by Magnus Isberg 26.1.1982.
71. Interview with Claes Eklundh 15.9.1982.
72. 'Allvarligare historia än vad vi först trodde'. *Dagens Nyheter* 13.3.1981.
73. 'Vi förhandlar om avveckling'. *Dagens Nyheter* 13.3.1981.
74. Isberg (1982), p. 68.
75. 'Telub-araberna reser hem'. *Nordisk Kontakt* 1/82, p. 66.
76. HM 4:49 (26.4.1957/176).
77. Frank Stacey, *Ombudsmen Compared.* Oxford: Clarendon Press, 1978, p. 5.
78. HM 4:49.
79. *The Parliamentary Ombudsman in Finland. Position and Functions.* Helsinki: Valtion painatuskeskus, 1976; *Report of the Parliamentary Ombudsman. Summary and Annotations.* Helsinki 1977, pp. 12–13.
80. RF 12:6.
81. Hans Esping, 'Politisera förvaltningen!' *Konkret* 3–4, 1967, pp. 66–9.
82. M. Donald Hancock, *Sweden: The Politics of Postindustrial Change.* Hinsdale, Illinois: Dryden Press, 1972, p. 205.
83. Isberg (1982), pp. 78–82.
84. Ibid., p. 80.
85. Stacey (1978), pp. 9–10.
86. RO 8:10:1, 2.
87. RO 3:13:1.
88. VJ 5:59.
89. Stacey (1978), p. 233.
90. Cited in Loewenberg & Patterson (1979), pp. 269–70.
91. Ibid., p. 268.

CONCLUSION

> 'Of recent decades, the Riksdag has encountered competition from such great economic and professional organisations as the Federation of Trade Unions, the Employers' Union and the Farmers' Union. This competition has chiefly taken the form of agreements concluded between the Government and the organisations, eg in respect of the pay of public servants or agricultural prices. As a rule, the Riksdag has had no option but to approve the agreement retrospectively.' — Elis Håstad, *The Parliament of Sweden* 1957, p. 138

The aim of this book has been to describe, analyse and compare the participation of the Nordic parliaments in the national policy process. What sorts of variation in parliamentary involvement have emerged from our examination of the three main policy stages — formulation, adoption and implementation? Can any tentative conclusions about relative influence be drawn from the differing patterns? Further, do the Nordic parliaments possess the political power to make their views heeded in the decisions of governments? Or can it be concluded, along with Richardson and Jordan's appraisal of the situation in Britain, that 'by and large the big decisions in society are not made in Parliament at all'?[1]

In Part I our central thesis was that the formal engagement of Nordic parliamentarians on the myriad executive structures of policy consultation and preparation has been low with the notable exception of Sweden. Due to the extensive representation of government delegates and, more notably, opposition delegates on Swedish commissions of inquiry, the Riksdag has participated in a unique way in the formulation of legislative programmes. Elsewhere in the region, delegates have been restricted to using members' request proposals to press for the creation of a commission of inquiry and, if they are not appointed to serve on it, may attempt to bring their opinions to bear through the spokesmen of kindred organised interests. A Social Democratic delegate would thus seek to work through the trade union members on a commission, and so on. Outside Sweden, however, the direct involvement of Nordic parliamentarians in the formulation of policy has been extremely limited.

Two further points need emphasis. First, the important legislative function of organised groups: as the state has become involved in ever wider areas of legislative activity, so the affected interests have increasingly been allowed to participate in and consent to proposed changes. Hence interest groups play a central role in policy-making and enjoy continuous and regularised access to government. Their spokesmen are extensively represented on the commissions that constitute the primary instruments of inter-élite bargaining and which also provide the institutional framework of the corporate channel. So much is commonplace in Nordic analysis: partly because it is the accepted wisdom but, more important, because of the parliamentary focus of this book, the significant policy contribution of interest groups has not been subject to detailed elaboration. Secondly, the cabinet should be viewed as one of many actors in the policy process and one which in a number of 'routine' legislative areas — e.g. social policy matters — has not necessarily been the most influential. In this context, the role of civil servants in coordinating the activities of commissions and in the detailed drafting of proposals needs recognition. Indeed, there is obviously a real sense in which, as the Swedish commission report in autumn 1983 — 'Political Direction — Administrative Independence' put it, 'the government governs too little'.[2]

Part II demonstrates that because the overwhelming proportion of measures they adopt are government proposals, the Nordic parliaments clearly belong to the family of deliberating assemblies. The possible exception is Iceland where the comparatively large proportion of private members' bills that become law (albeit a declining one since the Second World War) make the Althing closer to a legislating assembly than probably any other in Western Europe. We were able to see a number of distinctive features in the patterns of parliamentary involvement in the enactment process: the absence in Norway and Sweden of a pre-committee Reading at which the general principles of a bill are aired. (cf. the Second Reading in the House of Commons); the right of standing committees in Sweden and Iceland to initiate proposals invariably amending government bills; the traits of modified unicameralism in Norway, Finland and Iceland enforcing an 'upper chamber' consideration of measures; the historic system of qualified majorities applying to most economic legislation in Finland; and the provision in the Danish constitution allowing a minority of parliamentarians to submit to a popular referendum a measure already approved in the Folketing. The active participation of Nordic delegates in standing committee work emerged as a notable characteristic of the parliamentary culture of the region. The majority of Nordic delegates are 'legislators' rather than 'advertisers' in J.D. Barber's familiar typology.

Although the implementation of policy has traditionally been a function of the executive, Part III illustrates the way the Nordic parliaments have developed procedures for the inspection and control of government outside the enactment process. The government review functions of the Riksdag's Constitutional Committee and the work of the Parliamentary Ombudsman in Sweden deserve mention for their longevity alone, as indeed do the distinctive

Parliamentary Advisory Councils on Foreign Affairs in the three constitutional monarchies and the unique role of the Folketing's Market Relations Committee. The unusual bifurcation of the government machine in Sweden and Finland into policy-formulating bodies (departments) and policy-implementing organs (central boards and agencies), and the proscription of assembly scrutiny of public agencies, have plainly restricted parliamentary participation in oversight activities in those two countries. Throughout the region, however, delegate involvement appears to be more extensive in the interrogative work of the legislature than in the formulation of legislation, although the influence of the Nordic parliaments over policy implementation is weak when compared with the United States Congress or even the House of Commons in recent years.

Propositions about the influence of the Nordic parliaments are inevitably hazardous. It is not possible to make simple deductions about influence from the patterns of participation in the policy process, although the variations do indicate a varying potential for influence. Swedish parliamentarians, for example, will be generally better equipped to engage in the deliberation of bills in standing committee, having participated on the preparatory commission of inquiry, while opposition groups in the Eduskunta derive extra weight from the fact that only 34 delegates are required to prevent legislation being enacted in the lifetime of a whole parliament. Potential influence is one thing, but its realisation is quite another. The calculus must contend with the changing dynamics of political situations. In general the policy influence of all the Nordic parliaments seems integrally tied to the positions of the parties in the assembly — and in particular whether these militate towards the formation of majority governments.

When the legislative-executive balance is inclined in favour of parliament, the influence of the assembly is strengthened at every stage in the policy process. At the formulation stage, for instance, a significant increase occurred in the number of delegates from the parliamentary opposition parties represented on multi-member commissions of inquiry during Ullsten's Liberal minority cabinet in Sweden between 1978–9. The government was less able to resist parliamentary requests for commissions, and anyway sought to build a measure of cross-party consensus by the heightened incorporation of opposition delegates on them. In the absence of a majority administration, moreover, government proposals are invariably modified and compromises reached either before the formal presentation of a bill to parliament or at the standing committee stage. This type of *ad hoc* 'log-rolling' for support in the adoption of legislative measures has become a perennial feature of Danish parliamentary politics. Outside the enactment process, parliamentary control of the executive is also enhanced when the government lacks majority support in the assembly: the role of the Danish MRC in the fisheries dispute with Britain and the EC during Schlüter's minority administration well illustrates the point.

During conditions of majority government, the position appears reversed: the government controls the commission system, the majority in the assembly ensures the adoption of government bills, and government ministers are protected on the 'control committees' of parliament. Yet majority governments have not been the norm in the region in recent years, and even when the balance of power has favoured the cabinet, the Nordic parliaments cannot be considered weak assemblies acting merely as procedural devices for the legitimation of government decisions. True, the experiment introduced in Finland in 1980 of the government putting the main themes of the budget before the Eduskunta in June before the detailed parliamentary consideration of the Finance Bill in the autumn has proved largely ineffectual: in its inaugural year, the Finance Minister began the proceedings by reading verbatim a 24-page report already distributed to delegates and took an hour to do so.[3] But throughout the region it has become customary for a number of amendments to be made to the budget during its passage through the House. However, more far-reaching changes have not been made for, as Higley, Brofuss and Groholt's interview survey of Storting Finance Committee members has shown, delegates lack sufficient technical knowledge of the underlying economic concepts to make a true evaluation of the main guidelines of the budget as laid down by the civil service experts in the Finance Department (ministers suffer from a similar handicap).[4]

On occasions, one of the specialist standing committees in the region has contrived a collective, subject-based opposition to a bill which has led to amendments being recommended. Although this has generally been rare, a united Riksdag Finance Committee did take the unprecedented step in November 1977 of reproaching Fälldin's non-socialist majority government, during its preparation of the budget, over the decision announced by the Budget Minister not to incorporate certain key defence items into the next budget, but to include a 15% investment grant to non-priority buildings like sports centres and swimming halls.[5] More commonly, the Nordic parliaments have served as arenas for the registration of intra-party dissent, particularly over questions of regional economic policy and issues with a moral dimension. Deep-seated factionalisation within one or two parties has reinforced this picture: at times, half of a party has participated in government, while the other has remained in opposition. The Finnish People's Democratic League since 1970 and the Icelandic Independence Party since 1981 are cases in point. In short, the predominant pattern of government-opposition voting has been limited by intermittent manifestations of individualistic voting and the much more frequent incidence of multi-party coalitions.

It is also vital to avoid a simplistic picture of legislative-executive relations in the region. Irrespective of the partisan balance in the assembly, the Nordic approach to parliamentary politics has been far removed from the adversarial style of Westminster. A range of informal interactions and controls have operated. In Sweden a tradition of leadership conferences, born of war-time co-operation between the leaders of the four parties comprising the National Government of 1939–45, characterised politics up to the mid-1960s and a brief attempt was made to revive them when the non-socialists came to power in 1976. According to a Conservative Party chairman, these leadership conferences provided a means whereby the opposition could exercise a direct influence on government policy.[6] Typical of the Swedish approach (albeit one not unrelated to the logistics of the legislative-executive balance) was the Prime Minister Olof Palme's call in the autumn of 1983 for ten-day talks involving all the Riksdag parties as well as other organisations to explore ways of getting the country out of the economic crisis. Outside Sweden this type of well-publicised, high-level consultation between government and opposition leaders has been less in evidence; however, it has occurred, particularly with regard to major economic policy.

To sum up, there have been a series of minority governments in the region in recent years forced to search for legislative coalitions to back their proposals: for example, opposition approval has generally been a pre-condition of success for the broad packages of measures which have become a feature of Danish politics. There has been a web of interaction between government and parliament — *ad hoc* discussions with opposition leaders, liaison between ministers and the chairmen of the parliamentary standing committees, informal contacts between the staff of a standing committee and the corresponding government department, and consultations between ministers and the backbenchers in their parliamentary party groups. The existence of an incompatibility rule in Sweden and Norway and the force of strong convention elsewhere has meant a separation of the personnel of government and parliament which does not exist at Westminster where about 90 voting members of the House of Commons are at the same time members of the government. British- or French-style whipping arrangements have been absent from the Nordic assemblies; the level of partisan cohesion has been high, but Left-Right, socialist-nonsocialist voting has by no means monopolised legislative behavior. The subject-specific standing committees have fostered a level of delegate expertise (consolidated in the Swedish case by membership of a commission of inquiry in the same policy area) which has facilitated the cross-examination of witnesses in standing committee and strengthened the capacity of the parliaments in the region to scrutinise legislative proposals. All in all, while the situation is dynamic and ever-changing, the Nordic parliaments do not appear mere rubber-stamps meekly authorising government proposals: their influence, particularly at the deliberation and adoption stage, is not insignificant. Indeed the Nordic parliaments may be placed, along with the West German Bundestag, at the midpoint of a continuum with the 'delegate-centred' United States Congress at one end and the 'government-dominant' House of Commons and French National Assembly at the other.

It might, of course, be countered that in one respect the Nordic parliaments appear singularly weak — namely, that the indigenous institutions of the legislative process, the standing committees and plenary readings of bills prescribed by law in the Standing Orders, have been largely displaced as effective organs of policy deliberation by a counter-apparatus created by the political parties and centred on the parliamentary party group. The regular meetings of the parliamentary party group, it would be argued, determine the party line on a bill; standing committee spokemen report back to a full meeting of party delegates; and it is significant that it is within the parliamentary group that individual delegates feel most able to exert influence. In sum, the parliamentary party groups appear to be miniature parliaments within parliament. This picture perhaps needs to be presented with greater sophistication. It may be feasible to detect a two-stage transference of influence in policy deliberation — from the standing committees and plenary sessions of parliament to the parliamentary party groups and then within the parliamentary party group from its regular full meetings to the various internal policy committees. There seems, after all, to be a tendency for party group meetings to discuss broader questions of tactics and strategy and for the group policy committees to focus on substance and detail. Moreover, the existence of overlapping membership between the standing committee systems of the Nordic parliaments and the group policy committees makes it possible to speak of specialist sub-systems within the parliamentary group based on delegate expertise. These sub-systems appear to limit the capacity of the parliamentary group as a whole to scrutinise legislative proposals effectively.

The tendency for the detailed deliberation of measures to devolve to internal policy committees does not in itself detract from the importance of the parliamentary party group within the institutional framework of the legislature. Rather, it points to developing practice within the parliamentary group and one which reflects the existence of specialist sub-systems within the legislature at large — sub-systems based on membership (often long-standing) of a standing committee and which bring delegates in a real sense closer to the corresponding executive structures than those of the rest of the legislature. Anyway, policy committees are mainly confined, for obvious numerical reasons, to the bigger parties, particularly those on the left, while the executive committees which contain the group chairman, standing committee spokesman and a number of elected members represent an alternative source of authority within the parliamentary group.

Unquestionably the role of the parliamentary party group is important, although the significance of the standing committee as a deliberative arena should not be underestimated: there is a two-way flow of influence between parliamentary group and standing committee, and the former may be cast in the reactive role. What is questionable is the feasibility of divorcing the parliamentary group from the basic infrastructure of the Nordic assemblies so as to demonstrate the subjugation of the fundamental institutions of parliament to those of party. In recent years, there has been a progessive legitimisation of parliamentary group activity, which is increasingly acknowledged in practice in the work procedures of the assemblies and in law through the state subventions which are distributed to the parties on the basis of the number of parliamentary delegates they possess. Nor is the party-politicisation of parliament necessarily enervating: in the Nordic Council it has stimulated proceedings, and the same may also be said of the devolved assemblies, particularly in the way parties have organised around vital political issues like full independence and EC membership. In short, much parliamentary influence is mediated through the political parties in the assembly and the legislative apparatus they have created, but it is not at all clear that this has had damaging implications for the capacity of parliament to deliberate on and modify government bills. In parliamentary executives like the Nordic states, the crucial determinant of assembly influence is the legislative-executive balance: while the strength of partisan allegiance has tended to erode the force of the native parliamentary machinery of plenaries and standing committees as independent deliberative forums, it has been through the agency of the partisan balance in the legislature as a whole that the Nordic parliaments have at times been able to exert significant political influence at the adoption stage.

It might be thought that our focus in this concluding chapter hitherto has been misleadingly narrow and that irrespective of whether the cabinet enjoys majority or minority status, important economic policy — the primary target of corporatist attention — has been made by the government in conjuction with the leading sectional interests. Thus it might appear that parliamentary influence has been minimal.

It will readily be conceded that parliamentary involvement on the consultative machinery of economic policy-making has been at best minimal. The incomes policy systems are a case in point. Thus the Danish Economic Council, set up in 1962 on the Dutch model, comprises representatives of all the important labour-market organisations along with a number of expert economists, but contains no Folketing members. The same is true of the Technical Calculation Committee which was made permanent in Norway in 1969,[7] and was partly inspired by the French style of long-range economic planning as well as the Economic Council in Finland, the origins of which date back to the 1930s. Typically, the purpose of the Finnish Economic Council was defined in 1980 as 'a discussion forum with the aim of diffusing information, moulding public opinion, advising governments and handling incomes policy questions'.[8] However, although the major corporate interests are represented on all these three organs, the latter should not be thought of as economic parliaments comparable to the Social and Económic Council in the Netherlands in its heyday in the 1960s. The permanent structures of the incomes policy systems have been confined to a few government-appointed boards and councils with technical functions, particularly issuing expert reports and conditioning a favourable climate of opinion.

In general, the main economic bargaining occurs informally in largely *ad hoc* meetings of the peak federations. On occasions, meetings may be convened by the Prime Minister or Finance Minister, and these may also involve leaders of the opposition parties in parliament. In May 1983, for example, Olof Palme revived Tage Erlander's tradition of inviting leaders of the main labour-market organisations to an informal high-level conference at Harpsund designed to achieve a broad consensus on the major lines of economic policy. However, neither the significance of these much-publicised gatherings nor the cohesion of the bargaining process between the peak 'corporations' should be exaggerated. In Denmark, for example, the government was forced in 1963 to use statutory means to impose an incomes policy when the blue-collar and employers' organisations failed to reach agreement on the terms of a wage-freeze. Fifteen years later the historic Social Democratic-Liberal coalition fell when the central labour organisation, LO, made it clear to the Danish Prime Minister Anker Jørgensen that it was prepared to consent to a statutory incomes policy only at the price of the introduction of a compulsory profit-sharing and employee co-ownership scheme. In Finland in 1970 President Urho Kekkonen made an unprecedented intervention to secure an incomes agreement against the background of politically-motivated opposition to a settlement from the large Communist-controlled Metalworkers' Union and three years later a central agreement was not achieved at all. It is plain, given the common politico-economic base of the main sectoral groups and political parties (blue-collar organisations/Social Democrats and Labour, employers/Conservatives, farm producers/Centre) that the outcome of bargaining is often affected, and differences triggered off, by changes in parliamentary conditions — the fall of a government, the withdrawal of one party, a change in policy direction etc. Stable majority government, particularly of the left, has been most conducive to corporate agreements; minority conditions have jeopardised the smooth working of the economic bargaining process.

As to the locus of such agreements, Rokkan was obviously right in saying that the crucial decisions of economic policy are rarely taken in parliament — 'the central arena is the bargaining table where the government authorities meet directly with trade union leaders, representatives of the farmers, the smallholders and the fishermen and the delegates of the employers' association.'[9] The Nordic parliaments, indeed, play little or no role in the formulation and implementation of macro-economic policy. During periods of majority government, moreover, it will be extremely difficult to amend the details of a corporate agreement, and rank-and-file delegates will in all likelihood have a vested interest in supporting a deal which appears in the best interests of their 'core' votes. In recent years, however, two factors have contributed to promoting the influence of parliament in the deliberation and adoption of economic policy. The first is recession which by complicating the task of economic management has tended to reduce the cohesion of the corporate bargaining process and to elevate the importance of parliamentary consultation in generating the necessary support for a government's economic measures. Secondly, the advent of non-socialist governments in Denmark, Norway and Sweden after decades of Social Democratic ascendancy has also tended to diminish cohesion between the government and sectoral interests — austerity programmes and neo-monetarist policies have been unacceptable fare for the peak labour organisations — and again to place a premium on parliamentary support in economic management. The typical non-socialist minority governments of recent years, in particular — Finland 1976–7, Sweden 1978–9, 81–2, Denmark 1982–4 and Norway 1981–3 — have been forced to wheel and deal with fellow non-socialist groups in the assembly in order to preserve the main lines of their economic policy. Hence the Centre-led minority in Finland made concessions to both Conservative and Christian parties within the framework of the 1976–7 budget, and similar concessions were made to the Christian People's Party in Norway by the governing Conservatives over the 1983 budget. In short, the legislative-executive balance is the vital factor in determining parliamentary influence over economic policy: although decisions on major economic policy are not made in parliament, they have been influenced and modified by parliament.

It would not be justifiable on the basis of our analysis of parliamentary participation in the policy process to refer to the Nordic states as 'post-parliamentary democracies'. In the words of a standing committee secretary, 'the Riksdag is no longer the government's transport company' conveying its bills safely onto the statute book (the turning point was the end of the long era of Social Democratic majority rule) and neither can the other assemblies in the region be described as merely "government-controlled".' Rather, all the Nordic parliaments in recent years have been able to exercise an influence over the course of events.

We have considered a number of cases where this has happened. There was the Swedish parliament's refusal in 1980 to sanction the rundown of the state-owned Öresund shipbuilding yard, a setback which prompted the Industry Minister Nils Åsling to contend, in the debate on the future of shipbuilding the next year, that it was potentially harmful to the long-term planning of the industry to be bound by a decision of parliament. Fälldin's majority government did not resign over the Öresund defeat, but this was precisely what Jørgensen's Social Democratic minority administration in Denmark did in the autumn of 1982 when it became apparent that parliamentary backing for a crisis package of economic measures was not forthcoming. There was the decision of the centre-left majority government in Finland to withdraw its Surname Bill before the 1983 general election, following amendments tabled in the Grand Committee and a threat from the opposition to use the qualified majority provisions to delay the measure; the defeat of the Åland executive in a vote of no confidence in the Landsting in March

1983; and finally, the legislative coalitions entered into by Willoch's Conservative minority government in Norway in 1981–3 which enabled opposition groups to influence such contentious measures as the postponement of legislation extending the right of employees to representation on the boards of official organs and the restoration to shareholders of their majority on the controlling boards of commercial banks. Moreover, as its leader Johan Jakobsen stressed in the Storting, the Centre Party was backing the new administration to ensure itself some political influence — influence which presaged government compromises over tax policy and public spending, and prevented the incorporation of far-reaching cuts in the budget. Most dramatically of all, there was the Folketing's refusal via the Market Relations Committee to accede to the Danish government's position in the fisheries dispute with Britain early in 1983 which led to a serious international crisis. In all the aforementioned cases, 'big decisions' in Richardson and Jordan's terms have been taken in parliament and ones which the government has not been able to control.

All the Nordic parliaments have also exerted an indirect and/or longer-term influence over the course of events which it is not possible to measure in terms of the withdrawal, renegotiation, amendment or defeat of a government bill. In the area of 'invisible politics', a government (whether in a majority or a minority) might discreetly adopt the gist of a private member's bill, postpone a measure likely to provoke a hostile reaction in the assembly (particularly as an election approaches), or enter informal discussions with opposition spokesmen. After all, the overwhelming majority of cabinet ministers have been (or still technically are) members of parliament and regard the legislature as their natural locus for negotiating. Equally, the Nordic parliaments have performed an agenda-setting function by providing a platform for airing and publicising alternative ideas. Thus in the last decade or so, the values related to sustained economic growth have necessarily been re-examined, and parliament has provided a forum for the articulation of new thinking and the presentation of different scenarios — particularly in the energy, environmental and defence fields. Hence the importance of Fälldin's proposed embargo on nuclear development announced in the Riksdag in 1975; the election of two Green delegates in Finland in 1983; and the adoption by the left in Norway of many of the ideas of the peace movement especially its espousal of a nuclear-free Nordic area. In January 1983, proceedings in the Storting revealed that the cross-party consensus on defence and security policy had disintegrated for the first time since Norway joined NATO in 1949.

As this last Norwegian case illustrates, parliament remains a primary forum for debating major issues. On occasions it concentrates the attention of the whole nation, as with the dramatic vote in the Althing early in 1983 by which Iceland agreed to abide by the international moratorium on commercial whaling fixed to operate from 1985. The narrowest of parliamentary majorities in favour (29 votes to 28) followed intense public debate and a threat by Greenpeace to organise a boycott of all Icelandic fish products. At other times, parliament has been the target of popular movements and those pressure groups without an established position in the executive machine — the prohibitionists in the 1920s and, more recently, the Finnish 'beer marchers', feminists, the campaign against the Alta river hydroelectric development in northern Norway, and the lobby against the welfare cuts proposed by the Fälldin government in 1982. Throughout, the Nordic parliaments have lent legitimacy and stability to their political systems by creating an outlet for the expression of popular grievances and a platform on which to challenge the government of the day.

Our focus has been on parliament as a policy actor: the role of other actors in the policy process, the cabinet, civil servants, pressure groups, experts, mass publics and so on has necessarily taken second place. The inevitable (and in view of the absence of a comparative study of the Nordic parliaments) legitimate parochialism of this approach should not of course be allowed to disguise the importance for the initiation of legislation of the institutionalised relationships between government and pressure groups. The predominantly consultative style of policy-making and the broad-ranging involvement of representatives of relevant interests, including (to varying extents in the region) parliamentarians, has been little affected by alternations in government and/or the transition from majority to minority rule. However, something of an analytical pre-occupation with this group-government axis, the commission system and the corporate bargaining between the peak economic federations, has tended unfairly to relegate parliament to little more than a postscript in the policy process. Much of the influential corporatist literature (Rokkan, Heisler and Kvavik *et al.*) was after all produced in the 1960s, a period of stable government, economic growth and a basic élite consensus over goals — in short, it was a product of an era characterised by Daniel Bell in the United States as the 'end of ideology'.

Since then, a widespread polarisation in the party systems, the displacement of social democracy as a monopolistic governing party in the 'metropolitan' states in the region (Denmark, Norway and Sweden), the regular incidence of minority, especially non-socialist minority, governments and the assault on the old consensus from highly-mobilised groups focusing on new issues have combined to challenge the 'decline of parliaments' orthodoxy and to create the conditions for a modest revival of parliament in the Nordic states. The Nordic parliaments have had the political power to make their views heard in the deliberation and adoption of government bills and have at times asserted themselves to influence the course of events. It can scarcely be said of the Nordic parliaments in the mid-1980s, as was said of the parliaments in the small Western European democracies more than a decade earlier, that they have 'come to resemble a rubber-stamp in many of the most important policy areas.'[10] Take the case of the Danish Prime Minister Poul Schlüter: his crucial package of spending cuts was passed in an extraordinary session of the Folketing in September 1983 thanks to the support of the opposition-based Progress Party and in turn of its absent leader Mogens Glistrup — serving a $3\frac{1}{2}$-year prison sentence for tax fraud — who, from his temporary residence, advised his colleagues to back the government so as to avoid a general election at which their party stood to be decimated!

REFERENCES

1. Richardson & Jordan (1979), p. 121.
2. 'Politisk styrning — administrativ självständighet', SOU 1983:39, cited in Starkare politisk styrning möjlig, *Från Riksdag & Departement* 9.9.1983.
3. 'Hallitus tuhoaa selontekomenettelyn.' *Uusi Suomi* 6.6.1980.
4. Higley, Brofuss & Groholt (1975), pp. 265–71.
5. 'Ovanligt initiativ av finansutskottet'. *Nordisk Kontakt* 15/77, p. 904.
6. Ingvar Amilon, 'Party Leadership Conferences: A Study in Swedish Parliamentary Practice', in Herbert Hirsch & Donald Hancock (eds), *Comparative Legislative Systems. A Reader in Theory and Research.* New York: The Free Press, 1971, p. 329.
7. Nils Elvander, 'Collective Bargaining and Incomes Policy in the Nordic Countries: A Comparative Analysis'. *British Journal of Industrial Relations* 12, 3, pp. 417–37.
8. 'Talousneuvosto on herännyt'. *Suomen Kuvalehti* 23.1.1981. 'Talouspoliittisia toimintalinjoja soviteltiin yhteen'. *Uusi Suomi* 11.6.1980.
9. Cited in Richardson & Jordan (1979), p. 164.
10. Heisler & Kvavik (1974). pp. 62–3.

INDEX